NAPA VALLEY

Land of Golden Vines

Help Us Keep This Guide Up to Date

Every effort has been made by the authors and editors to make this guide as accurate and useful as possible. However, many things can change after a guide is published—establishments close, phone numbers change, hiking trails are rerouted, facilities come under new management, and so on.

We would love to hear from you concerning your experiences with this guide and how you feel it could be made better and be kept up to date. While we may not be able to respond to all comments and suggestions, we'll take them to heart and we'll also make certain to share them with the authors. Please send your comments and suggestions to the following address:

The Globe Pequot Press
Reader Response/Editorial Department
P.O. Box 833
Old Saybrook, CT 06475

Or you may e-mail us at:

editorial@globe-pequot.com

Thanks for your input, and happy travels!

HILL GUIDES™ SERIES

NAPA VALLEY

Land of Golden Vines

by Kathleen Thompson Hill
&
Gerald Hill

Old Saybrook, Connecticut

Hill Guides is a trademark of The Globe Pequot Press.

Cover painting entitled *Zinfandel Evening* by Judy Theo Lehner, M. F. A. Studio address: 679 First Street West, Sonoma, CA 95476. Medium: monotype.
Cover and text design by Lana Mullen
Maps by Mary Ballachino
Illustrations by Mauro Magellan
Photos by Kathleen and Gerald Hill
Historical illustrations by an anonymous newspaper illustrator, circa the 1800s.

Library of Congress Cataloging-in-Publication Data
   Hill, Kathleen.
     Hill Guides: Napa Valley / by Kathleen Thompson Hill and Gerald Hill.
  — 1st ed.
      p.   cm. — (Hill guides series)
     Includes index.
     ISBN 0-7627-0306-7
     1. Napa Valley (Calif.)—Guidebooks.   2. Wine and wine making—California—Napa Valley—Guidebooks.   I. Hill, Gerald N.
  II. Title.   III. Series: Hill, Kathleen. Hill guides.
   F868.N2H55   1999
   917.94'190453—dc21   98-48365
                                                CIP

Manufactured in the United States of America
First Edition/First Printing

CONTENTS

PREFACE

o our delighted surprise, we mostly found extremely nice, informative, and urbane winery owners, winemakers, staff, chefs, and helpers in the Napa Valley. We also discovered after never having looked at the Valley objectively before, that it is stunningly gorgeous especially with the help in 1997–1998 from El Nino's extended rains, which kept the grasses and mustard blooming in the vineyards longer than is the norm in dry years.

We found small, rustic, family-run wineries as well as some of the largest corporate-owned wineries in the world. We also found New York and French chefs cooking world-class food for world-class prices, as well as ethnic and home cooks sharing their best cultural traditions with the public at extremely reasonable prices.

Movie directors and cartoon developers, video-game and computer-program inventors, traditional vintners, and pilots and doctors all nurse their vineyards and wineries in their own way, each offering their personal taste and expression to the public. The contrasts are astounding and wonderful.

Napa Valley has more restaurants, more people, more money, more wineries, more applauded wines, more visiting movie stars, and more attention than Sonoma Valley. Things are often done with much greater flair and at greater expense in Napa. The Napa wineries tend to have more expensive and dramatic designs; some wineries' art collections are brilliant and extensive, drawing more viewers than the local art galleries and museums.

A friendly rivalry exists between the Napa and Sonoma Valleys. Sonoma resident and comedian Tommy Smothers' line, "Sonoma makes wine, Napa makes auto parts," adorns T-shirts and posters and fuels the fires to keep this good-natured competition going. Still, vintners have grafted and traded vine cuttings, winemakers, and *phylloxera* back and forth between Napa and Sonoma for decades.

But each valley has its special charms. We encourage you to visit both Napa and Sonoma to maximize your pleasure!

—Kathleen Thompson Hill
—Gerald Hill

ACKNOWLEDGMENTS

We particularly want to thank our old friends Janet and Senator John Dunlap for their historical and personal insights into the Napa Valley and for spending so much time with us.

Our friend Jane Mosier of Napa, whom we met initially through politics, gave us incomparable assistance by faxing us piles and piles of facts she collected with her usual energetic and intellectual care. Dear friends Susan Weeks and Sue Holman helped us with the arduous duty of joining us to sample restaurants, and Ada Press of On the Vine in St. Helena sacrificed herself as deputy taster. Our kids Erin and Mack gave their tolerant support, as usual.

And, of course, we thank the hundreds of winemakers, winery staff, chefs, restaurateurs, and shopkeepers for giving us their time, their stories, their soul, and their recipes. Thanks, too, to the people of Napa Valley for their encouragement and hospitality.

"... where ... the wine is bottled poetry. .."

—Robert Louis Stevenson, *Silverado Squatters*

INTRODUCTION

*N*apa Valley stretches about 30 miles from its northwestern end to its southeastern end, sprawling between the Mayacamas Mountains on the west and the Vaca Range (sometimes called the Silverado Range of hills) on the east. It is widest (5 miles) in the south around the city of Napa and narrowest (1 mile) in the north near Calistoga. The Napa River is widest around the city of Napa, which it often floods in the winter—but the river is just a trickling stream where it begins in the north. Napa Valley ranges from windswept flats, to the Palisade Cliffs at the foot of Mount St. Helena, to the forests of the Mayacamas Mountains.

Napa Valley's mildest climate is in the south, which benefits from breezes off the San Pablo Bay. The farther north you go, the rainier it gets, and the more extreme the temperatures. Microclimates are everywhere and contribute to some of the Valley's most unique wines.

The Napa Valley has two principal north–south roads: Highway 29 (locals prefer to call it the St. Helena Highway as it gets closer to St. Helena) and the Silverado Trail. A number of smaller roads connect the two.

In this guide, we first take you on a route up one side of the Napa Valley, on Highway 29. After meandering up Highway 29, you'll cross the Valley at Tubbs Lane, north of Calistoga, through Calistoga, and then head back south on the gorgeous Silverado Trail.

On each route, we recommend that you criss-cross the highway as few times as possible, for your safety and that of others. These busy roads can be quite dangerous. (Remember, other drivers have been sipping wine, too.)

On the way you will find restaurants judiciously interspersed with wineries. Napa Valley is one place where you will never go thirsty for wine or hungry for good food. Or is it hungry for wine and thirsty for food?

Napa Valley's towns are as attractive to visit as the wineries. Each has its own personality. We take you street by street, shop by shop, gallery by gallery through Napa, Yountville, Oakville, Rutherford, St. Helena, and Calistoga. We review every restaurant, from drive-up hamburger and taco stands to The French Laundry and the Culinary Institute of America, as we go along the route.

APPELLATIONS

Several microclimates and soil characteristics have been identified in the Napa Valley, and more attention is now paid to the unique terrain and terroir, a French term that reflects the effect that a particular vineyard site, the earth, and its sociology have on its wine.

Within the original Napa Valley Appellation, several sub-appellations have become recognized and named. These include the Stag's Leap District, Atlas Peak, Howell Mountain, Los Carneros, Mt. Veeder, Oakville, Rutherford, St. Helena, Spring Mountain, and Wild Horse Valley.

This guide also takes you mile by mile through the quasi-industrial auxiliary wine businesses south of the city of Napa—the part of the Valley you come to first if you come from Oakland, Berkeley, the rest of the East Bay, or Sacramento. In addition, you will explore the fascinating Los Carneros District, in the southern part of the Valley between the two main roads. (Carneros extends from Napa Valley into Sonoma Valley.)

In this guide we also offer the only concise and complete history of the Napa Valley. Read about the trials and travails of Robert Louis Stevenson, winemaking, wine lore, and wine fights.

And watch for elegant recipes throughout the book, provided by generous winemakers and chefs from throughout the Napa Valley. These luscious gems will allow you to bring some of your Valley experience into your own home.

How to Get Here

Napa Valley is only about an hour from San Francisco or forty-five minutes from Berkeley and Oakland. But there's a catch: You cannot reach the Valley by traveling via public transportation. You must have a car or private airplane to get here. (The only bus from the Bay Area airports is the Evans Airporter, a private bus service. It makes eight trips from Oakland International Airport and eleven trips from San Francisco International Airport to the Napa Valley daily. Fares on all runs are $18.)

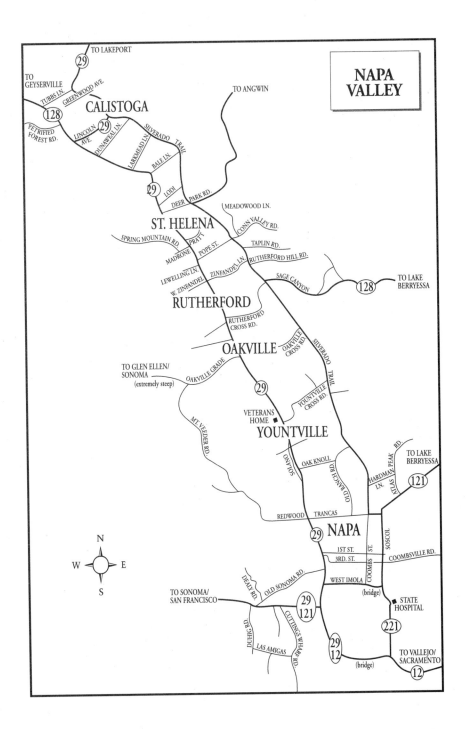

Getting Here by Car

From San Francisco: Take the Golden Gate Bridge north and continue on Highway 101 past San Rafael and through Marin County for about 30 miles. Turn east on Highway 37 toward Napa. Turn left (north) onto Highway 121 at Sears Point Raceway, heading toward Napa and Sonoma. Here you enter the prized and highly esteemed Carneros Wine District, which traverses the county line between Sonoma and Napa.

At the Schellville Fire Station, Highway 12 goes north into Sonoma, while 121 from here is also Highway 12 and goes east to Napa. So, to get to Napa, continue eastward (straight) toward Napa from the intersection of Highways 12 and 121. This segment of road is known locally as Fremont Drive. It takes you to or past the Cherry Tree plant and store, Babe's Drive-In (great hamburgers), eventually Clover-Stornetta Dairy (where Laura Chenel makes wonderful Chevre cheeses), and on to Napa.

After you pass (or even visit) Carneros wineries, turn north (left) onto Highway 121, which also becomes Highway 29. Highway 121 will turn eastward on Imola Avenue in Napa, and then will eventually become the Silverado Trail and run along the eastern side of the Napa Valley.

At this point you have two Napa wine-touring choices: Follow Highway 29 northward along the western side of Napa Valley, or follow Highway 121 to the Silverado Trail and the eastern side of the Valley. We suggest that you explore both.

From Berkeley, Oakland, and the East Bay: From Berkeley and Oakland take Highway 80 east (it says east, but you are actually traveling north) through El Cerrito, Crockett, and across the Carquinez Bridge. Get in the left lanes of the bridge, because just after the toll gate you can turn leftish toward Napa and Highway 29, which will take you northward through Vallejo and American Canyon (no canyon in sight) to Napa.

Or you can follow Highway 80 to the Columbus Parkway exit and head toward Marine World Africa U.S.A. From Marine World continue westward on Highway 37 to Highway 29 in Vallejo's outskirts. Turn right (north) on Highway 29 and follow it into Napa.

Just past the intersection of Highways 29 and 12, you can stop at the Hakusan Sake Company, Seguin Moreau cooperage, and Napa Brewing Company before you even get to the city of Napa.

From Downtown Sonoma: From Sonoma Plaza in the middle of downtown Sonoma, go south on Broadway, then turn left (east) on Napa Road. Follow this road through two flashing red lights, and on through the hills to the stoplight and intersection of Highway 12. Turn left onto Highway 12/121 toward Napa and take the road through the hills. Off to wineries you go!

Getting Here by Air

Napa Valley Airport, "Skyport to the Wine Country," is located conveniently south of the City of Napa and west of Highway 29 across from its intersection with Highway 12. (While no commercial jets land at the airport, Japan Airlines maintains an enormous flight-training school here.)

From Other Airports via Private Aircraft: Twenty-nine nmi NW of Oakland International (OAK) airport, 30 nmi SE of Sonoma County (STS) airport, 17 nmi NW of Concord (CCR) airport, and 18 nmi SW of Nut Tree (045) airport, Napa Airport is 4 nmi south of the City of Napa, 1nmi(-) east of the Napa River, and 1 NM west of Highways 12 and 29 intersection. The control tower is south side of runway 06/24, with rotating beacon east side of airport and a golf course 2 NM east.

Communication Frequencies: Napa Tower 118.7, Napa Ground Control 121.7, Napa Atis 124.05, Scaggs VOR (SGD) 112.1, Napa ILS Localizer 111.3, KVON (BDCST) 1440 KH 153, 4 NM to airport, Oakland Center 127.8, Oakland Radio 122.1T/112.1R.

Airport Information (APC): Field elevation 33 ft MSL; TPA: 1,033 ft MSL; Tower operates from 0700 to 2000 daily (may vary with season); VOR and localizer approaches available through Oakland Center (127.8); runway lights pilot activated. Key 118.7-3,5, or 7 times; San Francisco Sectional and L1-L2 Chart; Latitude 38-13; Longitude 122-17; Reil Runway 06; Papi runway 18R.

Winds at Napa generally favor the use of either Runway 18 or 24. Landings and takeoffs are frequently conducted simultaneously from several runways, so pilots should be alert for other traffic.

The instructions to expect, listed below, are based on the normal wind condition.

From southeast: Make LEFT traffic Rwy 18L, report downwind, or enter LEFT base Twy 24, report 2 mile LEFT base.

From north: Make straight in Rwy 18L or 18R. Report 2 mile final.

From northeast: Make straight-in Rwy 24, report the Water Tanks, or enter LEFT base Rwy 18L, report 2 mile LEFT base.

From west: Make RIGHT traffic Rwy 18R, report downwind.

At the airport, **Bridgeford Flying Service** (707–224–0887 or 707–644–1658) offers multitudinous goods and services, including Chevron fuel, flight instruction, ground school, pilot supplies, flying club, Cessna Pilot Center, maintenance, sales, and charter and scenic tours and rides. Office manager Adriann Harpst, a pilot herself, is most helpful and knowledgeable. Her office doubles as supply and gift shop, which includes pilot necessities, souvenirs, and an unusual collection of flying-related manuals and history books.

GETTING AROUND ONCE YOU'RE HERE

Once you arrive at the airport, you have to rent a car, which you can arrange at the airport or at your hotel, or take a taxi escorted tour.

Car Rental Agencies

AFFORDABLE AUTO RENTAL, 473 Soscol Avenue, Napa; (707) 257–1911
BUDGET RENT-A-CAR, 407 Soscol Avenue, Napa; (707) 224–7845
ENTERPRISE RENT-A-CAR, 230 Soscol Avenue, Napa; (707) 253–8000
HERTZ, 1895 Salvador Avenue, Napa; (707) 226–2037
RENT-A-WRECK, 555 Main Street, St. Helena; (800) 300–3213
SEARS RENT-A-CAR, 407 Soscol Avenue, Napa; (707) 224–7847
ZUMWALT FORD, 21 Main Street, St. Helena; (707) 963–2771

Taxi Companies

NAPA VALLEY CAB ("The Red Ones"), (707) 257–6444
TAXI CABERNET, (707) 942–2226, (707) 963–2620, or (888) 333–TAXI (8294)

Public Transportation

NAPA VALLEY TRANSIT, (800) 696–6433 or (707) 255–7631, runs its route between ten towns along Highway 29 from Vallejo in Solano County to Calistoga at the northern end of Napa Valley, Monday–Saturday. Buses also stop at Oakville Grocery, Beaulieu Winery, Freemark Abbey, and Bothe Napa State Park.

THE V.I.N.E. (Valley Intracity Neighborhood Express), (707) 255–7631, follows five routes within the city of Napa.

BEAR FLAG EXPRESS, (707) 944–4815, provides bus service within Yountville.

HOW TO BE A VISITOR AND NOT A TOURIST IN NAPA VALLEY

Don't worry about looking like a tourist in Napa Valley. The Valley is made for tourists! The wineries and restaurants thrive on your visit and are well aware of that fact, so you will be treated well. Just dress comfortably and bring your taste buds and money. There's no currency exchange—everyone's must be green or plastic.

It does help to know a few of the local rules, however. Smoking is not allowed in tasting rooms or restaurants, but it's occasionally okay outdoors. A few wineries even sell cigars. In addition, be sure to make dinner and accommodations reservations—this is a popular region.

CHAPTER 1

LOS CARNEROS DISTRICT

Los Carneros, a world-famous wine region, runs from the southern part of Sonoma Valley across the hills to the southern end of Napa Valley. Less formally known as just plain Carneros, it also has its own appellation.

The Carneros region is cooler than most other parts of the Napa and Sonoma Valleys due to the cool breezes and summer fog from the San Francisco Bay. These elements also provide for the slow maturation of the grapes—enhancing their flavor, color, and character—and are the ideal conditions for growing and producing Pinot Noir, Chardonnay, and Merlot.

In 1846 General Mariano Vallejo granted 18,000 acres of what is now known as Carneros to his brother-in-law, Jacob Leese. At that time the land was called Rancho Huichica; a nearby, smaller grant of 2,500 acres known as Rincon de los Carneros gave its name to the region.

In the mid-1850s many farmers planted grapes on their parcels of land in Carneros. A stagecoach ran between the farms and Sonoma along what is now Highway 12/121, known locally as the Carneros Highway. In 1870 the first winery in the region opened (first known as Winter Winery and subsequently as Talcoa Vineyards).

In the late 1800s and early 1900s, the first wave of *phylloxera*, and then Prohibition, temporarily eliminated wine growing in the Carneros. After the repeal of Prohibition in 1933, a winery named Garetto began making wine again. Louis Martini and Beaulieu both planted in the Carneros from the 1940s to the 1960s. And in the 1970s Carneros Creek, Saintsbury, and Acacia all achieved recognition as a new breed of winery.

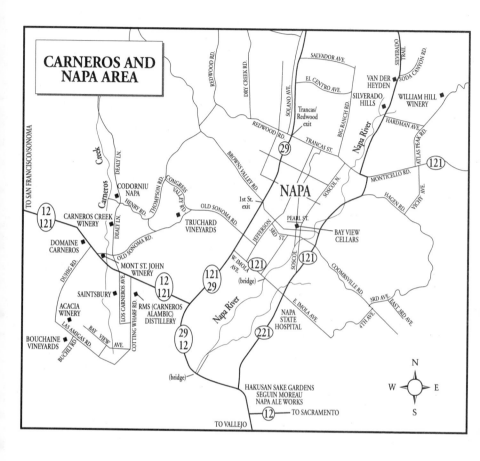

How to Get to the Carneros District

To get here from San Francisco, take the Golden Gate Bridge and Highway 101 north, turn east on Highway 37, left at Sears Point Raceway to Highway 12/121 and follow toward Napa. The Domaine Carneros chateau, vineyards, and sign on the right mean soon you will take an extremely sharp hairpin right onto Duhig Road and the first winery on our tour. From Oakland/Berkeley, take I–80 east, take Highway 37, north on Highway 29, and left on Highway 12/121. In about 1 mile Domaine Carneros and Duhig Road will be on your left. Before stopping at Domaine Carneros, however, you should make an appointment to visit the di Rosa Preserve, which is right across the way. When you see wooden cutouts of animals against the hillside and a newish corrugated metal building, turn right (north) into the di Rosa driveway.

Wineries and Distillery of the Carneros Region

Wineries and grape growers in the area have created The Carneros Quality Alliance, an organization dedicated to improving and promoting the wines of Carneros with dignity and gusto. A small group, its members believe intensely in their mission and group individuality. In Napa Valley's part of the Carneros, you can visit Domaine Carneros, Acacia, Saintsbury, RMS (formerly called Carneros Alambic) Distillery, Mont St. John, Carneros Creek, and Codorniu Napa.

Just west of the wineries, though, you come to the fascinating DI ROSA PRESERVE: ART & NATURE, on the north side of Highway 12/121, a highly unusual and personal collection of unconventional and experimental indoor and outdoor art. These pieces are dramatically presented throughout Rene di Rosa's fifty-three-acre property, which includes Winery Lake, the Gatehouse Gallery, and the Main Gallery.

Rene di Rosa collects San Francisco Bay Area artists' work and exhibits his 1,500-piece collection according to his own instincts, not according to curator's school standards. So you might find an unknown artist's work next to William Wiley's, an artist from San Jose next to Napa's Earl Thollander, or perhaps a lesser piece next to the drama of Joan Brown.

What many critics miss in describing Rene as a collector is the mission he feels to help artists. A former journalist who bought 460 Carneros acres when "experts" said you couldn't grow grapes here, di Rosa and his late wife Veronica took tremendous pleasure from helping artists by buying their work—a kind of sponsorship of the arts.

Veronica was the backbone of the restoration of the Napa Opera House. Tragically, she fell over a cliff in France while collecting flower seeds for her garden in Carneros. (Our mutual friend, the late Bob Ernest, who designed the di Rosa's chapel and some of the gardens, had told the di Rosas exactly where to find the seeds.) Veronica died as a result of the fall, just after Bob passed away.

Rene di Rosa sold most of his vineyards to Joseph E. Seagram & Sons in 1986 for a few million. He then created the Rene and Veronica di Rosa Foundation, part of whose mission is to support and inspire the work of Bay Area artists.

We guarantee that you will have an artistic experience at the di Rosa Preserve unlike any you will have in a museum—or anywhere else, for that matter. Di Rosa's collection will wake up your mind and your senses and stimulate your imagination as well as your funny bone.

 Fine points: Call for an appointment to take the two–hour tour. Everyone is welcome, and guides limit each group to twenty-five. Park in the lot below the corrugated-metal Gatehouse Gallery; the tours begin at the Gatehouse. Open your receptors and enjoy!

✴ *Di Rosa Preserve, 5200 Highways 12/121, Napa 94558; phone (707) 226–5991. Tours start at 9:25 A.M. and 12:55 P.M. Monday, Wednesday, and Thursday; 12:55 and 6:25 P.M. Tuesday; 9:25 and 10:25 A.M. Saturday. Admission is $10, but free to Napa County residents with photo ID. Visa and MasterCard. Wheelchair-accessible.*

The first winery you come to—and one of the grandest of Carneros—lies right across from di Rosa's property. The fabulous DOMAINE CARNEROS is owned by the Taittinger family of France.

In 1931 Pierre Taittinger acquired the venerable Champagne house Fourneaux, founded in 1734, and established Champagne Taittinger, which today is the last major French Champagne house still controlled by its founding family. Pierre Taittinger created a lighter Champagne wine, which now is the elegant wine that other producers emulate.

His son, Claude Taittinger, now president of Champagne Taittinger, selected this 138-acre parcel in Carneros in 1970 to build his American enterprise, a joint venture with Taittinger's distributor, Kobrand Corporation. Following his father's death in 1965 Claude Taittinger established the Prix Culinaire International Pierre Taittinger, now the ultimate recognition of a chef's skills.

Domaine Carneros was established in 1987. The building's design, inside and out, was inspired by the Taittinger family's French residence in Champagne, Chateau de la Marquetterie. Beautiful and slightly imposing, it is set on a knoll overlooking Carneros and the Napa Valley from the southwest.

Domaine Carneros' entrance deck

As you enter the elegant winery, a grand portrait of Madame de Pompadour greets you. Turn right to the tasting room, with its vast views of the di Rosa Preserve and Codorniu Napa. Enjoy well-known designer Mary Steer's interior decoration, featuring blue upholstered maple chairs, glass and brass tables, maple walls, an exquisite collection of wine and food books, and a warm and welcoming tasting bar.

If the ambience here seems familiar to you, there's an excellent reason: Winemaker Eileen Crane contributed to the design of both Domaine Carneros and Gloria Ferrer Champagne Caves in the Sonoma Valley part of the Carneros. An exceptional person who taught nutrition science in Venezuela, Eileen has a master's degree in nutrition and graduated from both the University of California at Davis enology program and from the Culinary Institute of America. She left Gloria Ferrer for Domaine Carneros to help design, develop, and lead this facility.

Fine points: Mother's and Father's Day celebrations include music and treats with wine tasting. Vineyard tour at 11:15 A.M. Friday morning, $10 per person for tour and tasting. Winery tours hourly at 11:00 A.M.–4:00 P.M. daily, May–October; same hours on Friday–Saturday, rest of the year; with tours at 11:00 A.M. and 1:00 and 3:00 P.M. Monday–Thursday, winter. Featured wines: Sparkling wines made in the *methode champenoise*, including Brut Cuvee, La Reve Blanc de Blancs, and

Famous Gate Pinot Noir. Tasting fees: $4.50–$7.50 a glass. Managing Director/Winemaker: Eileen Crane. Cases: 65,000. Acres: 138 here, 70 at Pompadour Vineyard.

❧ Domaine Carneros, 1240 Duhig Road at Highway 12/121, Napa 94559; phone (707) 257–0101, fax (707) 257–3020, Web site http://www.domaine.com. Open 10:30 A.M.–6:00 P.M. daily. MasterCard, Visa, and American Express. Wheelchair-accessible from upper parking lot.

As you come out of the Domaine Carneros driveway, turn right up Duhig Road. Follow it for about 2 miles, up the hill, down, and past a Mondavi vineyard on the right. Turn left on Las Amigas at Beaulieu's vineyard, and in 0.3 mile turn left into the driveway of ACACIA WINERY, the Carneros sister of the Chalone Wine Group.

Acacia Winery is a surprise, located in a pleasant, adobe-colored stucco building with leaf-green trim. It is surrounded by cow pasture and Beaulieu Vineyard across the road.

In 1988 Chalone Wine Group founder Dick Graf and Phil

CHEVRE AND HERB MOUSSE

from Eileen Crane, Director/Winemaker, Domaine Carneros

INGREDIENTS:

½ cup parsley leaves
½ tsp crushed garlic
1 bunch (about 1/4 cup) of tarragon leaves
1 cup Chevre (goat cheese)
1 ½ lbs cream cheese

PREPARATION:

Chop parsley leaves, crushed garlic, and tarragon leaves in a food processor, turning on and off in short pulses until finely minced but not liquefied. Remove to a small bowl. Blend the Chevre and cream cheese in the food processor until creamy and smooth. Add the herb/garlic mixture and lightly combine the ingredients by turning on and off the processor in short pulses.

The mousse can be piped or spooned into a serving dish. Present with mini toasts, crackers, or bread. Makes 25 small ramekin-size servings. Serve with Domaine Carneros' Famous Gate Pinot Noir or sparkling wines.

Woodward bought Acacia from Mike Richmond and partners, adding it to their Chalone Vineyard near Soledad, California; Edna Valley Vineyard near San Luis Obispo; Carmenet in Sonoma; and Canoe Ridge Vineyard in eastern Washington.

The Acacians, as Acacia's loyal and jovial staff members call themselves, stress their sensitivity to terroir, the French concept that each vineyard has a character different from others. That character emanates from its geography, geology, climate, and biological and sociological influences, and it should not be disturbed. Acacians call themselves "a friendly if a bit eccentric bunch" who "have never had a black tie event . . . and intend to keep it that way." The staff here are taught that no matter what the request, the answer is "yes." The Acacians clearly enjoy themselves, their work, and their wine, and they will do everything possible to be sure that you do, too. But please, be sure to call ahead for reservations.

Acacia has a small, cozy tasting room with Willi's Wine Bar. It also has a restaurant kitchen and two dining rooms, giving a hint of the winery's belief in the importance of food and wine. While you can't just walk in for lunch, Acacia will cater for groups from ten to one hundred people and "can do the whole range, from hot dogs to haute cuisine." They even have a rare permit to use the kitchen, "which in Napa County is harder to obtain than a concealed-weapons permit." Napa County tries to limit winery tourist traffic by restricting uses of, and visits to, wineries.

Acacia gives killer tours, with barrel tastings and technical tours. In the "Sky's the Limit" attitude, the staff put on Famous Chef Dinners, bicycle tours, "picnics, breakfast with the winemaker, bowling for Pinot, bar crawling, horseshoes, old wines, young wines, old dogs, new tricks. You name it we'll try it."

Fine points: Acacia bottles its wines with private labels for Tra Vigne, Spago, the Mauna Kea Beach Hotel, Ruth's Chris Steak House, Burlingame Country Club, and the Claremont Country Club. Tasting fee: none, except $5.00 per person for groups of 10 or more. Featured wines: Chardonnay, Viognier, Viognier Grappa or Brandy,

ACACIA WINERY IN CARNEROS

Pinot Noir, Petit Syrah, Zinfandel, Brut. Winemaker/General Manager: Dave Lattin. Cases: 60,000. Acres: 100.

꙳ *Acacia Winery, 2750 Las Amigas Road, Napa 94559; phone (707) 226–9991, fax (707) 226–1685, e-mail stock@chalonewinegroup.com. Open "by appointment" 10:00 A.M.–4:30 P.M. Monday–Saturday, noon–4:30 P.M. Sunday. MasterCard, Visa, and American Express. Wheelchair-accessible.*

RMS (CARNEROS ALAMBIC) DISTILLERY
WITH SWALLOWS CIRCLING

From Acacia continue east on Las Amigas, turn left (north) onto Cuttings Wharf Road until you reach **RMS DISTILLERY** (called Carneros Alambic Distillery until 1998), which makes American luxury brandies. (You can also get here by turning south on Cuttings Wharf Road from the Carneros Highway [Highway 12/121] 1.3 miles west of Highway 29, or by coming eastward across Withers Road from Saintsbury on Los Carneros.)

RMS president and CEO Pierre-Michel Alsac, who is also president and CEO of the Grand Vin de Gironde division of Remy-Cointreau, changed the name to RMS, meaning Rare, Mature, and Special. (We wonder why they don't just call it Remy Martin Carneros so that people will know what it is.)

As you approach RMS, be sure to notice the lush fields and ponds, pine trees, and French-looking gray stone buildings with red tile roofs. Hundreds of swallows nest under the buildings' eaves, dotting the parking lot and paths with surprisingly uniform little white splats!

You truly feel as if you might be in France in this protective complex of stone buildings with lawns and patios in the center and housing the Visitor Center, Still House, Barrel House, and offices. Enjoy the Visitor Center's soft blue sofa and fireplace, Gail Chase-Bien's three-panel painting called "Angels of Carneros," angel wind chimes, brandy maple syrup, Vine Village oils and vinegars, and French Prairie marionberries in brandy, pears in brandy, and black cherries. Here you can also view a display of French brandy making and a traditional Alambic Charentais pot.

Alambic Still House and Barrel House tours are a real treat. They provide a rare chance to see the centuries-old *methode charentaise* or traditional Cognac method of double wine distillation, culminating in the Aroma Room.

 Fine points: RMS affords the affluent among us the chance to select personal brandy blends and to create signature barrels. These can cost from $6,000 to $30,000 and come from French Colombard, Chenin Blanc, Pinot Noir, Palomino, Folle Blanche, and Muscat grapes. Featured brandies: SR, Carneros QE (Quality Extraordinaire), Pear de Pear from North Coast California Bartlett pears, Folle Blanche, Trilogy, and Heavenly Pear. Cellarmaster: Rick Estes. Cases: Undefined. Acres: 30.

RMS Distillery, 1250 Cuttings Wharf Road, Napa 94559; phone (707) 253–9055, fax (707) 253–0116. Open 10:00 A.M.–5:00 P.M. daily. MasterCard, Visa, and American Express. Wheelchair-accessible.

On the south side of the Carneros Highway (12/121), don't miss SAINTSBURY, renowned producer of Carneros Pinot Noir and Chardonnay. To get there, turn right (south) from the highway onto Los Carneros Avenue. Turn left (east) onto Withers Lane and then turn south into Saintsbury's driveway.

Saintsbury has a Ned Forrest–designed, elegant rural barn with gray stucco walls and beamed ceilings. An English garden of native plants and blonde pebbles provides a charming setting.

As you enter the Mexican tiled office and tasting area, you are struck with the quality of art everywhere, much of it from the San Francisco Museum of Modern Art Rental Center.

UC Davis enology classmates David Graves and Dick Ward discovered in 1977 that they liked "knocking back a decent glass of Morey-Saint-Denis." In 1981 they moved their wine friendship into a wine partnership. Original winemaker Bill Knuttel joined them in 1983, and Byron Kosuge came in as "Bill's right hand man."

Dick and Dave both named their winery for "the old codger" George E. B. Saintsbury (1845–1933), a Scottish professor of literature at the University of Edinburgh and wine fan. In his *Notes on a Cellar Book*, first published in 1920, Saintsbury wrote: "Well! A cellar is an interesting place to fill, to contemplate when filled, and to empty in the proper way."

Dick and Dave believe, and hopefully they are correct, that Carneros is the Beaune of California. They were among the first wineries to produce 100 percent malo-lactic Chardonnay, which means that the wine goes through malo-lactic fermentation, in which the conversion of malic acid to lactic acid makes the wine softer and richer. While their first devotion is to their exceptional Pinot Noirs, their reality also includes the fact that, as Dick puts it, "You need to have something for the fish course."

Fine points: Featured wines: Carneros Chardonnay, Pinot Noir, Garnet, Marc Brandy, and Vin Gris of Pinot Noir. Winemaker: Byron Kosuge. Cases: 48,000. Acres: 55.

❧ *Saintsbury, 1500 Los Carneros Avenue, Napa 94559; phone (707) 252–0592. Call for appointment. No credit cards. Wheelchair-accessible.*

On the north side of Highway 12/121 you will find three more wineries with vastly different and distinct personalities: Mont St. John, Carneros Creek, and Codorniu Napa.

To get there from Napa, Cuttings Wharf Road, or Los Carneros Avenue, turn right off Highway 12/121 onto Old Sonoma Road. (If you decide to forgo Saintsbury and go there from Domaine Carneros, get back onto the highway and immediately turn left onto Old Sonoma Road.)

MONT. ST. JOHN CELLARS, with its arched windows, is at the northeast corner of Old Sonoma Road and Highway 12/121, so turn right into its driveway. The Bertolucci family founded the winery in 1922 in the shadow of Mt. St. John near Oakville. They were among the first to plant premium grape varieties in the Napa Valley.

Andrea (Andy) Bertolucci came to the United States from Italy in 1913 expressly to make wine. He settled in St. Helena in 1919. In 1922 he purchased a twenty-four-acre vineyard and winery, where he made sacramental wines and sold grapes to home winemakers during Prohibition. He made his first table wine with his son Louis in 1933, selling the 5,000 gallons for 20 cents a gallon. Louis studied enology at U.C. Davis, began to modernize Madonna Winery, bought out his father, and began production of wines under the Mont St. John label. By 1947 Mont St. John Cellars was the twelfth-largest winery in California.

MONT ST. JOHN CELLARS

Louis's son, Andrea (Buck) Bertolucci, grew up in Louis's varietal specific vineyards, studied viticulture and enology at Cal State University at Fresno, and came home in 1967 to work as assistant winemaker to his father. When Louis and his brothers sold the winery in 1970, Buck bought and planted 160 acres in the not yet "discovered" Carneros Region, which he still farms organically and dry—meaning nature runs things. Buck's Madonna Vineyards is one of the few vineyards in Napa County with the California Certified Organic Farmers Association designation and produces the fine pesticide- and herbicide-free wines of Mont St. John. Buck believes that "herbicides and pesticides . . . are shortcuts that ultimately throw things in the vineyards out of balance, causing more problems down the road."

As you enter the tasting room with its wood-paneled walls and obviously linoleum floors, you instantly know that this is a casual, fun place with warm hospitality and humor. "No question's too dumb; the only dumb question is the one unasked." Here you can purchase one of our favorites: Angelo's garlic-stuffed olives, garlic marinara sauce and salsa, mustard, Cuisine Perel pastas, grapeseed oils, Vine Village vinegars and olive oils, Brent's Cabernet Chocolate Sauce, "Life Is a Cabernet" mouse pads, espresso shortbread cookies, and wine-country posters and books.

Fine points: Reserve ahead to spend some entertaining time with Buck or other wine guys on their vineyard and tasting tours, particularly on the second and fourth Saturdays of the month. These exceptionally personal tours and informative tours of organic farming and wine tasting cost $10 for tour and tastings. Featured wines (all estate-bottled): Chardonnay, Pinot Noir, Cabernet Sauvignon, Johannisberg Riesling, Gewürztraminer, Muscat di Canelli, Pinot Grigio. Owner: Andrea (Buck) Bertolucci. Winemakers: Buck Bertolucci and David Higgenbotham. Cases: 10,000. Acres: 160.

❧ *Mont St. John Cellars, 5400 Old Sonoma Road, Napa 94559; phone (707) 255–8864, fax (707) 257–2778. Open 10:00 A.M.–5:00 P.M. daily. MasterCard, Visa, and American Express. Wheelchair-accessible.*

CARNEROS CREEK winery is next on our tour. As you leave Mont St. John, turn right up Old Sonoma Road. (If you skipped Mont St. John, just continue up the road.) Turn left (west) onto Dealy Lane 0.3 mile from Mont St. John, and travel west 1 mile. After you pass a golf course (it's a private one belonging to David Wolper), watch for the Irish and American flags near what looks like a yellow wood house, which it was before it became Carneros Creek. Turn left into Carneros Creek's parking lot at the flags.

An Irishman making wine? You bet! In fact, Carneros Creek Pinot Noir is the official wine of the Irish city of Cork, one of San Francisco's Sister Cities. Here's the story.

Owner Francis Mahoney's parents left County Cork in the 1920s for California. Their families, the O'Mahoneys and O'Riordans, still farm around Cork. In the 1960s Francis took off to work the family

---

JOHANNISBERG RIESLING CUSTARD
from Buck Bertolucci, Mont St. John Cellars

INGREDIENTS:

    6 Tbs superfine sugar

    3 large egg yolks

    ½ cup Mont St. John Johannisberg Riesling

    ¼ cup grated lemon peel

    1 tsp orange marsala

PREPARATION:

    Whisk sugar and egg yolks in the top of a double boiler until sugar is dissolved. Simmer water and cook, whisking continually until eggs begin to thicken (3–4 minutes). Gradually add Riesling. Continue to whisk until mixture has thickened and has tripled in volume (about 7 minutes). Whisk in lemon and orange marsala. Pour into champagne glasses. Garnish with orange slices and serve quickly. Serves 4.

CARNEROS CREEK WINERY

farms and travel the wine regions of France, Germany, and Italy. After carefully developing his affinity for Burgundian wines, Francis taught for a while and then decided to follow his true love: wine. He studied enology at UC Davis, worked at Connoisseur Wine Imports in San Francisco and as vineyard manager for Mayacamas Vineyards, and established his own winery in the Carneros district in 1972. His goal was to make wines that would stand up to French Burgundies. Eventually he cofounded the Carneros Quality Alliance.

In a brilliant move, Francis offered his land for a UC Davis field study to improve grape varietal quality. He selected the Enology Department's top student, Melissa Moravec, to lead the clonal research project. Francis learned along with the researchers, hired Melissa as enologist, and then winemaker, and now sets a standard for Pinot Noir.

 Fine points: The tasting fee of $2.50 goes toward your purchase of wine. Featured wines: Fleur de Carneros Chardonnay, Fleur de Carneros Pinot Noir, Merlot, Mahoney Estate Chardonnay and Pinot Noir, Cabernet Sauvignon. Owners: The Mahoney Family. Winemaker: Melissa Moravec. Cases: 34,000. Acres: 108 planted, 108 new.

❧ *Carneros Creek, 1285 Dealy Lane, Napa 94559; phone (707) 253–9463, fax (707) 253–9465, e-mail wineinfo@carneros-creek.com, Web site http://www.carneros-creek.com. Open 10:00 A.M.–5:00 P.M. daily. MasterCard, Visa, American Express, and Discover. Wheelchair-accessible.*

As you leave Carneros Creek, turn left onto Dealy Lane to visit CODORNIU NAPA, an architectural and artistic heaven and sparkling-wine treat. After a curve in the road, turn left onto Henry Road and drive for about 0.5 mile. Turn left into Codorniu's long driveway, well marked with gate and gray cement walls. No—the cute old house on the left is not it. Keep going. Notice the peaceful lake just below what appears to be a knoll topped by a mound of long grass. *That* is Codorniu Napa.

Designed by Barcelona architect Domingo Triay and assisted by Napa Valley architect Earl R. Bouligny, this manmade local landmark features water cascading down the building and staircase edges, reflecting pools, smoky quartz–colored windows, an art gallery featuring exceptional Spanish and American artists (including the decorative glass and sculpture of permanent resident artist Gordon Huether), and winemaking artifacts. Barcelona craftspeople designed and built the custom furniture and fittings to express contemporary Catalan culture.

With their abundant resources the Raventos family built this remarkable winery. Part of a hill was removed and set aside while the production facility, offices, and visitor center were constructed. Then the complex was re-covered with the reserved earth, and the new winery's height was matched with the top

CODORNIU NAPA'S ENTRANCE AND WINERY
UNDER NATIVE GRASSES

Grilled Rack of Lamb Dinner
from Codorniu Napa

Ingredients for the Rack of lamb:

rack of lamb, approximately 2 lb
2–3 Tbs olive oil
1–3 cloves of garlic, split

Preparation:

Rub meat with olive oil and garlic. Arrange barbecue to achieve a hot, indirect open fire. Place lamb in center with coals around outside, or place opposite side of grill from coals. (Lamb should not be directly over coals.) Grill 10–15 minutes on each side. Serves 4.

Make batter for zucchini pancakes while the barbecue coals are heating, and start the herbed potatoes. Brown pancakes during the last 20 minutes that the lamb is grilling.

Ingredients for the Herbed Potatoes:

12 small red potatoes
2 Tbs butter
1 tsp crumbled dried rosemary

Preparation:

Wash potatoes, trim, and remove eyes. Cut in half. Melt butter in skillet. Add potatoes and sprinkle with rosemary. Pan roast, covered, 35–40 minutes, lifting cover from time to time to turn potatoes and prevent overbrowning. Serves 4.

Ingredients for the Zucchini Pancakes:

1 lb fresh zucchini
½ cup flour
½ cup grated Parmesan cheese
1 tsp garlic salt
1 egg, beaten

Preparation:

Coarsely grate zucchini, discarding juice. Mix with remaining ingredients. Twenty minutes before dinner is to be served, spoon batter onto preheated, non-stick griddle to make 2 ½–3-inch-diameter pancakes. Brown 10 minutes on each side. Serves 4.

of the original hill. Native grass was planted over the top so that the exterior changes with the seasons in tune with the surrounding hills, with the grass drip-irrigated from ponds on the estate. Talk about environmental sensitivity!

If you are lucky you will encounter Hospitality Coordinator Kay Malaske, who elegantly answers all questions. Enjoy excellent biscotti, a beautiful selection of books, Vine Village oils, and interesting glassware.

The family made the first *methode champenoise* sparkling wine in Barcelona in 1872 and began making elegant and delicate California sparkling wine here in 1991. They have been making still wines in Spain since the 1500s and today are Spain's foremost maker of Cava. They now also produce a still white wine here, with the goal of making a full range of table wines.

 Fine points: The Raventos family also own Bach, Bodegas Bilbainas, Rondel, and Raimat wineries. Featured wines: Brut, Brut Rose, Blanc de Blanc, Reserve Cuvee. Tasting fee $4.00–$6.00 for a full pour. No picnicking. Owners: The Raventos Family. Winemakers: sparkling wines–Todd Graff; still wines–Don Van Staavern. Cases: 30,000. Acres: 350.

❧ *Codorniu Napa, 1345 Henry Road, Napa 94559; phone (707) 224–1668, fax (707) 224–1672. Open 10:00 A.M.–5:00 P.M. daily. Tours at 11 A.M. and 2:00 P.M., or call ahead. MasterCard, Visa, and American Express. Wheelchair-accessible by elevator at southern entrance.*

SOUTH OF NAPA

As you approach Napa on Highway 29 coming from Berkeley/Oakland or the East Bay, you may want to stop at three interesting places that most people miss: Hakusan Sake Gardens, Seguin-Moreau Cooperage, and Napa Ale Works. They, and a Lafitte cork production facility, are all in a newish industrial complex in a triangle formed by the Kelly Road cutoff between the junction of Highways 12 and 29.

To get to these spots, take Kelly Road off Highway 12 or 29 and follow the signs into the complex. Take the northern road (Camino Dorado) entrance to Seguin-Moreau and Napa Ale, and the southern entrance (Executive Way) to Hakusan Sake.

Directly across from HAKUSAN SAKE GARDENS' parking lot and past the cherry trees is an unusual tasting room with plenty of tables and garden views. Here you can taste at least seven sakes, served warm or cold in small glasses that resemble shot glasses. Made from California's finest rice, these premium sakes contain no sulfites, which reduces the possibility of headaches (if you limit intake).

HAKUSAN SAKE GARDENS ENTRANCE
WITH SPRING CHERRY BLOSSOMS

If you sit in the tasting room, you can also take in the beauty of the Japanese gardens and American sculpture just south of the building and also facing the brewery. Since Hakusan is owned by Kahnan Inc., holders of a large Coca-Cola franchise in Japan, it is not a sake maker with etched-in-stone traditions that can't be broken. With such independence Hakusan has experimented and created sake six-packs as well as sake-filled chocolates and dessert sakes—moves disdained in Japan as being too American. When we visited we suggested Hakusan infuse some sake with gas to make a carbonated sake to compete in the beer market.

When founder Toyokichi Hombo introduced Coca-Cola to Japan, he met resistance because the Japanese thought it looked suspiciously like soy sauce. Eventually overcoming that problem, he decided that the next-hardest project might be to talk Americans into liking sake.

Take the self-guided tour of the adjoining brewery, where you can view the process through windows and read excellent explanations of the brewing steps. If you buy some sake, you can take a sake recipe booklet.

SESAME SPROUT SALAD AND FRESH APPLE MIRIN CUPS
from Hakusan Sake Gardens

INGREDIENTS FOR SESAME SPROUT SALAD:

1 tsp Hakusan Sake	*1 tsp sugar*
2 tsp Hakusan Mirin	*1 tsp sesame oil*
½ cup soy sauce	*1 tsp sesame seeds*
¼ cup rice vinegar	*1 lb bean sprouts*

PREPARATION:

Mix everything but the bean sprouts together. Rinse bean sprouts in colander. Drain. Heat a saucepan of water to a boil, then add sprouts. Cook for 1 minute, then drain. In a bowl, toss the bean sprouts with the dressing until thoroughly mixed. Served chilled. Serves 4.

For variety, use the dressing over a salad of noodles, cucumber slices, and shredded chicken. Serve with chilled Hakusan Premium Sake.

INGREDIENTS FOR FRESH APPLE MIRIN CUPS:

8 Tbs Hakusan Mirin	*cinnamon powder*
½ cup butter sliced in 8 pats	*8 large red apples, sliced and peeled*
8 tsp raisins	

PREPARATION:

Prepare apples and arrange one apple each in a dessert dish. Add 1 pat of butter, 1 Tbs of Hakusan Mirin, a dash of cinnamon, and 1 tsp raisins to each dish. Microwave on high, 4 dishes at a time, for 5–7 minutes or to desired tenderness. Serve chilled with Hakusan Sweet Blossom (dessert) Sake. Serves 8.

Fine points: Perhaps sake should be called "the other white wine." Tasting fee $1.00 total. Featured sakes: Premium Sake, Napa Hakusan, Mild Draft Sake, Sweet Blossom and Plum dessert sakes, three kinds of sake-filled chocolates ($1.00 per piece), Mirin cooking sake, and assorted gift baskets. Owners: Kohnan, Inc. (Toyokichi Hombo). Brewmaster: Hirotaka (Hiro) Sugiura. Cases: 200,000. Acres: Sacramento Valley.

❧ Hakusan Sake Gardens, One Executive Way, Napa 94558; phone (707) 258–6160 or (800) HAKUSAN, Web site http://www.hakusan.com. Open 10:00 A.M.–5:00 P.M. Thursday–Tuesday. MasterCard, Visa, and Discover. Wheelchair-accessible.

We highly recommend that you visit the Seguin Moreau Napa cooperage to view the craft of making wine barrels in the French tradition from American oak. In the cooperage across from Seguin Moreau's offices, you can watch from a walkway so close to the process that you can feel the heat of the flames and inhale the smoke and sawdust.

Huge signs explain the process, from cutting wood and stoking the fires with oak chips to the cooper's art of using water and dancing flames to mold the barrels. Like witches' caldrons, the flames seem to toast the barrels and the coopers' hair, sending a vanilla aroma into the air. Watch the hammer blows shape the metal bands in the "barrel-maker's dance."

Fine points: T-shirts, books, and other souvenirs are available here. Barrels: 80 per day.

❧ Seguin-Moreau Napa, 151 Camino Dorado, Napa 94558; phone (707) 252–3408. Open 8:00 A.M.–6:00 P.M. Best time to watch: 9:00 and 11:00 A.M., 1:00 and 3:00 P.M. MasterCard and Visa. Wheelchair-accessible.

SEGUIN-MOREAU COOPER HEATS WOOD
SO IT CAN BE FORMED INTO BARRELS

If you turn right as you leave Seguin-Moreau and then left onto Camino Ortega, you'll find NAPA ALE WORKS on your left. In a truly symbiotic environmental relationship, Napa Ale saves its shredded paper and gives it to neighbor Seguin-Moreau to start its fires.

Dwayne Mathews and Elaine St. Clair started making beer at home in 1988, a natural result of Elaine's Scottish heritage and UC Davis Fermentation Studies. While an assistant winemaker at Domaine Chandon, Elaine joined with John Wright, chairman of Domaine Chandon, to build this brewery.

Napa Ale makes beer "faithful to the German Rhenheitsgebot," an ancient Bavarian purity law that allows only malted barley or wheat, yeast, hops, and water as ingredients, with hops from the Washington's Yakima Valley.

Fine points: Be sure to call ahead for an appointment to visit this hands-on brewery for a down-and-wet experience. You can get Napa Ale Works brews at restaurants, better lounges and groceries, and Beverages and More. And be sure to check out the NAW merchandise. Featured beers: Napa Red Ale, Napa Wheat Ale, Napa Oatmeal Stout. Owners: Dwayne Mathews, Elaine St. Clair, and John Wright. Brewmaster: Elaine St. Clair. Barrels: 2,000.

Napa Ale Works, 110 Camino Ortega, Napa 94558; phone (707) 257–8381, fax (707) 257–2436, e-mail aleworks@aol.com, Web site http://www.aleworks.com. 8:00 A.M.–5:00 P.M. Monday–Friday. Tours by appointment. No credit cards. Wheelchair-accessible.

CHAPTER 2

IN THE CITY OF NAPA ITSELF

G ood news, folks. Downtown Napa is about to undergo an Oprah-style makeover. But in this case, it's a Mondavi-style makeover.

The Napa County Seat, complete with historic courthouse, big post office, and excellent new library, has suffered predictably from the development of outlying shopping centers and discount chains in ticky-tackey big boxes. But to the rescue, riding white stallions and wearing twenty-five-gallon white hats, come Robert Mondavi and friends, including many city of Napa residents.

Until recently, private redevelopment of downtown storefronts and historic buildings has been slow, because the Napa River has flooded drastically a few times in recent years, making any new investments vulnerable to disaster. But in June 1998 Napa voters decided to spend $155 million to control the river's flooding. This is great news for everyone because investors will feel that they can safely put money toward the redevelopment of the downtown without fearing disaster, and Napa will be revitalized.

Even before the people of Napa cast this life preserver into the water, Robert Mondavi's powerful safety net had begun to spread. When the restoration of the Napa Opera House seemed to have bogged down, for instance, he pledged millions of dollars to finish the project. (Mondavi has also pledged money to create the Oxbow School, a residential art school scheduled to open in 1999.) And, aware that the "Up Valley" towns of Yountville, St. Helena, and Calistoga really couldn't bear any more tourism and that the city of Napa was dying on the vine, Mondavi inspired, organized, and hired staff to raise funds to develop an enormous and fascinating American Center for Wine, Food and the Arts.

Located on thirteen acres on the banks of the Napa River on First Street, the Center already enjoys support from the biggest names in American food and wine, including Julia Child. Its purpose will be to promote the best of American culture and play a significant role in the advancement of America's achievements

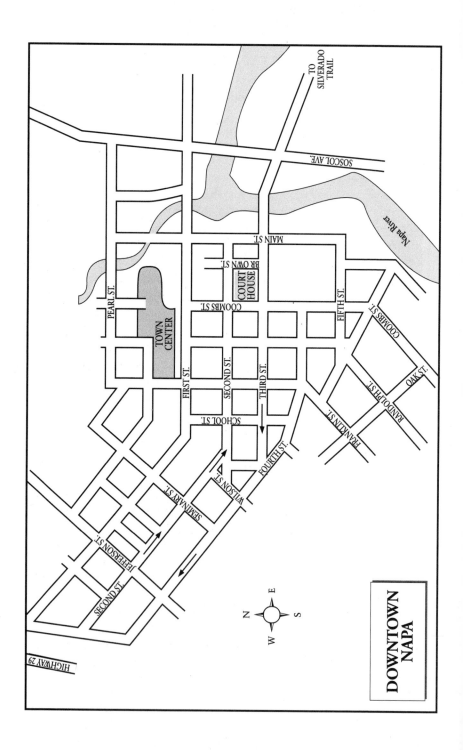

DOWNTOWN NAPA

in wine, food, and the arts. There will be exhibitions and educational programming to cover traditional and experimental programs in viticulture, enology, agriculture, cuisine, artistic and literary expression, the study of history, the science and politics of food, nutrition and health, sustainable agriculture, and the world food supply. Mondavi has already brought in as affiliated organizations The American Institute of Wine & Food, the University of California at Davis, and the Cornell University School of Hotel Administration.

All of this activity suggests a very exciting future for Napa.

Of course, the present isn't all that bad, either.

MAIN STREET, FIRST STREET, AND NAPA TOWN CENTER

Most of what you will want to visit on foot or wheelchair is along Main Street, First Street, and adjoining Napa Town Center, a collection of mall stores that snake around older buildings. Here is where most of Napa's interesting shops and restaurants are clustered, along with the Firemen's Museum and some intriguing import shops.

Beginning at Main Street's south end, take a look at the construction and new developments going on at the Napa Mill. Then, from Second Street on Main heading north, you might want to try one of several small restaurants, such as Pico Rio, P. J.'s at the corner of First Street, Peking Palace, and Downtown Joe's.

DOWNTOWN JOE'S, named for owner Joe Peatman, has been voted "Best Outdoor Dining," "Best Bar," "Best Night Spot," and "Best Place to Meet the Opposite Sex" by Napa residents. Downtown Napa's only microbrewery/restaurant, the restaurant and outdoor dining area look out over the river, a Napa park lawn, and Main Street action (such as it is). We enjoyed the best brew pub grub we've ever had here, ranging from a roasted-garlic Caesar salad and pulled pig, to burgers, grilled veggie pannini, flank-steak sandwich, pastas, and pizzas.

Fine points: Featured beers: Lickety Split Lager, Ace High Cream Ale, Dancin' Feet Red Wheat Beer, Tail Waggin Ale, Past Due Dark Ale, Golden Thistle Bitter Ale, and Slipknot Stout. Owner: Joe Peatman. Brewmaster: Lance McLaughlin. Chef: Paul Croshal. Barrels: 1,000.

Downtown Joe's, 902 Main Street, Napa 94559; phone (707) 258–2337, fax (707) 258–8740. Open 11:00 A.M.–11:00 P.M. daily, Sunday brunch from 8:30 A.M. Full bar. Visa, MasterCard, American Express, Discover, and JCB. Wheelchair-accessible.

A couple of doors north on Main Street is Napa's best coffee place, the **NAPA VALLEY COFFEE ROASTING COMPANY**, where you can inhale the mouth-watering aromas of roasting coffee, sit and read while you enjoy a cup, nibble on light foods, and feel slightly urban.

Our only complaint is that the place closes at 6:00 P.M. Perhaps when downtown development is further along it will stay open later.

Fine points: Enjoy the Roasting Company's other cafe in St. Helena, at Oak and Adams Streets, 1 block west of St. Helena's Main Street (Highway 29).

❧ *Napa Valley Coffee Roasting Company, 948 Main Street, Napa 94559; phone (707) 224–2233. Open 7:00 A.M.–6:00 P.M. daily. No credit cards. Wheelchair-accessible.*

Next, again north on Main Street, you might want to browse through **BREWSTER'S ARMY NAVY STORE** for a historic look at a huge collection of Ben Davis clothes, Dickies and Georgia boots, and everything you could need for camping, skiing, and work outfits. We hope Larry and Rachel Friedman stick around for another forty years.

❧ *Brewster's Army Navy Store, 1006 Main Street, Napa 94559; phone (707) 224–4121. Open 9:00 A.M.–5:00 P.M. daily. Visa, MasterCard, and American Express. Wheelchair-accessible.*

Just past Brewster's is the Main Street Exchange Building, through or around which you can walk to our favorite Napa restaurant, **CELADON**, which hangs over the creek and has not flooded recently. Owner/chef Greg Cole considers Philippe Jeanty, formerly of Domaine Chandon and currently of his own Bistro Jeanty in Yountville, to be his mentor. And are we lucky! You can also get to Celadon over the footbridge from the public parking lot (home to downtown Napa's Farmers' Market) adjacent to the Cinedome Movie Theater.

In what was once the Cecil Hotel, built in 1905, Greg and his wife Elizabeth Fairbairn have created an extremely comfortable dining room with industrial angles and celadon colors. There are blonde floors and celadon-colored chairs, trim, ducts, even vases and pitchers. Those lucky patrons who sit in the padded high chairs at the slate-covered counter get to watch all of the kitchen action in a small corner of the room. David Goines' Chez Panisse posters decorate the walls.

A graduate of the Culinary Institute of America, Greg worked for Jeanty at Domaine Chandon, opened Piatti's Sonoma restaurant in 1990, and served as chef at Robert Sinskey Vineyards for five years, having started at Sinskey

MAINE CRAB CAKES WITH SWEET CORN AND PEPPERS AND GRAINY MUSTARD SAUCE
from Chef Greg Cole, Celadon

INGREDIENTS FOR THE CRAB CAKES:

½ lb Maine crab meat, cleaned   *1 tsp Worcestershire sauce*

¼ cup mayonnaise   *½ tsp Tabasco sauce*

2 eggs   *½ tsp salt*

1 ½cups fresh white-bread crumbs   *pinch black pepper*

PREPARATION:

Combine all the ingredients and mix well. Divide the crab-cake mixture into 12 even portions. Pan fry in salad oil until golden brown on both sides. Remove onto absorbent paper and drain. Serve with Grainy Mustard Sauce. Serves 4.

INGREDIENTS FOR THE SWEET CORN & PEPPERS:

2 Tbs salad oil

1 Tbs olive oil

1 medium onion, finely diced

2 celery ribs, finely diced

1 ear white corn, husked, cut off cob

1tsp garlic

1 red bell pepper, finely diced

1 Tbs Italian parsley, chopped

zest of ½ lemon

PREPARATION:

Heat the olive oil in a small skillet and sauté the onion, celery, and corn kernels for 3 minutes. Add the garlic and cook for 1 minute. Add the red bell pepper and cook for an additional minute. Remove from heat and add the Italian parsley and lemon zest. Allow to cool. Serves 4.

INGREDIENTS FOR THE GRAINY MUSTARD SAUCE:

1 cup sour cream   *3 Tbs whole grain mustard*

¼cup white wine   *pinch salt and black pepper*

PREPARATION:

Combine all ingredients and mix well.

working in the wine cellar. In March 1998 (Celadon's first year), *Wine Spectator* named Greg one of "America's Hottest Young Chefs."

Besides serving some of the best, most honest food in Napa Valley, Celadon's menu is extremely reasonably priced. Maine crab cakes are perfect ($8.00), as is the grilled cheese and porcini-mushroom polenta with chard and balsamic glaze ($7.50). Salads are perfect and filling; the Caesar is available in both $3.50 and $7.00 sizes. The oyster po'boy and grille d'portobello mushroom sandwich with eggplant (the best vegetarian sandwich Kathleen has ever eaten) are both $8.00. The steak frites ribeye with perfectly crisp fries is $16.50, while the horseradish-roasted half chicken with vegetables and saffron broth is succulent and delectable ($13.50).

Oh, another thing: Be sure to watch for Greg and Elizabeth's Cole's Chop House up the block on Main Street.

❧ *Celadon, 1040 Main Street, Napa 94559; phone (707) 254–9690, fax (707) 254–9692. Open for lunch 11:30 A.M.–2:00 P.M. Monday–Friday, dinner 5:00–9:00 P.M. Monday–Saturday. Visa, MasterCard, and American Express. Wheelchair-accessible.*

Continuing our walk north on Main Street, a little Berkeley-style import shop called INTI, named for the Peruvian Sun God, sells pottery, jewelry, tapestry bedspreads, candles, incense, scarves, beads, and masks.

❧ *Inti, 1138 Main Street, Napa 94559; phone (707) 258–8034. Open 11:00 A.M.–6:00 P.M. Monday–Thursday, Saturday; 11:00 A.M.–10:00 P.M. Friday; 11:00 A.M.–5:00 P.M. Sunday. Visa and MasterCard.*

Be sure to take the time to cross Main Street and visit the NAPA FIREFIGHTERS MUSEUM, which really should be called the International Firefighters Museum. A volunteer staff has collected donations of antique fire engines, equipment, uniforms, photos, carriages, badges, hats, and stories from around the world. The collection grows constantly as firefighters from everywhere hear of the museum and send contributions. This is a great place for families and anyone who every followed a fire engine.

❧ *Napa Firefighters Museum, 1201 Main Street, Napa 94559; phone (707) 259–0609. Open 11:00 A.M.–4:00 P.M. Friday–Sunday. No admission fee. Wheelchair-accessible.*

Now go back to First Street, heading west from Main Street. Significant places to stop include Rod Covington's Napa Wine Merchants (1146 First Street), where you can find the best wines of the Napa Valley, in case you don't have time to explore the wineries yourself, and Bookends Bookstore at 1014 Coombs street between First Street and the Napa Town Center.

AMERICAN BISTRO is a comfortable, all-American bistro in a turn-of-the-century bank building at the corner of First and Coombs Streets. Here you can revive with clubhouse, grilled chicken, and roasted eggplant sandwiches, eight-ounce burgers, and good house salads and pastas. Nothing is over $8.00. Hearty breakfasts, too.

❦ *American Bistro, 1202 First Street, Napa 94559; phone (707) 226–1286. Open 8:00 A.M.–9:00 P.M. daily. No credit cards. Wheelchair-accessible.*

We especially enjoy Peggy Erridge's THE BEADED NOMAD for masks, Oriental rugs, beading and handcrafting magazines, great heavy rugs from Afghanistan, Raj travel jewelry from northern India, South African key chains, and lots of goodies from the Czech Republic, Bohemia, India, Africa, Italy, China, and hemp twine from Hungary.

❦ *The Beaded Nomad, 1238 First Street, Napa 94559; phone (707) 258–8004. Open 10:00 A.M.–5:30 P.M. daily. Visa, MasterCard, Discover, and American Express. Wheelchair-accessible.*

On the south side of First Street, check out Napa Children's Book Company with toys, stuffed animals, books and author readings; Copperfield's Books, an excellent North Bay independent book chain featuring used and new books; and Anette's Chocolate and Ice Cream Factory for Bud's Ice Cream, old-fashioned hand-made candies, and espresso drinks.

SIGNIFICANT OTHERS

The immediate downtown center is not the only place in the city of Napa for good shopping and dining.

ALEXIS BAKING COMPANY AND CAFÉ is a hidden treasure in downtown Napa. Few visitors find it, but it is worth searching for. Alexis is a popular place to drop in for breakfast pastries and breads, tea-time pastries and cakes, lunchtime daily special salads and soups, and adventurous burgers (love that gorgonzola!). The same informal goodies and two tasty specials ($10–$11) are offered for dinner Thursday and Friday. Alexis is a great place to stop before or after a movie at the downtown Uptown Theater.

❦ *Alexis Baking Company and Café, 1517 Third Street, Napa 94559; phone (707) 258–1827. Open: 6:30 A.M.–6:00 P.M. Monday–Wednesday; 6:30 A.M.–8:00 P.M. Thursday–Friday; 7:30 A.M.–3:00 P.M. Saturday; 8:00 A.M.–2:00 P.M. Sunday. No credit cards. Wheelchair-accessible.*

The ATLAS PEAK GRILL is everyone's favorite secret steakhouse, especially for those of us who claim that we no longer eat meat. At the northeast side of old Napa and near the Silverado Country Club, Atlas Peak is in a charming storybook cottage surrounded by flowers and greenery. Here you can sink your teeth into juicy, corn-fed beef that reflects another era, when Americans cared about whether their steak cuts were in the New York or Chicago style. Everything carnivorous here is perfect, from pork loin to filet mignon. Famous also for its perfect martinis, Atlas Peak provides an excellent chance to enjoy the best of Napa Valley's wines.

Atlas Peak Grill, 3342 Vichy Avenue at Monticello Road (Highway 121), Napa 94559; phone (707) 253–1455. Open for dinner only at 5:30 P.M. daily, summer; Wednesday–Sunday, winter. Full bar. Visa and American Express. Wheelchair-accessible.

Often voted "Most Romantic Restaurant in the Napa Valley," CHANTERELLE is reliable, pleasant, and plush. There are huge upholstered chairs, lots of room to spread out, and plenty of space between tables. Located on First Street at Soscol (near the Napa Valley Wine Train's terminus), Chanterelle offers no surprises and very good food, warranting its strong local following.

Sunday Champagne Brunch is sumptuous, with a full range of entrees— from pasta to Petrale sole, calamari steak, leg of lamb, and eggs Florentine with Hanns Kornell Extra Dry—at about $15. Here the Caesar salads actually have anchovies. The pastas are excellent, the Dungeness crab risotto is memorable ($12.95), and you might want to try the pork tenderloin with cognac-soaked currants ($14.75). Or how about crispy roasted duck ($16.75), herb-crusted filet of venison with sun-dried apricots and cranberries, or the hazelnut-crusted rack of lamb with wild mushrooms ($19.75). All entrees are available *prix fixe* at $32, with appetizer, soup or salad, entree, dessert, and coffee or tea.

Chanterelle, 804 First Street, Napa 94559; phone (707) 253–7300. Open lunch and dinner daily. Full bar. Visa, MasterCard, and American Express. Wheelchair-accessible.

The DEPOT HOTEL is something else entirely. The "longest continuously serving restaurant in Napa," this Depot Hotel (in contrast to the elegant one in Sonoma) is a T-shirt and elbows-on-the-table after-work-on-Friday-night kind of place. The main dining-room walls have olive-green, floral-print wallpaper above fake wood paneling, and green-squares linoleum on the floors. Waitresses who have been serving and living for a while engage in brief, matter-of-fact conversation and bring your dinner Italian "family style," which here means bowls of thick minestrone accompanied by an entire bowl of Parmesan cheese, a bare-bones salad, a choice of pastas (try the malfatti or paper-thin ravioli, or both), and an entree (choices range from veal marsala to chicken livers, lamb chops, and steaks). And the whole dinner costs just $12.

You can't miss here if you want to run into lots of locals mixed with winery owners having a good time. The wine list is local, limited, and inexpensive, offering Robert Mondavi Pinot Noir at $18.00, Louis M. Martini Cabernet Reserve at $10.00, and Sutter Home White Zinfandel at $9.50.

Depot Hotel, 806 Fourth Street, Napa 94559; phone (707) 252–4477. Open for dinner daily. Full bar. No credit cards. Not wheelchair-accessible.

Many locals go to Jerry Shaffer's FOOTHILL CAFÉ for his baby-back ribs, said by many Napa and Sonoma chefs to be the best in the country. But everything on the menu is tantalizing. Located in an unlikely little strip mall northeast of many Carneros wineries on Old Sonoma Road, Foothill Café is open only for dinner, alas, and is "closed for therapy Monday and Tuesday."

Jerry's humor shows everywhere, from decor to menu. The walls are bright mustard yellow with silver grape leaves. Round mirrors seem to enlarge the tiny room, and a red-framed window hangs free just inside the door. The total effect is to suggest you are going to have fun here. Jerry suggests in print, "If our food, drinks and service aren't up to your standards…please lower your standards."

Be sure to try the "world renowned baby back ribs" ($13.50), half smoked chicken ($11.50), or braised lamb shank ($14.50). The Thai spinach and Caesar salads are excellent ($6.50 each). Desserts such as creme brulee, cobblers, crisp, and chocolate indulgences are each $5.00. Enjoy—but be sure to call for reservations in advance.

Foothill Café, 2766 Old Sonoma Road, Napa 94559; phone (707) 252–6178. Open 4:30–9:30 P.M. Wednesday–Sunday. Wine and beer. "We like cash and take Visa, MasterCard, American Express, and checks that don't bounce." Wheelchair-accessible.

GENOA DELICATESSEN & RAVIOLI FACTORY is one of our favorites and has been ever since Kathleen was growing up in Berkeley and her mother used to go to the original Genoa Deli in Oakland (here since 1926) to get ravioli. Located in a strip mall on Trancas Boulevard, Genoa is worth tracking down for picnic supplies or an informal lunch or dinner. Here you will find the best in deli salads, minestrone and other soups, roasted chicken with garlic bread ($4.29), pastas, an excellent espresso and juice bar, and a wine shop with Napa Valley's best. Oh yes, and huge sandwiches ranging from $4.50 to $5.25, featuring maple turkey, Virginia baked ham, crab salad, head cheese, domestic prosciutto, bresaola, beef tongue, coppa Veneziana, and just about anything else you can imagine (but no peanut butter). Delivery is available.

Genoa is also a great place to buy dried pastas and olive oils, and it sells its famous pastas and sauces, frozen, in a case against the wall. Long live the DeVincenzi family, please!

❧ *Genoa Delicatessen & Ravioli Factory, 1550 Trancas Street, Napa 94558; phone (707) 253–8686, fax (707) 253–2487. Wine and beer. Open 9:00 A.M.–6:30 P.M. Monday–Saturday, 9:00 A.M.–5:00 P.M. Sunday. Visa, MasterCard, Diners Club, and JCB. Wheelchair-accessible.*

OLD ADOBE BAR AND GRILLE is in the second-oldest adobe building in Northern California (1840), with 3-foot-thick walls, low ceilings and beams, loads of character and characters, and surprisingly good food thrown in. Locals go for the steaks and prime rib, and Reuben and French dip sandwiches. We also enjoy the Mexican food, like Lupe's Puerco Verde ($9.95), prawn fajita enchiladas ($10.95), and the Santa Fe Taco Salad ($8.95). Maybe you'll like the grilled pork-loin chops with rosemary-merlot butter ($13.95). Sunday brunch ranges from omelettes to French toast with ham, bacon, or sausage ($6.25), Tom's Prospector Scramble ($5.50), filet mignon and eggs ($14.95), and Crepes a la Reine ($7.25). The Old Adobe also has an interesting wine list.

❧ *Old Adobe Bar and Grille, 376 Soscol Avenue, Napa 94559; phone (707) 255–4310. Open for lunch and dinner daily. Full bar. Visa, MasterCard, American Express, and Discover.*

You might want to stop at the RED HEN CANTINA and Red Hen Antiques, which you can't miss on the west side of Highway 29 between Napa and Yountville. Turn west on Oak Knoll and then immediately right on Solano (Frontage Road). Despite its glitz and large chicken on top of the roof, the Red Hen Cantina is a locally popular Mexican restaurant, where the bar and patio are after-work gathering places. Nachos and other ample appetizers go well with margaritas and salads, omelettes, and enchiladas. The Pollo Mexicano ($11.50), Chili Colorado ($9.50), Steak Rancheros ($11.50), and the Red Hen Burger ($8.50) are all enormous and satisfying.

❧ *Red Hen Cantina, 5091 St. Helena Highway (Highway 29) via west turn on Redwood (or Oak Knoll to Solano), Napa 94559; phone (707) 255–8125. Open for lunch and dinner daily. Full bar. Visa and MasterCard. Wheelchair-accessible.*

While you are at the Napa Valley Airport, don't miss JONESY'S FAMOUS STEAK HOUSE and its sidekick Café. Often rated the "Best Beef in the Napa Valley" (read: steaks) by locals, Jonesy's takes us fifty years back to another era, when it was cool to smoke and drink Manhattans. You can actually order a cottage cheese and peaches salad (small or large), shrimp Louies, Caesar salads, shrimp cocktails, or calamari ringers.

So many locals come here for lunch that tables in the lounge are reserved for the Café's overflow crowd. For a real steak-house experience, eat in the dining room where you'll find linen tablecloths. Jonesy's Famous Steak Dinners are "Hand-carved on Premises." Top Sirloin steak, "service for two" starts at $19.75 including tossed green salad with Jonesy's Bleu Cheese Dressing or soup, choice of potato or rice pilaf, and a "½ Service" for one of Top Sirloin for $10.50. There are other steak meals on the menu as well as chicken and seafood dishes. The children's menu is equally generous from grilled cheese sandwiches at $3.75 to steak at $5.75 with salad or soup, French fries, and Jello included!

A short but well-selected local wine list ranges from Hakusan Sake at $6.50 a bottle and Beringer Gamay Beaujolais at $12.00 to exceptional Silver Oak Cabernet Sauvignon at $45.00.

*⌘ *Jonesy's Famous Steak House, 2044 Airport Road (in the airport building), Napa 94558; phone (707) 255-2003. Open from 11:30 A.M. Tuesday–Sunday. Full bar. Visa, MasterCard, and American Express. Wheelchair-accessible.*

CHAPTER 3

HIGHWAY 29 (THE ST. HELENA HIGHWAY)

*W*e will now take you up Highway 29—known locally *and more fashionably as the St. Helena Highway. Road signs say 29 but merchants prefer to use St. Helena Highway in their addresses. Try not to be confused by the fact that Highway 29 is also called South St. Helena Highway, Main Street in St. Helena, St. Helena Highway North, and North St. Helena Highway. It is all the same road. If you don't want to explore the Napa Valley's wineries, restaurants, towns, and galleries quite this thoroughly, and decide to cut the tour short and head down the other side, just leap ahead in the book to the winery or restaurant you want.*

We must emphasize, yet again, the danger of turning left across Highway 29. Please make the crossing as few times as possible.

NAPA TO YOUNTVILLE

Four-and-a-half miles north of the intersection of Highways 121 and 29, you'll come to a stoplight at an intersection, announced on overhead signs as Trancas Boulevard. What it doesn't tell you is that Trancas goes to the east from Highway 29, and Redwood Road goes to the west.

Take Redwood Road to the fabulous HESS COLLECTION—the ultimate expression of owner and Swiss entrepreneur Donald Hess's two passions, wine and art. Get into the left lane so that you can ease left in 0.9 mile. Continue up Redwood about 4.5 miles and turn left into The Hess Collection and Mont La Salle Christian Brothers Monastery and Retreat House. The Hess Collection is just beyond the monastery. It belonged to the Christian Brothers until Donald Hess bought the facility in 1985.

ENTRANCE TO THE HESS COLLECTION

The Hess Collection is an *absolutely do not miss!* destination. The architecture, the art collection, and the wines are among the best in California.

There's a bike rack for cyclists in the upper parking lot. Follow the wide brick path lined with oleander trees to the Visitors Center entrance on the right at the back of the courtyard. You will be struck by the elegant vestibule, with white walls and railings and blond wood floors. The round window in the stairway between the second and third floors evocatively frames the round tops of the punch-down fermentation tanks, and the windows in the shop and tasting room frame the wine barrels.

Explore the art collection, which rotates, showing about 25 percent of Hess's private collection at a time. It includes works by Francis Bacon, Robert Motherwell, Georg Baselitz, Magdelena Abakanowicz, Franz Gertsch, Bruce Robbins, Henri Michaux, Emilio Vedova, Frank Stella, and many other great artists.

Hess Holding has an extended family of prominent wineries on other continents, including MontGras in Chile, Glen Carlou and Impala in South Africa, Castello Vicchiomaggio in Italy, and Bodega Norton in Argentina.

 Fine points: You *must* visit the shop here; it is the best in the wine country. The tasting fee is $3.00. Featured wines: Chardonnay, Cabernet Sauvignon, Merlot, Meritage, Zinfandel; from South Africa, Merlot, Chardonnay, and Classique Reserve. Owner: Hess

Holding. Winemaker: Randle Johnson. Executive Chef: Katie Sutton. Cases: 240,000. Acres: 400.

The Hess Collection, 4411 Redwood Road, Napa 94558; phone (707) 255–1144, fax (707) 253–1682. Open 10:00 A.M.–4:00 P.M. daily. Visa, MasterCard, and American Express. Wheelchair-accessible.

As you leave The Hess Collection driveway, turn right down Redwood Road to Highway 29, and turn left (north).

Now we have you traveling northward on Highway 29, barely out of town, and if you're already hungry for lunch, stop immediately at one of our favorites, BISTRO DON GIOVANNI. As soon as you see the mud-colored building on the right, turn off Highway 29 into the driveway. As you walk onto the restaurant's deck from the parking lot, you can decide whether to choose an outdoor table or to walk inside. The deck wraps around the northern and eastern sides of the building, away from highway traffic. Wine-industry locals hang out here to see who's arriving with whom.

When we ask locals for their favorite restaurants, nearly everyone starts the list with Don Giovanni, and for good reason. When you walk in you are greeted by unpretentious hosts in an unpretentious atmosphere that reeks of confidence in taste and style. Don't miss the large painting on Italian newspapers of a cutlery set hanging against soft yellow walls in one corner of the dining room. Gigantic arrangements of blue, yellow, and white flowers set the tone.

Owners Donna and Giovanni Scala were opening chefs at the original Piatti in St. Helena and basically set the chain's standard for Claude Rouas and his partners. Here at their own bistro, they have the luxury of doing it their own Italian–French way. What a relaxing pleasure! The staff is experienced, fun, loose, and efficient.

The wood-burning oven and pantry fill one corner in the room, with the mesquite grill and rest of the kitchen behind glass, off to the side. Donna serves the perfect Caesar salad ($7.50), complete with an actual anchovy and large enough to share as an appetizer; and the beet-and-haricots-verts salad ($6.95) is always a memorable treat. The Maine crab cakes ($8.75) are elegantly light— topped with avocado salsa and accompanied with a fennel slaw dressed in oil and vinegar. Even if you usually don't like clams, try Donna's Spaghetti Clams ($13.95), a dish she prepared for Giovanni's mother in Naples—who exclaimed that they were actually better than her own! All pastas and breads are house-made. We have friends who come here for drinks in the evening and happily make a meal of appetizers with terrific celebrity sightings.

Bistro Don Giovanni, 4110 St. Helena Highway, Napa 94558; phone (707) 224–3300. Open for lunch and dinner daily. MasterCard, Visa, and American Express. Wheelchair-accessible.

GRILLED PORTOBELLO WITH BRAISED GREENS AND BALSAMIC JUS

from Giovanni and Chef Donna Scala, Bistro Don Giovanni

INGREDIENTS FOR THE BALSAMIC JUS:

2 cups balsamic vinegar	1 bunch thyme
3 cups chicken stock, reduced	salt to taste
4 shallots	pepper to taste
2 bay leaves	2 tsp sugar

PREPARATION:

Simmer balsamic jus ingredients 5–10 minutes until reduced by half.

INGREDIENTS FOR THE GRILLED PORTOBELLO:

4 portobello mushrooms, medium size	4 cloves of garlic, sliced
	¼ cup extra virgin olive oil
5 bunches spinach, well washed	salt to taste
4 bunches broccoli rabe	pepper to taste
4 bunches of chard, red or Swiss	

PREPARATION:

Lightly oil and salt and pepper portobello mushrooms, and grill, gill side down. Place a pot of salted water on high heat until boiling. Blanch spinach, broccoli rabe, and chard in the water and cook for 2–3 minutes.

Meanwhile, place a sauté pan on medium-high heat. Add the extra virgin olive oil and sliced garlic, and cook until garlic is lightly browned—approximately 1–1 ½ minutes. When garlic is browned, reduce heat, strain greens, and add to the sauté pan. Cover the pan, turn heat to low, and cook greens for 3 minutes.

To serve, place greens on the plate and the portobellos on the greens. Spoon the balsamic jus over the mushrooms and garnish with onion rings and chopped chives. Serves 4.

TREFETHEN ESTATE VINEYARDS is the first winery you come to north of here; it is also one of the most congenial and fun. To get here, turn east onto tree-lined Oak Knoll Avenue off Highway 29. One-half mile later, turn left onto Eshcol Drive, named for the Eshcol Ranch vineyard and winery located here from 1886 to 1940. Notice the labels on vineyards to help you know what varietals you're passing. Turn left at the large oak tree onto Trefethen Lane, and continue until you reach the pink wood winery with brown trim.

As you get out of your car, enjoy the large, 500-year-old Valley and Cork Oaks and the gardens full of old farming equipment, along with marked and identified plants and rows of herbs, from anise to rosemary. Built by James and George Goodman and designed by Captain Hamden McIntyre in 1886, the winery is listed in the National Register of Historic Places.

While Gene Trefethen was still president of Oakland's Kaiser Industries, he and Katie spotted this run-down old treasure and couldn't resist. Gene had only overseen construction of Hoover Dam and the San Francisco-Oakland Bay Bridge—that's all! So what was a mere 600 acres to replant, rebuild, and organize? After son John got his MBA at Stanford, he and his wife, Janet, joined the winery. Both serve as managing director, making Trefethen the largest contiguous family-owned and -operated vineyard acreage in the Napa Valley. Whew!

The brick floors and cedar walls in the tasting room set the mood, framing an excellent selection of cookbooks and guidebooks. The Trefethens attract cooking celebrations and classes and Julia Child even cooked Thanksgiving dinner here for "Good Morning America" in 1992. Reflecting the Trefethens' community and political involvement, their wines were served at Reagan and Clinton White House dinners for Queen Elizabeth II, the queen of Thailand, and a French president. Trefethen remains the only wooden gravity-flow winery and the largest estate-vineyard winery in the Napa Valley.

TREFETHEN ESTATE VINEYARDS

TREFETHEN CIOPPINO
from Janet Trefethen, Trefethen Estate Vineyards

INGREDIENTS:

2 whole fresh crabs (preferably Dungeness), cooked, cracked, and cleaned

1 ½ lb fresh firm white fish (cod, snapper, sole) cut into 2-inch cubes

6–8 fresh clams in shell, scrubbed and cleaned

½ lb fresh shrimp, cleaned and deveined

2 cans clams with juice

2 cans bay shrimp, drained

1 8-oz bottle clam juice

3 Tbs olive oil

1 ½ cups onions or shallots, chopped

2 16-oz cans whole tomatoes

1 16-oz can tomato sauce

1 ½ cups Trefethen Eshcol Chardonnay

1 bay leaf

3 Tbs fresh parsley, finely chopped

3 Tbs fresh basil, finely chopped; or 1 Tbs dried basil

1 1/2 Tbs fresh oregano, finely chopped; or 1 Tbs dried oregano

3 cloves garlic, minced

3 drops Tabasco sauce

salt and pepper to taste

PREPARATION:

Remove crab meat from bodies and from a few of the legs. Set aside with clams, fish, and shrimp.

Sauté onion in olive oil until limp, abuot 8 minutes. Add garlic and cook 2 minutes more. Add whole tomato, tomato sauce, bottled clam juice, herbs, and wine. Cover and cook for 25–30 minutes over medium heat, stirring occasionally.

Add whole crab legs, crab meat, fish chunks, canned clams, and canned shrimp, and simmer on low heat for 25 minutes. Add fresh shrimp and clams and cook 10 minutes. Discard any unopened clams. Add salt, pepper, and Tabasco to taste. Serves 6–8.

Serve with tossed green salad, crusty French bread, and Chardonnay or Cabernet Sauvignon.

Aside from the wine biz, John is a pilot and motorcyclist. Once a Miss Rodeo California, Janet is an expert in food and wine matching, a leader of the quest for a local appellation designation, and an occasional speaker at the Culinary Institute of America's Hyde Park campus.

Under Janet Trefethen's leadership, the Napa Valley Cooking Class, featuring great chefs from around the United States, has taken place at the winery for more than twenty-five years. For Trefethen's thirtieth anniversary, in 1998, Trefethen held a cooking class given by four thirty-year-old chefs teaching thirty students, sponsored a Club 30 Recipe Contest for culinary professionals, and celebrated dinners honoring some of the country's top chefs' thirty-year-old protégés, with all proceeds from the dinners benefiting charitable causes fighting world hunger.

Oh yes, the wine. Try to get a bottle of the Thirtieth-Anniversary Chardonnay Cuvee. To hint at the quality, Trefethen's 1976 Chardonnay ranked number one in the world at the 1979 World Wine Olympics, sponsored by the French magazine *Gault Millau*. The next year Burgundy winemaker Joseph Drouhin challenged the '79 results, resulting in a second competition, this time at the esteemed Hospice de Beaune. Guess what? Trefethen won again, much to the disappointment of Monsieur Drouhin (who also once challenged the results when Oregon's Eyrie Pinot Noir finished in the top three at a Paris blind tasting. After Eyrie's wine finished a close second in re-tasting, Drouhin opened his own winery in Oregon's Dundee Hills.)

 Fine points: Featured wines: Chardonnay, Dry Riesling, Cabernet Sauvignon, Merlot. Owners: The Trefethen Family. Winemaster: David Whitehouse, Jr. Winemaker: Peter Luthi. Cases: 110,000. Acres: 650.

✴ᴗ *Trefethen Estate Vineyards, 1160 Oak Knoll Avenue, Napa 94558; phone (707) 255–7700 or (800) 556–4847, fax (707) 255–0793, e-mail winery@ trefethenwine.com, Web site www.trefethen.com. Open 10:00 A.M.–4:30 P.M. daily. MasterCard, Visa, and American Express. Wheelchair-accessible.*

Back to Highway 29. Just north of Trefethen and on the other side of Highway 29 you will find NEWLAN VINEYARDS & WINERY on Solano Avenue, which parallels the highway. Newlan is definitely a family affair, with founder Bruce Newlan and winemaker Glen Newlan almost always available to talk about their exciting wines.

To get here, turn left across Highway 29 at Oak Knoll (or straight across the divided highway, ½ highway at a time please, from Trefethen) and turn north (right) onto Solano Avenue. Or turn west (left) from Highway 29 onto Darms Lane and left again onto Solano.

Bruce told us, "It doesn't take a rocket scientist to make wine," with an enticing twinkle in his eye. Yes, he is a rocket scientist for Lockheed Missiles in Sunnyvale. He worked on the *Polaris, Poseidon,* and *Trident* programs. Ultimately, his family's farm roots grow deeper, though. Bruce and son Glen used to buy grapes near Gilroy and ferment them in the garage. After working as a computer whiz in Santa Clara, Glen moved to Napa with his wife, Jerri-Lynn. Their young son, Ryan, is "a train fanatic who watches the Wine Train ride by the vineyard every day."

The Newlans bought their first acreage in Napa Valley in 1967 and turned the thirteen-acre mess of a walnut orchard into a Cabernet Sauvignon vineyard. Bruce took courses at UC Davis, read viticulture texts, and soon began selling his grapes to Inglenook, Clos du Val, and Robert Mondavi. When he discovered that his grapes usually ended up in the wineries' reserve or cask bottlings, he decided that he should make his own wine, if they were that good.

As you enter the California-style stucco building, you immediately run into a railing, which overlooks the small winery and the cozy tasting room. You are at eye level with wine barrels. Walk down the few stairs to the left to see everything.

Fine points: Newlan's Cabernet Sauvignon and Zinfandel have been rated in the 90s by Robert Parker, Jr., and Jerry Mead, creating a great demand nationally. Bruce and Glen manage their own vineyards and make their own wine from their own grapes. Simple and slow. No tasting fee. Featured wines: Chardonnay, Pinot Noir, Cabernet Sauvignon, Zinfandel, Late Harvest Riesling. Owner: Bruce Newlan. Winemaker: Glen Newlan. Cases: 10,000. Acres: 30.

❧ *Newlan Vineyards & Winery, 5225 Solano Avenue, Napa 94558; phone (707) 257–2399 or (800) 500–9463, fax (707) 252–6510, e-mail napa wine@wine.com, Web site www.winecom/nvw. Open 10:00 A.M.–5:00 P.M. daily. MasterCard and Visa. Not wheelchair-accessible.*

Your next stop could be Yountville, or you can just drive north 2.7 miles on Solano Avenue and cross California Drive at the Veterans Home to visit Domaine Chandon.

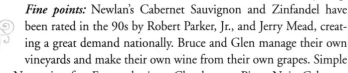

YOUNTVILLE

Just over 4 miles north of the Highway 29–Trancas Boulevard intersection, take the Yountville exit for elegant small-town wine-country shopping, dining, wine tasting, and the new Napa Valley Museum on the grounds of the Veterans' Home. As you turn off the highway to the right, turn right again and then immediately left at the stop sign and Washington Street to tour "downtown"

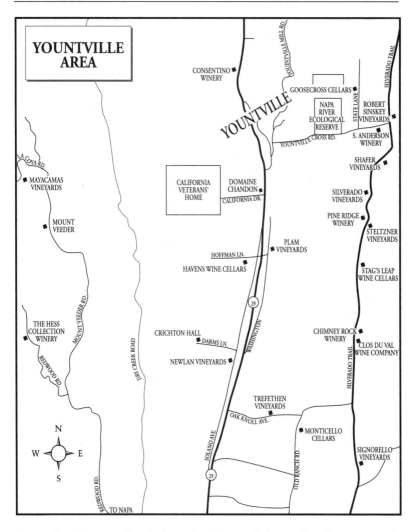

YOUNTVILLE AREA

CONSENTINO WINERY

YOUNTVILLE

YOUNTVILLE MILL RD.

GOOSECROSS CELLARS

SILVERADO TRAIL

NAPA RIVER ECOLOGICAL RESERVE

STATE LANE

ROBERT SINSKEY VINEYARDS

YOUNTVILLE CROSS RD.

S. ANDERSON WINERY

LA CONA RD.

MAYACAMAS VINEYARDS

CALIFORNIA VETERANS' HOME

DOMAINE CHANDON

CALIFORNIA DR.

SHAFER VINEYARDS

SILVERADO VINEYARDS

PINE RIDGE WINERY

MOUNT VEEDER

STELTZNER VINEYARDS

PLAM VINEYARDS

HOFFMAN LN.

HAVENS WINE CELLARS

STAG'S LEAP WINE CELLARS

29

MOUNT VEEDER RD.

THE HESS COLLECTION WINERY

CRICHTON HALL

DARMS LN.

NEWLAN VINEYARDS

WASHINGTON

CHIMNEY ROCK WINERY

CLOS DU VAL WINE COMPANY

REDWOOD RD.

DRY CREEK ROAD

SILVERADO TRAIL

TREFETHEN VINEYARDS

OAK KNOLL AVE.

N
W — E
S

SOLANO AVE.

MONTICELLO CELLARS

OLD RANCH RD.

SIGNORELLO VINEYARDS

29

REDWOOD RD.

TO NAPA

Yountville. New resort hotels abound, as Yountville has made a decision to welcome visitors with open arms.

A historic town along the wine trail, Yountville is now known for its outstanding restaurants, such as The French Laundry, Bistro Jeanty, Domaine Chandon, Pacific Blues Café, the Napa Valley Grille, Gordon's Café and Wine Bar, and Campadres. The Veterans' Home of California was established here in 1882 by veterans of the Mexican and Civil Wars as a home for all veterans west of the Rocky Mountains. In 1900 the State of California bought it for a twenty-dollar gold piece. You can visit the Veterans Home Museum as well as the Napa Valley Museum here.

We will take you up the right (east) side of Yountville's Washington Street, and then back down the west side.

Between the two palm trees on the right just as you enter Yountville from the south end jumps out THE DINER, decorated with Coca-Cola signs on the outside and Fiesta ceramic pitchers on the inside, ceiling fans and brown and beige linoleum floors. Choose the counter, with its round wooden seats, or the booth or table seating.

While locals swear by this place, we were slightly disappointed. It may be the best breakfast at this end of Yountville (try Gordon's at the north end), but we found the highly recommended portobello mushroom plate a bit dry, the cheeseburger flavor-free, and the fries limp. But the shakes are so thick they don't stir (yum!) and you get to finish off what's left in the metal glass it was blended in. The apple crisp, flan, sundaes, and banana splits are all great, as is the Mexican food, cooked by Mexicans. Here's an unusual chance to try Mexican eggs and German potato pancakes all in one meal.

This place served as the local Greyhound Bus Station and diner in the 1950s, and local adults and kids have been hanging out here ever since.

❧ *The Diner, 6476 Washington Street, Yountville 94559; phone (707) 944–2626. Open for breakfast all day, lunch, dinner daily. Beer and wine. No credit cards. Wheelchair-accessible.*

LEMON CREAM SAUCE
from Claude Rouas,
Ristorante Piatti

---

13 oz heavy cream
1 lemon, zest and juice
½ cup grated Parmesan cheese
⅛ tsp white pepper
½ tsp kosher salt

Bring all ingredients to a boil and strain through a fine strainer. Pour immediately over ravioli or other pasta.

Right next door is the original RISTORANTE PIATTI, the first in Claude Rouas's vast and successful upscale chain, contrasting drastically with The Diner in appeal, design, food, and price. This is where Donna and Giovanni Scala set the menu and formula before they went on to their own Bistro Don Giovanni.

The fabulous mesquite wood aroma you smell from the street and as you enter the dining room emanates from the open kitchen and oven, where Piatti pizzas toast. The California–Italian decor soothes, as does the food. Always reliable and innovative are Piatti's salads, pastas (here's that light lemon creme sauce on ravioli again), and the roasted chicken is exceptional. We also enjoy the Dungeness crab salad when it's available. The tiramisu is always good, as is the amaretto cheesecake with warm chocolate sauce. Entrees usually range from $12.50 to $20.00.

The Improvisator David Auerbach plays every Wednesday night, and you just might see Danielle Steele, Val Diamond, Sonoma resident and star of "Beach Blanket Babylon," or former San Francisco mayor Frank Jordan.

❧ *Ristorante Piatti, 6480 Washington, Yountville 94599; phone (707) 944-2070. Open for lunch and dinner daily. MasterCard, Visa, and American Express. Wheelchair-accessible.*

The local phenomenon RANCH MARKET supplies locals and transients with basic food needs like blood oranges and a few veggies, brooms, soap, etc. Many office workers slip in the side door facing Bistro Jeanty's parking lot for a deli sandwich ($3.65) and Bud's ice cream. A true country store with red-and-white checked curtains, Ranch Market makes you feel like you're really on vacation.

❧ *Ranch Market, 6498 Washington Street, Yountville 94599; phone (707) 944-2662. Open 6:00 A.M.–10:00 P.M. No credit cards. Wheelchair-accessible.*

One door up the street is the new, sensational BISTRO JEANTY, the creation of former Domaine Chandon executive chef Philippe Jeanty, who enjoys one of the greatest followings in the Napa Valley. The Champagne native shed the corporate umbrella to strike out on his own and give birth to a "homey place where my little daughter can come in anytime." Philippe is back in the tiny kitchen, to the good fortune of his new and loyal customers. Auberge du Soleil and Piatti co-founder Claude Rouas's daughter, Bettina, came from Niebaum-Coppola Winery to Bistro Jeanty to manage the dining room.

One of the greatest benefits of this new bistro is that we can enjoy Philippe's food at prices lower than at Domaine Chandon. He truly wants you to come by regularly, be comfortable, and greet your friends. On the door facing Washington Street, Philippe has hand-written the hours and specials, making the whole greeting reminiscent of a Paris neighborhood bistro, with half curtains and little floor tiles. Outdoor tables face south and the parking lot, while French antiques fill the dining rooms. Terracotta flower pots planted with miniature roses decorate the tables. Framed French posters hang on the walls, and recorded Edith Piaf warbles reach even the patio tables, creating an even greater allure to us than spraying garlic into the fans.

You enjoy the same menu at lunch and dinner, featuring appetizers of smoked trout and potatoes in olive oil at $7.50, rabbit pate and salad at $6.00, grilled quail and salad at $7.50, beet salad with feta and asparagus at $6.50, and tomato soup in puff pastry at $5.00. Main courses may include mussels in white-wine pastis and frites at $9.00, tuna steak au poivre, and cassoulet at $14.50. Desserts and dessert wines, ports, cognacs, and brandies are all very special.

Bound to be a success for a long time!

❧ *Bistro Jeanty, 6510 Washington Street, Yountville 94599; phone (707)*

944–0103, fax (707) 944–0370. Open for lunch and dinner daily. MasterCard,
Visa, and American Express. Wheelchair-accessible.

Next door, to the north of Bistro Jeanty, is the ANTIQUE FAIR, a collection
of interesting French antiques and furnishings, some from estates in Lyon and
Paris. This is a great spot to find interesting old beds, silverware, armoires, jewelry, and figurines. Locals and visitors have found the antiques here intriguing
for almost thirty years. Browse with care. Be sure to catch the "Noel Francaise"
here from Thanksgiving to December 31, 10:00 A.M.–9:00 P.M., during
Yountville's Festival of Lights.

Antique Fair, 6512 Washington Street, Yountville 94599; phone (707)
944–8440, Web site www.antiquefair.com. Open 10:00 A.M.–5:00 P.M. daily.
MasterCard, Visa, and American Express. Wheelchair-accessible.

As you progress up the right side of Washington Street, the left side of the
fork at the intersection with Oak Leaf Road, a couple of restaurants have
changed hands, with Brava Terrace opening a spinoff and the French Laundry
and Fleur de Lys Keller brothers opening a new bistro sometime soon.

Wine fans should not miss GROEZINGER'S WINE SHOP, for the very best of
rare French and local wines. You can taste at the tasting bar in back, after you
have wound your way through the Old World–feeling shop, which sells 96 percent of its wine by phone orders. Owners Martin and Rick have built a reputation and private lists for fifteen years. Groezinger's also sells old issues of the
Wine Spectator for 99 cents. If you live too far from the Napa Valley to purchase
wine in person, you can rely on Groezinger's to provide the best of small-lot
wines. Get on their mailing list.

Groezinger's Wine Shop, 6528 Washington Street, Yountville 94599; phone
(707) 944–2331. Open 10:00 A.M.–6:00 P.M. Monday–Saturday. MasterCard,
Visa, and American Express. Wheelchair-accessible.

North of Groezinger's Wine Shop, wander among a small complex of shops
and galleries in Beard Plaza, including Images Fine Art, Artistry in Gold, Raku
Ceramics, Raspberry's Art Glass Gallery, and Visions-Nature's Art.

Just for the heck of it, visit fun and charming Peggy Murray at her
MOSSWOOD, a shop to enhance your garden. Peggy recently left the fast-paced
world of public relations and bought Mosswood just two days before we
visited. There she offers exquisite garden sculpture and statuary, Jack
Willoughby's stone-and-iron tall birds from Nanaimo, British Columbia,
European frog and butterfly stakes, objets d'art, fresh plants and flowers, porcelain eggs, Gracie Knight's hand-painted furniture, and Ed McGillicutty's redwood bird aviaries with copper roofs.

Peggy gives garden tours and plans to hold garden events in the courtyard behind Mosswood. Check it out.

Mosswood, 6550 Washington Street, Yountville 94599; phone (707) 944–8151. Open 10:00 A.M.–5:30 P.M. daily. MasterCard, Visa, American Express, and Diners Club. Wheelchair-accessible.

THE FRENCH LAUNDRY

If you're ready for a splurge, make reservations to have lunch or dinner at THE FRENCH LAUNDRY, another block north on Washington Street at Creek Street, in a century-old, two-story stone house with no sign. The James Beard Foundation named owner/chef Thomas Keller the best chef in the United States in 1997. Keller's wry humor means to deceive and intrigue with occasional simplified names attached to complex dishes.

Originally a bar and brothel and then (yes) a French laundry, the building and exquisite tranquil gardens with raised beds of daffodils and vegetables melt away any anxiety if you have to wait for your table. Reservations are mandatory for the eleven-table dining room.

Lunch is served only Friday through Sunday, but it is the more economical way to experience this special culinary treat, at $44. The four-course orgy forces you to make several decisions, so you must come back to try other possibilities. First-course choices range from wild watercress soup to Tongue-in-Cheek braised beef-cheek-and-veal tongue. Second courses may include Atlantic skate wing or Maine lobster "pancake," followed by Hoffman Farm "poussin" with herbed risotto cake, liver and onions, lamb saddle with ravioli of "ris d'agneau et joue d'agneau." Sweet treats could be "coffee and doughnuts" with cappuccino semifreddo, mango sorbet with Maui pineapple and sauce "a l'impiratrice," followed by a tasting of vegetables.

Dinner, at a prix fixe of $65, might include Dungeness crab salad, panroasted calf's brain, or cream of Savoy cabbage soup. Next taste herb-roasted monkfish, filet of spiny lobster, or Maine diver scallop, followed by filet mignon of veal, Hoffman Farm squab, or Elysian Fields Farms lamb chop. Fruits and salads follow, finishing with desserts, which may include creme de farine, or a "floating island" of Swiss meringue with vanilla-bean custard sauce and bittersweet-chocolate "salad."

As an alternative, you may want to try the Chef's Tasting Menu of ten tastes that add up to a full meal of orgasmic small plates at $80.

❧ *The French Laundry, 6640 Washington Street, Yountville 94599; phone (707) 944–2380. Open for lunch Friday–Sunday, dinner daily. MasterCard, Visa, and American Express. Wheelchair-accessible.*

On a more economical but still high culinary level, don't miss GORDON'S CAFÉ AND WINE BAR, another block north on Washington. The sign says GORDON'S MARKET.

Sally Gordon first visited the store run by the Tenaci family in 1967. She moved to the Napa Valley in 1977. We first met her as the public relations director at Domaine Chandon when we accompanied M. F. K. Fisher there for lunch every year to celebrate her birthday and Bastille Day.

Gordon's is immensely popular with locals at breakfast and lunch, and its Friday Dinners sell out every week. When you walk in you feel as if you're entering a cozy country store. On your right, Chef Mari Tola, formerly of Mustards Grill and Table 29 (now Bistro Don Giovanni), and friends cook right in the room, and to the left shelves of well-selected delicacies line the wall. You will find Tazo teas, Potluck Studios bowls, V. G. Buck olive oils, The French Press Virgin Filbert Oil, Sparrow Lane vinegars, the *San Francisco Chronicle* and the *New York Times*. Along the back of the left wall is an admirable collection of local wines for sale. And, miracle of miracles, when you select a bottle to accompany your Friday dinner, Sally sells it to you at the shelf price, without the customary restaurant increase!

Gordon's sells and uses our favorite della Fattoria and Acme breads and serves elegant sandwiches and salads ranging from $3.75 to $6.95. If it happens to be on special, try the sandwich of roasted eggplant with sweet red peppers;

Italian tomato, sausage, and lentil soup; corned beef and Gruyere on rye; and always the genuine Croque Monsieur at $5.95. The homemade raspberry lemonade is a must-try. Locals play chess or cards while eating huge bowls of oatmeal at 1:30 P.M., and we love the espresso bar beyond the kitchen. Sally cooks and bakes on weekends.

Fine points: If you need a stiffer drink than wine, there's always Pancha's bar next door. Book reservations for Gordon's Friday Café supper, usually under $30 for three exquisite courses, which may include French-style sweet spring onion soup with Gruyere cheese or organic field greens with beets, toasted walnuts and crumbled Stilton, pan-seared Atlantic salmon with Beluga lentils, spring garlic, and fava beans; or Atkins Ranch Australian rack of lamb with pan-roasted Yukon gold potatoes, artichokes, and olives de Provence; and dessert and coffee or tea. Don't forget the greatest part of the deal: Wines at regular retail prices off Gordon's shelves in the same room!

Gordon's Café and Wine Bar, 6770 Washington Street, Yountville 94599; phone (707) 944–8246. Open 7:30 A.M.–6:00 P.M. Tuesday–Saturday, later Friday, 7:30 A.M.–5:00 P.M. Sunday. Beer and wine. MasterCard, Visa, American Express, and Discover. Wheelchair-accessible.

At this point Washington Street veers leftish and back to Highway 29. If, instead of going left with it, you decide to go straight ahead (north) on Lincoln, you can explore YOUNTVILLE PARK and a bit of Yountville history at the George C. Yount Pioneer Cemetery & Ancient Indian Burial Grounds.

Yountville Park offers colorful children's play equipment, good barbecues, public rest rooms, and lots of grass to play or lounge on.

Yountville Park, Washington and Lincoln Streets, Yountville 94599. Open 6:00 A.M.–10:00 P.M. No pets, animals, or motor vehicles.

Just beyond the park, GEORGE C. YOUNT PIONEER CEMETERY & ANCIENT INDIAN BURIAL GROUNDS gives a short and fascinating history of Yountville lesson, as do most old cemeteries. Ironically, George Yount was the first white settler in the Napa Valley and is buried here with Napa and Pomo Indians and some much more current immigrants.

George C. Yount Pioneer Cemetery & Ancient Indian Burial Grounds, Lincoln and Jackson Streets, Yountville 94599.

Back toward Yountville proper (we're talking a total of about 5 blocks) and across from Gordon's Café & Wine Bar, you might want to take the kids to

FRANKIE & JOHNNY & LUIGI TOO, a good, solid Italian restaurant with pastas, pizzas, veal, and fun for the kids. Featuring "homestyle Southern Italian cooking," FJ&L serves big portions, family-style dinners, all food to go, and lots of outdoor seating in good weather.

❧ *Frankie & Johnnie & Luigi Too, 6772 Washington Street, Yountville 94559; phone (707) 944–0177. Open: 11:30 A.M.–10:00 P.M. daily. MasterCard, Visa, American Express, Diners, and Discover. Wheelchair-accessible.*

Just south of Frankie etc. is the intriguing Burgundy House five-room inn. Once a brandy distillery built in 1891, the rich little building's 22-inch thick local stone walls keep it cool in the summer, perfect for sipping the decanter of wine that greets you in your antiques-furnished room on arrival. (See the chapter on *Where to Stay*.)

The Washington Square shopping center's primary attraction is the renowned NAPA VALLEY GRILLE, which is part of a group of California grill–style restaurants, but Chef Bob Hurley has total independence to use his massive talents, previously enjoyed at San Francisco's Masa's and Domaine Chandon.

This is a non-snooty California-cuisine delight, with an openness of both decor and menu selections. Plan time to wait for your meal, but we found the wait worthwhile. The Thai chicken salad is the best anywhere, the fish is usually grilled over a wood fire and yummy, if occasionally dry. Hamburgers are great, and the polenta is sumptuous. Be sure to try the specials to experience Bob's substantial talents. Enjoy the patio in good weather.

❧ *Napa Valley Grille, Madison and Highway 29 (approach from Washington Street), Washington Square shopping center, Yountville 94599; phone (707) 944–8686. Open for lunch and dinner daily, Sunday brunch. MasterCard, Visa, and American Express. Wheelchair-accessible.*

COMPADRES MEXICAN BAR & GRILL is the only Mexican restaurant in Yountville, so if you truly have the urge, this is it. Campadres bills itself as "A Great Place to Party" for breakfast, lunch, and dinner, and it is. If that's your goal, go for it. This place is super-California and huge, with loads of indoor and outdoor seating. Watch for the daily fish specials, seafood tacos, enchiladas galore, and several Jaliscan specialties. Margarita variations abound, but we prefer the originals.

❧ *Compadres Mexican Bar & Grill, 6539 Washington Street, Yountville, 94599; phone (707) 944–2406. Open 8:00 A.M.–10:00 P.M. Sunday–Thursday, 8:00 A.M.–11:00 P.M. Friday–Saturday. MasterCard, Visa, and American Express. Wheelchair-accessible.*

Before we get you inside the Vintage 1870 complex, we want to introduce you to Pacific Blues Café. Hold your horses, folks. We completely agree with the local vote making this the "Best New Restaurant of Napa Valley–1997." Jeff Steen, formerly of Piatti and Compadres, and Frank Cox have created the most fun casual restaurant in the Napa Valley. They serve consistently hearty "maverick American" taste surprises in what was once the train station. Hence the train and blues themes, which carry into the old train posters on the walls and train names on the menu, while blues music pipes softly through the restaurant and deck facing Vintage 1870 during the week, replaced by live blues bands on the weekend. Portions are large and prices are small.

Breakfasts are classic and innovative, from Flatcar Flapjacks with whipped orange butter and hot maple syrup for $1.00 each, buttermilk biscuits and Frank's gravy at $3.95, and vanilla-cinnamon French toast with bananas and walnuts at $5.50, to the Rocky Rail Scramble of turkey, spinach, onions, and egg whites at $6.25, the Healthy Car Scramble with poached veggies and egg whites at $5.00, and the engineer's Hearty Breakfast of grilled New York steak with eggs and hashbrowns at $10.25.

Lunch and dinner share the same menu, with ribeye and other excellent steaks, several veggie specialties (from fancy baked potatoes to dim sum and hot veggie chili and veggie pastas), humungous double-layered, tricolored nachos at $6.95, Caesar and spinach salads, a fab iceberg-lettuce wedge with thick, creamy, chunky bleu cheese dressing for $4.00, burgers galore, finger-licking ribs, and Kathleen's favorite—the Blues Burger, with ground turkey, bleu cheese, and jalapeño jam, served with perfect slaw or French fries (go for the garlic ones with fresh, crushed garlic). Outlandish desserts and a child's menu make this a place we come back to again and again. Pacific Blues also has one of the best-selected local wine lists and good espresso drinks.

᠉ *Pacific Blues Café, 6525 Washington Street, Yountville 94599; phone (707) 944-4455, fax (707) 944-2453. Open for breakfast (6:30–11:00 A.M.), lunch, and dinner. Beer and wine. MasterCard, Visa, and American Express. Wheelchair-accessible.*

The large brick building across the patio is Vintage 1870, loaded with specialty shops and art galleries. Originally the Groezinger Wine Cellars, the building is listed in the National Register of Historic Places and is built on the original land grant made to Salvador Vallejo by the Mexican government in 1838. In 1870 G. Groezinger purchased it from George C. Yount's estate for $250 in gold coins and it was used as a winery from up to 1954.

Vintage 1870 offers refreshingly high-quality businesses, one of the most tempting of which you encounter just to the right of the door. Gillespie's Ice

CREAM & CHOCOLATES serves Double Rainbow ice cream and made-before-your-eyes chocolates, including sugar-free peanut clusters. Smoothies, shakes, and sundaes steel you for shopping till you drop. CRAVINGS GOURMET & COOKWARE sells wine stuff like drip stoppers, cookbooks, cool drinks, and picnic baskets. KINYON! RESTAURANT invites you in with hardwood floors, colored napkins, and cobalt-blue glasses, to say nothing of the Thanksgiving turkey sandwich ($9.75), Holy Cow roast beef on French roll, a grilled chicken sandwich called Last Mango in Paris, a veggie Griller Thriller, To Brie or Not to Brie, salads galore, and a Here's the Skinny menu.

Notice the plaque marking the old Chutney Kitchen's cutting board. You can still get the once-famous chutney at Cravings. TILTON'S RENDEZVOUS 1870 has attractive turquoise jewelry, pottery, and beaded leather, while MIRA BOUTIQUE sells replica jewelry (also in Sonoma). THE TOY CELLAR carries trains, stuffed Breyer bears and other animals, toys, Beanie Babies, yo-yos, everything Madeline, and a 1-cent box of goodies. GALLERY 1870 features Thomas Kinkade paintings (he's all over the wine country).

We especially like GENERATIONS . . . a fine art gallery, with interestingly designed space and involvement in the community. Generations features art of the West, Judith Gaulke's (former food editor of *Sunset* magazine) French waiter series, Mikki Senkauk, and other Northern California artists. Also on the first floor are ROSALIA'S FOR SHOES and TOUCH OF GOLD BATH SHOP.

We particularly encourage you to visit the WORKING ART STUDIOS (upstairs) of Eric Christensen and Steven Gordon, who is married to Sally Gordon of delightful Gordon's Café and Wine Bar at the other end of town. The second floor also highlights i-ELLE BOUTIQUE, GAMI'S SCANDIA IMPORTS, CHATEAU STE. SHIRTS (also in Calistoga), DOMAINE HOME & GARDEN, HANDWORKS art accessories for the home, YE OLDE CANDLE SHOPPE, A LITTLE ROMANCE, HANSEL & GRETEL CLOTHES LOFT for children, high-quality American furniture at MANDRAKE'S ANTIQUES, and WOOD-U-LUV woodworks, including wine racks.

❧ *Vintage 1870, 6525 Washington Street, Yountville 94599. Open 10:00 A.M.–5:30 P.M. daily. Credit cards vary by shop.*

Just south of Vintage 1870, and across the street at the junction of Oak Leaf and Washington, stop at the Whistle Stop Center, a collection of shops in another train station beside a collection of railroad cars that make up the Napa Valley Railway Inn (see *Where to Stay*). If you like leather, the OVERLAND SHEEPSKIN COMPANY is a must-see for waxed coats, sheepskin pelts, purses, briefcases, bicycle-seat covers, suede skirts and vests, slippers, Western belts, and wallets. While it is one of twelve stores, this Overland at least feels local.

❧ *Overland Sheepskin Company, 6505 Washington Street, Yountville 94599; phone (707) 944–0778. Open 10:00 A.M.–7:00 P.M. Monday–Thursday, until 8:00 P.M. Friday, and until 6:00 P.M. Sunday. MasterCard, Visa, and Discover. Wheelchair-accessible.*

Right behind Overland Sheepskin you will find the YOUNTVILLE FITNESS AND HEALTH CLUB, which offers personal training, physical therapy, and general fitness at only $8.00 per day and open to all.

❧ *Yountville Fitness and Health Club, 6505 Washington Street, Yountville 94599; phone (707) 944–9345. Open 6:00 A.M.– 9:00 P.M. Monday–Friday, 7:00 A.M.–6:00 P.M. Saturday, 8:00 A.M.–5:00 P.M. Sunday. MasterCard, Visa, and American Express. Wheelchair-accessible.*

Go under the highway at the south end of Yountville and up California Drive to the Veterans' Home, Napa Valley Museum, and Domaine Chandon winery and restaurant, all of which are off this main little road and within pea-shooting distance of one another. While only a chainlink fence separates the Napa Valley Museum and Domaine Chandon, their staffs rarely visit each other in this cozily nestled complex.

Just before the Veterans' Home entry post, you will see DOMAINE CHANDON'S arch over California Drive. Turn right and follow the signs to the

DOMAINE CHANDON

parking lot. You can either park in the first lot, cross the little bridge over peaceful ponds with waterfalls and lilies, and walk into Domaine Chandon's dramatic entrance; or you can drive to a lot above and enter at the restaurant level. Ramps and elevators help you get from floor to floor.

Domaine Chandon deserves attention for both its winery and the restaurant. California's early Champagne wine prospects turned sharply better in 1973, when Moet-Hennessy of France built this dramatic and state-of-the-art sparkling-wine facility, which it now owns with Louis Vuitton. Moet & Chandon, the French Champagne house founded in 1743 and parent company of Domaine Chandon, uses the same methods that the monk Dom Perignon discovered as cellarmaster at the Benedictine Abbey in Hautvillers in 1690.

Domaine Chandon has integrated modern innovations with those traditional methods, including sustainable agriculture in its Carneros and Mt. Veeder vineyards. According to the 1920 Treaty of Madrid, which the United States did not sign during Prohibition, only sparkling wines made from Chardonnay, Pinot Noir, and Pinot Meunier grapes grown in Champagne and using *methode champenoise* could be called Champagne. "Sparkling wine" applies to all wines containing effervescence created by natural fermentation. Out of deference to its French founders, Domaine Chandon calls its California product sparkling wine, even though it is made by the same methods as are their Moet & Chandon French Champagnes and legally can be called Champagne.

As you enter the winery, you can enjoy a vast shop of Domaine Chandon wines, beautiful books, aprons, glasses, wine goodies, mustards, shortbread cookies, and shirts even in kids' sizes. Along the hallway is a museum-style, lighted instructional display of the Champagne-making process, and stairs or elevators take you up to the next level.

On the mezzanine visit the Pavillion, an elegant, glassed-in tasting bar and the restaurant. Chef Robert Curry continues the cuisine he mastered as sous-chef to Philippe Jeanty, who left after twenty years to start his own Bistro Jeanty, "downtown" in Yountville. After graduating from the Culinary Institute of America in Hyde Park, Robert also worked as sous-chef at Citrus in Los Angeles.

The menu changes weekly and may include mesquite appetizers of grilled asparagus ($9.00), duck foie blond pate ($10.00), home-smoked salmon tartare ($11.00), or Caesar salad ($9.00). Entrees can be pan-seared yellowfin tuna ($21.00 at lunch, $27.00 at dinner), rack of local lamb, Black Angus steak or beef tenderloin, Laura Chenel goat cheeses ($9.00), or French cheeses ($18.00 for two).

Claiming the oldest and largest wine club, the Chandon Club has 100,000 members, who receive for free an unlisted telephone number for restaurant

Black Mussels Steamed in Chandon Brut and Rabbit Terrine with Sliced Apples and Baguette

from Robert Curry, Executive Chef, Domaine Chandon

Ingredients for Black Mussels Steamed in Chandon Brut:

4 ½ lb black mussels
3 cups dry sparkling wine
3 shallots, diced
3 garlic cloves, chopped
½ bunch thyme, chopped

1 cup Italian parsley, chopped
½ cup tomatoes, peeled, seeded
   and diced
2 lemons
⅓ lb butter

Preparation:

Sweat the shallots and ⅔ of the garlic in a little butter. Add the thyme. Add the mussels and the sparkling wine. Cover and steam until mussels open, about 2 minutes. Remove the cooking liquid from the mussels. Bring the liquid to a simmer and whisk in the butter. Add the parsley and tomatoes. Adjust the flavor with the lemon juice and chopped garlic. Pour the liquid over the mussels and serve. Serves 4.

Ingredients for Rabbit Terrine with Sliced Apples and Baguette:

2 lb 3 oz boneless rabbit meat
1 Tbs + 2 tsp salt
1 tsp pepper
3 garlic cloves, peeled and sliced

1 bunch thyme, washed and dried
2 oz virgin olive oil
2 baguettes
4 of your favorite apples

Preparation:

In a bowl, mix the rabbit, garlic, thyme, and olive oil. Cover and refrigerate overnight. The next day, remove the garlic and thyme.

Season the rabbit with salt and pepper and grind the meat through a meat grinder. Line a 5-cup terrine mold with plastic wrap and pack the ground meat into the mold. Fold over plastic wrap to cover. Place the cover on the terrine mold. Place terrine in a water bath and bake in a 300° F oven for 1 hour 20 minutes. Refrigerate overnight.

Slice and serve terrine with thinly sliced apples and baguettes. Serves 8.

reservations, a newsletter, special invitations, cruises, and discounts on Chandon logo merchandise.

Winemaker Dawnine Dyer graduated in biology from UC Santa Cruz, worked at Robert Mondavi Winery and Inglenook Vineyards, and studied enology at UC Davis. She joined Chandon in 1976, makes regular visits to Moet & Chandon in Epernay, France, and consults to Moet's Australian winery.

 Fine points: In the restaurant, you may also want to try the Tasting Menu, at $60 or $80, which includes four ounces each of five wines. In 1998 Domaine Chandon released its first still wines— Pinot Meunier, Pinot Noir, and Pinot Blanc—all made in small lots and available only in its shop, restaurant, and by direct mail. Featured wines: Brut Cuvee, Carneros Blanc de Noirs, Reserve Cuvee, Etoile Cuvee, Chandon Fleur de Vigne, Chandon Pinot Meunier, Pinot Noir, and Pinot Blanc. Owners: Moet-Hennessy-Louis Vuitton. Winemaker: Dawnine Dyer. Executive Chef: Robert Curry. Cases: 450,000. Acres: 1,600.

⋆⋏ *Domaine Chandon, 1 California Drive, Yountville 94599; phone (707) 944–2280, fax (707) 944–1123, e-mail dchandon@napanet.net, Web site www.dchandon.com. Winery open 10:00 A.M.–9:00 P.M., tours on the hour 11:00 A.M.–5:00 P.M., departing from the bottom of the stairs in the entry hall. Restaurant open lunch 11:30 A.M.–2:30 P.M. daily May–October, dinner seatings from 6:00 P.M. Wednesday–Sunday year-round. Winery and restaurant are closed Monday–Tuesday November–April. MasterCard, Visa, American Express, Diners, and Discover. Wheelchair-accessible.*

Just up the tree-lined divided road, about half a block from Domaine Chandon's entrance, is the new NAPA VALLEY MUSEUM. The new state-of-the-art edifice, designed by architects Fernau and Hartman to resemble two thirds of a farm shed, serves as a regional museum that features wine-industry history, art, and local culture. This 10,000-square-foot vaulted structure represents the first phase of the 40,000-square-foot museum project.

Here you can visit the $1.5 million "California Wine: The Science of an Art" exhibit, which was moved here from the earthquake-unsafe California Museum of Science and Industry in Los Angeles and redesigned by Academy Studio for the Industry Gallery of the Napa Valley Museum. Explore the information provided on twenty-six video disc players, nine micro-computers, twenty-four monitors, and eleven audio speakers for a definitive wine-history experience.

Collections include works of Napa Valley painter Sofia Alstrom Mitchell, The Johnson Collection of Minerals and Fossils, Native peoples of the Napa Valley including Wappo relics and folk culture, local viticultural materials, and historical and contemporary works by artists who live or have lived in the Napa

Valley or use the Napa Valley as subject matter. We particularly enjoy the work of Earl Thollander, a favorite book illustrator for *Gourmet* and *Sunset* magazines.

The museum's unique Trunk Collection evolved as a way to take art and history to school children when the previous building in St. Helena was declared seismically unsafe. Trunks include features on kites, Chinese culture, Wappos, historic ranchos, pioneer settlements, viticulture, Napa River, and La Maleta Mexicana on the history of Napa Valley Mexican culture.

 Fine points: Be sure to visit the museum shop downstairs. It has one of the best collections of Napa history books and souvenirs anywhere.

❧ *Napa Valley Museum, 55 Presidents Circle, Yountville 94599; phone (707) 944–0500, fax (707) 945–0500, Web site www.nvmuseum.org. Admission fees adults $3.50; seniors 60 and up and students over 17, $2.50; children $1.50; free 5:00–8:00 P.M. first Thursday of the month. Open 10:00 A.M.–5:00 P.M. Wednesday–Monday, until 8:00 P.M. first Thursday. Wheelchair-accessible.*

As you visit the museum, you are surrounded by the CALIFORNIA VETERANS HOME, "established in 1882 by Veterans of the Mexican and Civil Wars as a home for all veterans west of the Rockies." Sold in 1900 to the State of California for a $20 gold piece, the vast home has been remodeled and updated (sort of) and has served veterans of the Mexican, Civil, Indian, Spanish–American, Korean, and Vietnam Wars, and of course World War I and World War II.

Fine points: The fascinating little museum behind the main building, south of the Napa Valley Museum, is unfortunately open only on Friday afternoon from noon to 2:00 P.M. If you plan lunch around those hours, you might see interesting rotating (changing, not moving) exhibits of historic uniforms, weapons, documents, models, and photographs.

❧ *California Veterans Home, 180 California Drive, Yountville 94599; phone (800) 404–8387, fax (707) 944–4542, e-mail vets@fcs.net, Web site www.blink.com/vets.*

As you work your way northward on Highway 29 from Yountville, four interesting stops on the west (left) side of the highway break our first recommendation of not turning left across this two-lane highway. Brix, Mustards Grill, Cosentino Winery, and Napa Cellars all tempt.

When we ask local winery people or anyone else in the Napa Valley what their favorite places for lunch are, they invariably respond, "Don Giovanni or Brix."

Seattle residents and visitors are used to "Asian Fusion" cuisine, a blend of Asian and traditional Northwest seafoods. In 1996 Executive Chef Tod Michael Kawachi brought his version of Asian Fusion from Roy's in Hawaii to BRIX, in a building known for years as The Christmas Store.

General Manager Curtis Jones and the Brix staff set the casually elegant tone in a restaurant where warm, comforting yellows and woods with beamed ceilings and large windows frame vegetable gardens, vineyards, and the Mayacamas Mountains. Brix makes olive oil from its trees' olives, grows vegetables and herbs for your meal, and grows ten acres of Chardonnay and Cabernet Sauvignon grapes (which it sells to Caymus Vineyards).

At lunch, starters may include crunchy coconut seafood cigars with sweet 'n' sour pineapple-chili sauce ($8.50), prosciutto-fennel sausage, cambozola, spinach-and-roasted-garlic pizza ($9.00), or chopped romaine hearts with creamy lemon Parmesan dressing, ($6.50). Main courses include pepper-seared tuna salad with Ponzu vinaigrette ($12.00), smoked-salmon spaghettini with fennel, capers, Maui onions, and orange gremolata ($12.00), Kasu grilled salmon with soba noodles and miso sauce ($13.50), and loads of Angus beef possibilities.

Dinner offers the same appetizers plus some others, a warm macadamia-nut-crusted goat-cheese salad ($8.00), Hawaiian mahi mahi with roasted-banana-and-coconut curry sauce ($21.50), Thai pesto–smoked rack of lamb with spicy peanut saté and zinfandel glace ($23.50), fennel-dusted bay scallops with Meyer lemon beurre blanc and truffle oil ($23.50), plus the Angus beef options.

 Fine points: The wine list is exceptional. Be sure to stop in at the interesting gift shop with wine country goodies and excellent travel and cook/food books. Feel free to stroll through the vegetable gardens and vineyards.

✤ Brix, 7377 Highway 29, Yountville 94599; phone (707) 944–2749, fax (707) 944–8320. Open lunch and dinner daily. MasterCard, Visa, American Express, Diners, Discover, Carte Blanche, and JCB. Wheelchair-accessible.

Practically next door to mustard colored Brix, the better known and noisier white MUSTARDS GRILL, is the original outpost of the Real Restaurants group, which now includes Fog City Diner, Tra Vigne and Tomatina in St. Helena and elsewhere, and the Buckeye Roadhouse in Mill Valley.

Mustards' roadside signs claim COCKTAILS, PORK CHOPS—ALMOST A MILLION SOLD, WAY TOO MANY WINES, GARDEN PRODUCE, CHOPS, RIBS. Just to the left of the front door is a small patio labeled MUSTARDS CIGAR & WILDLIFE PRESERVE, so park your stogies and stogie smokers here.

A fast-paced, clanking restaurant with attractive art, Mustards serves good-sized portions of hearty and occasionally healthy comfort food (speaking of which, you must try the off the diet stacks of crisp, thin onion rings with "homemade ketchup"). White walls, dark wood, and white tile floors give the feel of a city bistro.

The Caesar salad is good at $6.95, the lemon-and-garlic chicken with mashed potatoes ($12.95) is better, and the half-slab of barbecued baby back ribs with crispy yams and sweet-and-sour slaw ($13.95) can be terrific. If you eat such things, try the grilled Mongolian pork chop with garlic mashed potatoes ($15.50) or the calf's liver with caramelized apples, onions, and pancetta ($10.95). The wild-mushroom "burger" with jicama and apple salad, and the regular hamburgers, are deals at $7.75, as is the ahi tuna steak sandwich with basil mayonnaise and ginger for $9.95.

 Fine points: The "New World" wine lists includes 12 pages of fun reading and excellent wines, even some of Oregon's best Pinot Noirs. No photos of the restaurant without permission from manager Michael Kim Wolf personally.

❦ *Mustards Grill, 7399 St. Helena Highway, Napa 94558; phone (707) 944-2424, fax (707) 944-0828. Open lunch and dinner daily. MasterCard, Visa, Diner's Club, Carte Blanche, and Discover. Wheelchair-accessible.*

Immediately next door, to the north, is charming and small COSENTINO WINERY, the pride and joy of one-time assistant golf pro and wine distributor Mitch Cosentino. Possibly the only vintner to sell golf balls in his tasting room, Mitch plays golf in the Napa Valley with pals and pros (often at Chimney Rock Golf Course), including Miller Barber and Walter Morgan.

Cosentino's Pinot Noir and Chardonnay are highly rated by most critics. Its 1995 The Poet Meritage red blend and the 1996 Reserve Merlot both won double gold awards at the Tasters Guild International Wine Judging, and its 1996 Cabernet Franc garnered a gold medal. It is one of the few wineries that prints and offers visitors the whole list of its *Wine Spectator* ratings and wine awards so that you can learn other people's opinions of its wines.

Taste for yourself. Oh yes, you might also enjoy the autographed Steve Young football in Cosentino's ribbon and trophy case.

 Fine points: Cosentino's "Rare Art Series," which include "The Sculptor," "The Poet," and "The Novelist," are all "stylistically more 'old world' European than the California wines of that day. Each name was chosen to honor a type of artist whose approach to his medium best reflected the winemaker's approach to the development of these individual wine types." There is a tasting fee of $4.00, which is refundable with a purchase, and you get to keep the glass. Featured wines: Chardonnay, White Meritage, Gewürztraminer, Nebbiolo, Tenero Rosa, Pinot Noir, Il Chiaretto, Tenero Rosso, Il Tesoro Sangiovetto, Cabernet Sauvignon, Zinfandel, Cigarzin, Cabernet Franc Port, Francesca d'Amore aperitif/dessert wine. Owner and winemaker: Mitch Cosentino. Cases: 20,000. Acres: 3 Merlot, buy from others.

❧ *Cosentino Winery, 7415 St. Helena Highway, Yountville 94599; phone (707) 944–1220, fax (707) 944–1254. Open 10:00 A.M.–5:30 P.M. Visa, MasterCard, and American Express. Wheelchair-accessible.*

Now, walk next door to **Napa Cellars** in the interesting six-sided wooden building. As you enter, you face a corner of the tasting counter. Permanent Christmas-tree lights and dried flowers dangle over the six-sided bar. Enjoy the excellent book selection on the table to the left as you enter.

Napa Cellars is a new endeavor of Koerner Rombauer of Rombauer Vineyards and former Academy of Motion Pictures president Richard Frank, who are also involved in ownership of Hanns Kornell Champagne Cellars. Try the wines and stay tuned.

 Fine points: Marc Chagall and Guy Buffet posters decorate the walls. Tasting fee $5.00. Featured wines: Chardonnay, Merlot, Petite Syrah, Sangiovese, Cabernet Sauvignon, Muscat Canelli. Owners: partnership including Koerner Rombauer and Richard Frank. Winemaker: Matt Cookson. Cases: 10,000. Acres: 50.

❧ *Napa Cellars, 7481 St. Helena Highway, Oakville 94562; phone (707) 944–2565 or (800) 535–6400, fax (707) 944–0250. Open 10:00 A.M.–6:00 P.M. Friday–Sunday. Visa and MasterCard. Wheelchair-accessible.*

Across Highway 29, just north of Napa Cellars, visit the "two-fer" of **Cardinale** and **Pepi Wineries** in the same building. Both are owned by Jess Jackson of Kendall-Jackson Winery. To get there, turn right (east) at the Cardinale Estate sign, proceed for 0.4 mile, and turn right up the hill to cement-block and then stone buildings. (You enter the tasting room from the parking lot.) Cardinale will remain in the stone building, while Pepi will be moving to a new structure growing down the hill. Jackson is filling in his own reservoir to build a 500,000-case underground winery.

Jess Jackson established Cardinale to make Cabernet Sauvignon and Merlot in Oakville, in the heart of the Napa Valley, to use the exceptional hillside and benchland vineyards in Napa and Sonoma Counties. Cardinale's handcrafted and unfiltered wines are aged 100 percent in French oak barrels.

Since 1966, Robert Pepi has grown and produced outstanding

NAPA CELLARS

Sangiovese and Sauvignon Blanc from Pepi's original cuttings of Sangiovese Grosso, brought from Italy's Tuscany region. Pepi's Colline di Sassi comes from the "Hill of Stones" on the Pepi property. Jess Jackson bought Pepi in 1994 from Robert Pepi.

Fine points: The tasting room itself is small, with a redwood-and-white interior, a small wood tasting bar, and fabulous views of the Napa Valley. Tasting fees are $2.00 for Pepi, $4.00 for Cardinale; a souvenir glass is $2.00. You will find a limited but excellent selection of wine and cookbooks here, as well as handsome hand-carved wooden bottle stoppers. In *The Wine Advocate*, Robert M. Parker, Jr., rates Cardinale's Cardinale a 90–92. Featured wines: Cardinale: Royale Meritage, Cardinale Meritage, Due Baci. Cases: 5,000. Robert Pepi: Sauvignon Blanc, Arneis, Malvasia Bianca, Pinot Grigio, Chardonnay, Tocai Friulano, Barbera, Sangiovese, Colline di Sassi Sangiovese. Winemakers: Cardinale: Charles Thomas; Robert Pepi: Marco DiGiulio. Cases: 30,000. Acres: 70+, and is the largest purchaser of Cabernet Sauvignon grapes in Napa Valley.

❧ *Cardinale* and *Pepi Wineries, 7585 Highway 29, Oakville 94562; phone (707) 945-1391, Web site www.pepi.com. Open for retail sales 10:30 A.M.–4:00 P.M. MasterCard, Visa, Carte Blanche, and Diners Club. Wheelchair-accessible.*

North of Cardinale and Pepi, the Oakville Grade heads west from Highway 29 and winds almost treacherously to Glen Ellen in Sonoma County. There are several good reasons to make this turn: Pometta's Deli, an Episcopal church, the Carmelite House of Prayer and Religious Shop, and La Famiglia di Robert Mondavi Winery and Italian Marketplace. Many more signs guide you to the Carmelite mission than to any of the other attractions.

At Pometta's Delicatessen and Catering, owner Susan Potgeter and staff make sandwiches and picnic lunches for locals and tourists and cater most Robert Mondavi Winery staff lunches (a hint of the high quality of food here). Pometta's serves down-home Italian and Napa Valley specialties, barbecue chicken, salads, soups, and huge portions of good humor.

Sandwiches range from the Pometta Club and Muffaletta to the Sicilian, with salami, pastrami, sauteed zucchini, Swiss cheese, olive oil, and wine vinegar. You might try the vegetarian sandwich or the barbecued chicken or beef, the Hot Texan, or Mama's Homemade Meatloaf.

Picnic lunches include such choices as roasted chicken or boneless chicken breast with pesto, salads, cheese, fruit, cookies, and other goodies. Prices range from $10.50 to $35.00 for two.

Be sure to pick up a jar of Pometta's highly rated Special Garlic Sauce or pasta sauces (which are also sold at Oakville Grocery). And don't miss a walk into the "dining rooms" with red-and-white-checked tablecloths to the left of the door to see the chickens in the shower, and head outside to play horseshoes or enjoy your lunch on the lawn.

POMETTA'S DELI, OAKVILLE

❧ *Pometta's Delicatessen and Catering, Highway 29 and Oakville Grade, Oakville 94562; phone (707) 944–2365. Open 9:00 A.M.–6:00 P.M. Beer and wine. MasterCard and Visa. Wheelchair-accessible.*

As you continue westward on the flat part of the Oakville Grade through acres of vineyards, notice the historic little St. Stephen's Episcopal Church on the right. It's worth getting out of the car if you're interested in local history. The next stop is also religious: the Carmelite House of Prayer and Carmelite Religious Store. Turn right up Mount Carmel Drive, and Stations of the Cross shrines lead you up the mission's driveway. Park at the top, respect the quiet, and explore the historic chapel to your left, the mosaics, and the popular shop.

Another 500 feet up the winding grade, turn left into LA FAMIGLIA DI ROBERT MONDAVI WINERY AND ITALIAN MARKETPLACE. As of 1998, Tim Mondavi, part of La Famiglia di Robert Mondavi, took over this winery and tasting room from another Robert Mondavi enterprise, Vichon, which moved to the Languedoc-Rousillon region of France. La Famiglia specializes in "Cal–Ital" wines—Italian in origin and Californian in style.

As you approach the winery overlooking the Napa Valley, picnic tables and bocce-ball courts are to your left, the tasting room to your right. (If you buy some wine, you can use the bocce-ball courts and picnic tables.) As you wander around the building, you can soak in the views and enjoy the beautiful flower beds.

Inside the newly remodeled marketplace and tasting room, you will find the most engrossing collection of Italian cookbooks and travel books we have seen gathered in one place, as well as the most attractive souvenir shirts around. There's an expansive mural by San Francisco painter Jennifer Ewing.

Fine points: Tastes of these new Italian-style wines are real treats, as are the good humor and vast knowledge of the hosts. Some tasting is free; $5.00 for Reserves. Featured wines: Bocce Rosato, Bianco, and Rosso; La Famiglia Malvasia Bianca, Moscato Bianco, Pinot Grigio, Tocai Friulano, Barbera, Nebbiolo, Rosato, Sangiovese, and Sangiovese Riserva. Owners: Robert Mondavi Family. Winemaker: Heather Pyle. Executive Chef: Annie Roberts. Cases: 65,000. Acres: 4.5 here, many elsewhere.

❧ *La Famiglia di Robert Mondavi Winery, 1595 Oakville Grade, Oakville 94562; phone (707) 944–2811, fax (707) 944–2607, Web site www.ROBERT-MONDAVI.COM. Open 10:00 A.M.–4:30 P.M. daily. Tours by appointment. MasterCard, Visa, American Express, and Diners Club. Wheelchair-accessible.*

Pork Scaloppini
with Pinot Grigio, Caper Sauce
from Executive Chef Annie Roberts, La Famiglia
di Robert Mondavi

INGREDIENTS:

1 ½ lb boneless pork tenderloin
3 Tbs olive oil
3 Tbs butter
½ cup flour
½ cup Pinot Grigio
2 Tbs capers, rinsed and drained
1 Tbs Italian parsley, chopped
¼ cup green onions, white part only, chopped
salt
freshly ground black pepper

PREPARATION:

Slice the pork across the grain into ½-inch slices. Place the slices between 2 sheets of waxed paper or parchment paper. With a meat pounder, lightly and evenly pound the pieces of meat to ¼-inch slices.

Heat all the oil and 1 Tbs butter in a large sauté pan. Coat the meat in flour and, when the oil is hot, brown the meat on both sides, then remove and set on a warm plate. Add the greeen onions to the pan and cook for about 1 minute. Add the wine and reduce slightly. Add the capers and the remaining butter and return the meat and any juices back to the pan.

Season with salt and pepper and cook just until the meat has been heated through. Sprinkle with Italian parsley and serve with Pinot Grigio. Serves 4.

OAKVILLE

As you come into Oakville, please slow down, both for your safety and for that of pilgrims gathering at the Oakville Grocery Mecca.

At the southern end of this three-building metropolis is NAPA WINE COMPANY, which is not in most books but is fun to visit. Turn right onto the Oakville Crossroad just before the Oakville Grocery Café, and right again into the winery's driveway.

The original winery on this site was built in 1877 by Adolph Brun and Jean Chaix as Nouveau Medoc Winery and California Bonded Winery No. 9. After passing through many winemaking hands before and after Prohibition, the property was bought by Heublein in 1986 and turned into Inglenook's Chardonnay Cellar. It closed three years later. The northwest corner building was built in 1892 for the Bartolucci Brothers' Modanna Winery, also passing through several hands and ending up with Heublein. The Andrew Pelissa family bought the whole works in 1993 and re-opened under the name Napa Wine Company.

This is an unusual, custom-crush facility to which fifty small wineries bring their own winemaker, grapes, and barrels and use the equipment and space to crush, ferment, age, and bottle their wines. Here you can sample and buy hand-crafted wines from family wineries whose wines are rarely available in stores or restaurants, including a 1985–1994 vertical Marilyn Merlot for a mere $4,000. In this case, "vertical" refers to one bottle of each vintage, and not to Ms. Monroe.

 Fine points: If you have ever fantasized about starting your own small winery, check this out. It's full of learning opportunities. The tasting fee is $5.00. Wines from wineries you might sample and purchase in the salesroom here include Bayview Cellars' Cabernet Sauvignon, Chardonnay, and Merlot; Fife Vineyards' Cabernet Sauvignon, Merlot, Petite Syrah and Zinfandel; Lanborn Family Vineyards' Zinfandel, Liparita's Cabernet Sauvignon, Chardonnay, and Merlot; Mason Cellars' Merlot and Sauvignon Blanc; Napa Wine Company's Sauvignon Blanc; Nova Wine Group's Marilyn Merlot and Marilyn Cabernet Sauvignon with luscious Marilyn portraits on the labels; Oakford Cellars' Cabernet Sauvignon; Pahlmeyer & Co. Chardonnay, Merlot, and Red Table Wine; and Philippe Lorraine Cellars' Chardonnay and Cabernet Sauvignon. Owners: Andy Hoxsey, Dawne Dickenson, and the Harris family. Winemaker: Rob Lawson. Acres: 650.

Napa Wine Company, 7840 St. Helena Highway, Oakville 94562; phone (707) 944-1710, fax (707) 944-9749, e-mail retail@napawineco.com, Web site www.napawineco.com. Open 10:00 A.M.–3:30 P.M. Wednesday–Sunday. MasterCard and Visa. Wheelchair-accessible.

Next door to Napa Wine Company are two of our favorites: the OAKVILLE GROCERY CAFÉ and the OAKVILLE GROCERY itself. These are great places for food lovers and lovers of food lovers.

Oakville Grocery took over what had been Stars Oakville Café in 1997, creating an instant casually elegant hit. It feels as if you have just entered an informal country kitchen here, with historic signs on the walls, fresh pizzas, an island "counter," fresh pizzas and sandwiches under $10, crispy shoestring potatoes (a must-try) and housemade potato chips.

SPINACH SALAD AND FELICITAS VINAIGRETTE
from Oakville Grocery Café

INGREDIENTS FOR SPINACH SALAD:

1 lb spinach, washed and torn into bite-size pieces
½ large red onion, sliced thin
2 medium-size pears
¼ lb Oakville Grocery Spiced Pecans
¼ lb firm blue cheese, like Maytag Blue
½ lb pancetta, cooked crisp (optional)

PREPARATION:

Toss the spinach, onion, and optional pancetta with Felicitas Vinaigrette (recipe follows). Serve on individual plates topped with slices of pear, the spiced pecans, and crumbled blue cheese. Serves 8 as a first course.

INGREDIENTS FOR FELICITAS VINAIGRETTE:

½ cup Felicitas Virgin Olive Oil
½ cup Felicitas Rose of Pear Vinegar
1 Tbs Oakville Grocery Sundried Tomato & Curry Mustard
1 tsp Sonoma honey
salt and pepper to taste

PREPARATION:

Whisk ingredients together or shake them in a jar. This vinaigrette can also be used as a marinade for chicken or fish.

You can stop by for an espresso and sensational muffin at 7:30 A.M. Full breakfast is served from 8:00 A.M. Those having lunch or dinner might want to partake of the excellent wine list.

We particularly enjoy the grilled fillet of salmon and leg of lamb sandwiches, the hearts of romaine with creamy anchovy–lemon vinaigrette at $6.95 or $4.25, a salad Niçoise with grilled tuna ($8.95), and the wild-mushroom pizza. Iced-tea choices include caffeinated or decaffeinated.

Everything here is fabulous. Plan plenty of time to wait your turn.

OAKVILLE GROCERY AND U.S. POST OFFICE, OAKVILLE

❧ *Oakville Grocery Café, 7848 St. Helena Highway, Oakville 94562; phone (707) 944–0111. Open for breakfast 7:30 A.M.–11:00 P.M., lunch 11:00 A.M.–3:00 P.M. except until 5:00 P.M. Thursday–Sunday, when they are open for dinner 5:00–9:00 P.M. Beer and wine. MasterCard, Visa, and American Express. Wheelchair-accessible.*

Just north, where it looks as if busloads of people have been dropped off but they all actually arrived in their own gorgeous cars, is the original **OAKVILLE GROCERY**, California's leading specialty-food store. Built in 1881 by James and Jennie McQuaid as the "mercantile" for the bustling town of Oakville, Oakville Grocery supplied essentials to locals for generations. Listed in the National Register of Historic Places, the store was owned from 1978 to 1980 by vintner Joseph Phelps, who sold it to current CEO Steve Carlin and partners.

It is worth braving the crowds for tastes of oils and della Fattoria, Artisans and Acme breads; classic sandwiches to go, from Mediterranean chicken and smoked turkey and brie to Ozark peppered ham, vegetarian, curried turkey salad, and mom's tuna salad; or focaccia sandwiches of turkey pesto, roast beef and blue cheese, or house-roasted pork loin. All are under $7.00. Feast your eyes upon eight Italian pastas, Chinese noodle salad, citrus chipotle salsa, twenty kinds of

OAKVILLE POLENTA CROSTINI
WITH SUN-DRIED TOMATO PESTO
from Executive Chef Richard Hoff, Oakville Grocery

INGREDIENTS:

3 cups water
1 cup milk
1 tsp salt
1 cup Oakville Grocery Organic Polenta
2 Tbs McEvoy Ranch extra virgin olive oil
¼ cup grated Vella Dry Jack cheese (can substitute Parmesan cheese)
2 Tbs Italian parsley, chopped
pinch of freshly ground black pepper
1 9.5-oz jar of Bella Cucina Sun-Dried Tomato Pesto

PREPARATION:

In a medium-size saucepan, combine the water, milk, and salt and bring to a boil. Sprinkle the polenta slowly into the boiling liquid and stir with a whisk until fully incorporated to avoid lumps. Lower the heat so that the mixture simmers slowly rather than boils. Switch to a wooden spoon and stir frequently for 20–25 minutes. The polenta should be very thick and smooth and free of lumps. When the grains are tender, add ¼ cup of cheese, olive oil, parsley, and pepper to taste. Stir until incorporated.

Carefully pour the polenta into a rectangular 8-by-12-inch cake pan that has been brushed lightly with olive oil. Spread polenta with a spatula until it is about ½ inch thick. Cover with plastic wrap and allow to cool for 2 hours.

Cut into 24, 2-inch squares and arrange on lightly oiled cookie sheets. Brush tops with oil and set under preheated broiler until the tops brown lightly. Top each square with a dollop of pesto and sprinkle with reserved cheese. Place back in broiler to warm and serve immediately. Serves 6–8.

---

olives, crab cakes with remoulade sauce, and, my God, chocolate-covered apricots, teeny cherry pies, hazlenut mousse chocolates, and Graffeo coffees.

Be sure to notice the wines in the back, especially the unusual collection of splits of local wines, as well as Oakville Grocery's own oils, vinegars, mustards, preserves, honeys, and wines.

Fine points: The Oakville U.S. Post Office is still in the building, as are public telephones.

☙ *Oakville Grocery, 7856 St. Helena Highway, Oakville 94562; phone (707) 944–8802. Open 9:00 A.M.–5:00 P.M. daily. Beer and wine. MasterCard, Visa, and American Express. Wheelchair-accessible, but difficult to get around due to closeness of aisles.*

The greatest concentration of wineries is between Oakville and St. Helena, which means that you might want to plan your route carefully, with full awareness that some of your favorites might be between St. Helena and Calistoga or on the Silverado Trail.

OAKVILLE TO RUTHERFORD

OPUS ONE is the perfect child created by Robert Mondavi and the late baron Philippe de Rothschild of Bordeaux's Chateau Mouton-Rothschild, combining France's best with California's champion of wine. Open for tasting and tours by appointment only, Opus One's secrecy and mystery, and Robert Mondavi's unequaled skills at promotion, have contributed to wine fans' heightened desire to gain admission to this shrine. To get here, turn east (right) off Highway 29 into Opus One's driveway, 0.4 mile north of Oakville.

Designed by Johnson, Fain & Perreira of Los Angeles, who also designed San Francisco's once controversial TransAmerica Pyramid, the building resembles a cross between a Mayan temple and a spaceship. Partially buried by grasses and plantings, the redwood and limestone winery was built in 1991 for about $26.5 million. It has a dramatic courtyard entrance and a breathtaking open pavilion overlooking Napa Valley's finest vineyards.

Fine points: Old World traditional gravity flow methods merge with advanced California technology here to produce some of the finest wines anywhere. This is one appointment worth making ahead to plan your trip around. While the tasting fee is the highest we know of ($15), it is also worth it. (The wines you taste here sell for about $65 per bottle.) Featured wines: Opus One (Cabernet Sauvignon, Cabernet Franc, and Merlot blends) and Overture. Owners: The Mondavi and Baron Philippe de Rothschild families. Winemakers: Tim Mondavi and Patrick Leon. Cases: 30,000. Acres: 130.

☙ *Opus One, 7900 St. Helena Highway, Oakville, 94562; phone (707) 944–9442. Open by appointment. MasterCard, Visa, and American Express. Wheelchair-accessible.*

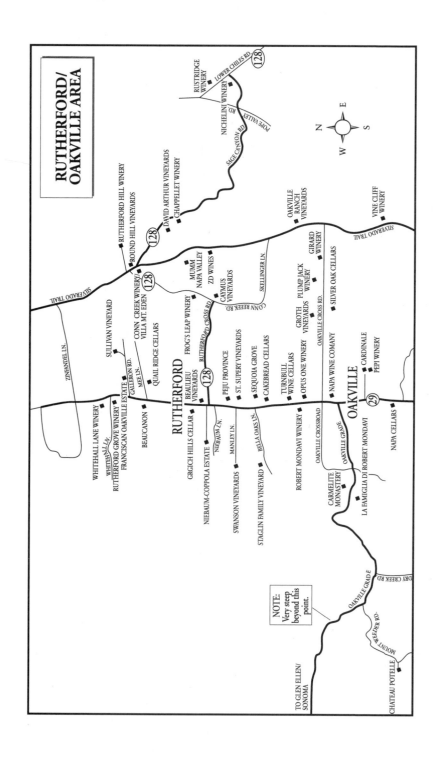

The next winery as we progress northward on Highway 29 is ROBERT MONDAVI WINERY, on the west side of the road. Then we have, in succession on the east side, Turnbull, Cakebread, Sequoia Grove, St. Supery, and Peju Province. Niebaum-Coppola is on the west side just before the intersection from the east of the Rutherford Cross Road.

Robert Mondavi is both the man and the winery. He is completely tied to his winery's image, because he promoted it and developed it, while also warning loudly of his perception of a new Prohibition coming from America's political right. His sons Michael and Tim now run the winery, while Robert continues, in his late eighties, to educate consumers and promote wine.

Upon leaving the Mondavi family–owned Charles Krug Winery, Robert Mondavi built and began his own winery in what was, in 1966, an avant-garde California–Italian building that stood out dramatically from the undeveloped, natural surrounding landscape. The winery now includes an elegant art gallery and dining rooms, reserve tasting room, and learning rooms, in addition to winemaking facilities. The layout resembles a California mission.

Besides its vast array of interesting wines, special events here are exceptional and well worth your attention. Robert and Margrit Mondavi and family work constantly to fulfill their goal of educating the public about wine and "its role as a mealtime beverage of moderation and to promote a gracious way of life."

The summer music series has included the biggest names in American music. Kathleen particularly likes The Great Chefs at Robert Mondavi Winery series, which since 1976 has included Simone Beck, Jean Troisgros, Roger Verge, Gaston Lenotre, Julia Child, Paul Prudhomme, Larry Forgione, Paul Bocuse, Wolfgang Puck, Barbara Kafka, Alice Waters, Diana Kennedy, Paula Wolfert, Martha Stewart, Jeremiah Tower, Joyce Goldstein, Giuliano Bugialli, Lydia

---

SMOKED SALMON AND CAPER CROSTINI
from Executive Chef Annie Roberts, Robert Mondavi Winery

INGREDIENTS:

> ¼ lb smoked salmon, sliced thinly into strips
> 2 Tbs capers
> ¼ cup red onion, chopped
> ¼ cup Italian parsley, chopped
> 2 Tbs mayonnaise
> 1 long, thin baguette

PREPARATION:

Combine ingredients in a bowl. Transfer to a food processor and pulse briefly until chunky-smooth.

Slice baguette into ¼-inch slices, brush lightly with olive oil, season with salt and pepper, and bake in 375° F oven until golden. Spread salmon mixture on toasted baguette and serve with Chardonnay. Makes 12 appetizers.

Shire, Marion Cunningham, Marcella Hazan, Charlie Trotter, Joachim Splichal, Roy Yamaguchi, and Jacques and Claudine Pepin.

Mondavi Picnics in the Vineyards begin at 10:00 A.M. on Mondays from May to October. They require reservations forty-eight hours in advance. The picnics are limited to ten people ($30 each) and include a four-hour tour and tasting, focusing on viticultural practices and tastings of wines selected to complement the day's picnic lunch.

Fine points: Other tours: Vineyard and Winery Tour (daily); Essence Tasting (Tuesday at 10:00 A.M.); Advanced Winegrowing Tour for guests who have already taken the Vineyard and Winery Tour ($15, Sunday and Wednesday, 10:00 A.M.); The Art of Wine and Food ($55, Friday, 10:00 A.M.–2:00 P.M.); Robert Mondavi Winegrowing Experience of on-site tours, tastings, and discussions ($295); To-Kalon Room for reserve-wine tasting, cigars, and Riedel Sommelier crystal stemware (daily from 10:30 A.M.); The Rose Garden for new releases outdoors (weekends June–October). Call the winery for tour information and reservations. Tasting fees vary. Featured wines: Chardonnay, Fume Blanc, Sauvignon Blanc, Brut Reserve, Cabernet Sauvignon, Merlot, Zinfandel, Pinot Noir, Moscato d'Oro, and the La Famiglia di Robert Mondavi wines. Owner: Robert Mondavi. Winemaker: Genevieve Janssens. Cases: 600,000. Acres: information not available.

✢✧ *Robert Mondavi Winery, 7801 St. Helena Highway, Oakville 94562; phone (707) 226-1335 or (800) MONDAVI, Web site robertmondavi.com. Open 9:00 A.M.–5:00 P.M. daily May–October, 9:30 A.M.–4:30 P.M. November–April. MasterCard, Visa, and American Express. Wheelchair-accessible.*

If you continue nothward from Robert Mondavi, please be extremely careful as you turn left across the road. Each attempt is dangerous.

Just north of the Oakville Cross Road on the east side of Highway 29, in a building with striking vertical redwood siding, is TURNBULL WINE CELLARS, founded in 1979 by famed architect William Turnbull, who died in 1997. Turnbull sold the winery in 1993 to publisher Patrick O'Dell, who rotates exhibits of his vast personal collection of Ansel Adams photographs in the tasting room, where the light gray walls and wine barrels show off the collection magnificently.

A 1998 addition to the winery on its southwest side was designed in the same style as the winery in homage to Bill Turnbull. Don't miss the small old Ford truck collection in the parking lot.

Fine points: There is a tasting fee of $3.00, which is refundable with a purchase. Featured wines: Old Bull Red (Cabernet Franc and Syrah blend), Sangiovese, Cabernet Sauvignon, Syrah, Zinfandel, Merlot, Nebbiolo, Rhone. Owner: Patrick O'Dell. Winemaker: Jon Engelskirger. Cases: 20,000. Acres: 300.

TURNBULL WINE CELLARS

✣ *Turnbull Wine Cellars, 8210 St. Helena Highway, Oakville 94562; phone (707) 963–5839 or (800) 887–6285, fax (707) 963–4407, Web site www.turnbullwines.com. Open 10:00 A.M.–4:30 P.M. daily. Visa, MasterCard, American Express, and "checks that don't bounce." Wheelchair-accessible.*

As you leave Turnbull, turn right and go 0.4 mile to CAKEBREAD CELLARS, one of the most upbeat and friendly wineries in the entire Napa Valley. Turn into Cakebread's driveway when you see vertical redwood siding like Turnbull's, but where the address number 8300 is written in red on a stone wall. There is no Cakebread sign.

Having left their mechanics garage in Oakland for greener vineyards, charming Jack and Dolores Cakebread bought the Sturdivant Ranch and started this winery in 1973. Bunches of friends helped them pound nails, trim roses, and generally build and fix up the place. Dolores cooked dinner for the weekend volunteer troops for several years, as the list of food and wine enthusiasts grew.

Now Chef Brian Streeter of Cakebread, who formerly worked at Domaine Chandon with Philippe Jeanty, gives four cooking classes a year. Culinary Director Dolores Cakebread hosts the annual fall American Harvest Workshop, featuring five chefs giving public classes. A winery with five kitchens and the tiny Cakebread Cellars Produce Center (which sells the extras from Dolores's 1 ½-acre vegetable and herb garden), Cakebread produces excellent wines. Instead of selecting a wine to go with food, the Cakebreads prefer to choose a wine and "cook to it."

LAMB BROCHETTES WITH ROSEMARY AND POMEGRANATE
from Delores Cakebread, Culinary Director, Cakebread Cellars

INGREDIENTS FOR THE BROCHETTES:

 2 lb leg of lamb, boneless
 ½ pint cherry tomatoes (preferably Sweet 100s)
 salt and freshly ground pepper
 4 oz pomegranate molasses (a Middle Eastern condiment found
  in some gourmet food markets)
 24 bamboo skewers, 6 inch length

INGREDIENTS FOR THE MARINADE:

2 Tbs olive oil	*1 tsp marjoram, chopped*
3 cloves garlic, minced	*1 Tbs flat leaf parsely, chopped*
1 tsp rosemary, chopped	

PREPARATION:

Mix all marinade ingredients. Trim lamb of any fat and connective tissue and cut into 1-inch cubes. Combine the lamb cubes with the marinade. Allow to marinate for 3–4 hours—preferably overnight.

The next day, thread lamb onto skewers, alternating 4 pieces of lamb with 3 cherry tomatoes. Heat a large, nonstick skillet over high heat. Season brochettes with salt and peppr and place a layer across the bottom of the skillet without crowding. Cook on first side for about 2 minutes, until they start to lightly caramelize. Turn over and cook for another minute or two. Right before removing from pan, brush liberally with pomegranate molasses.

Serve immediately while still hot. Serves 8. Enjoy with a glass of Zinfandel.

As you walk into the barrel room, the tasting bar is to your left.

  Fine points: The Cakebreads have assembled two exquisite binders containing Napa Valley restaurants' menus and chefs' histories for the convenience of visitors and staff. The binders are placed on two wine barrels in the back of the tasting room. Be sure to get on the mailing list for cooking classes, new wines, and special events. Cakebread's own little cookbook, created to celebrate their first 25 years, is yours free for the asking. Cakebread enthusiastically serves alternative beverages to designated drivers. No tasting fee. Featured wines: Sauvignon Blanc, Chardonnay, Cabernet

Sauvignon, Rubaiyat, Merlot, Zinfandel, Pinot Noir, Vin de Porche. Owners: Jack and Dolores Cakebread. Winemaker: Bruce Cakebread. Chef: Brian Streeter. Cases: 75,000. Acres: 85. *❧ Cakebread Cellars, 8300 St. Helena Highway, Rutherford 94573; phone (707) 963–5221 or (800) 588–0298, fax (707) 963–1067, e-mail cellars@cakebread.com, Web site www.cakebread.com. Open 10:00 A.M.–4:30 P.M. Visa, MasterCard, and American Express. Wheelchair-accessible.*

SEQUOIA GROVE WINERY

Just 0.1 mile up the line is SEQUOIA GROVE WINERY, the baby of Jim Allen, who holds degrees in psychology and political science; mined gold in Alaska; served as an interpreter for the United Nations in Germany, Australia, and Greece; worked as a correspondent for UPI in Europe; and taught at a college in Santa Fe, New Mexico.

    Having thoroughly sipped and researched wine everywhere his travels took him, Jim is joined in this adventure of the soul by his brother, Stephen, and their wives, children, and mother. Turn right at the carved redwood burl sign.

    The "sequoia grove" consists of seven trees surrounding the modest barn, a contrast to the flamboyant style of the Robert Mondavi Winery. Walking into the barn/tasting room, you will find the tasting bar to the right, barrels and hoses everywhere, and a welcoming committee of a couple of house dogs waddling through.

    The personality and sociology of a winery really do contribute to the wine and aura of the endeavor—to say nothing of the local "Rutherford Dust" believed to yield the outstanding Cabernets grown on this Rutherford Bench. (Hence the local effort to get the Bureau of Alcohol, Tobacco and Firearms to establish a Rutheford Bench appellation.)

    With his robust, earthy energy, Jim transformed a more than century-old farmhouse into a winery whose wines have received platinum, gold, and silver medals throughout France and the United States. He also built "the first completely underground cellar in the floor of Napa Valley" to create perfect conditions for aging his wines—enduring criticism because of Napa's high water table, but resulting in excellent wines stored and cooled naturally at 55° F.

Fine points: Dan Berger named Sequoia Grove the 1988 American Winery of the Year, just twenty years after the winery's beginning! Wine writers from the *Wine Spectator* and from Berger to Jerry Mead, Joe Pollack, and Bob Thompson rave about Sequoia Grove's Cabernet Sauvignon and Chardonnay. Tasting fee $3.00 for 4 tastes. Featured wines: Cabernet Sauvignon, Chardonnay, Red Table Wine, Gewürztraminer. Owners: Jim and Steve Allen. Winemaker: Jim Allen. Cases: 25,000. Acres: 20. ֍ *Sequoia Grove Winery, 8338 St. Helena Highway, Rutherford 94573; phone (707) 944–2945, fax (707) 963–9411, Web site www.sequoiagrove.com. Open 10:30 A.M.–5:00 P.M. daily, tours by appointment. MasterCard and Visa. Wheelchair-accessible.*

Next up the line is the St. Supery Vineyards & Winery Discovery Center, 0.2 mile north of Sequoia Grove. In stark contrast to Sequoia, St. Supery is a highly technical and marketed establishment owned by French agri-businessman Robert Skalli, who bought the property once owned by Edward St. Supery. Skalli built the winery next to Atkinson House, the white Queen Anne Victorian house built by Joseph Atkinson more than a hundred years ago.

As you drive into St. Supery, the Victorian and an educational vineyard are to your right, and the winery and Discovery Center are straight ahead. Offices are in a charming old wood pump house to your left. Notice the iron vine sculp-

St. Supery Vineyards & Winery

ture to the left of the door, and the Helene Minelli painting of all the California missions just inside the front door of the Winery Discovery Center.

St. Supery's self-guided and guided tours are famously popular—including the SmellaVision Tour, where you can learn to discern those elusive "cherry" and "chocolate" flavors that cause wine writers to rhapsodize. Galleries of panoramic murals, photos, models, and interactive displays illustrate wine lore, to the delight of children and grown-ups alike. Check out the historic wine-bottle collection in the front lobby.

CEO Michaela Rodeno came to St. Supery in 1988 after fifteen years with Domaine Chandon. Michaela is founder of Women for WineSense. She chaired the 1998 Napa Valley Wine Auction, holds an M.A. in French literature, and an M.B.A. from UC Berkeley. She lives on a vineyard in Oakville with her husband, Gregory, and their two children, and grows grapes in Pope Valley. Michaela's mission is to take the snobbishness out of wine and make it fun.

In one of the busiest tasting rooms anywhere, you will find not only great wines but also olive oils, dipping sauces, mustards, aprons, Gil's olives, Elena's pastas, books

CRISPY & TANGY LEMON CHICKEN
from CEO Michaela Rodino, St. Supery

INGREDIENTS:

4 cloves garlic, minced
1 Tbs minced fresh ginger
2 tsp soy sauce
2 tsp lemon juice
½ cup nonfat yogurt
1 tsp ground coriander
2 tsp ground cumin
1 tsp turmeric
1 tsp ground pepper
4 whole (including thigh) chicken legs, skinless
2 cups breadcrumbs

PREPARATION:

Combine the first 9 ingredients in a bowl, stirring to blend thoroughly. Cover the chicken legs with the marinade and refrigerate for 1–2 hours, or overnight for stronger flavor.

Preheat oven to 375° F. Remove chicken legs from marinade and coat in breadcrumbs. Bake chicken legs on a rack for 40–50 minutes until the juices run clear. Serves 4. Serve with Sauvignon Blanc.

Note: Removing the skin of the chicken eliminates about half of the fat. The lemony yogurt marinade replaces the fat with flavor.

galore, corks, and videos. You can sit outside on the patio on green iron tables and chairs and check out St. Supery's booklet "Techniques for Living Well," available in the tasting room.

Fine points: Besides its St. Supery and Bonverre labels, St. Supery's Mount Maroma wines are the only certified Kosher for Passover and mevushal wines made in the Napa Valley. Israeli prime minister Binyamin Netanyahu enjoyed the 1992 Mount Maroma Chardonnay at the White House. Be sure to get on the winery's mailing list for the funniest newsletter in the wine business. No tasting fee. Guided tour with tasting $2.50, wine by the glass $2.50. Featured wines: St. Supery Sauvignon Blanc, Chardonnay, Merlot, Cabernet Sauvignon, Meritage Red, Meritage White, Moscato; Bonverre Chardonnay, Merlot, Cabernet Sauvignon, Viognier, Syrah, Zinfandel; Mount Maroma kosher Chardonnay, Cabernet Sauvignon. Owner: the Skalli family. CEO: Michaela Rodino. Winemaker: Michael J. Scholz. Chef: Sunny Cristadoro. Cases: 180,000. Acres: 635.

St. Supery Vineyards & Winery Discovery Center, 8440 St. Helena Highway, Rutherford 94573; phone (707) 963–4507, fax (707) 963–4526, e-mail divinecab@stsupery.com, Web site www.stsupery.com. Open 9:30 A.M.–6:00 P.M. daily. Visa, MasterCard, and American Express. Mostly wheelchair-accessible.

Next door, to the north, is PEJU PROVINCE, a lovely garden and winery that make you feel as if you have just walked into a home winery in Provence. What do you know? Madame Peju calls the trees down the driveway "Peju sycamores" because her husband trims the sycamores to look like a strong Mistral wind blew the leaves and branches off one winter.

PEJU PROVINCE

PEJU BREADED TURKEY SLICES AU CABERNET
from Herta Peju, Peju Province

INGREDIENTS FOR THE MARINADE:

> *juice of 1 large lemon or ¼ cup of lemon juice concentrate*
> *¼ cup Cabernet Sauvignon (optional)*
> *1 small onion, shredded*

INGREDIENTS FOR THE BREADED TURKEY:

> *1 lb turkey-breast slices, pounded flat*
> *3 whole eggs, lightly beaten (add salt)*
> *1 cup breadcrumbs, unflavored, spread on wax paper*
> *½ cup flour*
> *vegetable oil (should measure ⅜ inch up the side of a skillet)*
> *salt and pepper to taste*

PREPARATION:

Prepare marinade by mixing the ingredients in a bowl.

Pound turkey pieces very thin and place in the bowl with marinade, add salt and pepper. Leave for at least 2 hours in the marinade.

Dredge each turkey slice in flour to coat well. Dip each slice in the egg mixture. Coat with breadcrumbs. As you turn each slice over, place a piece of wax paper over the slice and tap it into the breadcrumbs with the palm of your hand to get a better adherence of the crumbs to the meat. (You may prepare slices up to this point a few hours ahead of time.)

Heat the oil, preferably in a heavy skillet, over medium-high heat. Make sure oil is hot enough—it should sizzle—before you begin cooking. Cook as many slices at one time as will fit loosely in a single layer in the skillet. Remove them just as soon as they are brown and crisp on both sides, which will be very quickly because they are so thin.

Place the browned meat on paper towels, to absorb any excess oil. Serve piping hot with lemon wedges and cranberry sauce. Serves 4–6.

Notice Mendocino sculptor Welton Rotz's statuary in the parking lot and throughout the grounds. Enter through the brass-and-iron gate and enjoy the fountain and bell, Herta Peju's much-photographed, multicolored flowers, and French sculptured gardens.

Named the "Top Artisan Winery of the Year" in 1994 by *Wine & Spirits* magazine, its 1994 Cabernet Sauvignon was in the "100 Best Wines of the Year" at the 1997 World Wine Championships, and among the "50 Best American Red Wines" by *Wine & Spirits Buying Guide–1998*; Peju should be on your must-stop list.

Anthony Peju grew up in Aix-en-Provence, studied film direction at UCLA, and owned an extremely successful nursery and garden supply business in Los Angeles. Tony and his wife, Herta, from Salzberg, Austria, scoured California from Mexico to Napa Valley. They selected this site, finding it perfect.

We found an outstanding selection of wine and cookbooks, Jacques Pepin's pepper sauce, Sparrow Lane vinegars, and Peju Cabernet-filled chocolates.

 Fine points: If you are lucky, Events Coordinator Alan Arnopole, who considers every visit to be an event, might yodel for you in the barrel room. Claiming to have learned to yodel by jumping over cactus, he sings to the wine and claims it just may be what makes Peju's wines so exceptional. Tasting fee $3.00. Featured wines: Chardonnay, Cabernet Sauvignon, Merlot, Cabernet Franc, Provence table wine, and Carnival (French Colombard). Owners: Anthony and Herta Peju. Winemaker: Anthony Peju. Cases: 10,000. Acres: 30 planted.

✿ *Peju Province, 8466 St. Helena Highway, Rutherford 94573; phone (707) 963–3600, fax (707) 963–8680, Web site www.wines.com. Open 10:00 A.M.–6:00 P.M. daily. Visa and MasterCard. Wheelchair-accessible.*

Before you get into "downtown" Rutherford, Francis Ford Coppola's NIEBAUM-COPPOLA is on your left. *Do not* turn west on Niebaum Lane. This is a road that does not lead to any wineries. Take the next left (west) off Highway 29 at the signs.

Flush with earnings from *The Godfather*, Eleanor and Francis Ford Coppola went to the Napa Valley to find a one-acre retreat, a place perfect for writing and creating. Instead they found this elegant estate, planted with vines in 1872 and acquired in the late 1870s by Finnish sea captain and Alaska fur trader Gustave Niebaum, who named the estate Inglenook. Niebaum's property was subdivided in 1969. Eventually, Heublein produced mass-market Inglenook wines in the winery facility. Coppola bought the Victorian estate home in 1975 and began to lust after the Inglenook Chateau to reunite the properties.

With *Bram Stoker's Dracula* profits, he paid most of the $10 million for the winery parcel in 1995, fulfilling his dream. The Coppolas turned the chateau into the Niebaum-Coppola Estate Winery and the Centennial Museum to showcase both the history of winemaking and Coppola's film career.

As you walk toward the chateau from the parking lot, you just know you have entered a movie set, complete with expansive walkways, decorative columns, and fountains. The only incongruity is the electronic sign at the south end of the chateau beaming out event notices. Once inside the heavy, cool building, notice the sweeping staircase made of exotic woods Coppola brought from Belize, where he owns a resort, Blancaneaux Lodge, in a remote rain forest. The Coppola-conceived stained-glass window over the staircase depicts the historic estate's reunification.

As you turn right inside the front doorway, first you come to the tasting room, and then to the retail shop. We were struck with the warm elegance of the Belize woods in these two vast rooms, as well as with the casual friendliness of the entire Niebaum-Coppola staff. You are welcome to sit at the long tables, sip wine, and enjoy the atmosphere and music, the latter of which comes from a player piano that sounds out songs written for _The Godfather_ by Coppola's father, music publisher Carmine Coppola. The retail shop has such things as excellent Coppola herbed olive oils and pastas, Italian ceramics, linens, candles, copperware, cigars and accessories, and the best selections of French and Italian food books we have seen.

Be sure to pick up a copy of _Coppola's Zoetrope: All Story_ tabloid magazine of short fiction.

Not incidental to all the movie jazz are some of America's finest vineyards and wines. Winemaker Scott McLeod (a well-known Italian name) received his B.S. in fermentation sciences at UC Davis and worked at Fattorie Isole e Olena in Tuscany's Chianti region; and as winemaker at Fattorie Badia a Passignano in Tuscany, Robert Mondavi, Cain Cellars, and Charles Shaw and now Niebaum-Coppola.

Fine points: Academy Award statues for _Patton_, _The Godfather_, and _The Godfather, Part II_, Coppola's 1948 Tucker from the film _Tucker_, Don Corleone's desk and chair from _The Godfather_ and Oscar-winning costumes from _Bram Stoker's Dracula_ are all on display. Tasting fee $7.50 (and you may keep the glass). Featured wines: Rubicon (mostly Cabernet Sauvignon), Francis Ford Coppola Family Wines including Chardonnay, Merlot, and Cabernet Franc, Edizione Pennino Zinfandel, Niebaum-Coppola Claret, and Francis Coppola Presents: Bianco and Rosso. Owners: Francis and Eleanor Coppola. Winemaker: Scott McLeod. Cases: 40,000. Acres: 195 planted of 1,654.

Niebaum-Coppola, _1991 St. Helena Highway, Rutherford 94573; phone (888) COPPOLA, fax (707) 967–4178, e-mail rosso@aol.com, Web site www.niebaum-coppola.com. Open 10:00 A.M.–5:00 P.M. daily. Visa, MasterCard, American Express, and Discover. Wheelchair-accessible._

Cross Highway 29 very carefully when you leave, turning left to go north only when it is clearly safe. Almost immediately you come to the Rutherford Cross Road, Rutherford Grill, and Beaulieu Vineyards on the right (east) side of the highway.

From the outside the RUTHERFORD GRILL looks like an ordinary roadside plastic-menu kind of place. It sits in front of Beaulieu Vineyards. Drive in Beaulieu's driveway and park either in its parking lot or behind the restaurant in a small lot shared with the tiny U.S. Post Office. Walk between the buildings to the patio and a bar (a poolside feeling without the pool), and on the right you will come to the dining-room entrance. Are you in for a surprise!

Dark wood, comfy leather booths, leather-covered counter stools, and beamed ceilings with skylights set the tone. Opened linen napkins serve as "tablecloths" at the counter, where many singles drop in and enjoy a hearty, adventurous lunch or dinner. Expect lots of noise and action, with waiters and cooks shouting and repeating orders.

The food is California hearty with a twist, and they "take rotisserie cooking very seriously." Try the roasted chicken with mashed potatoes ($12.00) or sliced leg of lamb ($17.00). You can get the same chicken as a chicken dip sandwich ($9.00) with cole slaw or in a "very wild rice" salad, or ask for a little of both for a unique salad orgy. Knife and Fork Barbecue Ribs are grilled over hardwood and basted with Texas Hill Country BBQ sauce and served with cole slaw and chips.

"This and Thats" include house-smoked-salmon appetizer ($10.00), Chicago Style Spinach and Artichoke Dip ($8.00), and Maytag Blue Cheese Potato Chips ($7.00). The menu warns that "The California legislature has determined that eating is a dangerous endeavor. At Rutherford Grill we serve rare tuna, use raw eggs in our Caesar salad and grind chuck roast in house for all burgers. Upon request, we will be happy to change what we feel is a safe and delicious presentation and serve your food consistent with California Codes 113995, 113996, and 113998." Roast prime rib bones for your dog available.

Vegetarians also enjoy the Napa Valley Vegetable Platter or club sandwich. The Caesar Salad (with raw egg) comes with homemade Challah bread croutons. The Grill has a good Napa and Sonoma wine list.

Rutherford Grill, 1180 Rutherford Road, Rutherford 94573; phone (707) 963–1792. Open 11:30 A.M.–9:30 P.M. daily. Visa, MasterCard, and American Express. Wheelchair-accessible.

Seemingly behind the Rutherford Grill is the original champion of California Cabernet Sauvignon, BEAULIEU VINEYARDS, known in the local vernacular as "B.V." which, to some people, confuses it with Sonoma's Buena Vista Winery. Beaulieu is the oldest continuously producing winery in the Napa Valley.

BEAULIEU VINEYARDS

The tasting room is in the newish, peaked-roof octagon building at the southeast corner of the Beaulieu complex. To the left of the entrance is a tree donated and planted by the *Wine Spectator* in memory of Beaulieu's longtime winemaker and Napa wine guru, Andre Tchelistcheff.

Georges de Latour immigrated from Bordeaux, France, in the late 1800s to San Francisco, where he developed a successful cream-of-tartar business. After he and his bride, Fernande Romer, began their four-acre vineyard and named it Beaulieu ("beautiful place"), the dreaded *phylloxera* invaded, sending Georges back to France to find resistant rootstock. He brought some back to the Napa Valley, establishing a nursery and selling healthy vines to other vintners.

Surviving Prohibition by selling sacramental wines to the Catholic Church in San Francisco, Georges switched from hard-to-get French oak barrels to American oak for his Cabernet Sauvignon, and he recruited Russian-born enologist Andre Tchelistcheff from Paris's Pasteur Institute in 1938. Two years later, Georges de Latour died, having won a gold medal and Grand Sweepstakes Award at the 1939 Golden Gate International Exposition for his 1936 Cabernet Sauvignon.

Having worked side-by-side with her husband, Madame de Latour took over management of the winery and named the Cabernet "Georges de Latour Private Reserve" in his honor. Relying on Tchelistcheff's expertise, she ran the winery until her death in 1952, expanding its prominence to the tables of Franklin D. Roosevelt and Winston Churchill.

Tchelistcheff gained worldwide fame and taught many prominent Napa winemakers, including Joseph Heitz, Miljenko Grgich, and Tom Selfridge. In 1963 he planted B.V.'s original Carneros vineyard, one of the first to realize the Carneros region's potential for fine grapes.

Beaulieu was sold to giant Heublein in 1969, which sold it in 1998 to Industrial Distillers & Vintners (IDV Wines), which also owns Glen Ellen Winery in Sonoma Valley.

 Fine points: You can see Madame de Latour's influence in wine-making through the photos of Beaulieu Vintners' women and the placard honoring the "Women of Beaulieu." No tasting fee in main tasting room; $10 for four tastes of Special Reserve Wine in separate elegant building. Featured wines: Georges de Latour Private Reserve Cabernet Sauvignon, Tapestry Reserve Red Table Wine, Reserve Chardonnay, and Pinot Noir; the Signet Collection of Zinfandel, Ensemble (Rhone blend of Mourvedre, Grenach, Carignane, and Syrah); Napa Series of Cabernet Sauvignon, Merlot, Chardonnay, Pinot Noir, and Sauvignon Blanc; and Beautour Cabernet Sauvignon, Merlot, Sauvignon Blanc, Chardonnay, Pinot Noir, and Gamay Beaujolais. Owner: IDV Wines. Winemaker: Joel Aiken. Cases: 750,000. Acres: 1,500.

❧ *Beaulieu Vineyards, 1960 St. Helena Highway, Rutherford 94573; phone (707) 967–5200, Web site www.bvwine.com. Open 10:00 A.M.–5:00 P.M. daily. Visa, MasterCard, and American Express. Wheelchair-accessible.*

Just across the highway, in a slightly run-down, long wooden building, try Dione Carston's HACIENDA HARDWARE—COLECCION MEXICANA, where you will find a labyrinth of rooms crammed with great old peasant Mexican furnishings and home accessories, from huge, heavy wooden doors to light fixtures, furniture, a wooden highchair, an antique brass crib that swings, enormous pottery, and general house and garden doodads.

❧ *Hacienda Hardware–Coleccion Mexicana, 1989 St. Helena Highway, Rutherford 94573; phone (707) 963–8850, fax (707) 963–8877, Web site www.haciendahardware.com. Open 10:00 A.M.–6:00 P.M. daily. Visa, MasterCard, American Express, and Discover. Not wheelchair-accessible.*

Try to visit both Hacienda Hardware and Grgich Hills when you are driving south, so that you stay on the same side of Highway 29.

On the west side of the highway is GRGICH HILLS CELLAR, the baby of Miljenko (Mike) Grgich, a native of Croatia and champion of its independence from the late Yugoslavia, and Austin Hills of San Francisco's Hills Brothers Coffee family and fortune. As you turn across the railroad tracks, notice the Croatian flag flying. You will also see the Croatian shield on Grgich Hills wine labels.

Mike Grgich brought to this 1977 wine marriage a degree in viticulture and enology from the University of Zagreb, as well as long stints as chemist at Beaulieu Vineyards; chief enologist at Robert Mondavi Winery; and limited partner, winemaker, and vineyardist at Chateau Montelena, where he created the Chardonnay that won "Best Chardonnay" at the 1976 Paris Tasting and put Grgich firmly on the world wine-celebrity map. As a result of this triumph, his Chardonnay has been served to President Bill Clinton at the California Café in Los Gatos, Queen Elizabeth II, King Juan Carlos of Spain, and President Jose Sarney of Brazil. President Ronald Reagan took four cases to Paris for President François Mitterrand.

For his contribution to the wine marriage, Austin Hills brought money, a fine coffee taster's palate, a refined sense of business management, and a reserved manner that allows Grgich to create and promote great wines. Hills' wife, Erika, owns Erika Hills Antiques, just south of St. Helena.

Together, Grgich and Hills agreed on the European tradition of concentrating on quality instead of quantity of their wines, and has it paid off. Their Chardonnay is often called the best in the world, the Cabernet Sauvignon consistently receives high ratings, and the Fume Blanc has won several gold and silver medals. The Violetta, named for Grgich's daughter and manager, Violet, is

GRGICH HILLS CELLAR

a late-harvest dessert wine of Riesling and Chardonnay that received a 95 from the *Wine Spectator* in 1997.

Fine points: Enjoy the Old World feeling in the tasting room, with its dark wood, and take time to peruse the vast literature reprints and Croatian travel posters. You can also buy wooden boxes here for just $6.00 that are ideal for storing CDs. Tasting is free, but there's a $3.00 glass charge on weekends, because they can't get them all washed! Featured wines: Chardonnay, Fume Blanc, Cabernet Sauvignon, Zinfandel, Violetta Late Harvest. Owners: Mike Grgich and Austin Hills. Winemaker: Mike Grgich. Cases: 70,000. Acres: 200.

Grgich Hills Cellar, 1829 St. Helena Highway, Rutherford 94573; phone (707) 963–2784 or (800) 532–3057, fax (707) 963–8725. Open 9:30 A.M.–4:30 P.M. Visa and MasterCard. Wheelchair-accessible.

North of Beaulieu, on the east side of Highway 29 just 0.9 mile away, is QUAIL RIDGE CELLARS & VINEYARDS, whose ponds and gardens offer one of the most peaceful of winery settings. Turn right onto Mee Lane.

Barrels line the cream-colored winery's eastern wall. Walk around to the western side of the building and onto the deck facing the lake and Highway 29 to get to the tasting room's entrance.

Inside the small, fun tasting room, you can dip bread into French Press grapeseed, filbert, and olive oils for tastes or palette cleansers.

QUAIL RIDGE'S DECK AND POND

Fine points: Tasting fee is $3.50 for five tastes and you can keep the Quail Ridge crystal glass. Featured wines: Sauvignon Blanc, Cabernet Sauvignon, Merlot, Cabernet Franc. Owners: Rutherford Benchmarks. Winemaker: Anthony Bell. Cases: 30,000. Acres: 10.

❧ *Quail Ridge Cellars & Vineyards, 1155 Mee Lane, St. Helena 94573; phone (707) 963–9783. Open 11:00 A.M.–6:00 P.M. daily in summer; 10:00 A.M.–5:00 P.M. daily in winter. Visa and MasterCard. Wheelchair-accessible.*

On the west side of Highway 29, BEAUCANON NAPA VALLEY looks like an industrial cement building with a French flair, which it is, with parking lots at both ends. Even if you don't see any cars and the small window sign says Closed, try the door. And sometimes when the sign says Open, the door is locked. Persevere.

The de Coninck family has been producing fine wines in St. Emilion, Bordeaux, France, for more than 250 years. They bring part of the family and its knowledge and background to the Napa Valley. Intertwining French wine-making expertise with Napa Valley grapes, Jacques de Coninck established their La Crosse and estate Beaucanon labels in the 1980s.

Joyce Alcouloumre serves as hospitality director in the vast tasting room and is very knowledgeable about the de Conincks and Beaucanon wines. Hang around a while and you can learn from her.

Fine points: No tasting fee. Featured wines: Chardonnay, Cabernet Franc, Merlot, Cabernet Sauvignon, Late Harvest Chardonnay 1991 Envie desert wine. Owners: The de Coninck family. Winemaker: Louis de Coninck. Cases: 30,000. Acres: 250.

❧ *Beaucanon Napa Valley, 1695 St. Helena Highway, St. Helena 94574; phone (707) 967–3520, fax (707) 967–3527. Open 10:00 A.M.–5:00 P.M. daily. Visa, MasterCard, American Express, and JCB. Wheelchair-accessible.*

To get to FRANCISCAN VINEYARDS, just north of Quail Ridge, turn east onto Galleron Lane. Turn left immediately into Franciscan's driveway and parking lot. (Galleron Lane will also take you to Sullivan Vineyards, the next stop after Franciscan.)

The real story of Franciscan is far greater than just this winery, which has never had any relationship to Franciscan orders of the Catholic Church. Franciscan is owned by Germany's Eckes Family and its vintner–president, Chilean Agustin Huneeus. (Huneeus also owns other impressive properties, including the new Quintessa Estate in Rutherford, huge Veramonte in Chile's Casablanca Valley, Mount Veeder Estate on the western slopes of Napa Valley, and Estancia Alexander Valley in Sonoma County and Monterey County.)

FRANCISCAN VINEYARDS

Huneeus operates all of his vineyards on a sustainable-agriculture basis, proclaiming sensitivity to local *terroir*, which he defines as "that challenging merging of microclimate, soil, slope, and sun exposure," an old European approach newly discovered by California vintners.

As you approach the winery's entrance, enjoy the humor of the cement "Rutherford Bench," a pun on the Rutherford bench (land section) where the winery is located; the purple, lavender, and mustard banners; and a gigantic fountain, along with an eighteenth-century wine press in front. A peaceful, enclosed patio planted with roses, off the tasting room, provides a relaxing place to sample Franciscan wines and your picnic lunch.

 Fine points: Floor Manager Michael Colon offers tastes of Franciscan, Estancia, and Mount Veeder wines in the tasting room. Be sure to notice prize-winning artist David Lance Goins designs for the Mount Veeder Winery labels and posters. He also did graphics for Ravenswood Winery in Sonoma. The tasting fee of $3.00 can be applied to a purchase. Featured wines: Franciscan Chardonnay, Zinfandel, Merlot, Cabernet Sauvignon, Cuvee Sauvage Chardonnay, Magnificat; Quintessa; Veramonte Casablanca Estate Chardonnay, Cabernet Sauvignon, Merlot, and Primus Merlot; Mount Veeder Winery Cabernet Sauvignon, Merlot, Cabernet Franc, Malbec, Zinfandel, and Petit Verdot; Estancia Alexander Valley Estate Meritage, Cabernet Sauvignon, Merlot, and Duetto;

and Estancia Monterey County Estate Bottled Chardonnay, Fume Blanc, Pinot Noir, Reserve Chardonnay, and Reserve Pinot Noir. Owners: Agustin Huneeus and the Eckes Family. Winemakers: Larry Levin, Franciscan, and Janet Pagano, Mount Veeder. Cases: Franciscan 60,000; Mount Veeder 10,000; Veramonte over 1,000,000. Acres: nearly 4,000 worldwide.

❧ *Franciscan Vineyards, 1178 Galleron Lane, St. Helena 94574; phone (707) 963-7111, fax (707) 963-7867, Web site www.franciscan.com. Open 10:00 A.M.–5:00 P.M. daily. Visa, MasterCard, American Express, and Discover. Wheelchair-accessible.*

If you leave the Franciscan parking lot by the southern exit onto Galleron Lane, turn left (east) to SULLIVAN VINEYARDS. Turn left into Sullivan's gravel driveway. On your right will be the family's interesting two-story home with rolling lawns and a refreshing duck pond. The winery is to your left. Drive around to the south side of the winery and park. Boing, the blond Lab, greets you with a green tennis ball firmly planted in his mouth.

You taste Sullivan's wines with Sean Sullivan, co-winemaker and son of the founder, right in the middle of the winery with the inventory and barrels while Cellarmaster Lorenzo Garcia works around you. Sean's sister, Kelleen, is obviously a talented painter, as her winery poster demonstrates.

 Fine points: Check out the elegant etched-crystal glasses ($36) as well as the tasteful shirts and well priced hats ($15). Custom etched bottles are also available. Sullivan's special wines are all in the Bordeaux style and are promoted solely by word of mouth. The prized Coeur de Vigne is aged thirty-two months in oak. No tasting fee. Featured wines: Cabernet Sauvignon, Coeur de Vigne (80 percent Cabernet Sauvignon, 20 percent Merlot blend), Merlot. Owners: Jim and JoAnna Sullivan. Winemakers: Jim and Sean Sullivan. Cases: 3,500. Acres: 26.

❧ *Sullivan Vineyards, 1090 Galleron Lane, Rutherford 94573; phone (707) 963-9646 or (800) 501-4669, fax (707) 963-0377, e-mail sean@fes.com, Web site www.sullivanwine.com. Open 10:00 A.M.–5:00 P.M. Visa, MasterCard, and American Express. Wheelchair-accessible.*

As you leave Sullivan, turn right (west) onto Galleron to Highway 29. Turn right (north) to continue our tour.

The next three wineries moving north are on the west side of Highway 29. RUTHERFORD GROVE WINERY AND NAPA VALLEY GRAPESEED OIL COMPANY is tucked back in a grove of century-old eucalyptus trees that envelop a lush expanse of lawns and gardens, protected from highway traffic and noise. This is just part of the reason it is the new home of the Napa Valley Shakespeare

CAPONATA

Rutherford Grove Winery's Napa Valley Grapeseed Oil Company

Caponata is an excellent appetizer served with toasted baguette rounds or as a topping for pasta.

INGREDIENTS:

> ¾ cup Napa Valley Grapeseed Oil
>
> ¼ cup olive oil
>
> 1 ½ lb eggplant, peeled and cut into 1-in cubes
>
> 2 large green peppers, cut into 1-in pieces
>
> 2 large cloves garlic, minced
>
> 1 28 oz can solid pack tomatoes, undrained
>
> ⅓ cup red wine vinegar
>
> 2 Tbs sugar
>
> 2 Tbs capers
>
> 2 Tbs tomato paste
>
> 2 tsp salt
>
> ½ cup fresh chopped parsley
>
> ½ cup pimento-stuffed green olives, rinsed, sliced thickly
>
> ½ tsp freshly ground pepper
>
> 2 tsp crumbled dried basil or ¼ cup loosely packed fresh basil leaves, sliced into ribbons
>
> ½ cup pine nuts sauteed in Napa Valley Grapeseed Oil

PREPARATION:

In a large heavy saucepan, combine ¾ cup Napa Valley Grapeseed Oil and ¼ cup olive oil, eggplant, green peppers, onion, garlic, and tomatoes. Cook for about 20–30 minutes or until just tender. Add wine vinegar, sugar, capers, tomato paste, salt, parsley, basil, green olives, and pepper. Cover and simmer for 15 minutes. Add pine nuts and serve warm or at room temperature. Makes 12 appetizers. Serve with Cabernet Sauvignon.

Festival. Walking into Rutherford Grove is a cool, peaceful experience, thanks to its dark redwood walls, cement floors, rattan chairs, fireplace, and wrought-iron foot rail at the tasting bar. Vaulted ceilings and large windows showcase rotating art shows.

Rutherford Grove is worth a visit if only as a lesson in total-use recycling. In back of the winery, they make naturally cold-pressed grapeseed oil and compost residue from fifty vineyards, and sell back to vineyards for organic fertilizer. You can taste the grapeseed oils in the tasting room, but not the compost.

Founded by German-born Bernard Skoda, Rutherford Grove was eventually purchased by the Pestonis, originally a Swiss–Italian family from Monte Carasso. They have been in the Napa Valley since Albino Pestoni arrived four generations ago. Monte Carasso's thirteenth-century monastery appears on some of the Sangiovese labels. Bob and Marvin Pestoni carry on the family tradition at Rutherford Grove.

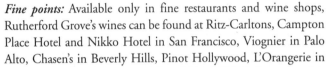

Fine points: Available only in fine restaurants and wine shops, Rutherford Grove's wines can be found at Ritz-Carltons, Campton Place Hotel and Nikko Hotel in San Francisco, Viognier in Palo Alto, Chasen's in Beverly Hills, Pinot Hollywood, L'Orangerie in Los Angeles, and many others. The tasting fee of $3.00 ($5.00 for reserves) is refundable with purchase. Featured wines: Johannisberg Riesling, Helena Rosé (Rosé of Cabernet Franc), Merlot, Sangiovese, Cabernet Sauvignon. Owners: Bob and Marvin Pestoni. Winemaker: Bob Pepi. Cases: 5,000. Acres: 30+.

❧ *Rutherford Grove Winery and Napa Valley Grapeseed Oil Company, 1673 St. Helena Highway, Rutherford 94573; phone (707) 963–0544, fax (707) 963–3150, Web site www.Rutherfordgrove.com or seedoil.com. Open 10:00 A.M.–4:30 P.M. Visa, MasterCard, and American Express. Wheelchair-accessible.*

WHITEHALL LANE WINERY has been under reconstruction and remodeling for a while to fulfill great expectations for a state-of-the art tasting and wine-making facility. Check out the tasting room's gift and logo-wear merchandise. We enjoyed tasting in the fermentation room during construction. The bar consisted of a board resting between two barrels. A real treat!

The Leonardini family of San Francisco bought the estate in 1993 and have been at work updating the wine and facilities ever since, first with winemaker Gary Galleron and now with Dean Sylvester. Sylvester comes to Whitehall Lane from Newton Vineyards, Chimney Rock Winery, and Mario Perelli-Minetti Winery. Besides being readily accessible at the winery, you might also catch Sylvester playing guitar as his therapy "outlet" on the nightclub circuit with musician Gary Yoder.

Fine points: Don't miss the barrel tasting tours at 1:00 and 4:00 P.M. or the characters who work here, including Kim Leonardini, who manages the tasting room. She also writes her own column in the Whitehall newsletter. Tasting fee $3.00, and you can keep the glass or apply fee to a purchase. Featured wines: Sauvignon Blanc, Chardonnay,

1995 WHITEHALL LANE NAPA CABERNET RED RISOTTO
from Whitehall Lane

INGREDIENTS:

1 bottle 1995 Whitehall Lane Napa Cabernet

¼ cup butter

2 Tbs chopped fresh thyme

1 ½ cups Arborio rice (risotto)

3 cups canned vegetable broth

¼ cup grated Parmesan cheese

1 14-oz can cannellini beans, rinsed and drained (any white bean will work)

1 ½ cups red onion, chopped

4 cups thinly sliced radicchio

1 ¾ cups 1995 Whitehall Lane Cab

1 cup toasted walnuts, chopped

salt and pepper to taste

PREPARATION:

Uncork the Cabernet, pour a glass for taste approval and for yourself! Remember, do not get too carried away in the enjoyment of the wine—you need 1 ¾ cups for the recipe itself, leaving approximately 2 glasses for dinner.

Melt the butter in a large saucepan over medium heat. Add onion and saute until soft and just beginning to brown, about 5 minutes. Mix in 1 ½ Tbs thyme. Add the sliced radicchio and the rice. Sauté until the radicchio wilts, about 3 minutes.

Meanwhile begin to simmer the vegetable broth in a separate pot. Slightly increase heat and add the beans and 1 cup of wine to the mixture. Simmer until the wine is absorbed and stir. Add remaining ¾ cup of wine, while continuing to simmer, for about 3 more minutes.

When all of the wine is absorbed in the risotto, add the vegetable broth to the mixture. Stir to combine, cover, and simmer until the liquid is absorbed and the rice is tender, but firm in the center. Stir in the remaining ½ Tbs thyme, the cup of walnuts, and add the ¼ cup Parmesan cheese. Season with salt and pepper and stir to combine. Transfer to a bowl, ready to serve with additional Parmesan at the table. Serves 4.

L'Etoile Zinfandel, Merlot, Cabernet Sauvignon, Johannisberg Riesling. Owner: Thomas Leonardi. Winemaker: Dean Sylvester. Cases: 25,000. Acres: 90.

Whitehall Lane Winery, 1563 St. Helena Highway, St. Helena 94574; phone (707) 963–9454, fax (707) 963–7035. Open 11:00 A.M.–6:00 P.M. daily. Visa, MasterCard, and American Express. Wheelchair-accessible.

For a little side trip, turn right (east) onto Zinfandel Lane to RAYMOND VINEYARD & CELLAR. At 0.6 mile east of Highway 29, turn right (south) at Raymond's signs, go through the gates, and go another 0.2 mile. The "Pepto Bismol colored" house on the left belongs to Romy Gould, widow of Paco Gould, one of the Napa wine industry's late gurus.

On the outside, Raymond looks like a large California ranch house with grey vertical wood siding and stone walls and gorgeous renunculas in the garden. Inside, the tasting room and hospitality feel like someone's living room, with carpeting and a dining table. You will find green-and-burgundy aprons, pastas, VinTea, Vintners Kitchen food products, Vine Village and French Press oils, and a Raymond Vineyard 550-piece puzzle.

Roy Raymond, Sr., began working in the barrel room of Beringer Winery in 1933, married winemaker Otto Beringer's daughter, Jane, worked his way to manager, and left Beringer when Nestlé Corporation bought it. Raymond bought ninety acres here on Zinfandel Lane in 1971, with the first grapes harvested in 1974, developing highly revered Cabernet Sauvignons. Even though Roy Sr. had sold the winery to Kirin Beer of Japan, he was often seen on his tractor mowing the winery's lush lawns, right up until his death in 1998. Roy Jr., Walter, and Craig Raymond, great-grandsons and great-great-grandson of Beringer, continue to manage Raymond.

 Fine points: Tastings free except $2.50 for limited-production or hard-to-find wines. Featured wines: Sauvignon Blanc, Chardonnay, Pinot Noir, Cabernet Sauvignon, Merlot; Amber Hill Chardonnay, Cabernet Sauvignon, Merlot; Generations Chardonnay and Cabernet Sauvignon; Private Reserve Meritage. Owner: Kirin Beer. Winemakers: Walter Raymond, Kenn Vigoda, Kathy Chase. Cases: 250,000. Acres: 460.

Raymond Vineyard & Cellar, 849 Zinfandel Lane, St. Helena 94574; phone (707) 963–3141 or (800) 525–2659, fax (707) 963–8498. Open 10:00 A.M.–4:00 P.M. daily. Visa, MasterCard, Diners Club, and JCB. Wheelchair-accessible.

MILAT VINEYARDS is one of the few remaining old wineries still run by the original owner family. Bob and Mike Milat and their wives Joyce and Carolyn run the whole show; in fact, they are the show. Bob and Mike grew up on the prop-

MILAT VINEYARDS

erty where their family has been growing and selling grapes since 1949, eventually realizing that their high-demand grapes might just make good wine for them, too. They started making wine in 1986, and you can buy these personal and reasonably priced vintages only here in the tasting room. Be sure to stop.

 Fine points: The Milat family also offers three guest rooms in cottages in the vineyard and a converted loft in the barn, with queen beds, full baths and patios, coffeepots, and refrigerators from $80–$95. Tasting fee of $2.00 for logo glass. Featured wines: Chardonnay, Chenin Blanc, Sweet Chenin Blanc, Zivio blush table wine, Zinfandel, and Cabernet Sauvignon. Owners: The Milat Family. Winemakers: Bob and Mike Milat. Cases: 3,000. Acres: 22.

❧ *Milat Vineyards, 1091 St. Helena Highway, St. Helena 94574; phone (707) 963–0758 or (800) 54–MILAT, fax (707) 963–0168, Web site www.milat.com. Open 10:00 A.M.–6:00 P.M. daily. Visa, MasterCard, American Express, and Discover. Wheelchair-accessible.*

As we approach the city of St. Helena, the winery and specialty food forests thicken. Winery buildings range from expensive cement blocks to expensive charming old Victorian homes and wood barns. Locals refer to this area as St. Helena Highway South, with St. Helena as the center of the universe, of course. To mapmakers, it is simply Highway 29.

But whatever it's called, it is an engrossing (interesting as well as fattening!) food-and-wine mecca that even the most casual food-and-wine fans will enjoy.

On the left (west) side of Highway 29, heading north, FLORA SPRINGS has a brand new tasting room. To get there turn west into the driveway just past Zinfandel Lane and Inglewood Avenue.

Owner John Komes commissioned Richmond, Virginia, artist Happy the Artist to paint the cartoonish murals depicting wine growing and the wine-making process on the tasting-room walls.

If you want to visit Flora Springs' 1888 winery, founded by Scots James and William Rennie and later housing Louis Martini's sherry and wine-aging operations, you will find Jerome and Flora Komes' treasure at 1978 West Zinfandel Lane in St. Helena.

The Komes purchased the "old ghost winery and vineyard in the western foothills of the Napa Valley" in 1977. Komes' children, John and Julie, got caught up in the venture. John used his skills as a contractor and businessman to renovate the historic buildings and begin the winery, and Julie's husband, Pat Garvey, left his job as a college administrator to tend the vineyards. After two vintages of learning and making the wine themselves, the family invited Ken Deis to become winemaker, with impressive results.

 Fine points: No tasting fee. Flora Springs' 1991 Reserve Cabernet was selected #3 wine in the world in the *Wine Spectator's* "Top 100 Wines of the Year." Flora Springs' featured wines: Chardonnay, Sauvignon Blanc, Soliloquy, Cabernet Sauvignon, Merlot, Sangiovese, Trilogy. Owners: Jerome and Flora Komes, Winemaker: Ken Deis. Cases: 50,000. Acres: 350.

Flora Springs, 677 St. Helena Highway, St. Helena 94574; phone (707) 967–8032, fax (707) 963–5711. Open 10:00 A.M.–6:00 P.M. daily summer, 10:00 A.M.–5:00 P.M. winter. Visa and MasterCard. Wheelchair-accessible.

Behind Flora Springs is **29 JOE'S COFFEE HOUSE**, which also joins Dean and DeLuca by parking lot. Enjoy the mosaics at the cafe's entrance. This spot features good coffee, coffeebeans, Sweetie Pies cakes and pastries (the best!), sandwiches, salads, local art and music, checkers that you can pick up at the coffee bar and take to your table (chess is already set up), frozen drinks, and poetry readings. We particularly like the green chairs and tables right outside the cafe on the patio, on the non-parking-lot side. Use the drive-up window if you're in a hurry.

29 Joe's Coffee House, 677 St. Helena Highway, St. Helena 94574; phone (707) 967–0820. Open 5:30 A.M.–5:30 P.M. Monday–Friday, 6:30 A.M.–3:30 P.M. Saturday, 7:30 A.M.–3:30 P.M. Sunday. No credit cards. Wheelchair-accessible.

Right next door, and in dramatic contrast to 29 Joe's, is famed **DEAN &
DELUCA**, the Manhattan "Purveyors of Fine Food and Kitchenware" founded
on Prince Street in SoHo by former publishing executive Joel Dean and former history teacher and son of a food importer Giorgio DeLuca. Leslie Rudd,
who also owns Girard Winery on the Silverado Trail, now owns a controlling
interest in Dean & DeLuca and is responsible for its successful expansion,
with Giorgio DeLuca continuing day-to-day management and his global
search for the finest food products.

POLENTA WITH WILD MUSHROOMS
Executive Chef Tom Gray, Dean & DeLuca

INGREDIENTS FOR THE POLENTA:

1 cup polenta	*1 tsp white pepper*
2 cups whole milk	*¼ cup Parmesan cheese, grated*
2 cups water	*2 oz unsalted butter*
2 tsp salt	*2 Tbs chives, finely chopped*

PREPARATION:

Bring milk, water, and salt to a boil. Slowly whisk in polenta to avoid lumps.
Cook approximately 30–45 minutes on low heat until polenta is soft. Remove
from heat, stir in butter, cheese, and chives. Pour into molds or pour into a ½-
sheet pan, then chill and cut into desired shapes. Reheat with roasted mushrooms on top.

INGREDIENTS FOR THE WILD MUSHROOMS:

8 Shiitake mushrooms, stems removed and cut in quarters
12 oyster mushrooms, stems removed and cut in quarters
2 portobello mushrooms, stems removed, diced
3 cloves garlic, finely diced
1 sprig rosemary, cleaned, stems removed, chopped
1 sprig thyme, cleaned, stems removed, chopped
enough olive oil to lightly coat

PREPARATION:

Combine mushrooms, garlic, herbs, and olive oil. Season with salt and white
pepper. Roast in 350° F oven approximately 7–9 minutes, or saute.

Serve over polenta. Serves 4.

You can enter Dean & DeLuca from the parking lot to the store's south; or through the southern front door, which takes you into the fresh local produce, breads, and delicacies sections; or through the northern front door into the wine shop, where Hyde Park CIA graduate John Hardesty oversees 1,200 California wines, cognacs, armagnacs, mezcals, and cigars in a walk-in humidor, where his best customers have their own lockers.

In the produce department you might find Black Trumpet or Hedgehog mushrooms ($14.00 per pound), red and white Belgian endive ($5.95 per pound), and Della Fattoria and Artisan breads. The deli is like no other and offers cherry peppers stuffed with provolone and prosciutto ($1.25 each), Ozark and Serrano hams, salted capers, thirteen types of olives, duck confit ($11.95 per pound), foie gras, and various herrings.

Forty of the world's best olive oils, mustards, and other delicacies lead you to the kitchenware section and finally to the cooked food case in the back, created by Executive Chef Tom Gray, formerly of Zoe in New York, Sous Chef Jeff Cierciello, formerly of The French Laundry, and their highly qualified crew. You might find rotisserie pork loin with stoneground mustard and apricot preserves, chicken salad, yellow corn polenta with roasted mushrooms, or green-chile potato salad. You can even get elegant sandwiches to go for your picnic. The take-home dinner menu changes weekly.

The espresso bar offers fresh fruit smoothies, shakes, and coffees, with stand-up cafe tables, and excellent rest rooms down the hall.

Dean & DeLuca, 607 South St. Helena Highway, St. Helena 94574; phone (707) 967–9980, fax (707) 967–9983. Visa and MasterCard. Wheelchair-accessible.

THE SPOT, in all its glory, is next to Dean & DeLuca. You can't miss the pink arch, with the patio's turquoise railing and Coca-Cola umbrellas facing the parking lot and highway and neon signs everywhere. Portraits of Elvis, "Leave It to Beaver," and old movies welcome you to this retro joint where you order at the neon-lighted counter and choose between grease and grease. Thousands of Napa Valley locals stream in here daily for their burgers, fries, onion rings, and a pretty good salad bar (brought back from oblivion by public demand).

The floors are black-and-white-checked linoleum, and you can sit at red plush booths or on red-seated padded chairs at gray formica tables. Beef, turkey chicken, emu, or veggie burgers come with fries or onion rings; and fried chicken, fries, and slaw in a basket cost a whopping $6.25. You can enjoy eight microbrews and local wines. Breakfast has its regulars, too.

The Spot, 587 South St. Helena Highway, St. Helena 94574; phone (707) 963–2844. Open 7:00 A.M.–9:00 P.M. Sunday–Thursday, 7:00 A.M.–10:00 P.M. Friday, Saturday. Beer and wine. Visa and MasterCard. Wheelchair-accessible.

On the east side of Highway 29 (here called St. Helena Highway South), you will find three great wineries right next door to one another. The first one you will come to going north is the venerable and fun **V. SATTUI WINERY**. Turn east onto White Lane and go over the railroad tracks to the winery's cool lawns and warm welcomes. If the parking lot is too crowded, drive farther east on White Lane to additional parking.

Sattui is under-known for its fabulous delicatessen, pastries, and, of course, prize-winning wines, which are sold only here at the winery.

Vittorio Sattui came to California from Carsi, near Genoa, Italy, and eventually made wine in San Francisco's North Beach Italian neighborhood—but who wasn't making their own wine then? Purchasing grapes from the Napa Valley, Sattui moved his operation to Bryant Street, and then closed down during Prohibition.

Vittorio's great-grandson, Daryl Sattui, began to reestablish the family winery, this time in the Napa Valley, in 1975, with the goal of making "wines my great-grandfather Vittorio would be supremely proud of." He even slept in a sleeping bag on the tasting room floor and took showers from the winery's hose, since he couldn't afford housing rent.

V. SATTUI WINERY

Opening the winery to the public on March 4, 1976, Daryl served wine tastes from a wooden plank bridging two barrels, sold cheese from a $200 used deli case, kept the money in a wooden-box "cash register," and lived in terror that he might fail and have to go back to cleaning wine tanks at Christian Brothers winery.

Daryl used a hand bottler and his great-grandfather's ninety-year-old corking machine to bottle his first wines, and traded several cases of wine to a college friend to modify the original, historic label. Having no money to advertise, he hoped the wine would sell itself, and it has. And, since all Sattui wines are sold here, a near-cult of devotees has developed of people who clamor to buy their wines directly from the winery.

In addition to the original winery building, where the delicatessen and tasting room are now, Sattui built a historically accurate, elegant stone winery building in 1985. It looks like one from the 1890s, with 3-foot-thick, hand-hewn stone walls and heavy rustic timbers. Be sure to take yourself on a self-guided tour of the stone building's underground cellars and small caves, where you will find a fascinatingly musty historical museum chronicling Sattui's and California's wine history.

Two acres of lawns, picnic tables and century-old oak trees invite hundreds of picnickers to enjoy themselves daily. Kids run and scream, grandparents bask, and parents watch them all, eating and sipping wine all the way.

As you enter the old winery, the first thing you smell is cheese, not wine. And for good reason. An enormous Swiss Emmenthaler wheel and 200 varieties of imported and a few domestic cheeses greet you to the left of the door, along with Molinari salami, Sciambria and Acme breads, strawberries, apples, Dijon mustards, French cornichon pickles, Kalamata olives, Italian pepperoncini, and an entire wall of prepared-daily deli foods. Be sure to check out Sattui's own chocolate sauce and their Monastero Le Vallesi extra virgin olive oil from Tuscany. The charming staff offer you a choice of the day's cheese-tasting selections. Cheese Shop Manager Jean Varner came to Sattui from Oakville Grocery, where she served as assistant manager in charge of "charcuteries," specialty foods, and meats.

One of our most astounding food discoveries in the Napa Valley is Sattui's delicatessen, for which Daryl hired Executive Chef Charlotte Combe, the only American ever to apprentice (for nearly twenty years) under PBS television chef Jacques Pepin. Charlotte, whose delightful Scottish brogue surprises visitors to an Italian–American winery, ran the Charlotte Combe Cooking School in Woodside, California. There she hosted celebrity chefs such as Marcella Hazan, Lorenza De Medici, Diane Kennedy, and Jacques Pepin. Charlotte trained primarily in Bologna in Italy's Emilia-Romagna province, thought by many to produce the finest food in Italy.

Charlotte told Kathleen that "Daryl Sattui gave me carte blanche to do it my European way." And has she ever. Feast your eyes upon fresh foods and reasonable prices of fresh artichokes ($2.95), oven-roasted salmon with remoulade ($4.95), smoked trout, Russian and American caviar, marinated and roasted beef, oven-roasted vegetables, Gulf prawns with mustard sauce ($1.50 each or five for $6.95), steamed asparagus with olive oil ($6.95 per pound), and grilled rosemary-lemon chicken breast. Finish all that off with elegant pastries and sumptuous macaroons, displayed at the end of the cheese case.

If you attend one of Sattui's Harvest Balls, held two weekends in late September, often you can arrive three days early and participate in Charlotte Combe's cooking schools to learn how to prepare the dinner served at the Balls.

Watch for annual Tax Relief and Crush Parties, full of music, fine foods, fine Sattui wines, and added discounts on case purchases. This is one mailing list you must get on.

Fine points: Don't miss Saturday wine-and-cheese pairings at 11:30 A.M. March–April ($7.50). Sattui's Preston Vineyard Cabernet Sauvignons often win medals, including a best Cab in California at the California State Fair. According to Sattui's brochure, the *Wine Spectator* recently noted that V. Sattui has "garnered more gold medals in the big taste-offs than any other single winery in the Napa Valley." A must-stop! No tasting fee. Featured wines: Chardonnay, Sauvignon Blanc, Johannisberg Riesling, White Zinfandel, Gamay Rouge, Suzanne's Vineyard Zinfandel, Merlot, Cabernet Sauvignon including three vineyard designates, Blanc de Noirs Champagne, and dessert wines Muscat, Madeira, Colli del Trasimeno, Felicita, and Vin Santo. Owner: Daryl Sattui. Winemaker: Rick Rosenbrand. Cases: 45,000. Acres: 750.

✢⤷ *V. Sattui Winery, 111 White Lane, St. Helena 94574; phone (707) 963–7774 or (800) 799–2337, fax (707) 963–4324. Open 9:00 A.M.–6:00 P.M. daily, closes 5:00 P.M. November–February; Visa, MasterCard, and American Express. Tasting room is wheelchair-accessible, museum is not.*

Right next door, to the north, is HEITZ WINE CELLARS, which is now just the winery's tasting room, with the actual winery currently located in a restored, 1898 stone cellar originally built by Anton Rossi on a 160-acre property on Taplin Road, east of St. Helena. This is the original, where Alice and Joseph Heitz built his reputation and cult following for both his wines and his interesting personality.

Joe was from Illinois and Alice from South Dakota. They met in California in the 1940s. Joe earned two degrees in enology at UC Davis and spent seven years as understudy to the famed wine guru Andre Tchelistcheff at Beaulieu Vineyards. Joe and Alice purchased their first vineyard (eight acres) in 1961.

The three Heitz children grew up in the vineyards and business, and now David serves as winemaker, having made the 1974 commemorative bottling of Heitz Cellars' now famous Martha's Vineyard Cabernet Sauvignon as his first solo effort. Kathleen directs national and international sales and marketing, working with a biology degree from studies in Switzerland and at the University of Oregon. And Rollie oversees the company's finances and properties with his business degree from Santa Clara University.

When we visited the tasting-room, our host's blue Rolls Royce Corniche was the lone automobile in the parking lot. The redwood structure looks like a mountain cabin on the outside and an elegant parlor on the inside. The teensy, carpeted, and subdued tasting room, with interesting corkscrews and calming classical music, focuses on a glass-topped table, where you are served.

In the Heitz's case, "Martha's Vineyard" refers to vineyards owned by Tom and Martha May near Oakville, while "Bella Oaks" refers to Barney and Belle Rhodes' vineyard abut 3 miles north of Martha's Vineyard, on the southwest side of Rutherford.

 Fine points: Joe Heitz actually pioneered single vineyard designation wines in California. He has been feted as one of the world's thirty top winemakers at La Tour d'Argent in Paris. No tasting fee.
Be sure to get on this mailing list so you hear about the next Martha's Vineyard Cabernet Sauvignon release, expected in January or February 2001, and get in line with other Heitz devotees. Other wine releases and tastings occur in February. Another must-stop. Featured wines: Chardonnay, Joe's White, Martha's Vineyard Cabernet Sauvignon, Napa Valley Cabernet Sauvignon, Bella Oaks Cabernet Sauvignon, Zinfandel, Grignolino, Ryan's Red (named for redheaded, first Heitz grandchild Ryan Thomas Heitz) and Grignolino Rose, Grignolino Port. Owner: Joseph Heitz. Winemakers: Joseph and David Heitz. Cases: 40,000. Acres: 200.

Heitz Wine Cellars, 436 St. Helena Highway South, St. Helena 94574; phone (707) 963–3542. Open 11:00 A.M.–4:30 P.M. daily. Visa, MasterCard, American Express, and JCB. Wheelchair-accessible.

Just north of and next door to Heitz Cellars you will find LOUIS M. MARTINI, one of the oldest wineries in the Napa Valley. Three generations of colorful Martinis (men, that is) have dedicated themselves to finding the best land for growing grapes and matching soils and microclimates, following the old country Italian traditions.

In 1906, the year of the San Francisco earthquake and great fire, Louis M. Martini and his father Agostino made their first wine in San Francisco. They eventually built a 60,000-gallon winery in the Bayview District. Louis M. took

PASTA PRIMAVERA
from Carolyn Martini,
Louis M. Martini

INGREDIENTS:

1 sweet red pepper, chopped

1 cup snow peas, chopped

6 tomatoes (preferably home-grown), peeled, seeded and chopped

1 leek, sliced thinly

3 Tbs fresh herbs, chopped (basil or dill, for example)

1 Tbs olive oil

1 cup white wine

2 cloves fresh garlic

8 oz fettucine

chives, chopped, to taste

Parmesan cheese, grated, to taste

PREPARATION:

Blanch red pepper and snow peas in boiling water for a minute or two. Sauté tomatoes with leek and herbs in olive oil for 5 minutes. Add white wine to the sauté and let simmer another minute.

Boil fettuccine al dente according to directions and drain.

Put sauté mixture in a large bowl along with the blanched vegetables and cloves of fresh garlic. Add fettuccine to sauté in bowl, toss it all together and garnish with chopped chives and fresh Parmesan cheese.

his wine on his market wagon when he was selling clams and mussels on Polk Street and sold his first gallon to the fish-shop owner, who gave a taste to the chicken-shop owner. Then *he* bought a gallon and gave a sample to the butcher next door, who also bought a gallon, and off to the wine races went Louis M. Martini. He opened the L. M. Martini Grape Products Company in Kingsburg, California, in 1922, to make sacramental and "medicinal" wines and grape concentrates.

Anticipating the repeal of Prohibition, the Martinis moved to the Napa Valley in 1933 to build their winery, one of the first to use cold fermentation. Five years later Louis M. purchased the Goldstein Ranch in Sonoma Valley and made it Italian–American by renaming it Monte Rosso. By 1942 Louis M. owned the Stanley Ranch in Carneros, forseeing the potential of the now-famous winegrowing region that flops on both sides of the Napa–Sonoma County border. In the early 1950s Louis M. introduced wind machines to protect vineyards from winter frosts and worked with UC Davis enologists to pioneer clonal research on Chardonnay, Pinot Noir, and Riesling grapes. By 1954 Louis P. Martini became the second-generation Louis Martini winemaker, introducing gondolas for grape harvesting in 1957. In the late '60s he bottled the first Merlot in the United States. (Sadly, Louis P. Martini died in September 1998.)

After Louis M. died in 1974, his granddaughter, Carolyn Martini, joined the company. She is now president. Louis P.'s son, Michael, graduated from UC Davis in enology and eventually became the third-generation Martini winemaker.

While the winery building itself has a slightly industrial Italian–American look, it's what's inside that counts. Just as you walk in the door, stop for a minute and stare at the historic cases in the vestibule. Placards in the cases give a quick, succinct course in winemaking. The Louis Martini "Food First" aprons tell the Martini story: Its wines are made to accompany food, to enhance its flavor, and to celebrate the sharing of mealtime among family and friends.

Pick up a wicker basket in the tasting room to load up with pasta sauces, salsas, cherries, and the Louis Martini video.

 Fine points: Ask about the Los Ninos Series, dedicated to the births of Michael's and

---

MARTINI FAMILY RECIPE FOR SHERRY WINE CAKE
from Carolyn Martini, Louis M. Martini

INGREDIENTS:

> *1 package yellow cake mix*
> *1 package vanilla pudding (3.4 oz)*
> *½ tsp nutmeg*
> *4 large eggs*
> *¾ cup Cream Sherry*
> *¾ cup oil*
> *powdered sugar*

PREPARATION:

Combine cake mix, pudding mix, and nutmeg in a large bowl. Add remaining ingredients. Mix at low speed until moistened, then at medium speed for 3 minutes. Pour into greased, floured Bundt pan. Bake, below oven center, at 350° F for 40–45 minutes.

Remove from heat and let stand in pan 10–15 minutes, then turn out onto wire rack. Dust with powdered sugar.

Carolyn's children with labels designed by the kids. Enjoy a picnic (bring with you) and Martini wines in Martini Park, the winery's garden courtyard. No tasting fee for most wines; the $6.00 fee for reserves includes logo glass. Featured wines: Louis' White Blend, Sauvignon Blanc, Zinfandel Heritage Collection, Cabernet Sauvignon, Reserve Chardonnay, Barbera, Merlot, Gewürztraminer, Dry Sherry, and Cream Sherry. Owners: The Martini Family. President: Carolyn Martini. Winemaker: Michael Martini. Cases: 150,000. Acres: 580.

Louis M. Martini, 254 St. Helena Highway, St. Helena 94574; phone (800) 321–WINE, fax (707) 963–8750, Web site www.louismartini.com. Open 10:00 A.M.–4:30 P.M. daily. Visa, MasterCard, and American Express. Wheelchair-accessible.

GARDEN PAELLA

from Project Manager Ron Mangini, Edgewood Estate Winery

INGREDIENTS:

¾ cup olive oil

1 large onion, chopped

1 red pepper, chopped

4 cloves garlic, crushed

½ tsp thyme

¼ tsp oregano

2 bay leaves, whole

salt and pepper to taste

1 ½ cups short grain rice

3 ½ cups vegetable or chicken stock

pinch of saffron

1 zucchini squash, cut into
    ¼-inch slices

2 artichoke hearts, quartered

1 summer squash, cut into
    ¼-inch slices

6 broccoli florettes

4 cherry tomatoes

¼ cup small green peas

PREPARATION:

In a large pan, heat olive oil and sauté onion, red pepper, and garlic. Add thyme, oregano, bay leaves, salt, and pepper.

In a paella pan or similar pan, heat 1 Tbs oil. Brown rice until coated and opaque. Add mixture from the first pan. Mix well.

Add saffron to chicken or vegetable stock. Place in paella or other pan and bring to boil. Lower heat. Arrange zucchini, summer squash, broccoli, tomatoes, and artichoke hearts on top of rice. Cover and simmer for 20 minutes. Uncover, add peas, and simmer 5 more minutes. Let settle for a few minutes before serving. Serves 4. Serve with Malbec.

Between Heitz Cellars and Louis M. Martini, on the west side of Highway 29, you might want to try EDGEWOOD ESTATE WINERY. (In fact, we advise that you go into St. Helena proper, have lunch and shop, and then come back south to visit Prager Winery and Port Works, Sutter Home, and Edgewood Estate.)

Giant Golden State Vineyards (California is the Golden State), "California's largest vertically integrated grape growing and wine processing company," is developing its premium-wine division, Edgewood Estate Winery, by restoring what used to be the Napa Valley Cooperative.

Captain William Peterson, a New England sea captain, built the original winery on a forty-acre tract called Vineland, with the Vineland School in back of Edgewood Estate. For 60 years, beginning right after the end of Prohibition, the Napa Valley Cooperative served 128 growers and resurrected viticulture in the Napa Valley. Its purchaser, Golden State Vineyards, is now the largest grape grower and exporter of wines in the United States.

In 1985 many of the original vines were removed to create a parking lot. In 1998 Edgewood removed most of the parking lot and entry drive, replanted 2,880 Cabernet Sauvignon vines in front of the winery, and moved seventy-eight 20- to 40-foot-high mature trees around the property "to return the frontage to its agricultural beginnings and to create a grand entry to this historical site," according to Project Manager Ron Mangini.

A gravel path leads from the parking lot to the quaint tasting room. Notice the high vaulted ceilings, local cut stone and clapboard walls, and the herb garden in back. The actual winery is next door to the north and encloses Captain Peterson's original winery building.

Fine points: No tasting fee. All of Edgewood's wines are made in small lots of less than 1,500 cases, and many are available only in the tasting room. Featured wines: Chardonnay, Malbec, Cabernet Franc, Merlot, Cabernet Sauvignon, Zinfandel, Petite Syrah, and Petite Syrah Port. Owner: Golden State Vineyards, Jeffrey O'Neill President and CEO. Winemaker: Eric Laumann. Cases: 6,400. Acres: 40.

❧ *Edgewood Estate Winery, 401 St. Helena Highway South, St. Helena 94574; phone (707) 963–7293, fax (707) 963–8537. Open 11:00 A.M.–5:30 P.M. daily. Visa, MasterCard, American Express, and Discover. Wheelchair-accessible.*

SUTTER HOME WINERY, the next winery on the west side of the highway, going north, dates from 1874, and the name from 1900, when pioneer John Sutter's daughter named it for him, although Italian immigrants John and Mario Trinchero bought it in 1946 (still early by Napa standards) and majored in bulk wines until about 1970. They were well known for their mantra that, if you could bring it through the front door, they would fill it with wine.

Wine industry innovator Bob Trinchero eked a rosé-style wine out of some Zinfandel grapes and called it White Zinfandel, which, as an almost "pop" wine, became the best-selling wine in the United States. Bob also developed the single-service 187 ml. bottles you get on airplanes and Amtrak and can even buy commercially now (for a picnic, we suppose).

While they have three vineyards in the Napa Valley, most of Sutter Home's grapes come from the Sierra foothills, the flat Delta area near Sacramento, and the hot Sacramento Valley, which is what many locals assume to be the source of the name Sutter Home. All Sutter Home vineyards are farmed organically or by sustainable farming practices.

SUTTER HOME WINERY

When you drive up to Sutter Home, you will be struck by the lovely Victorian home and gardens with their hundred varieties of roses, forty varieties of day lilies, and a camellia at the Victorian Inn's entrance that was planted in 1876. The large palm tree was brought from the Canary Islands in the 1940s. Our late, great friend, landscape architect Bob Ernest, designed the current gardens, using all natural fertilizers and predatory insects to control pests.

The spacious, wood-walled tasting room is to your left. Here there are lots of serious wines—and humorous other stuff and staff. You can take a "Blend Your Own Wine" forty-five-minute seminar, learning the differences among varietals and learning how to blend your own personalized wine, all for just $10.

Admire the historic General Electric fridge on legs and covered with magnets, Sutter Home cigar boxes, Triple Cream Chocolate sauce or Triple Cream Dessert Wine, Soleo white and rosé Sangria, an abundance of pasta sauces from Spicy Mediterranean to Roasted Garlic, Sutter Home Premium Wine Vinegar, fudges, olive oils, peace salsa, Queso Quatexa Cheese Sauce, teriyaki and peanut sauces, coleslaw and dipping sauces, and roasted-garlic oil. Don't forget to enter the "Build a Better Burger" recipe contest, for which Sutter Home flies the finalists in for the cookoff.

Fine points: Sutter Home is one of the few wineries that produces alcohol-free wine; it is available here under the Fre label. The winery also announces special sale deals on the blackboard daily, so you have to be here to know about them. Tasting fee: "zip, zero, nada." Featured wines: various Zinfandels, Gamay Beaujolais, Sauvignon Blanc, Chardonnay, Chenin Blanc, Cabernet Sauvignon, Merlot, Gewürztraminer, Barbera, Sangiovese, Muscat Alexandria. Owner: The Trinchero family. Winemakers: Steve Bertolucci and Derek Holstein. Cases: 8,000,000. Acres: 5,500.

Sutter Home Winery, 100 St. Helena Highway South, St. Helena 94574; phone (707) 963–3104, Web site www.sutterhome.com/ Open 9:30 A.M.–5:00 P.M. daily. Visa, MasterCard, American Express, and Discover. Wheelchair-accessible.

One of our favorite discoveries is **PRAGER WINERY & PORT WORKS**, which is actually right behind Sutter Home's Victorian house off Lewelling Lane, a narrow little one-lane street.

Prager's tasting room is the downstairs of an old wooden barn at the rear of a small parking lot. Originally a carriage house and the John Thomann Winery and Distillery, built in 1865, the building must be very happy with its current tenant.

Jim Prager presides over his realm from a wooden bar stool and sees the cobwebs holding bottles on the windowsill as "the original web site." He sees the secondary "web site" as the one draping the picture of "my father's father's grandson." Hello? It's also fun to study the paper money wallpaper chipped in by Prager's visitors from all over the world. A huge musty Oriental rug, well-worn wooden captain's chairs, and a truly old corkscrew collection complete the stage setting.

In a stroke of genius, Jim and his wife, Imogene, left Orange County for Napa, developed a small shopping center (now the St. Helena Premium Outlets) north of St. Helena, and settled on his other true love, wine, and even more specially, Port. Imogene runs a small B&B adjoining their lovely home next to the winery, and their children, John, Jeff, Peter, and Katie, are all involved in this downhome and highly personal effort.

Fine points: Here you can taste at least three of the six styles of Port that Jim produces, all a blend of sweetness and brandy. Jim talks of evaporation as something "the angels love," and of his one-year-old Noble Companion Ultra Premium Port as "smooth as a baby's bottom." He recommends his Aria White Port, made from Chardonnay, as the perfect companion to an oyster appetizer. We recommend all of his Ports for an elegant taste experience, smooth even on a hot day. Don't

miss the Chocolate Drizzle, Chocolate Mousse Balls, and interesting cigars. Tasting fee $5.00. Featured wines: Chardonnay, Zinfandel, Cabernet Sauvignon, Aria White Port, Royal Escort LBV Port, Madeline (late harvest Johannisberg Riesling), Noble Companion Ultra Premium Port. Owner: James Prager. Wine and Port maker: "God—we just tend the land," with the help of Pete Prager. Cases: 3,600. Acres: none, buy from others in Napa Valley.

❧ *Prager Winery & Port Works, 1281 Lewelling Lane, St. Helena 94574; phone 963–PORT or (800) PORT, fax (707) 963–7679. Open 10:30 A.M.–4:30 P.M. Visa and MasterCard. Wheelchair-accessible.*

ST. HELENA

About 0.3 mile north of Sutter Home, on the same side of Highway 29, is Erika Hills' "THE PAINTED ILLUSION," one of the most fun and authentic emporia of antiques and collectibles in Northern California. Once a turn-of-the-century church, the building vibrates with memories. Austin and Erika Hills restored the building and put a new roof on top of the old one.

Don't miss the late-nineteenth-century Hills Bros. Coffee grinder, from Austin's family's business. He is now a partner in Grgich Hills winery.

Explore the seemingly unlimited niches and model living spaces full of eclectic period pieces. Lee Prosegger is the perfect guide around the shop, which includes painted furniture upstairs.

❧ *Erika Hills' "The Painted Illusion" Antiques and Furniture, 115 Main Street, St. Helena 94574; phone (707) 963–0919, fax (707) 963–8824. Open 11:00 A.M.–5:00 P.M. Thursday–Monday. Visa and MasterCard. Not wheelchair-accessible.*

Almost a mile north of Sutter Home and Prager you will find what has become an interesting cluster of buildings, which include MERRYVALE VINEYARDS, the Real Foods group's Ristorante Tra Vigne, Tomatina pizza restaurant, and the Inn at Southbridge. (You are still on Highway 29, which, as you noticed, was called St. Helena Highway and St. Helena Highway South, and is now called Main Street in St. Helena proper. Confused enough? We are.)

The Mondavi family's first wine venture began here in the lovely stone structure that now houses Merryvale Vineyards. The first Napa Valley winery built after Prohibition, the Sunny St. Helena Winery was purchased and founded in 1983 as Merryvale by San Francisco developer Bill Harlan and friends, who renovated it and, in 1996, sold 60 percent to Jack Schlatter and his son Rene from Switzerland, who again renovated the winery, while preserving its historic look.

When Harlan first bought the winery, the wine was made at Rombauer Vineyards, whose winemaker, Bob Levy, is now winemaker at Merryvale. World-renowned winemaster Michel Rolland, owner of Chateau Le Bon Pasteur in Pomerol, serves as consultant.

 Fine points: Don't miss the Tank Room, with its 22,000-gallon wooden cask, and the Cask Room, lined with two stories of century-old 2,000 gallon casks, usually used for private and group romantic parties. Book reservations to take the Wine Component Tasting Seminar, offered at 10:30 A.M. on Saturday and Sunday in the Cask Room, $10.00 per person. The tasting fee is $3.00 for Vintage selections, $5.00 for Connoisseur wines. Featured wines: Semillon, Chardonnay, Merlot, Antigua (Muscat de Frontignan); Connoisseur Vignette, Reserve Chardonnay, Reserve Merlot, and Profile. Owners: Jack and Rene Schlatter, Bill Harlan and partners. Winemaker: Bob Levy. Cases: 50,000. Acres: buy in Napa County.

Merryvale Vineyards, 1000 Main Street, St. Helena 94574; phone (707) 963–7777, fax (707) 963–3018. Open 10:00 A.M.–5:30 P.M. daily. Visa, MasterCard, American Express, and Discover. Wheelchair-accessible.

If you are famished, you are in Californian–Italian heaven, right within short walking distance of Merryvale. Across Charter Oak Street you will find TOMATINA, an upscale pizzeria that tries to fill the financial gap by offering reasonably priced food for both locals and visiting wine fans, including soups, salads, pastas, and desserts.

You'll notice the place by the huge red-tomato metal sculpture on the front porch. As part of the Real Foods group, Tra Vigne's well-known chef Michael Chiarello serves as executive chef.

The yummy piadine are un-rolled-up roll-ups made from pizza dough, with Caesar salad, lettuce, tomatoes, and other veggies combined with skirt steak, grilled chicken, or gorgonzola piled high. Just try to eat this politely! They even bring you a diagram of eating directions.

Pizzas and pizza crusts for the piadine are baked in a giant wood-burning brick oven. Be sure to notice that pizza prices start with a base of six slices ($7.95, or twelve for $12.95, all toppings are additional).

Order with the computer host at the counter just as you walk in the door, and then sit at a table and wait for your food and beverages to arrive. Enjoy your meal indoors or on the west-facing patio with black-and-white-striped umbrellas. Even the counter stools, shaped like screw-top tomato vines, keep the theme.

This is a great place for groups and kids. Cokes come with free refills if you go up to the bar/counter.

❧ *Tomatina, 1016 Main St. at The Inn at Southbridge, St. Helena 94574; phone (707) 967–9999. Open 11:30 A.M.–10:00 P.M. daily. Beer and wine. Visa and MasterCard. Wheelchair-accessible.*

Just up Main Street at its intersection with Charter Oak Avenue is TRA VIGNE, one of the Napa Valley's best-known restaurants. Real Foods group has succeeded in creating the feeling of a small Italian village with Tra Vigne, its courtyard, and the smaller Cantinetta Tra Vigne in an old sherry winery. Flowers brighten tables and spirits inside and out, even on rainy days.

TRA VIGNE AND CANTINETTA TRA VIGNE ENTRANCE FROM PARKING LOT

Tra Vigne itself feels Italian the minute you walk in, with 30-foot ceilings, heavily draped entry, a hand-carved bar, and Italian beaded light fixtures. Helen Berggruen's colorful paintings and Cinzano red posters decorate the walls. Service is meticulous, while the feeling is elegantly casual. The restaurant makes its own mozzarella and prosciutto, presses its own olive oil, and grows its own table grapes.

Some of Chef Michael Chiarello's signature dishes include appetizers, such as an antipasto of seafood–fried crisp in arborio rice flour ($7.75), oven-roasted polenta with wild mushrooms and balsamic game sauce ($7.95), and renowned risottos. Smoked Nieman-Schell beef short ribs with garlic soft polenta ($17.25), grilled Sonoma rabbit ($16.95), or roasted salmon ($18.95) are all exquisite. Passing of plates around the table and sharing are expected here. Do not leave without trying the Tiramisu do Cioccolata ($5.95).

Although there is a full bar, be sure to check out Tra Vigne's exceptional Italian and California wine list, with an exclusive selection of 1987 Cabernet Sauvignons commemorating the restaurant's tenth anniversary. Take time to venture downstairs (under the guise of finding the rest room, if necessary) to see the interesting historic photos, including a locally famous train derailment.

If you're in the mood for a less formal and less expensive lunch or dinner, try CANTINETTA TRA VIGNE for excellent Panini (sandwiches), including a tasty

ROASTED POLENTA AND BALSAMIC SAUCE

from Executive Chef Michael Chiarello, Tra Vigne

INGREDIENTS FOR THE ROASTED POLENTA:

3 cups chicken stock   1 cup polenta meal

3 cups heavy cream   1 cup semolina

pinch nutmeg   ½ cup grated Fontina

¼ tsp ground white pepper   1 cup Parmesan

1 tsp salt

PREPARATION:

Combine stock, cream, grated nutmeg, salt, and pepper in a large, heavy-gauge pot. Bring liquid to a boil, then add the polenta and semolina gradually while stirring. Continue to cook over moderate heat while stirring constantly. Polenta is ready when it begins to pull away from the sides of the pot (approximately 10–15 minutes).

Remove from heat and stir in all the fontina and ¾ cup Parmesan cheese until well incorporated. Spread polenta evenly on oiled sheet trays. Be sure to use trays that are not warped, and spread to a thickness of approximately ¾ inch.

Cool trays to room temperature, then cover with parchment and refrigerate. These may be prepared 48 hours in advance.

INGREDIENTS FOR THE BALSAMIC SAUCE:

1 pint balsamic vinegar   6 peppercorns

1 chopped shallot   2 bay leaves

2 quarts stock (roasted chicken, veal,   1 stick sweet butter
     rabbit, or canned; if using a canned
     broth, do not salt any portion of the recipe)

PREPARATION:

Reduce the vinegar with the chopped shallots to a syrup consistency. Add the stock, bay leaves, and peppercorns. Reduce to a sauce consistency and strain.

TO ASSEMBLE:

Cut polenta into squares or triangles. Put on a buttered sheet pan, sprinkle generously with leftover Parmesan cheese and put in a 500° F oven until golden brown. Remove from oven and finish sauce.

Bring reserved sauce to a simmer and whisk in butter, adjust salt and pepper to taste, and pour on plates before polenta. Serves 4.

Notes from Chef Michael Chiarello: "This is the very best recipe for polenta I have ever used. The ratio of liquid and dry ingredients is 3:1. For soft polenta try a ratio of 5 or 6 to 1. I encourage you to change the recipe as you see fit."

roasted vegetable one with eggplant, peppers, goat cheese, arugula, and garlic vinaigrette, smoked turkey, or warm corned beef (all $5.75); Pasta Fabioli soup ($4.25); salads from Caesar to roasted balsamic onions; veggie lasagna; spring tarts; stuffed focaccia; or five pizzas, all under $7.00.

Pastries, from the Tra Vigne kitchen, are divine. You can also purchase Tra Vigne's fresh mozzarella ($8.00 per pound) as well as its fresh stocks, sauces, and dressings. What a treat!

❧ Tra Vigne and ***Cantinetta Tra Vigne**, 1050 Charter Oak Avenue, St. Helena 94574; phone (707) 963–4444, fax (707) 963–1233. Visa, MasterCard, Discover, Carte Blanche, and Diner's Club. Wheelchair-accessible from patio.*

We want you to take the time to drive another block down Charter Oak behind Tra Vigne to Allison Street and the NAPA VALLEY OLIVE OIL MANUFACTORY. Leonora and Ray Particelli and Policarpo (Pol) Lucchesi are the current generation nurturing the family olive-oil business founded by Guillermo Guidi in 1930. As you might guess by their names, the owners are all from Lucca, Italy.

Surprisingly enough, when you walk into the old white-clapboard barn, you smell salami, seemingly tons of loose Molinari salami. Heaven! The two rooms' walls are covered with thousands of business cards, including ours on the door-frame. Wander through barrels and barrels of dried mushrooms, tubs of dried beans from French flageolet to Lupini and canellini, pickled everything, prosci-utto bones for $10.00, baggies of herbs, and containers of anchovies from small at $2.75 to major at $25.00. Check out the freezer in the front room full of delectable crab or lobster ravioli ($4.50), veggie or cheese tortillini or ravioli ($3.00) and lasagna ($6.75).

Be sure to notice the olive press brought from Lucca more than seventy years ago. The tracks in the wooden floor were caused by the cart (now filled with salami) that was used to move olives brought in from Napa fields by Carmelite nuns for pressing. The olive oil is now made in the Sacramento Valley and bottled here. It is available in regular or extra virgin, in sizes rang-ing from pints to generous gallons. The Extra Virgin (blue label) is quite potent, and Leonora recommends the regular Pure Olive Oil (white label) for most purposes.

*❧ Napa Valley Olive Oil Manufactory**, 835 Charter Oak Avenue, St. Helena 94574; phone (707) 963–4173. Open 8:00 A.M.–5:30 P.M. daily. No credit cards. Wheelchair-accessible.*

Across Main Street (Highway 29) from Charter Oak Avenue and Tra Vigne is one of St. Helena's local favorites, TAYLOR'S REFRESHER. Founded by pharmacist Lloyd Taylor when he stopped selling on the road in 1949, Taylor's famous special is the sourdough hamburger and fries, although Mexican regulars such as burritos and tacos have crept onto the posted menu. Among Taylor's best features are the enormous lawns and loads of picnic tables. Great place to stop with the kids.

Taylor's Refresher, 933 Main Street, St. Helena 94574; phone (707) 963–3486. Open for lunch and dinner. No credit cards. Wheelchair-accessible.

We will walk you up the right (east) side of Main Street as far north as Pairs Restaurant and Tivoli. Then we will cross Main Street and walk back down the west side, guiding you into every shop, bakery, and restaurant along the way.

St. Helena's few blocks of downtown are elegant yet homey, and the city is trying hard to keep it from becoming too touristy, while maintaining its usefulness to locals and allure to visitors. It feels like a step back several decades, with a gracious, relaxed ambience and elegant boutiques to suit most needs, mixed with a pharmacy and hardware store, important parts of a functioning downtown.

The first shop you encounter walking north is ST. HELENA CYCLERY. Here you can rent tandem bikes, road, mountain, or hybrid bikes, as well as helmets and maps. Be sure to make a reservation for ten or more riders.

St. Helena Cyclery, 1156 Main Street; St. Helena 94574 phone (707) 963–7736. Open 9:30 A.M.–5:30 P.M., Sunday 10:00 A.M.–5:00 P.M. Visa, MasterCard, and American Express. Wheelchair-accessible.

The CREATIVE NEEDLE sells anything and everything you need for knitting, darning, and crocheting projects, including Adrienne Vittadini yarns.

Creative Needle, 1210 Main Street, St. Helena 94574; phone (707) 963–7533. Open Tuesday–Friday 11:00 A.M.–4:00 P.M., Saturday 10:30 A.M.–2:00 P.M. Visa and MasterCard. Wheelchair-accessible.

Next door, CALLA LILY sells elegant fine linens and gifts.

Calla Lily, 1222 Main Street, St. Helena 94574; phone (707) 963–8188. Open Monday–Saturday 10:00 A.M.–5:00 P.M., Sunday 11:00 A.M.–4:00 P.M. Visa, MasterCard, and American Express. Wheelchair-accessible.

Two doors farther on, CRICKET sells playclothes versions of Reel, Avalon, Workshop, Citron, and Flax for luxuriating at resorts. Everything looks very comfortable.

Cricket, 1226 Main Street, St. Helena 94574; phone (707) 963–8400. Open 10:00 A.M.–6:00 P.M. daily. Visa and MasterCard. Wheelchair-accessible.

D. CHAMPAIGN, "Where you can relax your style," purveys elegant casual men's resort wear, including designers such as Barry Bricken, Haupt, North 44, Java Lava, Columbian, Lazo, Tallia shirts, and Teva and H.S. Trask shoes.

❧ *D. Champaign, 1228 Main Street, St. Helena 94574; phone (707) 963–1782. Open 10:00 A.M.–6:00 P.M. daily. Visa, MasterCard, American Express, and Diners Club. Wheelchair-accessible.*

Next door, AMELIA CLAIRE offers elegant ladies' shoes, bags, and belts.

❧ *Amelia Claire, 1230 Main Street; St. Helena 94574; phone (707) 963–8502. Open 10:00 A.M.–6:00 P.M. daily. Visa and MasterCard. Wheelchair-accessible.*

The next storefront was recently enlivened with the arrival of BERGMAN'S, the hottest new restaurant in St. Helena. "Serving good food since 1998," this is where the best Napa Valley restaurant staffs end up for a good meal after a long day of cooking so that they too can sit down and be served in a fun atmosphere.

Bergman's took over the space of Trilogy, a long-time well known California-French restaurant. Alexis and Bryan Bergman and Bryan's brother Andy have redone the place with bright colors, good music, and great food. You can now sit in a beautiful patio and enjoy the casual cafe atmosphere.

The Bergmans bring all the best local credentials, having cooked at Brava Terrace, Pinot Blanc, and Mustards, in addition to several top Atlanta establishments. Bryan and Andy handle the kitchen, while Alexis meets, greets, and delights.

The menu is simple and direct. Soups and salads, such as chicken noodle and "the other soup" and large salads range from $3.00–$6.00. Hot entrees come with your choice of three sides and range from All Vegetable Plate ($9.00) and Andy's Meatloaf or roasted chicken ($10.00) to A Piece of Fish ($11.00), The Pork Chop ($12.00), and grilled sirloin steak ($14.00). Sides include mashed potatoes, egg noodles and tomato gravy, squash casserole, spinach, cabbage, stewed tomatoes, macaroni and cheese, string beans, carrots, or applesauce. Is my mother here?

Desserts may include chocolate cream pie, apple crisp ala mode, jelly sponge cake, or Grapenut custard, all at $4.00. Lots of soda pop and an excellent short, local wine list complete the scene. Corkage fee if you bring in your own bottle of wine: "A taste of wine for the house."

The fun and young message is loud and clear. Don't miss it.

❧ *Bergman's, 1234 Main Street, St. Helena 94574; phone (707) 963–1063. Beer and wine. 5:00–11:00 P.M. Sunday–Tuesday, 5:00 P.M.–1:00 A.M. Thursday–Saturday. No reservations. Visa and MasterCard. Wheelchair-accessible.*

One of Kathleen's favorite shops in all of Napa County is Ada Press's ON THE VINE, a food-and-wine-lover's clothing and trinket boutique at the corner of Main and Hunt Streets. A New Yorker with tremendous merchandising savvy and cooking and catering experience, Ada turned a former travel agency into a smart, saffron-colored destination with sensuous curves, bordeaux carpeting, and terraced counters. The shop's design alone is worth going in to see.

Don't miss the wine-and-food-inspired jewelry and "wearable art," including silver asparagus pins, whisk earrings, silverware picture frames, and foody ceramics by Sonoma artist Cynthia Hipkiss. Puzzles and jack-in-the-boxes complement the lighthearted casual clothes perfect for traveling in the heat. Visitors from other countries have been known to come in, be astonished at the appropriateness of the clothing, and purchase whole racks of a style.

Hand-painted "Field of Grapes" silk jackets are $725, ties $100. Garnet Merlot grape earrings are only $38. You can even find grape cluster cufflinks and tuxedo studs. Be sure to get on Ada's mailing list to learn all the latest.

On the Vine, 1234 Main Street, St. Helena 94574; phone (707) 963–2209 or (800) 992–4339. Open 10:00 A.M.–5:30 P.M. daily. Visa, MasterCard, and American Express. Wheelchair-accessible.

For an alternative restaurant experience, wander around the corner from Main onto Hunt to find the MAGNOLIA CAFÉ, a whimsical emporium of mostly healthy eats where locals hang out regularly.

Michael and Betty Scott moved their baby across the street in August 1998 to a larger space. Michael made it more colorful, like no one else could or would. He covered awkward support posts with his trademark mosaics of plate pieces and rescued lamps from the dump. Mosaics run off the table edges and decorate the fireplace, and flashing tube lighting outlines the 1950s booths.

You can get the whole menu to go at the deli counter, including Magnolia's superb breads and pastries. A former nurse and nutritionist, Betty chefs it up, creating mouth-watering breakfasts (served until 3:00 P.M.) including lemon-ricotta pancakes (three for $6.25), French toast ($4.75), a Portobello Mash of sliced portobellos grilled with potatoes, peppers, onions, spinach, and cheddar cheese ($7.25), and all sorts of eggs and creative omelets.

Lunch ranges from small and large salads and soups (try the vegetarian black-bean chili) and classic veggie sandwich ($5.25) to grilled eggplant and roast beef and grilled cheese. Pastas are loaded with veggies with add-ons of chicken herb sausage, bacon, capers, and porcini-mushroom ravioli.

If you're in desperate need of a refreshing picker-upper, indulge in the Olallieberry of Pina Colada smoothie ($2.75). And then there are the cobblers, brownies, cookies, and carrot cake.

Beware of the occasional egg-throwing contest when the Wine Train goes by the back patio.

❧ *Magnolia Café, 1113 Hunt Street, St. Helena 94574; phone (707) 963–0748. Open 7:30 A.M.–3:00 P.M. for breakfast and lunch, 5:00 P.M. on for dinner daily. Beer and wine. Visa, MasterCard, and Trans Media. Wheelchair-accessible.*

Back on Main Street, continue northward on the right (east) side. Once the Wonderful Drug Store, according to brass letters in the sidewalk, REED'S offers comfortable ladies' clothing from Calvin Klein, Harari, Loose Threads, Kevo, Kathleen Sommers, and Joan Vass. This is a popular boutique both with locals and visitors.

❧ *Reed's, 1302 Main Street at Hunt, St. Helena 94574; phone (707) 963–0400. Open 10:00 A.M.–5:30 P.M. daily. Visa, MasterCard, and American Express. Wheelchair-accessible.*

Next door to Reed's are two fun and wonderfully different (and differently wonderful) restaurants. The first one you come to is ARMADILLO'S, serving fresh Californian–Mexican food. Fun primary colors permeate the atmosphere, with large murals, painted chairs and tables, and Michael Scott's (as in Magnolia Café) trademark mosaic-cornered tables. He has had a part in and of this restaurant, and his whimsical influence shows. Copper palm trees greet you at the door.

Both Mexican and gringo food are served including breakfast, with a special children's menu and crayons available. Locals come in here constantly on their lunch breaks, which tells you something about Armadillo's prices and consistency.

With Betty Scott's influence, and her penchant for healthy foods, no lard is used in the freshly made refried beans. Imagine! We particularly enjoy the Enchilada Pollo con Mole, fresh shredded chicken covered with house-made mole sauce. The best! Lots of vegetarian specialties grace the menu, popular with the large Seventh Day Adventist community in the area. The chips

---

RECIPE FOR A GOOD EVENING
from Michael and Betty Scott Armadillo's and Magnolia Café

2 shots tequila
8 oz salsa
2 baskets chips
good company

Dip chips in salsa, eat. Sip tequila. Enjoy.

are warm and the salsa is fresh, served in a metal ice cream dish.

🍴 *Armadillo's, 1304 Main Street, St. Helena 94574; phone (707) 963–8082. Open 11:00 A.M.–9:00 P.M. Sunday–Thursday, 11:00 A.M.–10:00 P.M. Friday–Saturday. Beer and wine. Visa and MasterCard. Wheelchair-accessible.*

Just one door up the street from Armadillo's is a small, narrow restaurant that is so good, popular with Napa Valley residents, and under-discovered that we hesitate to tell you about it. We don't want it spoiled.

TRATTORIA GREEN VALLEY AND GREEN VALLEY CAFÉ & TRATTORIA (both are on the front signs) is/are all the same Italian bistro.

International investment consultants drive from Calistoga for a weekly "best burger in the Napa Valley," members of local bocce-ball teams (with names like The Olive Oilers) come in for a pasta lunch, and winemakers sneak in without

---

GREEN VALLEY PASTA CRUDEOLA
from the Cherry Tree

INGREDIENTS:

> 1 cup tomatoes, chopped
> 1 Tbs roasted sliced garlic
> 1 Tbs red onion, chopped
> 1 Tbs Greek, Italian, or French black olives, chopped
> 1 Tbs capers
> good pinch of fresh basil, chopped
> olive oil
> fresh ground pepper
> pinch salt
> 8 oz pasta

PREPARATION:

Combine all ingredients except pasta and let set at room temperature for at least an hour to let juices and flavors merge. Cook pasta al dente according to package directions. Mix sauce and hot pasta together, saving a little sauce to pour on top. Serves 2.

---

letting outsiders know that this is one of the best restaurants in the Napa Valley. Locals bring in the *St. Helena Star* and sit on green padded stools at the green marble counter, soaking up the gossip, printed and verbal.

Turandot, Othello, and Verdi posters decorate the walls, and deals are made in the larger back room. Be sure to check the daily specials blackboard to the left of the door as you enter.

At lunch you can have exceptionally flavorful fresh salads and sandwiches, hot sandwiches such as a North Beach Burger, Italian sausage, or vegetarian grilled eggplant (drippy gooey and wonderful) with tomatoes, cheese, peppers, onions, and olives (with small salad for $6.95), and outrageously divine pastas. The canneloni stuffed with chicken, mushrooms, spinach, and artichokes is $9.95. If crudeola is on the specials board, it is a compulsory try. Otherwise, try the spaghetti aja e ojho—spaghetti with fresh garlic, virgin olive oil, red-pepper flakes and parsely, gnocchi with Gorgonzola cheese sauce ($8.75) said to be the "best not in Italy," or ricotta-filled spinach tortellini with smoked salmon, tomatoes, mushrooms, and cream. The fried calamari with garlic mayonnaise is mouth-watering ($9.00).

Dinner features some of the same salads and pastas, plus linguini with fresh clams ($12.75), braised chicken ($10.75), grilled New York steak ($16.00), braised lamb shank with polenta ($11.95), marinated and grilled lamb top sirloin ($16.00), and mussels steamed in white wine and garlic ($10.75). Espresso drinks are available, and you can split an entree for an extra $2.00. Local and Italian wines, of course.

& *Trattoria Green Valley, 1310 Main Street, St. Helena 94574; phone (707) 963–7088. Wine and beer. Open lunch and dinner. Visa and MasterCard. Restaurant is wheelchair-accessible; rest room is not.*

One door up from Green Valley, at ALAN'S FRAMES & PHOTOGRAPHY, you can get film, picture frames, photos developed in one hour, and chat with the owner, who restored and recently sold his house, which had been M. F. K. Fisher's home for two decades here in St. Helena.

This is a classic photography shop and studio. Alan's is scheduled to move across to 1375 Main Street, but has not done so, as of this writing.

& *Alan's Frames & Photography, 1312 Main Street, St. Helena 94574; phone (707) 963–9294. Open 9:00 A.M.–6:00 P.M. Monday–Saturday, 11:00 A.M.–4:00 P.M. Sunday. Visa and MasterCard. Wheelchair-accessible.*

Up one door from Alan's is St. Helena's good old stand-by local grocery store, KELLER'S MARKET, with green-and-white-checked linoleum floors. You can still see the lighted Stornetta's dairy picture across the back wall. You can also get decent deli sandwiches and warmable meals, and indulge in the latest Acme breads or *The New York Times.*

& *Keller's Market, 1320 Main Street, St. Helena 94574; phone (707) 963–2114. Open 8:00 A.M.–8:00 P.M. daily. Visa and MasterCard. Wheelchair-accessible.*

As you walk by the *St. Helena Star* newspaper offices next door to Keller's, pick up a copy of the visitor edition, a tremendous wealth of local information, including wine and food transitions and developments.

One door up from the newspaper, ladies especially will enjoy STYLE STATION for its abundance of grown-up kid stuff, including Mary Engelbreit magnets, stuffed puppies and kittens, and flower prints galore on stationery, clothes, and denim clothes.

✱↳ *Style Station, 1332 Main Street, St. Helena 94574; phone (707) 963–2154. Open 10:00 A.M.–5:30 P.M. daily. Visa, MasterCard, and American Express. Wheelchair-accessible.*

For an evening of cinema, the Cameo Theatre at 1340 Main Street is a classic theater providing a classic American movie-going experience. Enjoy it for what it was and is.

Marc Robbins and Wayne Bradshaw own and preside over both PATINA FINE JEWELRY, just north of the Cameo Theatre, and Paladium, between David's and Buchanan's on the west side of Main Street. Their personal delight and passion for their jewelry shows the minute you walk in the door. At Patina they sell estate jewelry, including platinum and diamonds, objets d'art, and antiques, ranging from the late 1700s through the 1960s and costing from $150 to $25,000.

✱↳ *Patina Fine Jewelry, 1342 Main Street, St. Helena 94574; phone (707) 963–5445. Open 10:00 A.M.–5:30 P.M. Tuesday–Sunday. Visa, MasterCard, American Express, and Discover. Wheelchair-accessible.*

SHOWPLACE NORTH, just one door north of Patina, feels like the elegant extension of San Francisco's wholesale furniture houses that it is. The ceilings are high, the rooms are large, and the furniture is massive in both size and impact. Ralph Lauren upholstery, leather armchairs from $1,000, mosaic dining tables at $2,625, beds, and lamps are enticing to look at or perhaps even to purchase to furnish your home!

✱↳ *Showplace North, 1350 Main Street, St. Helena 94574; phone (707) 963–5556. Open 10:00 A.M.–5:00 P.M. Monday–Saturday, 11:00 A.M.–5:00 P.M. Sunday. Visa, MasterCard, and American Express. Wheelchair-accessible.*

THE BOOK CELLAR is St. Helena's book lovers' comfort zone in an 1885 historic brick-and-stone building that once housed Steves' Hardware, which is now next door to the north. High ceilings, dark wood shelves, and enormous soft sofas make you want to buy a book and curl up for the afternoon or evening. The Book Cellar has an outstanding selection of wine-country travel and photo books as well as books about wine and food and all the general fiction and nonfiction you could want. Also music tapes and CDs, gift cards, and emergency reading glasses. A must-stop.

✱↳ *The Book Cellar, 1354 Main Street, St. Helena 94574; phone (707) 963–3901, fax (707) 963–0296. Open 10:00 A.M.–5:30 P.M. Monday–Saturday, 11:00 A.M.–5:00 P.M. Sunday. Visa and MasterCard. Wheelchair-accessible.*

STEVES' HARDWARE AND HOMEWARE, INC., at the corner of Main Street and Adams, is a fine social and business institution whose existence reminds us all of what life was like in Napa and Sonoma Valleys before big wine came. If you are lucky, Carol Rutherford (yes, as in town of Rutherford) will be presiding over the counter to the left of the entrance. She and the Steves family have the longevity and knowledge to tell you anything you could possibly want to know about the Napa Valley.

Steves' moved here in 1991 from next door (now The Book Cellar), where they had been for 107 years in a store 2,000 feet smaller than this one. You will find Good Housekeeping's *Household Encyclopedia* on a James Graham stove with Le Creuset and Calphalon cookware. Rifles, guns, warnings, and ammo are sold along with Winchester sign replicas, paint, nails, sandpaper, copper cookware, ceramic animal salt-and-pepper shakers, tiles, cannisters, pepper grinders, and wooden salad bowls. Well-selected cookbooks, toasters, tool belts, plumbing and garden supplies, glassware, and live fishing bait add to the good old hardware-store quality, disappearing at the hands of the chain stores but lovingly preserved at Steves'.

❧ *Steves' Hardware and Homeware, Inc., 1370 Main Street, St. Helena 94574; phone (707) 963-3423. Open 7:30 A.M.–6:00 P.M. Monday–Friday, 7:30 A.M.–5:30 P.M. Saturday, 9:30 A.M.–4:00 P.M. Sunday. Visa, MasterCard, and Discover. Wheelchair-accessible.*

We highly recommend that you go another half-block up Main across Adams Street, passing the most expensive gas station (Chevron) in the wine country, and have a look or taste at Pairs Parkside Café, Lolo's Consignment Shop, and Tivoli. We beg you.

PAIRS PARKSIDE CAFÉ has a light, casual, and airy feeling, with blonde wooden chairs and tables, soft saffron walls, and white boards that carefully explain in detail the tastes you might encounter with each dish and the compatibility of wines with those foods—hence making pairs.

Craig and Keith Schauffel's "Cal–Asian" menu changes monthly, and low-calorie or heart-healthy suggestions are marked with a pear. All desserts and breads are baked here daily.

At lunch, carnivores will enjoy the Grilled Basil Burger with smoked tomato ketchup and crispy shoestring pototoes ($6.95) or the cheddar-chicken BLT with creamy coleslaw and Gaufrette potato chips ($7.95). Everyone else will want to try the vegetarian picnic sandwich loaded on grilled pesto bread ($7.50), roasted root-vegetable macaroni and cheese ($8.95), or the wild-mushroom wholewheat lasagna with sage ricotta cheese and broccoli ($8.50).

Dinner offerings may include wild-mushroom filet mignon ($17.50), parmesan-crusted sea bass ($15.95), grilled sancho pepper ahi tuna ($16.95), or veal osso bucco topped with gremolata on basmati rice with caramelized root-vegetable ragout ($17.95).

Espressos and six herbal teas are available to complement the warm cinnamon apple crisp with vanilla bean ice cream or rice pudding, espresso bittersweet-chocolate sundaes, or strawberry-rhubarb cheescake custard. Are you hungry yet?

❧ *Pairs Parkside Café, 1420 Main Street, St. Helena 94574; phone (707) 963–7566. Open 11:30 A.M.–3:00 P.M. and 5:30–9:00 P.M. Wednesday–Monday. Visa, MasterCard, American Express, Diners Club, and JCB. Wheelchair-accessible.*

Just up the street from Pairs is LOLO'S SECOND TO NONE CONSIGNMENT SHOP, with used clothing, furniture, and eclectica.

❧ *Lolo's Second to None Consignment Shop, 1424 Main Street, St. Helena 94574; phone (707) 963–7972. Open 10:30 A.M.–5:30 P.M. Tuesday–Saturday, 10:30 A.M.–4:00 P.M. Sunday–Monday. Visa, MasterCard, American Express, and Discover. Wheelchair-accessible.*

Please go one shop farther and walk down the driveway to TIVOLI, as in gardens, in what used to be the town meeting hall and then funeral home. Dottie Richolson manages Tivoli for owner Tom Scheibal, who also owns Bale Mill Pine Furniture, south of Calistoga.

Tom designs and builds iron-and-pine furniture and carries handmade mosaic tables made with Morrocan tiles, huge iron chandeliers, and unusual Ira Yaeger paintings. (He also has luxurious vacation accommodations available near Calistoga.) Tivoli is a great place to browse and escape to another world in just a few steps.

❧ *Tivoli, 1432 Main Street, St. Helena 94574; phone (707) 967–9399, fax (707) 967–9397. Open 10:00 A.M.–5:00 P.M. daily, closed Tuesday in winter. Visa and MasterCard. Wheelchair-accessible.*

Here we cross Main Street and, contrary to our nature, we suggest you walk the few steps back to the crosswalk and light. Traffic along Main Street is heavy, and crossing mid-block creates confusion and infuriates local drivers.

It's worth it to drop into VANDERBILT & COMPANY–NAPA VALLEY, a shop and gallery of home and personal accessories, including Vietri Italian ceramic dishes and paintings, place settings, tablecloths and napkins, interesting cookbooks, Phoebe Ellsworth's St. Helena paintings and white flower scene collection, and Vanderbilt's Napa Valley Collection of hand-painted platters, flower dinner plates (inspired by the rich colors and textures of the Napa Valley), all work of local artists such as Sherman Nobleman, John Nyquist, and Charles Gautreaux. The colors of the ceramics and the bed, bath, and table linens make us happy. Be sure to check out the closeout table in the back corner of the back room.

❧ *Vanderbilt & Company–Napa Valley, 1429 Main Street, St. Helena 94574; phone (707) 963–1010. Open 9:30 A.M.–5:30 P.M. daily. Visa, MasterCard, American Express, and Discover. Wheelchair-accessible.*

As you come out of Vanderbilt's, turn right and go south on Main past the bank and turn right on Adams Street to Tantau, Tapioca Tiger, Sportago, Pat Quigle–Paper Tiger, and the Napa Valley Coffee Roasting Company, for a minor but interesting diversion.

TANTAU is an intriguing little boutique featuring "accents for living," from glorious French poster originals ($1,200), cards, ceramics, beautiful accessories for kids' rooms, personal shopping treats, and bridal registry, to coffee cups and quilts.

❧ *Tantau, 1220 Adams Street, St. Helena 94574; phone (707) 963–3115. Open 9:30 A.M.–5:30 P.M. Monday–Saturday, 11:00 A.M.–5:00 P.M. Sunday. Visa and MasterCard. Wheelchair-accessible.*

Next door, TAPIOCA TIGER appeals to kids of all ages, with Madeline Tea Sets, Curious George everythings, children's books (yeah!), clothes, and shoes.

❧ *Tapioca Tiger, 1224 A Adams Street, St. Helena 94574; phone (707) 967–0608. Open 10:00 A.M.–5:30 P.M. Monday–Saturday, 10:30 A.M.–4:00 P.M. Sunday. Visa and MasterCard. Wheelchair-accessible.*

One of our great surprise finds in St. Helena is SPORTAGO for great outdoor clothes and emergency sports equipment. Forget your tennis racket? This is the place.

Christine Miller and Christina Stephens converted what had been an automobile dealership into the most appealingly abstract designed shop we have ever seen. Sportago is an authorized Patagonia dealer and also sells Prince and Wilson tennis rackets, balls, books, clogs, and jazzy Arnelle sunglasses.

❧ *Sportago, 1224 Adams Street, St. Helena 94574; phone (707) 963–9042. Open 9:00 A.M.–5:30 P.M. Monday–Saturday, close at 4:00 P.M. Sunday. Visa, MasterCard, and American Express. Partially wheelchair-accessible.*

Just beyond Sportago, ladies especially might want to venture into PAT QUIGLE–PAPER TIGER–NAPA for B Country Clothes, Sigrid Olsen, Pringle and

Ballentine sweaters, Foxcroft Blouses, Bagit raincoats, Mari sweaters, and other fine wear from Nancy Rogers, Catherine Stewart, Mishi, and Corbin. We just had fun talking to the staff, all from the larger outside world and graduates of UC Berkeley.

❧ *Pat Quigle–Paper Tiger–Napa, 1234 Adams Street, St. Helena 94574; phone (707) 963–4336. Open 10:00 A.M.–5:00 P.M. daily. Visa and MasterCard. Wheelchair-accessible.*

Local coffee lovers hang out at the NAPA VALLEY COFFEE ROASTING COMPANY. Since not too many visitors venture to the end of this single block off Main Street, this is a great place to find out what's happening locally. Sister to the store in Napa, it has the best coffee in town and is worth the extra steps. All your favorite espresso drinks, scones, and biscotti are here. Enjoy!

❧ *Napa Valley Coffee Roasting Company (with entrances on both Adams and Oak), 1400 Oak Avenue, St. Helena 94574; phone (707) 963–4491. Open 7:30 A.M.–6:00 P.M. Visa and MasterCard with $5.00 minimum purchase. Wheelchair-accessible.*

Around the corner and half a block down Oak Street from the coffee roastery, dip into THE BIG DIPPER ("Ice Cream Parlor with an Old Fashioned Flavor"), across from St. Helena Elementary School. (Is this location or what?)

ST. HELENA HOME OF THE LATE M.F.K. FISHER

More than an ice cream parlor, this place is an informal shrine and museum to ice cream parlor and Coca-Cola memorabilia. Be sure to look up at the stuff covering the walls, from huge ice cream cone displays and a 1908 ice cream dipper, a 1920 ice cream sandwich maker, and early milkshake blenders. Return to your childhood or earlier at the penny candy counter, games, and a jukebox you can play with all those oldie favorites.

✥ *The Big Dipper, 1336 Oak Avenue, St. Helena 94574; phone (707) 963–2616. Open 11:30 A.M.–8:00 P.M. Monday–Saturday, noon–6:00 P.M. Sunday. Cash only. Wheelchair-accessible.*

We highly recommend that you return to Adams Street, follow it across Main Street for 2 blocks (or if you are on Main, turn east on Adams), and turn north on Library Lane to both the Silverado Museum and the George & Elsie Wood Public Library and Wine Library.

SILVERADO MUSEUM is a near shrine to one-time Napa Valley resident Robert Louis Stevenson, established in 1969 by Charlotte A. Strouse and Norman H. Strouse, a former executive with J. Walter Thompson advertising.

Stevenson came to the Napa Valley for health reasons, apparently respiratory-related. First he and his bride spent a week in one of Sam Brannan's cottages in Calistoga, and then the couple stayed for two or three months on Mount St. Helena at the old Silverado Mine, scene of Stevenson's *Silverado Squatters*. Local rumor insists that Stevenson drafted (or at least "germinated the idea for") *Treasure Island* and thought about *Dr. Jekyll and Mr. Hyde* while here. He also wrote *Kidnapped* and *A Child's Garden of Verses*.

The local air cure didn't work, and there is even speculation that Stevenson developed new allergies here, just like the rest of us. Jack London fans will be interested to know that London followed Stevenson's route through the South Sea islands, trips you can trace on museum maps.

The Silverado Museum is the largest of five museums dedicated to Stevenson (although Yale University has the largest collection of his manuscripts). There are loads of copies of various editions of his work for sale at the museum, which certainly heightened our interest in the author.

✥ *Silverado Museum, 1490 Library Lane, St. Helena 94574; phone (707) 963–3757. Open noon–4:00 P.M. Tuesday–Sunday. Visa, MasterCard, and American Express. Wheelchair-accessible.*

Beside and behind the Silverado Museum is the GEORGE & ELSIE WOOD PUBLIC LIBRARY and the Napa Valley Wine Library, an unusual effort resulting from private and public funding.

Two things that make this library worth a trip are the Wine Library and its accompanying food-book collection. For visitors deeply interested in California wine-industry history and gossip, this is the place. The library attempts to collect every book worth its salt on wine, and also has a substantial collection of food literature. A real treat to browse are the transcribed oral interviews done with all of the Napa Valley's prominent wine pioneers, from Maynard Amerine to Robert Mondavi, and many in between. To see these volumes, ask the librarian to unlock the glass doors. She might ask for your youngest child as a deposit, but it's only for a little while!

George & Elsie Wood Public Library, 1492 Library Lane, St. Helena 94574; phone (707) 963–5244 or call the Napa Valley Wine Library Association at (707) 963–5145. Open noon–9:00 P.M. Monday–Wednesday, 10:00 A.M.–6:00 P.M. Thursday–Friday, 10:00 A.M.–4:00 P.M. Saturday, 1:00–5:00 P.M. Sunday. Wheelchair-accessible.

Resuming our walk or roll down the west side of Main Street, at the corner of Adams you will find VASCONI'S DRUGS, a local Valu-Rite pharmacy, for all your emergency prescription and associated health needs, cards, trinkets, great postcards, and film and film processing. If you have the kids along, they can get crayons and other fun stuff to keep themselves occupied.

Vasconi's Drugs, 1381 Main Street, St. Helena 94574; phone (707) 963–1444. Open 9:00 A.M.–7:00 P.M. Monday–Saturday, 10:00 A.M.–5:00 P.M. Sunday. Visa and MasterCard. Wheelchair-accessible.

If you are thinking of taking home a colorful painting to remember your wine-country experience forever, be sure to stop at THE GALLERY ON MAIN STREET. Bright and cheerful colors depict local vineyard scenes, painted primarily by local artists. We also like the classic French art posters. English wine-bottle stoppers cost only $9.50.

The Gallery on Main Street, 1359 Main Street, St. Helena 94574; phone (707) 963–3350. Open 10:00 A.M.–5:00 P.M. daily. Visa, MasterCard, and American Express. Wheelchair-accessible.

South just one door from the gallery is a local favorite, THE MODEL BAKERY, a wonderful bakery–cafe where you can get fabulous Old World–style scones, muffins, croissants, breakfast pastries, and breads to go or eat here with teas or Spinelli espresso drinks. Light meals are also here to tempt, including daily specials such as fresh spinach soup ($3.75) and meat or veggie brick-oven pizzas ($5.00).

Soft-looking walls, ceiling fans, and black-and-white-checked linoleum set the mood. If you're lucky, you can get a window table and alternate between people watching and newspaper reading.

The Model Bakery, 1357 Main Street, St. Helena 94574; phone (707) 963–8192. Open 7:00 A.M.–6:00 P.M. Tuesday–Saturday, 8:00 A.M.–4:00 P.M. Sunday. Visa and MasterCard. Wheelchair-accessible

South of the bar you will find GAIL'S CAFÉ, a funky step into the past complete with soda fountain and ice cream parlor, player piano, jukebox, antiques, and collectibles. Gail and John Marshek's cafe's walls are covered with original old signs, the counter's stools are vinyl-backed, and the oak back bar over the espresso counter was built in 1861 in Sacramento. The mahogany apothecary cabinets were built in the 1900s in Oakland in a building that burned in the 1960s riots, near where Gail grew up.

Gail's features Bud's Ice Cream of San Francisco, unbelievable shakes, flavored cokes (always liked those cherry cokes), nonfat frozen yogurt, smoothies, daily special pastas, espressos, sandwiches, soups and salads, a killer grilled cheese ($4.25), and a mom's meatloaf sandwich ($5.95), with fries or homemade potato chips extra for $1.95. Loads of locals pile in here for daily lunch specials, especially corned beef and cabbage. Oh yes, the fudge is made here—chocolate, cappuccino, maple, or rocky road.

Great spot downtown for a full breakfast too, ranging from eggs and their friends to thick French toast and pancakes, and three-egg omelets. Nothing over $7.00.

Gail's Café, 1347 Main Street, St. Helena 94574; phone (707) 963–3332, Web site www.napavalley.com/gails. Open 8:00 A.M.–8:00 P.M., close earlier in winter. Beer and wine. Visa, MasterCard, and American Express. Partly wheelchair-accessible.

DAVID'S is St. Helena's authorized Rolex and Cartier jewelry dealer since 1976.

David's, 1343 Main Street, St. Helena 94574; phone (707) 963–0239. Open 10:00 A.M.–5:30 P.M. Tuesday–Saturday. Visa, MasterCard, and American Express. Wheelchair-accessible.

Wayne Armstrong and Marc Robbins, who have Patina across the street, recently opened another fine boutique featuring contemporary jewelry. Stop in at PALLADIUM just to soak up the ultra contemporary design—of both the store and its jewelry. Most of the latter is so beautiful that just viewing it is a peaceful experience.

❧ *Palladium, 1339 Main Street, St. Helena 94574; phone (707) 963–5900, fax (707) 963–5757. Open 10:00 A.M.–5:30 P.M. daily. Visa, MasterCard, and American Express. Wheelchair-accessible.*

BUCHANAN'S STATIONERY sells fine letter papers, artists' materials (in case you left sketch pads, pencils, watercolors etc. at home), cards, gifts, and wrapping paper.

❧ *Buchanan's Stationery, 1337 Main Street, St. Helena 94574; phone (707) 963–3198. Open 9:30 A.M.–5:00 P.M. Monday–Saturday. Visa, MasterCard, and American Express. Wheelchair-accessible.*

Don't miss GOODMAN'S SINCE 1879, just south of Buchanan's. The clothing is resort, the wine-country souvenir shirts resemble Hawaiian, the ceiling creaks, and the place is loaded with local history. Joking aside, those wannabe Hawaiian shirts are the best available in the Napa Valley.

Check out the historic-clothing display case toward the back of the store, the Abraham, Cecelia, Jacob, and Julius Goodman photos, the original articles of the 1906 incorporation of Goodman–Lauter Company, and the bargain balcony.

The women's clothing is natural fiber, loose and lovely, some in ample sizes, including Cut Loose dresses.

❧ *Goodman's Since 1879, 1331 Main Street, St. Helena 94574; phone (707) 963–1750. Open 10:00 A.M.–6:00 P.M. Monday–Saturday, 10:00 A.M.–5:00 P.M. Sunday. Visa, MasterCard, and Discover. Wheelchair-accessible.*

One door down, NATURE ETC. sells mood music, nature-learning toys and puzzles, and name bead bracelets in case you forget your name or your child's name.

❧ *Nature Etc., 1327 Main Street, St. Helena 94574; phone (707) 963–1706, Open 10:00 A.M.–5:30 P.M. Sunday–Thursday, 10:00 A.M.–6:00 P.M. Friday–Saturday. Visa and MasterCard. Wheelchair-accessible.*

Even if you aren't a chocoholic, you must go into NAPA VALLEY CHOCOLATES for a sensuous experience. Candy Cane Dryer (yes, that is the owner's name) and her son Adam Burns and daughter Elizabeth Dryer have been making candy the old-fashioned way by roasting the cocoa beans. They make all the caramels by hand (but occasionally use their new machine).

Voted the "Best of Napa Valley Place to Get Something Sweet" in 1998, this family is a group of zany artists whose medium is chocolate. Adam makes chocolate sculptures, like the hand-painted white-chocolate Madame Mustard

for the Napa Valley Mustard Festival, while Elizabeth puts tiny chocolate eye-
balls with pupils on white-chocolate-covered gummy worms.

❧ *Napa Valley Chocolates, 1325 Main Street, St. Helena 94574; phone (707)
967–0808. Open 10:00-ish–6:00-ish daily. Visa, MasterCard, American Express,
and Discover. Wheelchair-accessible.*

Wine fans should not miss the ST. HELENA WINE CENTER, where you can
taste and purchase the finest and most rare wines made and sold in the Valley,
often at discount prices. Many of the wines here are true collectibles.

The St. Helena Wine Center is primarily owned by the extremely knowledgeable and local Beringer family, founders of Beringer Winery who no longer
own it. We had a delightfully informative afternoon with Phoebe Beringer.

We highly recommend that you explore wines here, particularly if you don't
have enough time to visit many wineries. The best are here. Be sure to get on
the mailing list to receive their exquisite catalogue.

❧ *St. Helena Wine Center, 1321 Main Street, St. Helena 94574; phone (707)
963–1313 or (800) 331–1311, fax (707) 963–8069, e-mail shwc@aol.com.
Open 10:00 A.M.–6:00 P.M. daily. Visa, MasterCard, and American Express.
Wheelchair-accessible.*

Next door to St. Helena Wine Center, HEAVEN & EARTH majors in aromatherapy, essences and body, bath, and spirit goodies.

❧ *Heaven & Earth, 1313 Main Street, St. Helena 94574; (707) 963–1124.
Open 10:00 A.M.–6:00 P.M. daily. Visa and MasterCard. Wheelchair-accessible.*

MAIN STREET BOOKS is one of the smallest and most charmingly independent book stores in the world. This is a real book-person's bookstore, featuring
new and used books of literature, the classics, and nice, warm people. Because
of their space limitations, these folks have mastered the special-order process.

❧ *Main Street Books, 1315 Main Street, St. Helena 94574; phone (707)
963–1338. Open 10:00 A.M.–5:30 P.M. Monday–Saturday. Visa and MasterCard.
Wheelchair-accessible.*

One of St. Helena's landmarks is GILLWOOD'S CAFÉ, a local institution and
old-timey hangout for "homestyle cooking," even though it's only been here
since 1990. Flowered vinyl tablecloths cover the tables, surprisingly comfortable
wooden benches line the walls, and there's a "community table" down the middle of the dining room to "share with friends and neighbors." Locals sit reading
books and newspapers as long as they want. Breakfast is better than standard
and includes Dickinson's preserves.

This is where you get those all-American reliables like meatloaf with mashed potatoes, fresh vegetables, and mushroom gravy ($8.75), chicken fried steak with mashed potatoes and country gravy ($9.25), Yankee pot roast ($9.95), crispy boneless half chicken with creamed sweet Vidalia onions and country potaotes ($9.95), patty melts, BLTs, and a good old tuna-salad sandwich ($6.40). At lunch, all sandwiches come with green salad, French fries, or homemade soup. At dinner, salads are extra and come with a mini-loaf of multigrain bread.

❧ *Gillwood's Café, 1313 Main Street, St. Helena 94574; phone (707) 963–1788. Open for breakfast, lunch, and dinner. Visa, MasterCard, and American Express. Wheelchair-accessible.*

Eccola women's resort clothing occupies the front of the St. Helena Hotel, a character of a small hotel whose lobby is packed with dolls, a pack-rat heaven. Once a flop house, St. Helena Hotel is now a Victorian Bed & Breakfast. Walk down the short alleyway just to check out the lobby, complete with spittoons.

The next shop down the street is Sweet Pea, a great place for kids of all ages with Brio toys, trains, cars, and clothes. Its neighbor to the south is I-elle, which sells professional women's clothing both here and in Sonoma. My Favorite Things is a delightful shop with table settings, picture frames, and home accessories, perfect to take home as gifts.

THE WILLIAM PACIFIC COMPANY (Treasures of the Orient) offers fine gifts, including jewelry, antiques, objets d'art, porcelain garden seats, and even a Ching Dynasty kitchen cabinet from 1820–1900.

❧ *The William Pacific Company, 1269 Main Street, St. Helena 94574; phone (707) 963–6000. Open 10:30 A.M.–4:30 P.M. daily. Visa, MasterCard, and American Express. Wheelchair-accessible.*

One of the most professional and elegant galleries in the Napa Valley is I. WOLK GALLERY, which features dramatic large paintings, works on paper, photography, and sculpture.

❧ *I. Wolk Gallery, 1235 Main Street, St. Helena 94594; phone (707) 963–8800, fax (707) 963–8801. Open 10:00 A.M.–5:30 P.M. Wednesday–Monday. Visa, MasterCard, and American Express. Partially wheelchair-accessible.*

Plan to spend some time wandering through ST. HELENA ANTIQUES & OTHER FINE COLLECTIBLES, where you will find everything from old pots to huge and heavy statuary, a collector's treasure-hunt paradise.

❧ *St. Helena Antiques & Other Fine Collectibles, 1231 Main Street, St. Helena 94574; phone (707) 963–5878. Open 11:00 A.M.–5:00 P.M. Wednesday–Monday. Visa and MasterCard. Wheelchair-accessible.*

Just south of the antiques heaven is the W. J. Giugni Grocery, now GIUGNI'S DELICATESSEN, an extremely local deli purveying everything from jawbreakers to great sandwiches. Papers tacked to the walls flap in the air conditioner's breeze, photos on the back wall are signed by Daryl Hannah and Joe Montana (yes, it's that popular), and decades of old memories are collected and posted for all to enjoy. And then there are the plants, baskets, and Perot for President posters.

The sandwiches are huge and varied with twelve bread and roll choices, plus twenty-three meats, from turkey pastrami to mild or hot coppa. Cheeses are just as abundant, and the service is cheerful and irreverent, thank heavens. But then we know owner Lonny Dunlap from when he had the same sort of deli across from the mission in Sonoma, a space now occupied by Viansa's Lo Spuntino. Great pick ups for picnics at the wineries, since very few of them are allowed to sell food.

Giugni's Delicatessen, 1227 Main Street, St. Helena 94574; phone (707) 963–3421. Open 9:00 A.M.–5:00 P.M. Beer and wine. No credit cards. Wheelchair-accessible.

South of the OK Barber Shop, where the barber snoops behind a screen in the back so that he can see you if you come in (reminiscent of a confessional), is MARIO'S FOR MEN, a fashionable men's boutique with clothes from Jhane Barnes, Zanella, Nicole Miller, Mondo, Cole-Haan, Caruso sport coats, leather shoes and belts, tuxedo rental, and other elegant resort and dining wear. (This is a brother store to D. Champagne on the east side of Main Street.)

Mario's for Men, 1223 Main Street, St. Helena 94574; phone (707) 963–1603. Open 10:00 A.M.–6:00 P.M. daily. Visa, MasterCard, American Express, Diners, Discover, and JCB. Wheelchair-accessible.

The next store down the street is San Francisco's splendiferous WILKES SPORT, a resort-wear child of Wilkes Bashford, San Francisco Mayor Willi Brown's favorite clothier. Men and women will find the finest in fashion here from lots of Italian designers, including Zegna, Loro Piana, Biella, Piazza Sempione, Industria, and Yoshi Hishinuma. Wilkes Sport even provides treats for your dogs, who are most welcome here. How refreshing!

Wilkes Sport, 1219 Main Street, St. Helena 94574; phone (707) 963–4323. Open 10:00 A.M.–6:00 P.M. Visa, MasterCard, American Express, and Diners. Wheelchair-accessible.

R. S. BASSO HOME FURNISHINGS (1829) is a great place to stop for dramatic French posters, cigar music (sexy jazz) CDs, interesting furniture, and mosaic objects.

❧ **R.S. Basso Home Furnishings**, *1219 Main Street, St. Helena 94574; phone (707) 963–0391. Open 10:00 A.M.–6:00 P.M. Monday–Saturday, 10:30 A.M.–5:00 P.M. Sunday. Visa and MasterCard. Wheelchair-accessible.*

Now we come to ANA'S CANTINA, where El Salvador native Ana provides a unique hangout for bar regulars to spend their days and farm workers and winery owners stop by for breakfast or come in after work to play pool, throw darts, listen to music from country to reggae, and dine on Ana's special food. Francis Ford Coppola drops in to sing karaoke in Spanish on Monday and Thursday nights under a huge canvas portrait of Freda Kahlo that hangs in "Ana's Gallery," which means the walls of the bar and restaurant. Coming partly from an Irish background, Kathleen was slightly alarmed by the regular "Black and Tan Night," but here it just means one night when they officially mix Guiness light and dark ales.

Music nights (Thursday, Friday, and Saturday) have featured Dana Hubbard and Philip Claypool, among others. The margaritas are famous.

❧ **Ana's Cantina**, *1205 Main Street, St. Helena 94574; phone (707) 963–4921. Open for breakfast and lunch daily, dinner 6:00–9:00 P.M. Thursday–Saturday. Visa, MasterCard, and Diners. Wheelchair-accessible.*

At VALLEY EXCHANGE we found wonderfully priced imitation Fiestaware dishes, pottery, and fun local products. The book selection, which you'll find toward the back of the store, includes *The Hot Flash Cookbook* and *Getting in Touch with Your Inner Bike*, both prominently displayed. You will also enjoy Graffeo coffee beans and chocolates, Annette's Napa Valley Truffles, Napa Valley Herbs (Kathleen finds these to be among the best and definitely best priced for the quality), Napa Valley Cabernet sauce, loads of pepper mills, great tea towels, and floor lamps.

❧ **Valley Exchange**, *1201 Main Street, St. Helena 94574; phone (707) 963–7423. Open 10:00 A.M.–5:30 P.M. Monday–Saturday, open at 11:00 A.M. Sunday. Visa and MasterCard. Wheelchair-accessible.*

Some of the Napa Valley's best restaurants are on St. Helena's side streets, so now we will take you to them. Spring Street Restaurant is on Spring Street (surprise), one of the most southern cross streets in downtown St. Helena, and Terra and Showley's are next door to each other on Railroad Avenue, east of Main Street.

SHOWLEY'S AT MIRAMONTE never gets much publicity, simply because owner–chef Grant Showley concentrates his energies on his food instead of hype. Lots of locals mention this as one of their two or three favorites in the Valley.

With a historic 1860 building, Showley's looks like a country inn, indoors as well as on the pleasant brick patio. Simple linens cover the tables, and the excellent and unpretentious service contributes to a relaxing meal. If you like sweetbreads, you have arrived at your mecca, or try the monkfish, wild boar cassoulet for a new taste experience, or lighter pastas and salads. Showley's is also popular for business lunches.

Showley's at Miramonte, 1327 Railroad Avenue, St. Helena 94574; phone (707) 963–1200. Open for lunch and dinner Tuesday–Sunday. Visa, MasterCard, American Express, and Diners. Wheelchair-accessible.

TERRA is one of California's finest and most creative restaurants, and one that gets lots of publicity. Hiro (Hiroyoshi) Sone and Lissa Doumani have created the perfect blend of history and culture in their restaurant in this historic 1884 Taylor, Duckworth & Company Foundry Building, dignifying the stone walls and large arched windows with a comfortable decor that immediately makes visitors feel at home.

Hiro developed and directed the kitchen at Wolfgang Puck's Spago in Los Angeles, and Lissa is earth mother and pastry chef, with deep roots in wine-country vineyards. The food they create speaks for itself in an unabashed California–Asian–French way, the definition of which you will experience by dining at Terra.

TERRA RESTAURANT ENTRANCE

Appetizers may include home-smoked salmon with potato latkes ($13.50), braised beef tongue, leeks and Yukon gold potato salad ($9.00), sauteed Miyagi oysters on the half shell ($11.00), or petit ragout of sweetbreads, prosciuto, mushrooms, and white truffle oil ($10.50). If you are lucky, main-course experiences may include one of our favorites, broiled sake-marinated Chilean sea bass with shrimp dumplings ($19.00), grilled ranch quail with wild-mushroom risotto and Pinot Noir sauce ($21.00), New York strip steak with potato gnocchi in gorgonzola-cheese sauce ($24.00), or grilled lamb tenderloin and braised riblets with potato samousa and minted yogurt ($23.00). Our favorite dessert is the sauteed strawberries in black-pepper Cabernet Sauvignon sauce with vanilla-bean ice cream ($7.00); or maybe it's the baked-apple creme brulee ($7.00). Jerry likes the chocolate walnut brownie with chocolate bourbon ice cream and chocolate fudge sauce ($7.50), which may be death on a plate.

Terra's wine list is exceptional, which should be no surprise.

✤✥ *Terra, 1345 Railroad Avenue, St. Helena 94574; phone (707) 963–8931. Open for dinner Wednesday–Monday. Beer and wine. Visa, MasterCard, Diners, and Carte Blanche. Wheelchair-access down the alleyway to the back.*

PINOT BLANC, just south of St. Helena proper, is the northern exposure of famed restaurateur Joachim Splichal's Patina Restaurant in Los Angeles. Sean A. Knight executes the orders as executive chef. Many locals have been disappointed here while others love it, all with expectations raised by Splichal's reputation.

Pinot Blanc has one of the most soothing decors in the wine country, with its dignified dark wood walls, club-like bar, and private-feeling dining areas. Check out the great French magazine cartoons on the lounge walls and the wallpaper of actual wine labels on the walls down the hall to the rest rooms.

Pinot Blanc serves lunch and dinner, with daily "Plats du Jour." One of the most popular dishes is the grilled veal chop with pancetta-studded bean puree, portobello mushrooms, and herb veal jus ($23.95). Lunch may feature endive salad with Roquefort cheese and caramelized walnuts ($6.95), French onion soup ($5.95), high-cholesterol (but oh so good) foie gras ($13.95), big salads, burgers and sandwiches including a good Niçoise salad ($12.95), creative pastas, exotic fish, oxtail pot pie ($14.95), braised short ribs with horseradish mashed potatoes and wilted spinach and crispy onions ($14.95), or unorthodox peppered beef tenderloin with red wine risotto cake and poached bone marrow ($23.95).

Dinner usually includes many of the same dishes, plus wild-mushroom risotto with ragout of baby onions and shaved parmesan ($15.95), planked Atlantic salmon with apple smoked-bacon crust with roasted baby artichokes, white beans, and arugula ($17.95), spa specials, farm chicken with Yukon Gold and arugula potatoes ($14.50), and chestnut-crusted venison with truffled sweet potato puree ($22.95).

Regular nightly specials include Tuesday's Scottish mallard duck, Wednesday's roasted local squab, Thursday's Scottish pheasant, Friday's grilled veal chop, Saturday's lamb shank, and Sunday's Calistoga pig.

✤ *Pinot Blanc, 641 Main Street (Highway 29), St. Helena 94574; phone (707) 963–6191. Open for lunch and dinner. Visa, MasterCard, American Express, Discover, Diners, and JCB. Wheelchair-accessible.*

St. Helena to Calistoga

As we head north on Highway 29 from St. Helena, the first two major stops are on your left (west). Beringer Vineyards comes up quickly on the left barely outside St. Helena, and the Culinary Institute of America's western campus and its Wine Spectator Greystone Restaurant appears 0.4 mile farther.

Amidst what our children called "the tree tunnel" and Napans call the "Row of Elms," you enter BERINGER VINEYARDS, "the oldest continuously operating winery in the Napa Valley." Beringer is the most spectacular winery setting in the Valley, with exquisitely cultivated gardens, vast lawns (no picknicking, please), preserved historic buildings, fun tours, and ample wine tasting in three places. But the wine is made across the road where you can't go, so enjoy showtime here.

In 1876 German immigrants Jacob and Frederick Beringer bought land and founded Beringer Winery. Chinese laborers returning to the San Francisco Bay Area, after completing the transcontinental railroad, hand-chiseled rock tunnels 250 feet into the hills. Wines are still aged and stored here.

After the winery was built, Jacob lived in an existing 1848 farmhouse on the property, now restored and expanded and called Hudson House, which serves as Beringer Vineyards' Culinary Arts Center and home of the School for American Chefs.

Frederick began construction of the seventeen-room mansion to re-create the family home on Germany's Rhine River. Frederick's Rhine House is now listed in the National Register of Historic Places and serves as Beringer's hospitality center. We recommend just walking into Rhine House to experience its opulence. An excellent collection of books on wine and food are available in what was Frederick Beringer's library. Notice the stained-glass windows.

Premium-wine tastings take place upstairs in the Founder's Room (regular tasting and souvenir purchasing is in the Old Bottling Room toward the back of the property). Catch the Clark Gable photo, dusty historic bottles, and delicious tastes of breads, oils and sauces such as four dipping and marinade oils, olive and grapeseed oils, yummy mayonnaise, bread spreads (artichoke and garlic eggplant), pasta sauces, and beautiful recipe cards.

Fine points: Beringer is now owned by the Nestlé Corporation, while the Beringer family has the St. Helena Wine Center in downtown St. Helena on Main Street. No tasting fees. Featured wines: White Zinfandel, Johannisberg Riesling, Chenin Blanc, Gewürztraminer, Alluvium Blanc, Viognier, Chardonnay, Gamay Beaujolais, Pinot Noir, Zinfandel, Cabernet Sauvignon, and dessert wines. Owner: Nestlé Corporation. Winemaker: Ed Sbragia. Cases: Undefined. Acres: 600.

CAESAR SALAD WITH GARLIC OIL
from Beringer Vineyards

INGREDIENTS FOR THE DRESSING:

1 Tbs Dijon mustard	*1 anchovy fillet*
1 Tbs lemon juice	*1 Tbs Parmesan cheese, grated*
1 tsp salt	*1 tsp ground black pepper*
1 Tbs red wine vinegar	*½ cup Infused Garlic Grape Seed Oil*
1 tsp garlic, minced	

INGREDIENTS FOR THE CROUTONS:

1 cup sourdough bread cut into ¾-inch cubes
1 Tbs Infused Garlic Grape Seed Oil
salt to taste

INGREDIENTS FOR THE SALAD:

3 Tbs Parmesan cheese, grated
1 head Romaine lettuce (washed and cut into 1-inch pieces)

PREPARATION:

Combine first 9 ingredients in a blender to make the Caesar dressing.

Toss the bread cubes with Garlic Grape Seed Oil and salt to taste. Bake croutons in an oven at 450° F for 4–5 minutes until light golden.

Toss the romaine lettuce with the dressing. Add the croutons and the Parmesan cheese and toss again. Serves 4.

❦ *Beringer Vineyards, 2000 Main Street, St. Helena 94574; phone (707) 963–4812, fax (707) 963–8129. Open 9:30 A.M.–5:00 P.M. daily. Visa, MasterCard, American Express, and Discover. Old Bottling Room is wheelchair-accessible.*

As you progress northward you absolutely *must* stop at the CULINARY INSTITUTE OF AMERICA AT GREYSTONE, the thirty-acre Western campus for continuing education of the CIA–Hyde Park, New York, the foremost culinary educational institution in the United States.

While this campus welcomes professionals in a wide range of fields connected to food and wine (including writers, tra la!), home chefs are welcome to indulge in watching cooking demonstrations held in Greystone's exquisite Ecolab Theatre ($5.00, and you get a hat to take home). You can also attend kitchen viewings of the incredible 15,000-square-foot room full of teaching kitchens. After students prepare foods in the morning, the fruits of their labors take center stage on display tables in the Clover-Stornetta Dairy–sponsored dining room, and CIA staff get to enjoy. Leftovers go to local food-for-the-disadvantaged programs.

Built in the late 1880s for William Bourn and Everett Wise as a cooperative winery where Napa Valley growers could make wine and circumvent San Francisco's tightly controlled wine dealers, Greystone is built in the Richardsonian–Romanesque style with 22-inch-thick walls of locally quarried tufa stone. It is now listed in the National Register of Historic Places. Notice the cathedral ceilings, grand arches, tasteful antiques, and massive hand-crafted furniture, combined with the latest state-of-the-art cooking equipment.

First known as the Bourn and Wise Cellar, Bourn sold the building in 1894 to Charles Carpy, a founder of the California Wine Association, which then became one of the largest wine producers in California. At its peak under the CWA, Greystone could make 1,349,000 gallons of wine with a marvelous gravity system. Eventually passing through several owners, the Christian Brothers bought the property in 1950, making brandy and wine here for many years.

Heublein bought Christian Brothers' wine line and eventually closed down the operation at Greystone. The Culinary Institute bought the building from Heublein, which, in turn, made a magnificent donation to the nonprofit CIA, enabling it to embark on a fabulous restoration project you can now enjoy.

Do not miss the De Baun Museum, where you can view Christian Brothers' famed winery leader's Brother Timothy's fabulous Corkscrew Collections, winemaking artifacts, a Tuscan olive press, and an extensive collection of oak cooperage. In front of the building and to the left, stroll through the organic Cannard herb garden on little terraces and wander

SPICY PORK KEBABS WITH MOORISH FLAVORS
from Wine Spectator *Greystone Restaurant*
at the Culinary Institute of America in St. Helena

INGREDIENTS:

2 garlic cloves, sliced	¼ tsp crushed red pepper
salt to taste	1 tsp curry powder
freshly ground paper to taste	4 Tbs olive oil
1 tsp coriander seeds	1 Tbs lemon juice
¾ tsp paprika	1 Tbs parsley, chopped
¾ tsp cumin seeds	1 lb lean pork, cut into ¾-in cubes
½ tsp thyme, dried	1 lb red grapes

PREPARATION:

In a mortar, pound the garlic with a pinch of salt to make a paste.

In a dry skillet, heat the coriander seeds, paprika, cumin seeds, thyme, crushed red pepper, and curry powder until hot and aromatic, about 30 seconds. Remove from pan and put the mixture into a spice grinder or mortar and pestle. Grind to make a fine powder.

In a bowl, combine the garlic, spices, olive oil, lemon juice, parsley, ¾ tsp salt, pepper, and pork cubes. Toss well to coat completely and let marinate several hours, mixing occasionally.

Skewer the pork along with the red grapes and grill. Yields 12 skewers.

among culinary herbs, onion and garlic beds, edible flowers and herbal teas, and the salad-greens plot. This garden provides the teaching and restaurant kitchens with more than 145 different types of vegetables, sixty varieties of culinary herbs, twenty-seven types of fruit, and eleven varieties of berries.

The fifteen acres of Merlot grapes on the grounds result in custom-crushed and -bottled Greystone Cellars wine available at the Campus Store and in the *Wine Spectator* Greystone Restaurant. Ah, the Campus Store. Kathleen thought she had arrived in heaven: every cooking utensil imaginable, 2,000 cookbook titles including children's cookbooks, the CIA videotape series, all prices and colors of chef's uniforms and aprons, and a world market of unusual spices and ingredients. Check out the big stove imported from the Hyde Park campus.

Now to experience the *Wine Spectator* Greystone Restaurant, where every Adam Tihany–designed table has a view of the restaurant's chefs (no students) at work. You can dine and sip in front of the roaring fireplace or bask in the sun on the terrace overlooking Charles Krug winery and part of the Napa Valley.

An excellent eight-page wine list accompanies the creative menu, which offers you tastes of the Mediterranean from Spanish tapas, Italian antipasti, and eastern Mediterranean meze. With great pleasure we tried the grilled octopus ($7.00), cod cakes with Meyer lemon aioli ($5.25), grilled pork kebabs ($5.95), and the lamb kefta and kumquat skewers ($5.75). You can try the Tasting Extravaganza for your whole table at $7.95 per person.

The Greystone seafood paella ($9.50 for two or more) is excellent, as are the grilled Monterey Bay sardines ($9.00) and seasonal risottos as first courses. The pepper-crusted yellowfin tuna ($19.00) was sensational, as was the nearly fat-free breast of duck ($18.00). Wine devotees may select flights of wines to taste, usually consisting of three three-ounce pours, except dessert wines of three one-ounce pours.

There's even a cigar menu of fine and unique cigars. Servers provide cutters and matches so that you can indulge in the cigar in the terrace's designated smoking area.

❧ The Culinary Institute of America at Greystone, 2555 Main Street, St. Helena 94574; phones: restaurant (707) 967–1010, continuing education (707) 067–0600; Web site www.ciachef.edu and www.digitalchef.com. Restaurant open 11:30 A.M.–9:00 P.M. Thursday–Monday, December 1–March 31, and daily April 1–November 30; Campus Store open 10:00 A.M.–6:00 P.M. daily; Demonstrations and Kitchen Viewings 10:30 A.M., 1:30 P.M., and 3:30 P.M. Saturday and Sunday. Visa, MasterCard, American Express, Diners, and Discover. Wheelchair-accessible via parking lot and terrace at north end of building.

As you leave the Culinary Institute, turn left extremely carefully to continue north on Highway 29 to Charles Krug, St. Clement, Markham, Freemark Abbey, Folie á Deux, Ehlers Grove, Hanns Kornell Champagne, and Stonegate wineries, plus an entrance to Sterling—all before you get to Calistoga!

Turn right (east) just north of the CIA to CHARLES KRUG WINERY, the "oldest operating winery in the Napa Valley," founded by Prussian-born Charles Krug. Krug died in 1892, and San Francisco banker James Moffitt bought the winery from Krug's heirs. (Remember, Beringer claims to be the "oldest continuously operating winery," the key word being *continuously*.)

Rosa and Cesare Mondavi purchased the property from Moffitt in 1943. Their son, Peter Mondavi, Sr., named one of twelve "Living Legends" by the Napa Valley Vintners' Association, took over the winery in 1966 and instilled cold fermentation and use of French oak barrels, has now passed management duties on to his sons, Peter Jr. and Marc. They all live on the family estate.

Olive trees line the driveway to the historic buildings and the separate tasting room (be sure to try the Charles Krug Peter Mondavi Family Extra Virgin Olive Oil, based on Krug estate olives). Catch the fabulous view of Greystone and take time to picnic in the vineyards.

If you had any previous misgivings about Krug wines, try them again. They are again contenders, particularly the Cabernets and Pinot Noir. You will find Krug wines under both Charles Krug and C.K. Mondavi labels. Their Generations blend won gold medals in 1998 competitions at the National Orange Show, Monterey Wine Competition, and *Dallas Morning News* Wine Competition.

Fine points: Featured wines: Pineau, Chardonnay, Sangiovese, Cabernet Sauvignon, Merlot, and Generations (blend of Cabernet Sauvignon, Merlot, and Cabernet Franc. Owner: Peter Mondavi, Sr. Winemaker: Marc Mondavi. Cases: Charles Krug 100,000, C.K. Mondavi 1,000,000. Acres: 800.

❦ *Charles Krug Winery, 2800 North Main Street, St. Helena 94574; phone (707) 967–2200, fax (707) 967–2291, e-mail www.charleskrug@pmondavi.com. Open 10:30 A.M.–5:30 P.M. daily. Tasting fee $3.00. Visa, MasterCard, and American Express. Wheelchair-accessible.*

MARKHAM VINEYARDS will be on your right going north. Look for a rather industrial new building at the front with flagpoles, dramatic dripping fountains filled with floating lilies, and lovely marguerites in the entrance patio.

The historic building was built as La Ronde Winery in 1874 by prospector Jean Laurent, and passed through various owners over the decades. Bruce Markham bought the winery in 1977 and sold it in 1988 to giant Mercian, Japan's largest wine importer.

The tasting-room entrance is to the left at the rear of the entrance patio, with the daily Tasting Menu posted on a tripod at the door. Mercian has put millions into elegant blonde-wood floors, Calder prints, high ceilings, Robert O. Rowland ceramics, jazz background music—and obviously someone talented is in charge of display and color.

You might be interested in the Oaxacan pottery and posters, Napa Valley Wine Auction posters, olive oils, cookbooks, lead-free pewter flatware and corkscrews, jewelry, and wine bottles of doggie treats called Chateau Pooche.

Fine points: The Chardonnay, Sauvignon Blanc, and Merlot have all been rated tops in California by the *Wine Spectator*. Tasting fees run $3.00 for regulars, $5.00 for reserves. Featured wines: Chardonnay, Muscat Blanc, Merlot, Zinfandel, Cabernet

Sauvingon, and Petite Syrah. Owner: Mercian of Japan. Winemaker: Michael Beaulac. Cases: 150,000. Acres: 300.

Markham Vineyards, 2812 St. Helena Highway, St. Helena 94574; phone (707) 963–5292, fax (707) 963–4616. Open 10:00 A.M.–5:00 P.M. daily. Visa, MasterCard, American Express, and JCB. Wheelchair-accessible.

The next winery going north is ST. CLEMENT VINEYARDS in a big yellow and white Victorian house up the hill to the left (west) of Highway 29. Leave Markham and turn right, ready to turn left almost immediately and carefully. Park in the lot below and hike up the path, climb the steps, and rest and recover at the patio's wrought iron tables and chairs. If the hike didn't take your breath away, the view will. As you walk in the front door, turn right to the library and feast your eyes on a marvelous collection of wine books, which you are welcome to leaf through.

San Francisco glass merchant Fritz Rosenbaum built this elegant Gothic–Victorian in 1878 and lived in the house with his family while producing commercial wines in the stone cellar beneath the house, the eighth bonded winery in the Napa Valley.

Bill Robbins bought the property, restored the building, and started Spring Mountain Winery here. It was Robbins' Parrott Mansion, to which he

ST. CLEMENT VINEYARDS

moved Spring Mountain, that was the residence in the "Falcon Crest" nighttime soap. The name St. Clement refers to an island in the mouth of the Potomac River where interim owner Dr. Bill Casey, a Maryland ophthalmologist, loved to sail.

Japanese Sapporo beer company bought the property from Casey in 1987, and the winery's production facility in back of the Victorian and its wine reputation continue to grow.

 Fine points: Tasting fee: $2.00. Featured wines: Chardonnay, Sauvignon Blanc, Merlot, Cabernet Sauvignon, and Oroppas, a Bordeaux-style blend. Owner: Sapporo. Winemaker: Dennis Johns. Cases: 20,000. Acres 3.

St. Clement Vineyards, 2867 St. Helena Highway North, St. Helena 94574; phone (707) 967–3033 or (800) 331–8266, fax (707) 963–1412, e-mail sclement@napanet.com, Web site www.stclement.com. Open 10:00 A.M.–4:00 P.M. daily. Visa, MasterCard, American Express, and Discover. Wheelchair-accessible , although slightly precarious, by parking in lot at top of driveway.

GRANMA DIXON'S CHOCOLATE CAKE
from Nancy Carlson, Hospitality Coordinator, St. Clement Vineyards

INGREDIENTS:

3 cups flour

2 cups sugar

3 tsp soda

½ tsp salt

⅛ cup cocoa

1 cup oil

½ cup milk

2 eggs

2 tsp vanilla

1 cup boiling water

½ cup St. Clement Cabernet Sauvignon

PREPARATION:

Mix all ingredients except the boiling water in a large bowl. Beat until blended well. Slowly add boiling water and mix well. Pour into greased 9" x 13" pan. Bake at 350° F for 35–40 minutes. Although frosting of your choice is an option, this cake is so moist that it tastes great without it. Serve with another bottle of 1994 St. Clement Cabernet Sauvignon.

To get back on our tour, come back down St. Clement's driveway and turn left very carefully. At your next stop, you can visit Freemark Abbey, Hurd's Candle Factor, and superb Brava Terrace restaurant. You might also want to stop at Elrod Antiques.

FREEMARK ABBEY WINERY's name has nothing to do with the Catholic Church, although many of us grew up believing there were monks wandering around with smirks on their faces in long brown robes. The name is actually a combo of Southern Californians Albert "Abbey" Ahern, Charles Freeman, and Markquand Foster, who bought Lombarda Cellers in 1939.

Founder Josephine Marlin Tychson became the first woman to build and operate a winery in California in 1886, which she called Tychson Cellars. San Lorenzo, California, native Josephine and her Danish husband John Tychson, moved here in 1881 to cure his tuberculosis. They bought 147 acres, known as Tychson Hill on the west side of Highway 29, for $8,500. He died and Josephine built a 50-square-foot redwood winery and hired Nils Larsen as foreman to make wine, producing Zinfandel, Riesling, and a

FREEMARK ABBEY'S COMFORTABLY ELEGANT TASTING ROOM

Burgundy blend. When *phylloxera* attacked, she sold the winery to Larsen, who sold it to Antonio Forni, a friend of Josephine's who renamed it Lombarda Cellars in 1898.

A thinking man, Forni made Chianti and other Italian-style wines to sell to Italian immigrants working Barre, Vermont's marble and granite quarries. Using stones from nearby Glass Mountain, Forni expanded by building a new structure around the wooden one so he wouldn't have to move the tanks and later removed the redwood building. Prohibition shut Forni down, and along came the Freemark Abbey boys in 1939, who sold their wine primarily in San Francisco.

Freemark Abbey went through several owners, ending up for now with a group including the late Chuck Carpy and Jim Warren, Dick Heggie, Brad Webb, and Laurie Wood. Winemaker Ted Edwards also became a partner. Carpy is generally credited with resurrecting the winery.

Enjoy the living room feeling in the tasting room with large upholstered chairs, elegant wood furniture, and a roaring fire in the walk-in fireplace (on cold days, that is). Freemark Abbey was named "Winery of the Year" by *Wine & Spirits* magazine in 1994, 1996, and 1997.

 Fine points: Tasting fee: $3.00 and you keep the glass. Featured wines: Chardonnay, Sauvignon-Bosche, Cabernet Sauvignon-Sycamore, Cabernet Sauvignon, Merlot, Johannisberg Riesling, Cabernet Franc, Merlot, and Edelwein gold late harvest Riesling. Owners: the group. Winemaker: Ted Edwards. Cases: 40,000. Acres: 330.

❧ *Freemark Abbey Winery, 3022 St. Helena Highway North, St. Helena 94574; phone (707) 963–9694, fax (707) 963–9554. Open 10:00 A.M.–4:30 P.M. Visa, MasterCard, and American Express. Wheelchair-accessible.*

Right next to Freemark Abbey, and in the same building complex about two miles north of St. Helena, don't miss HURD BEES WAX CANDLES AND GOURMET. The sweet, musty smell of candles-in-progress permeates the air in this rambling emporium of everything to do with candles, including encased buzzing bees, honey, and women making and dipping candles. This is an aesthetic and educational experience in a casual but professional atmosphere.

❧ *Hurd Bees Wax Candles and Gourmet, 3020 St. Helena Highway North, St. Helena 94574; phone (707) 963–7211, fax (707) 963–4358. Visa, MasterCard, American Express, and Discover. Partly wheelchair-accessible.*

Just north of Hurd's is one of our favorite restaurants, the casually elegant and comfortable BRAVA TERRACE. Owner/Chef Fred Halpert has worked with the best: Chapel, Senderens, Verge, Jacques Maximin, and Louis Outhier for starters. His classic French training merges with California wine country realities and peppers and vegetables from the back garden to treat you to some of the most refreshing real food to survive the puddle and stacking schools of California Nouvelle Cuisine.

As you walk in the front door, which actually faces the back of the property, the small open kitchen is right ahead for you to watch and enjoy. To your left down the hall to the restrooms are framed letters to Fred Halpert from Paul Bocuse, James Beard House's late Director Peter Kump, and a Man Ray sketch of Halpert. Hardwood floors, big windows, and a cozy yet enormous stone fireplace make a cozy room, particularly on a rainy day.

For food starters, you absolutely must indulge in sampling the slightly salty homemade potato chips with melted Danish blue cheese and basil pesto ($4.75), and the seared skewers of Norwegian salmon with Japanese BBQ sauce ($3 each) were out of sight wonderful. The grilled vegetable melt sandwich was huge and yummy with plenty of portobello mushroom, zucchini, eggplant and cheddar ($8.75) sandwich were better than perfect and served with a light fennel cole slaw. Try the daily risottos or pastas ($13.95), the grilled filet of beef with roasted potato cake and ragout of mushrooms ($22.95), the half slab of BBQ ribs with corn and garlic bread ($16.95), superb braised veal shank osso bucco with garlic mashed potatoes ($16.95), or the positively no oil or butter penne pasta with chopped tomatoes, garlic, Balsamic vinegar, and basil ($13.95). Halpert's Napa Valley Ovens' breads from Calistoga are heavenly.

We blissfully tried all the "extras" including spicy fries, roasted potato cake, sauteed spinach, and garlic mashed potatoes—a potato lover's feast. Daily specials draw regular fans with fish on Monday, ribs and zin on Tuesday, braised short ribs on Thursday, 20-ounce T-Bone steak on Friday, coq au vin on Saturday, and crispy half chicken on Sunday.

✦❧ *Brava Terrace, 3010 St. Helena Highway North, St. Helena 94574; phone (707) 963–9300, fax (707) 963–9581. Beer and wine. Open noon–9:00 P.M. daily May–November, closed Wednesday December–April. Visa, MasterCard, and American Express. Wheelchair-accessible.*

On to more wineries and the St. Helena Premium Outlets. After you leave the Freemark Abbey complex, you turn right (north) and wind over a little hill, at the bottom of which is the driveway to FOLIE Á DEUX WINERY. Turn right (east) at the colored flags flying across from the St. Helena Premium Outlets, and right again at the oak tree. The little yellow century-old farm house serves as tasting room in this bucolic setting.

Please heed the warning about "uneven rock steps–please use caution," and enjoy your picnic at a table on the lawn under the old oak tree.

When the two psychiatrists who founded the winery told psychiatrist friends they were going to fulfill a mutual dream by starting a winery, their friends said the couple were showing classic symptoms of Folie Á Deux, a term that refers to two "batty individuals (who) share the same delusional ideas or fantasies about the real world." In other words, they were both crazy. Indeed.

Folie á Deux began producing wine in 1981 with grapes from its 12 acres, winning "Best of Show" at the 1985 California State Fair for its 1983 Chardonnay. In 1995, renowned winemaker Dr. Richard Peterson and friends bought the winery and hired winemaker Scott Harvey, named by wine writer

Dan Berger as one of the "Ten Best Winemakers in America" in 1990. Watch for his Amador Zinfandel from the 130-year-old Grandpere Vineyard. Be sure to taste their flavored oils and get a sample four-pack for $15.00. Notice the official *Newsweek* label.

Featured wines: Chardonnay, Chenin Blanc, Cabernet Sauvignon, Menage á Trois, Muscat á Deux, and "fantaisie" sparkling wine. Owners: Dr. Richard Peterson and group. Winemaker: Scott Harvey. Cases: 40,000. Acres: 21.

Folie á Deux Winery, 3070 North St. Helena Highway, St. Helena 94574; phone (707) 963-1160 or (800) 473-4454, fax (707) 963-9223, e-mail fantasy@folie-a-deux.com, Web www.flavorweb.com/folie.htm. Open 10:00 A.M.–5:00 P.M. daily. Visa, MasterCard, and American Express. Not wheelchair-accessible.

To get to EHLERS GROVE and CARTLIDGE & BROWNE wineries, turn right on Ehlers Road off Highway 29, and turn left at their sign to the small pinkish beige stone building with planters full of colorful flowers and a black iron rocking chair near the tall sliding wooden door. Notice the gorgeous wildflowers growing beneath the grove of olive trees next to the winery. You are welcome to picnic here, reminiscent of some extremely romantic French scenes. If no one seems to be around, ring the bell by the door.

Bernard Ehlers built the wonderful stone winery in 1886, and it has since been inhabited by ghosts, Saintsbury (now in Carneros), Vichon (now in

EHLERS GROVE AND CARTLIDGE & BROWNE

France), and Conn Creek. Now it is one of the most people-friendly wineries around. Paul Moser and British partner Tony Cartlidge bought the building in 1993 and began to renovate, first naming their enterprise Stratford Winery, and later changing the name to fit its historical origins. Partly because of Tony's contacts, Ehlers exports loads of wine to England and Norway.

Be sure to stop at this highly personal and cozy winery. Many of Ehlers' wines have received ratings in the high 80s from all of the major critics.

 Fine points: No tasting fee. Featured wines: Ehlers Grove Sauvignon Blanc, Chardonnay, Dolcetto, Zinfandel, Cabernet Sauvignon, and Cartlidge & Browne Pinot Noir and Zinfandel. Owners: Paul Moser and Tony Cartlidge. Winemaker: Paul Moser. Cases: 80,000. Acres: buy from others.

❧ *Ehlers Grove and Cartlidge & Browne, 3222 Ehlers Lane, St. Helena 94574; phone (707) 963–3200 or (888) 234–5377. Open 11:00 A.M.–5:00 P.M. daily. Visa, MasterCard, and JCB. Wheelchair-accessible.*

Three miles north of Brava Terrace and half a mile north of Ehler's Grove is BALE GRIST MILL STATE HISTORIC PARK, a wonderful place to take kids of all ages. Follow signs up the little hill and park in the designated lot. Then you walk or roll down an asphalt path (no dogs, please) through thick, luxuriant green growth. You can hear the water in Mill Creek as soon as you get out of the car.

The mill was built in 1846 by Dr. E.T. Bale, Grantee, Carne Humana Rancho. When settlers arrived in the Napa Valley in the 1830s and 1840s, they planted corn and wheat to replace the oats they found growing wild. To convert these grains to usable flour, they needed a mill, which also became the local social center and gathering place. The miller was the local bigshot, someone to whom everyone spoke, a collector of gossip, and an adviser on banking and business.

A real character, Bale shot at Salvador Vallejo twice on a Sonoma street during an argument over Bale's nonpayment of a debt. Bale barely escaped lynching, went to jail, and partly due to untrue rumors that settlers were going to storm the jail and get him out, the governor ordered him released. Somewhat sobered by the experience, Bale settled down on his rancho and sold off some land to finance building this mill. A subsequent owner of the mill and land, Mrs. Sara Lyman, deeded it all to the Native Sons of the Golden West in 1923.

Now George Stratton is the miller, and he does his thing four times a day on the weekends at unspecified times. Sometimes he even makes bread on the wood stove in the granary. You can buy (and we did) all sorts of ground-here rye, whole wheat, corn meal, and pastry flour, and polenta by the half or whole pound, as well as an excellent historic cookbook ($5.00). You can also follow a 1.02-mile trail from Bale Mill State Historic Park to Bothe Napa Valley State Park. The Culinary Institute of America at Greystone in St. Helena brings students here to learn the elementary process of making flour and bread.

꙳ *Bale Grist Mill State Historic Park, 3369 Highway 29, St. Helena 94574; phone (707) 942–4575. Open 10:00 A.M.–5:00 P.M. daily. Admission fee: $2.00 adults, $1.00 children, which is also good to get into Bothe Napa Valley State Park up the road and state historic buildings on Sonoma Plaza the same day. Wheelchair-accessible on paths to the park. The historic mill is not wheelchair-accessible.*

BALE MILL PINE FURNITURE on your left (west) going north is in a two story old white structure that was actually an inn, but feels more like a whore house with little rooms upstairs, escape routes, and creaky floors. Here you will find fabulous framed and large French posters, pine furniture made locally,

---

OLD BALE MILL CHEESE SPOON BREAD
from Bale Grist Mill State Historic Park

You can purchase a whole booklet of recipes from Bale Grist Mill State Historic Park, but we include here one of the miller's recipes that is not in that cookbook.

INGREDIENTS:

> 2 cups milk or buttermilk (buttermilk makes it even better)
> 2 Tbs butter
> 1 ½ cup cornmeal
> 2 eggs, separated
> 1 ½ cups grated cheddar cheese
> ½ tsp salt

PREPARATION:

Preheat oven to 375° F. Grease baking dish. Bring milk to just below boiling. Add butter. Gradually stir in cornmeal. Cook over medium heat, stirring constantly 2 minutes or until thick. Remove from heat, stir in egg yolks, cheese and salt. Beat egg whites until stiff. Fold into mix.

Place dish in oven and bake 35 minutes.

---

wrought iron, iron canopy beds upstairs, and the world's best straw sun hats. Owner Tom Scheibal also has Tivoli on the north end of St. Helena proper, and Dottie Richolson is design consultant and elegant hostess. Be sure to stop in.

🍇 *Bale Mill Pine Furniture (also known as Bale Mill Classic Country Furniture), 3431 St. Helena Highway North, St. Helena 94574; phone (707) 963–4595, fax (707) 963–4128. MasterCard and Visa. Not wheelchair-accessible.*

BOTHE NAPA VALLEY STATE PARK'S entrance is just a mile north of Bale Mill, and you can walk between the two parks on a trail. Bothe is nearly 2,000 acres of lush laurel, madrone, and oak trees that afford quiet campsites and non-vineyard views from the top of Coyote Peak. You can swim in the natural spring pool ($3.00) near the Visitor Center or ride horseback with Napa Valley Trail Rides. Be sure to visit the Native American Plant Garden, Wappo People next to the Visitor Center. Enjoy Redwood Trail along Ritchey Creek Canyon and picnics under the towering Douglas firs.

🍇 *Bothe Napa Valley State Park, 3801 St. Helena Highway North, Calistoga 94515; phone (707) 942–4575. Open 8:00 A.M.–sunset. Admission fee: $5.00 per vehicle, $4.00 senior's car or $2.00 per adult and $1.00 per child. Parts of the park are wheelchair-accessible.*

Practically across the road is Larmead Lane, which leads to HANNS KORNELL CHAMPAGNE CELLARS, one Marilyn Monroe's wine country hangouts. It was originally Larkmead Cellars from 1884–1938, when Hanns Kornell bought it. In the meantime, Treasury Department villains came in with sledge hammers during Prohibition and destroyed the wine tanks, sending a "river of red" wine flowing down the road. It is now owned by the Kornell family, grape-grower Richard Frank, and Koerner Rombauer of Rombauer Vineyards. Rombauer brings their crushing pad to this partnership, Richard Frank is president of the Academy of Television Arts and Sciences, and Kornell brings champagne making experience.

Marilyn Monroe was a very close friend of Hanns Kornell. When she used to visit the Calistoga baths when hubby Joe DiMaggio was off playing baseball, she would plant herself on a couch in what is now the outer tasting room and spend the afternoon sipping champagne and listening to Kornell's stories. Hence, the life-size portrait and Andy Warhol-esque series over the reserve wine bar in the back room.

 Fine points: Featured wines: Brut, Blanc de Blancs, Blanc de Noirs, and Extra Dry. Owners: Richard Frank, Koerner Rombauer, and the Kornell family. General manager: Koerner Rombauer. Cases: 10,000.

HANNS KORNELL TASTING ROOM ENTRANCE

❧ Hanns Kornell Champagne Cellars, 1091 Larkmead Lane, Calistoga 94515; phone (707) 942–0859 or (800) 574–WINE, fax (707) 942–0657. Open 10:00 A.M.–4:30 P.M. daily. Visa, MasterCard, and American Express. Tours are wheelchair-accessible, but the historic tasting room is not. The staff, however, is happy to help anyone needing assistance.

To visit prized SCHRAMSBERG VINEYARDS you must make an appointment ahead of time, according to Napa County regulations. It is well worth making the call ahead of time to experience its highly regarded sparkling wines. Turn left (west) off Highway 29 at Peterson Drive and wander through lush woods, turning onto Schramsberg Road and taking care around curves for about a mile, and watching for deer. Schramsberg's Blanc de Blancs was the first non-French champagne served in The White House.

German immigrants Annie and Jacob Schram founded the winery in 1862 as the first winery on the hillsides of the Napa Valley. Chinese laborers cleared the scrub oak and replaced them with vineyards, along with a network of two miles of tunnels and caves in the soft volcanic rock.

The Schrams built the large Victorian house as they prospered, and hosted Robert Louis Stevenson here in 1880. He later devoted a whole chapter to Schramsberg in his *Silverado Squatters.* The entire 200-acre Schram estate became a California Historical Landmark in 1957. Until his death in 1998, owner Jack Davies and his wife Jamie Davies dedicated themselves and Schramsberg to drawing on the best of the past to create premier sparkling wines in the *methode champenoise*. Jamie continues that tradition today.

As you arrive at the sloped parking lot, you are greeted by handsome and huge Dalmatian and Irish Setter dogs, who lazily get up to welcome you to their home. The cozy tasting room is to the left of the parking lot, just beyond the elegant little pond with its statue of a frog wearing a tuxedo and holding a champagne bottle and glass and floating lilies. Plan a little time to look at the fascinating photos and letters on the walls, and enjoy the high quality of shirts, ice buckets, hats, champagne stoppers, and even a flashlight and a copy of Stevenson's *Silverado Squatters* ($6.00).

Schramsberg certainly takes the sweepstakes for prestigious pourings of their wines, including dinners at The White House to Presidents Reagan and Bush, for Queen Noor of Jordan, for Princess Grace of Monaco (Grace Kelly), for Prince Charles and the late Princess Diana, for Mikhail Gorbachev, for President Richard Nixon and Chou En Lai, and at the North Pole.

Fine points: Tasting fee: $7.50 allows you to try three current releases. Featured wines: Blanc de Blancs, Blanc de Noirs, Brut Rosé, Cremant, J. Schram. Owner: Jamie Davies. Winemaker: Mike Reynolds. Cases: 40,000. Acres: 200.

SCHRAMSBERG POND AND TASTING ROOM ENTRANCE

Schramsberg Vineyards, 1400 Schramsberg Road, Calistoga 94515; phone (707) 942–4558, fax (707) 942–5943, e-mail schramsbrg@aol.com. Open 10:00 A.M.–4:00 P.M. daily by appointment only. Visa, MasterCard, and American Express. Wheelchair-accessible.

Go back to Highway 29 and turn left (north) to go to Sterling and STONEGATE WINERY, until recently one of the few small family wineries remaining in Napa Valley. The Spaulding family developed and ran Stonegate (notice the stone gate over the entry path) for more than 25 years and recently sold the winery (but kept the vineyard) to John Merritt (Bandiera) and the California Wine Company.

Teensy and far less publicized than its glamorous neighbors Sterling and Clos Pegase, Stonegate concentrates on wines made from grapes best grown on hillsides, which happen to be cluttered with stones. First they wanted to call it Stonewall, but it was Nixon time and they decided wisely on Stonegate for a name. Stonegate offers interesting wines in a very informal atmosphere.

 Fine points: Tasting fee: none weekdays, $1.50 for the glass on weekends. Featured wines: Chardonnay, Sauvignon Blanc from the Spaulding's vineyard around the winery, Cabernet Sauvignon, Merlot. Owners: California Wine Company. Winemaker: Andrew Schweiger. Cases: 15,000. Acres: 225.

Stonegate Winery, 1183 Dunaweal Lane, Calistoga 94515; phone (707) 942–6500. Open 10:00 A.M.–4:30 P.M. Visa, MasterCard, and American Express. Wheelchair-accessible.

The enormous white Moorish looking structure you see on a hill to the east of Highway 29 is STERLING VINEYARDS, a remarkably striking structure built in 1973. It is not a monastery, as many of us have grown up believing. To find your way there, turn right on Dunaweal Lane for .4 mile and turn right (south) at the white mausoleum-style arches. Even the divided driveway hints that something interesting is ahead.

Park in the parking lot and get in line to pay your tram fee ($6.00 adults). You cannot drive up to the winery, so you have to take the tram, except for handicapped visitors who can actually ride in a van. The Disney-esque experience again contributes to the mood.

Brace yourself for a spectacular view, relaxing tasting, and glorious balcony seating where servers bring the wine to you, truly unusual in this stand up to the bar and have a sip wine country. Take yourself on an excellent self-guided tour and enjoy the Three Palms Art Gallery. This is a must-stop experience like no other.

Peter Newton, an English paper broker, started the winery in 1964 and sold it to Coca-Cola in 1977, who later sold it to the Joseph E. Seagram & Sons group in 1983. Tremendous investment is obvious, but you can't miss the Old St. Dunstan's Church bells Newton brought to chime every half-hour to remind you of him and his English origins. This is one winery where you can also purchase film and Calistoga mineral water. Kids are served juices in the tasting room.

 Fine points: Tasting fee: included in $6.00 adult gondola fee, $3.00 children under 18. Featured wines: Chardonnay, Sauvignon Blanc, Semillon, Cabernet Sauvignon, Merlot. Owners: Joseph E. Seagram & Sons Chateau and Estate Wines. Winemaker: Rob Hunter. Cases: 360,000. Acres: 1,100.

Sterling Vineyards, 1111 Dunaweal Lane, Calistoga 94515; phone (707) 942-3344. Open 10:30 A.M.–4:30 P.M. daily. Visa, MasterCard, and American Express. Winery is wheelchair-accessible; tram gondola is not, and rest rooms at tram station are. A wheelchair-accessible van is available.

For a nearby wildly different art and wine experience, visit CLOS PEGASE across Dunaweal Lane and eastward from Sterling. You can also get to Clos Pegase easily by turning west from Silverado Trail.

Jan and Mitsuko Shrem's shrine to art and wine is a must-see on the Napa wine trail. Here several senses will be pleased. Just driving into the parking lot is a pleasure, so be alert to large abstract sculptures in the fields and vineyards surrounding the winery.

The whole place celebrates Pegasus, the winged horse who brought us art and wine by releasing the Spring of the Muses. Water flowing from the spring gave new life to the vines, inspiring the gift of poetry in those who drank the wine.

A native of Colombia with Jewish heritage, Shrem made his first fortune importing technical books to Japan and then translating and publishing them there. He hired famed Princeton architect Michael Graves to design his wine and art gallery in 1984 and acquired outstanding works including some by Dubuffet, Francis Bacon, Max Ernst, Tanguy, Miro, Kandinsky, Oscar Dominguez, Jacques Lipschitz, Matta, Auguste Herbin, and Appel. Many of the paintings in Shrem's collection, including his prized *Pegasus*, painted circa 1890 by French artist Redon, grace the winery and its wine labels.

Having broken out of a few accepted ruts himself, Shrem advocates that you break out of your wine rut and not allow yourself to be intimidated by wines or winemakers. Freeze good wine if you want to—Shrem does.

Fabulous sculptures greet you throughout the winery, including a sculpture at the end of the cave of Dionysus depicting his decision between wine and love.

ONE OF THE MANY FIRST IMPRESSIONS AT CLOS PEGASE

If you're really interested in art and wine, there's a free presentation on 4,000 years of art the third Saturday of every month at 11:00 A.M. Don't be so distracted by the art that you miss the fine wines, and they are.

 Fine points: Tasting fee: $2.00–$2.50. Featured wines: Chardonnay, Pinot Noir, Merlot, Cabernet Sauvignon, Claret, Hommage series blends. Owners: Jan and Mitsuko Shrem. Winemaker: Steven Rogstad. Cases: 40,000. Acres: 500.

Clos Pegase, 1060 Dunaweal Lane, Calistoga 94515; phone (707) 942–4981, fax (707) 942–4993, e-mail jishrem@aol.com. Open 10:30 A.M.–5:00 P.M. daily. Visa, MasterCard, and American Express. Wheelchair-accessible.

Let's head back west on Dunaweal Lane (turn right coming out of Clos Pegase and left out of Sterling) and turn right (north) on Highway 29 to Calistoga and some special wineries: Vigil Vineyards, Storybook Mountain, Chateau Montelena, Vincent Arroyo, and the Old Faithful Geyser.

As you drive into Calistoga, you can choose. You can pass the intersection of Highway 29 and Lincoln, Calistoga's main street, and continue northward as Highway 29 turns onto Lincoln, goes through Calistoga, and turns left (north) to Clear Lake. Highway 128 (straight ahead) takes us to the Petrified Forest,

MITSUKO'S LEG OF LAMB WITH VEGETABLE MEDLEY & LENTIL–RICE MIX

from Mitsuko Shrem, Clos Pegase

INGREDIENTS FOR LENTIL–RICE MIX:

3 cups rice	*1 cup lentils*
1 Tbs olive oil	*salt*

INGREDIENTS FOR LEG OF LAMB:

1-6 lb leg of lamb   *1 ½ cup chicken broth*

6 bay leaves   *olive oil*

6 garlic cloves, 4 cloves slivered   *salt and pepper*
and 2 cloves mashed

INGREDIENTS FOR VEGETABLE MEDLEY:

2 Spanish onions, large and chopped

3 lb potatoes; cut 2 lb in 1 ½ inch cubes, and 1 lb in ½ inch cubes

1 ½ lb carrots, cut lengthwise in 1 ½ inch strips

3–4 Tbs olive oil

2 pinches curry powder

chicken broth

4 pinches dried thyme

salt and pepper

PREPARATION:

Wash and soak lentils for 2 hours in water, then drain.

Preheat oven to 425° F.

Cut small slits in the leg of lamb and insert the 4 slivered garlic cloves. Mix the mashed cloves with 2–3 Tbs of olive oil and spread over meat with salt and pepper. Crush 3 bay leaves to cover bottom surface of the lamb. Place lamb in pan with fatty side up. Crush and sprinkle remaining bay leaves on the rest of the meat. Place lamb in hot oven for 15 minutes, then reduce heat to 350° F. Allow the lamb to cook for an additional 10 minutes per pound if you like it rare, 15 minutes for medium, and 20 minutes for well.

When the lamb has cooked to your liking, remove from oven and pour off excess fat. With a fork prick holes in lamb and pour chicken broth over it.

(Continued on next page)

Mitsuki's Leg of Lamb with Vegetable Medley & Lentil–Rice Mix (Continued)

Remove lamb to warm plate and cover with aluminum foil. Allow to rest for 20 minutes.

In rice cooker (or traditional) place rinsed rice and soaked lentils with olive oil and salt to taste. Fill with water to 4 cups and cook 15 minutes. Allow rice to rest an additional 15 minutes. Mix lentils and rice well before serving.

Meanwhile put roasting pan on stove top and deglaze meat drippings. Season to taste, optionally adding lemon juice, and strain into sauce boat.

Heat pressure cooker (wok or heavy pan) and stir fry onion and thyme in oil until translucent. Add additional vegetables and stir fry all, then add salt. Add broth to cover vegetables and cook for 15–20 minutes or until carrots are cooked. If liquid remains, reduce until almost dry. Mix so that small potato pieces crush to coat all the other vegetables.

Serves 12. Mitsuko says, "Dozo Meshiagate Kudasai—Please enjoy!" Serve with Clos Pegase 1995 Merlot.

Vigil Vineyards, and Tubbs Lane, where you will find Old Faithful Geyser and Chateau Montelena. If you take this route, you can easily continue .2 mile eastward to Highway 29 and turn right (south) back toward Vincent Arroyo Vineyards, Traulsen Vineyards, Calistoga, and the Silverado Trail. Or you can turn right (east) onto Lincoln Avenue at the flashing red light and enjoy downtown before continuing on to wineries and the Silverado Trail.

We will visit the wineries before strolling through town, taking you first to Vigil Vineyards, the farthest one north. At the flashing red light, continue straight ahead on Highway 128 instead of turning right (east) on Lincoln and Highway 29. You may want to stop .8 mile north of Lincoln at the Calistoga Pioneer Cemetery to learn a little local history.

If you want to take a four mile detour to the PETRIFIED FOREST, go ahead, following the signs west from Highway 128 one mile north of Lincoln. "Petrified Charlie" Evans happened upon a petrified tree stump while wandering with his cows and thus discovered the pertrified forest covered with volcanic ash. Now you can drive in, take a little tour of the important biggest and oldest trees, and visit the museum and store in the Ollie Bickee House for souvenirs

Petrified Forest, 4100 Petrified Forest Road, Calistoga 94515; phone (707)

942–6667. Admission fee $4.00 adults, $2.00 for kids 12–17, $1.00 for 4–11. Visa and MasterCard. Partially wheelchair-accessible.

In .8 mile north of Highway 128's intersection with Petrified Forest Road, you come to Tubbs Lane, with the light green Mitchell's Drive-In on the right (southeast corner). To get to Old Faithful Geyser and Chateau Montelena, turn right at Tubbs Lane. To get to VIGIL VINEYARDS, go another .7 mile northward on Highway 128 and turn right at the Vigil sign to the peach stucco and peach tile roof winery off in the near distance to the east of the road. Trumpet vines climb the trellis covering the tiled patio, and a young lemon tree looks pregnant with heavy lemons hanging. The small light tasting room feels like home.

Fluent in three languages, owner Jamie Pawlak graduated from Tulane in economics and is a California lawyer with the good fortune to have been born the grandson of the founder of Champion Spark Plugs, and has both Irish and Apache ancestors. Jamie has succeeded quickly in several careers.

Jamie started making wine in law school (of course), purchased and revitalized an abandoned fifty-year-old vineyard in 1989, and built his state-of-the-art winery in 1995. His Vigil Vineyards is a certified organic farm, in homage to the family's Apache respect for the land.

Enjoy free wine tastes and check out Sonoma food products such as Adamson's excellent chutneys and Koslowski Farms dressings.

 Fine points: Tasting fee: none. Featured wines: Terra Vin (Zinfandel and Carignane), Cabernet Sauvignon, Valiente, Zinfandel. Owner: Jamie Pawlak. Winemaker: Michael Loftus, Ph.D. Cases: 13,000. Acres: 10 and buy from others.

❧ *Vigil Vineyards, 3340 Highway 128, Calistoga 94515; phone (707) 942–2900, fax (707) 942–2902, e-mail vigilwine@aol.com. Open 10:30 A.M.–4:30 P.M. Visa, MasterCard, and American Express. Wheelchair-accessible.*

As you leave Vigil, turn left (south) on Highway 128, and then left (east) again at Mitchell's Drive-In, a light green grocery store, onto Tubbs Lane and head east to Old Faithful Geyser and Chateau Montelena.

OLD FAITHFUL GEYSER brings us a spectacle of nature every forty minutes right here on Tubbs Lane. Enter the parking lot and walk into the building to pay for your right to see the phenomenon. Now a private enterprise, free viewings are blocked by tall bamboo and pampas grass. This geyser is one of three legitimately called "Old Faithful;" the others are in New Zealand and Yellowstone National Park. This Old Faithful is also an official U.S. Weather Station.

Some parts of the year, somewhat unpredictably, the geyser spouts every ten minutes, varying by the weather, tides, earth stresses, and season. The water is always 350 degrees and shoots about 60 feet into the air. When the water erupts more frequently than every forty minutes, owner Olga Kolbek begins to be alert for earthquakes, since it has acted up before almost all of the major nearby earthquakes.

The little ticket and convenience store stocks film, postcards, drinks, microwave sandwiches, snacks, excellent brochures and information pamphlets in twenty-three languages, and lots of local lore and conversation from the family. You are welcome to bring picnics and use their tables near the geyser, just so you pay the admission price.

✤ *Old Faithful Geyser, 1299 Tubbs Lane, Calistoga 94515; phone (707) 942–6463. Open 9:00 A.M.–6:00 P.M. daily. Admission $6.00 adults, $5.00 seniors, $2.00 children 6–12. Visa and MasterCard. Wheelchair-accessible.*

As you leave Old Faithful, turn left (east) onto Tubbs Lane to CHATEAU MONTELENA, one of the Napa Valley's most majestic and respected wineries. It is an absolute must-stop on your personal wine tour. Six-tenths of a mile east of Old Faithful turn left (north) up Chateau Montelena's narrow paved driveway. Cyclists love the ride up here, but picnicking is by reservation only. The stone fountain rocks were cut out of the cliff now covered with moss, ivy, and ferns to the left of the winery entrance. To see the old chateau, go down the stairs to the right of the tasting room.

Along with Stag's Leap, Chateau Montelena is one of two Napa wineries to beat French Chardonnays in a blind Paris Wine Tasting. In 1976 Chateau Montelena's 1973 Chardonnay beat the best from Burgundy. Upon winning the tasting, owner Jim Barrett said, "Not bad for kids from the sticks." It was only his second vintage since resurrecting the winery, which had stopped bottling fifty years earlier.

Humor pervades this elegant establishment, including a life-sized chessboard painted on the barrel room floor, where players walk around to move their men. Three generations of Barretts work at every level of production, and the winery's brochure features Mary Breiner, who runs the office/business side of the place and hosts the staff for big deal sports events in "The Mary Dome," in front of her giant home television screen.

Alfred Tubbs began Chateau Montelena in 1882 by planting 254 acres of vines, built his chateau and by 1896 the winery was the seventh largest in the Napa Valley, out of how many is the question! The winery itself is carved into the north side of a hill, forming its own cave with walls three to twelve feet thick. In 1960 Chinese immigrant Yort Franks built a "moat" called Jade Lake around the winery and is now a beautiful fish and wildlife sanctuary inhabited by swans and geese and lucky picnickers. In 1972 James Barrett bought the

CHATEAU MONTELENA'S TASTING ROOM ENTRANCE

Chateau, brought in the latest winemaking equipment, and replanted the vineyard. You are welcome to explore the grounds and visit Jade Lake.

Be sure to indulge in this elegant experience. Robert M. Parker, Jr., in *The Wine Advocate*, said "This is a splendid winery at the top of its game."

Fine points: Tasting fee: $5.00. Featured wines: Chardonnay, Cabernet Sauvignon. Owners: James Barrett and family. Winemaker: Bo Barrett. Cases: 40,000. Acres: 120.

Chateau Montelena Winery, 1429 Tubbs Lane, Calistoga 94515; phone (707) 942–5105, fax (707) 942–4221, Web site www. montelena.com. Open 10:00 A.M.–4:00 P.M. daily. Visa, MasterCard, and American Express. Tasting room is wheelchair-accessible.

Now you can either return to Highway 128 the way you came and turn left on 128 to Lincoln Avenue and downtown Calistoga, or you can complete the winery loop by turning left (east) as you leave Chateau Montelena, go .2 mile to Highway 29, and turn right (south) toward Calistoga. In .4 mile you cross the 1902 Garnett Creek Bridge, and in another .5 mile turn right at Greenwood Avenue to VINCENT ARROYO WINERY. Turn right at their sign and go down the gravel driveway past the house to the beige barn winery. Notice the beautiful roses, lawns and picnic tables, all for your pleasure.

Vincent Arroyo is the owner's name, not the Spanish name of the Vincent Riverbed. Vince is a warm, earthy fellow who, fortunately, gave up life as a mechanical engineer in Silicon Valley to make wine here in the far north of the Napa Valley. He learned to make wine hands-on from his Spanish father, who was a home winemaker. Always accessible to tasters, Vince teaches visitors about wine and loves to talk with young couples who are just venturing into the wine field. The entire winery is in one little room, so visitors can learn a lot from the source.

Joy the black Labrador greets you and quietly dominates the whole scene. Having shown up on the Arroyo's doorstep in 1990 sick and starving, she now has her own wine label, Joy's Choice, and her own line of clothing (black shirts with white paws) available in the retail sales room. Vince says, "Joy sells more wine than anyone."

Vincent Arroyo wines are sold only here at the winery, so get them while you can. They host an annual open house featuring old vintage wines, food, and winemakers' dinners for $75. Be sure to get on their mailing list, because tickets usually sell out to their loyal fans within five days.

 Fine points: Featured wines: Chardonnay, Melange (red blend), Cabernet Sauvignon, Merlot, Zinfandel, Petite Syrah. Owner: Vincent Arroyo. Winemaker: Vincent Arroyo. Cases: 5,000. Acres: 65 (sell ⅔ to others).

VINCENT ARROYO AND JOY IN THE WINERY AND TASTING ROOM

❧ Vincent Arroyo Winery, 2361 Greenwood Avenue, Calistoga 94515; phone (707) 942–6995. Open 10:00 A.M.–4:30 P.M. daily. Visa, MasterCard, and American Express. Wheelchair-accessible.

To get to downtown Calistoga, go back out the Arroyo's driveway, turn left (east) on Greenwood Avenue, and then turn right on Highway 29, which becomes Lincoln Avenue in Calistoga. Or you can turn left and down the east side of Napa Valley on the Silverado Trail to many more wineries, Meadowood Club, and Auberge du Soleil.

CALISTOGA

Calistoga tops off the Napa Valley 75 miles from San Francisco. Founded over 130 years ago as a hot springs resort, Calistoga still feels like a small western town where you might expect to see horses tied at the sidewalk's edge and guys swaggering up to the saloon's swinging door. Calistoga generously provides a parking lot for residents and visitors that runs behind all the shops on the south side of Lincoln Avenue.

We begin our walking tour of Calistoga at the western end of Lincoln Avenue, where Highway 29 turns east and Highway 128 goes north. (*Note:* in downtown Calistoga Lincoln Avenue is Highway 29.) We will first take you up the south side of the street, and then back down the north side of Lincoln Avenue, with a one-block side track on Washington Street to Wappo Bar Bistro and the Sharpsteen Museum.

If you are coming from Chateau Montelena or Vincent Arroyo Winery, simply begin the walking tour by starting with the north side of Lincoln.

LINCOLN AVENUE, SOUTH SIDE

The first notable building you come to on your right is the venerable CALISTOGA INN AND RESTAURANT, whose dining room is everyone in town's favorite birthday celebration place, because "everyone knows and loves Rosie." Owner/chef/hotelier Rosie Dunsford is a member of the Calistoga City Council and hosts clusters of unofficial (of course) gatherings.

The 1882 hotel has 18 reasonably priced upstairs rooms ($49 midweek and $60 weekends) with shared baths, a restaurant, and "one small brewery," and its office is around the corner on Cedar Street, between window boxes draped with bright red geraniums.

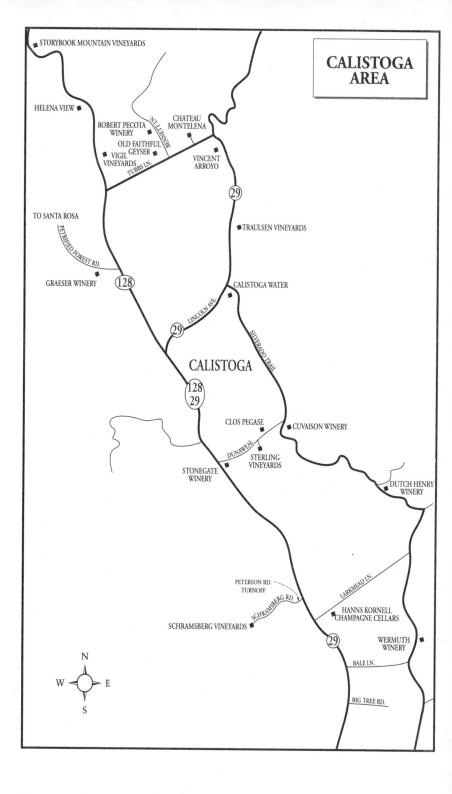

NAPA VALLEY BREWING
COMPANY PATIO AT THE
CALISTOGA INN

In the summer you can dine on the old, comfortable patio hanging over the river in front of the Napa Valley Brewing Company in the former pump house. The restaurant offers live music every night except Monday. Check out her collection of turkey platters rimming the dining room and dish towels hanging all over the place along with Christmas lights that "go outside in summer."

The reliables on the menu at lunch are the burgers with garlic fries ($8.50), the chicken livers sauteed with bacon and onions ($8.50), with lots of salads and vegetarian chili, curry, and sandwiches. Dinner is more expansive with a choice of chopped leaf or whole leaf Caesar salads, garlic crusted calamari ($7.25), peas and pasta ($7.50), a smokehouse plate, filet mignon ($17.50), 40-clove garlic chicken ($15.75), and Sonoma duck breast with leg confit ($16.25). Again, vegetarian specials are always on the menu.

Calistoga Inn and Restaurant, 1250 Lincoln Avenue, Calistoga 94515; phone (707) 942–4101. Open for lunch and dinner. Full bar. Visa, MasterCard, and American Express. Restaurant is wheelchair-accessible; the hotel is not.

As you progress eastward on Lincoln Avenue, the next interesting stop is the LEE YOUNGMAN GALLERIES, featuring national and Napa Valley artists, including Gene Zesch bronze sculpture, Neil Boyl, and Paul Youngman, local vineyard scenes, hand-made paper, Navajo turquoise and silver jewelry, Betty Carr and Howard Carr, Joe Beeler bronze sculpture, and early California paintings. Youngman also has a frame shop just beyond the auto parts store next door.

Lee Youngman Galleries, 1316 Lincoln Avenue, Calistoga 94515; phone (707) 942–0585. Open 10:00 A.M.–5:00 P.M. daily. Visa, MasterCard, Discover, and American Express. Wheelchair-accessible through the parking lot and back door.

Explore The Lane Mall shops to find Country Vines Clothing for casual clothes and body care, Trends Massage and Body Wraps, and you might even find Mother Dora East Indian Psychic in. We never have. Part of the building and a wonderfully funky café right at the front is the CAFFE SAN MARCO ESPRESSO COMPANY whose owners moved up from Sausalito to get away from it all. Locals stream in here for Graffeo coffee, Dreyers and Breyers ice creams, Peter Pan donuts, bran cakes, bagels, soups, salads, sandwiches, and quiche. The price is right.

❧ *Caffe San Marco Espresso Company, 1336 Lincoln Avenue, Calistoga 94515. Open 7:30 A.M.–8:00 P.M. or later. No credit cards. Wheelchair-accessible.*

Beyond Caffe San Marco, Silverado Pharmacy fills your emergency needs, including Beanie Babies, and A Volonte sells estate jewelry and antiques.

In this land of spas and mineral and mud baths, you will find many body care possibilities, including FREE TIME, which offers toys, lotions, soaps, walk-in massages and facials, and seasonal specials.

❧ *Free Time, 1348 Lincoln Avenue, Calistoga 94515; phone (707) 942–0210. Open 10:00 A.M.–6:00 P.M. Sunday–Thursday, till 9:00 P.M. Friday–Saturday. Visa and MasterCard. Wheelchair-accessible.*

Joel Guitron's very local TAQUERIA SANTA ROSA (SR Restaurant) has a spec-tacular chile relleño made from peppers roasted here, its beef and chicken dishes are made of hand-shredded meats, and they make their own mole sauce. Try the Parrillada for two cooked over charcoal in terra cotta and including chicken, carne asada, carnitas, roasted pork, and shrimp ($24.95 for two). McDougall style fat-free dishes are also available.

❧ *Taqueria Santa Rosa, 1350 Lincoln Avenue, Calistoga 94515; phone (707) 942–6468. Open 11:30 A.M. on. Visa, MasterCard, and American Express. Wheelchair-accessible.*

Next door is one of our favorites, and one voted Napa residents' favorites too, SOO YUAN CHINESE FOOD, serving Mandarin and Szechuan specialties. The owner had restaurants in Taiwan and Vallejo before moving here a few years ago. Their lunch at under $5.00 is a healthful bargain with no MSG, and includes a light soup, and several selections from their menu of fresh entrees. Portions are so large, two can almost share one lunch. Ironically, the narrow room and Chinese decor make us feel as if we are in a small restaurant in an Asian country. Napa residents drive for miles for the food, and Soo Yuan will deliver to your hotel room.

❧ *Soo Yuan Chinese Food, 1354 Lincoln Avenue, Calistoga 94515; phone (707) 942–9404. Open 11:00 A.M.–9:30 P.M. serving continuously. Beer and wine. Visa, MasterCard, American Express, and Discover. Wheelchair-accessible.*

Marjorie Brandon, Inc. unfortunately is open only by appointment for great collectibles. The dust on the Nixon photo in the window suggests she hasn't been here in a while.

BOSKOS RISTORANTE is definitely here, serving cafeteria style with windows open onto the sidewalk and a wheelchair ramp entry. A sign commands you to: ORDER WITH CASHIER BEFORE TAKING A SEAT. Choices include Bombay pasta salad, pizza from a wood burning oven in the back, a salad bar at $5.50 for a small plate and $7.50 for large, loads of fresh pastas, a roasted garlic chicken and other salads ($5.95 and $7.95), and their own garlic bread ($1.50–$3.00). A good informal place to go with the kids and still have some creative food. Lots of wines by the glass, or select a bottle from the rack across from the cashier and then pay for it at the register. Don't miss the historic photos in the hallway to the rest rooms.

*_Boskos Ristorante, 1364 Lincoln Avenue, Calistoga 94515; phone (707) 942–9088. Open 11:00 A.M.–10:00 P.M. daily. Beer and wine. Visa and MasterCard. Wheelchair-accessible._

Calistoga's newest restaurant is already one of our favorites. At the corner of Lincoln and Washington Streets, BRANNAN'S GRILL is named for Calistoga historical bigwig Sam Brannan, but it's owned by Ron Goldin and Mark Young, who also own Checkers up the street and in Santa Rosa. When Ron and Mark took on the building, which last housed the Silverado Restaurant and Tavern, they discovered huge beams beyond a false ceiling and created a meticulously crafted American Craftsman interior and a new terraced dining space with windows opening onto Lincoln Avenue. The nineteenth century Brunswick bar was discovered under layers of cigarette smoke and tar. Calistoga artist Carlo Marchiori created a tromp l'oeil mural as a backdrop for the dining room. Ron and Mark have also planted the Young–Goldin Truck Farm on their ranch to provide fresh produce for Brannan's year 'round.

Chef Greg Markey worked with Gary Danko to open Viognier, with Bill Gallaway and Julian Serrano at Masa's, and with Cindy Pawlcyn to hone his skills. Greg loves to mix regional specialties, as Brannan's menu reflects. You might try Senate bean soup, which is nearly right on, Gatton, Kentucky Country ham, Rhode Island clam fritters, New England Rum Tum Tiddy; Brannan's fried oyster Po-Boy with red chili remoulade is terrific. Entrees range from voodoo shrimp ($16.50) and open-faced wild mushroom ravioli ($12.50) to Yankee Pot Roast with dumplings ($13.95), Texas slow-smoked beef brisket ($15.95) and a whole selection of smoked and grilled meat specialties. Several excellent local wines are available by the glass at $6.00 or less. You can also enjoy an excellent bar menu and fabulous desserts at $5.50.

YANKEE POT ROAST WITH HERB DUMPLINGS
from Chef Greg Markey, Brannan's Grill

INGREDIENTS FOR THE POT ROAST:

4 lb flat iron roast (shoulder)	½ tsp cracked black peppercorns
salt and pepper to taste	6 cloves
1 Tbs canola oil	1 cup cranberries
2 cups apple cider	6 new potatoes
1 qt. beef stock or chicken stock	6 carrots
1 cup celery, diced medium	2 Tbs softened butter
1 cup onion, diced medium	2 Tbs flour
½ tsp ground allspice	¼ cup parsley, chopped
½ tsp ground ginger	¼ cup stone ground mustard

PREPARATION:

Season the flat iron roast with salt and pepper. In a hot cast iron pan add the canola oil and brow the roast on all sides. Remove the roast to a roasting pan and add the onion, celery, cranberries and spices after the meat is browned. Add the cider and the stock. Cover the roast and cook in a 300° F oven for 2 ½ hours. Remove the meat and strain the juice.

Cut the new potatoes in quarters, peel the carrots and cut into ½-inch slices. Brown the carrots and potatoes in a hot cast iron skillet with a little butter.

Add the vegetable to the meat and sauce and cook until tender, approximately 30 minutes. Place the juices in a sauce pot, knead the softened butter with the flour and add to the sauce; bring the sauce to a simmer until it's slightly thickened. Add half of the chopped parsley and the stone ground mustard.

INGREDIENTS FOR THE HERB DUMPLINGS:

2 cups flour	1 Tbs chives, sliced
4 tsp baking powder	½ tsp black pepper
1 tsp salt	½ tsp cayenne pepper
½ cup milk, heated	3 Tbs roasted garlic puree
1 Tbs parsley, chopped	

PREPARATION:

Heat the garlic with the milk. Combine the dry ingredients, add the herbs and spices. Stir in the warm milk just until the dough forms. Gently form the dumplings into 1-inch balls. Cook them in the simmering juices of the pot roast, or substitute any stock or broth. Serves 6–8.

To serve: Slice the pot roast and serve with plenty of sauce, vegetables and herb dumplings. Garnish the dish with chopped parsley.

❧ Brannan's Grill, *1374 Lincoln Avenue, Calistoga 94515; phone (707) 942–2233, fax (707) 942–2299. Open 11:30 A.M.–10:00 P.M. daily. Visa and MasterCard. Wheelchair-accessible.*

One of our secret favorites we almost hate to tell people about is the under-heralded ALL SEASONS CAFÉ AND WINE SHOP, also on Lincoln right across Washington from Brannan's. Located in the Del Mar Building, the All Seasons seems hidden right on Calistoga's prime corner. The interior feels like an old, unpretentious big city bistro, with black and white linoleum floors, wooden benches with restful cushions for your back, and views of the community's comings and goings. The lively paintings on the walls comes from I. Wolk Gallery in St. Helena. Feel free to have fun sitting at the counter.

Owned by Alex Dierkhising who also has Hydro Bar & Grill across the street, All Seasons has the mother of all wine lists in quality if not in quantity. Rosamond Mitchell, a former New Yorker who now loves to hike Napa trails, happily hosts and mothers customers just enough to steer you to the best of the day.

All Seasons' menu changes by seasons (natch), which are even broken down as far as "Almost Spring." You must try the warm spinach salad with café-smoked chicken, crumbled bacon and feta, which I praised beyond the ceiling to the server, who replied, "It's Robert Redford's favorite, too." Seems he was ensconced in a nearby home editing a movie, and is rumored to have bought a house near Calistoga. When in town, he comes in almost every night around nine and orders the warm spinach salad.

The "grilled lamb sandwich" is actually an elegant pile of sliced tender warm lamb laid ever so gently on a piece of thick rosemary toast, grilled onions, portobello mushrooms, red peppers, lamb jus and feta cheese ($8.50). There are always choices of pizzas, risottos and pastas, but try the fish of the day pan seared with North African sweet spices, grilled fresh rabbit with spring garlic mustard sauce ($16.50), and even the roast half chicken is sensational ($15.75). Desserts at $7.00 are just as superior as the rest of the menu. For all this we have Executive Chef John Coss and friends to thank.

What is truly unusual about All Seasons is its wine shop to the left at the back of the restaurant. This is the finest restaurant wine shop anywhere, as we discovered by looking for a few obscure bottles that happened to be here. The wine shop sponsors Wine Basics–A Down to Earth Tasting and Discussion that includes family-style All Seasons lunch and tasting.

❧ All Seasons Café and Wine Shop, *1400 Lincoln Avenue, Calistoga 94515; phone (707) 942–9111. Open lunch and dinner till 9:00 P.M. Beer and wine. Visa and MasterCard. Wheelchair-accessible.*

STEAMED CLAMS WITH PANCETTA, CHARDONNAY, APPLE JUICE, AND SAGE
from Executive Chef John Coss, All Seasons Café

INGREDIENTS:

3–4 lb Manila clams

cold water

1 Tbs cornmeal

¼ lb pancetta, diced

3 Tbs chopped shallots

1 cup Chardonnay

¾ cup apple juice, fresh if possible

¼ cup unsalted butter

2 Tbs fresh sage, chopped

2 Tbs parsley, chopped

PREPARATION:

Place clams in cold water and add cornmeal. Refrigerate for 1–2 hours. Drain and rinse.

Sauté pancetta in a large pot until almost crisp. Drain away half of the fat. Add shallots and sauté for 1 minute. Add clams, Chardonnay, and apple juice. Cover and cook over high heat until clams open, shaking pan occasionally. Add butter, chopped sage and chopped parsley. Serve immediately. Serves 4. Enjoy!

Note: Discard clams that don't open in cooking process.

Just east of All Seasons is the GOOD N AIRY ANGEL espresso bar featuring Son of Killer brownies, Beyond Killer brownies, and Killer Brownies, loads of candy, cool drinks and breakfast treats baked here daily.

✒ *Good N Airy Angel, 1408 Lincoln Avenue, Calistoga 94515; phone (707) 942–0714. Open 8:30 A.M.–6:00 P.M. daily. Wheelchair-accessible.*

The Surfwood Bar is exactly what it says for lots of locals, with good weekend music from the likes of Philip Claypool.

Beyond the Surfwood is CHECKERS PIZZA & PASTA restaurant, which is a great informal place for pizzas, wonderful salads, huge calzones, and vegetarian and carnivore sandwiches served on focaccia bread with soup or salad. Pizza add-ons of goat cheese, sun-dried tomatoes, and others are only $1.00. Yes, this Checkers is related to the one in Santa Rosa.

Enjoy the flying monsters hanging from the ceiling and the Pasta Piper airplane hanging over the wine bar. Lots of humor and color keeps you going while you wait for your food. Checkers is owned by the same great team as Brannan's, Mark Young and Ron Goldin.

Try the Nicoise tuna melt ($7.95), Roasted leg of lamb sandwich ($7.95), or a great Caesar salad. The braised lamb shanks are interesting with garlic mashed potatoes and braised chard ($14.95), and so are the butternut squash ravioli ($10.95).

✦❧ *Checkers Pizza & Pasta,* 1414 Lincoln Avenue, Calistoga 94515; phone *(707) 942–9300. Open 11:00 A.M.–10:00 P.M. daily. Beer and wine. Visa and MasterCard. Wheelchair-accessible.*

Next to Checkers, Calistoga Natural Foods sells sandwiches, wheat grass smoothies, health books, lotions, and vitamin supplements. Moreno's offers quickie burritos, tostadas, hot dogs and shaved ice, while the Smoke Shop and Liquor Store provides the obvious and emergency cork screws.

Don't give up. Keep walking to the old Calistoga Depot built in 1886 by Sam Brannan who brought the steam train and people to Calistoga. From 1912–1937 electric trains also came to Calistoga and terminated at what is currently the Calistoga Fire Station.

The Calistoga Depot was converted to historic exhibits and small specialty shops in 1976, and Greyhound Bus purchased the Napa InterUrban in 1936, took out the tracks and started running diesel-spouting buses up Napa Valley.

The station's original waiting room is now the Smokehouse Café, which you enter off the parking lot, featuring smoked meats and sausages including Acadian bacon and eggs, flat iron steak, Sacramento Delta crawfish cakes ($13.80), and Arkansas Slow Pig Plate ($12.95). Also look for Adell & Adela Yarn Shop, Treasures of Tibet, The Flower Lady, interesting Calistoga Wine Shop in a Central Pacific Coach, Le Artisan Gifts, and several other goodies.

If you're dying for a superb hamburger or chicken sandwich with fries and a shake, or a decent Philly Cheese Steak sandwich for only $3.95, or Aidell's fancy sausages, BIG DADDY'S DRIVE-IN is the place, just east of the Southern Pacific railroad cars next to the Calistoga Depot. All hamburgers are ⅓ lb and made from low fat Harris Ranch beef (which is wonderful if you don't mind feed lots), and the beer battered tempura onion rings are sensational and somehow seem less sinful than ones not called tempura. Watch for the blue and white striped awning. There are lots of flowers and umbrellas at picnic tables. Order at the window and wait for your number to be called on the loudspeaker.

BIG DADDY'S DRIVE-IN, CALISTOGA

✦❧ *Big Daddy's Drive-In, 1522 Lincoln Avenue, Calistoga 94515; phone (707) 942–9503. Open*

CALISTOGA GLIDERPORT

11:00 A.M.–6:00 P.M. daily (sometimes later in summer). No credit cards. Wheelchair-accessible.

You might also enjoy Tin Barn Antiques and Calistoga Gardens next to Nance's Hot Springs. Calistoga Gliders offers glider rides and truly majestic, breathtaking flights. (See *Beyond Wine Tasting,* page 235.)

LINCOLN AVENUE, NORTH SIDE

The **CALISTOGA COFFEE ROASTERY** coffee clinic is locals' and *The New York Times'* favorite coffee destination in Calistoga. Aussie Clive Richardson and Terry Rich roast thirty-five kinds of coffee beans, six of which are decaf and sell beans (whole or ground) as well as espresso drinks, poached eggs, sandwiches, bagels, and—surprise—Calistoga waters bottled right around the corner. They also make blends for the Culinary Institute of America's Wine Spectator Greystone Restaurant.

A sign on the wall quotes Clive, "Drink more coffee, you sleep when you are dead." New customers ask if there's a charge for the entertainment (Clive). In a cozy side room facing the street kids can sit at their own table and play with a plastic toy espresso machine. Enjoy the shaded deck on the east side of the "coffee clinic."

❧ *Calistoga Coffee Roastery, 1631 Lincoln Avenue, Calistoga 94515; phone (707) 942–5757 or (800) 879–5282. Open 6:30 A.M.–6:00 P.M. daily (closed Christmas) No credit cards. Wheelchair-accessible.*

Heading back west on Lincoln Avenue, Calistoga Photography will develop your film in one hour. Then we come to the wonderfully elegant MOUNT VIEW SPA and MOUNT VIEW HOTEL, home of Jan Birnbaum's Catahoula Restaurant & Saloon. In an attempt to bring the outside in, artists have painted ivy on the hotel's art deco lobby walls, surrounding thick, soft sofas and soothing music.

Once called the European Hotel, the Mount View was built in 1919 and now has a swimming pool and thirty-three rooms, suites and cottages with hot tubs, all extremely pleasant and ranging from $80–$250. Recently an impassioned guest shot out his room's windows and a few across the street.

❧ *Mount View Spa and Mount View Hotel, 1457 Lincoln Avenue, Calistoga 94515; phone (707) 942–6877. Visa, MasterCard, and American Express. Wheelchair-accessible.*

Jan Birnbaum's CATAHOULA RESTAURANT & SALOON features Jan's personal brand of southern-inspired American food in an ambience somewhere between Old West and Deep South. Named for the Catahoula hound dog, the official dog of Louisiana, and the only breed native to Louisiana, Jan says it is "a cross between a Spanish war dog and a Native American Red Wolf." Hence, all the photos, sculptures, and signage feature this spotted, webbed foot loyal guard and hunting dog.

Jan is, thankfully, from Baton Rouge, Louisiana and began his culinary apprenticeship under Chef Paul Prudhomme at K-Paul's Louisiana Kitchen. He left to become head chef at New York's Quilted Giraffe Restaurant, worked as sous chef at Denver's Rattlesnake Club, and as executive chef at San Francisco's five-star Campton Place Hotel Restaurant. He is one of the most widely praised chefs in America. It's a real treat to have his humor and creativity available in the wine country.

Try the bibb and arugula salad with teleme cheese, hot coppa and perfectly ripe pears ($7.50), seafood filé gumbo ($5.00 or $7.00), thick pizza pies, real Andouille sausage, pork Porterhouse steak with red eye gravy, soft sexy grits and pickled cabbage ($19.00), southern fried rabbit with dirty rice and collard greens ($17.00), cornmeal fried catfish with Mardi Gras slaw ($17.00), or roast chicken fricasse with white beans, artichokes and rosemary gremolata ($17.00).

Don't miss breakfast on the weekends for the usuals with a twist to crispy hominy cake with fried egg, Catahoula ham and sauce piquant ($9.00), Bubble Squeak with poached eggs and jalapeño gravy ($9.50), lots of eggs, sexy grits, and southern smoked meats. The fresh lemonade and gin fizzes are out of sight. ✢✧ *Catahoula Restaurant & Saloon, 1457 Lincoln Avenue, Calistoga 94515; phone (707) 942–2275. Open noon–2:30 P.M. and 5:30–10:00 P.M. Wednesday–Monday, breakfast 8:30–11:30 A.M. Saturday–Sunday. Full bar. Visa, MasterCard, and Discover. Wheelchair-accessible.*

South of Mount View and Catahoula are Calistoga Jewelers (every town has one), and North Star with T-shirts, bracelets and trinkets. Alex's Restaurant serves prime rib, steaks, liver, and pastas, specializing in Daiquiris and open for dinner only. The Evans Ceramics Studio Outlet branch sells ceramics at a discount.

L. FUNKE & SON DEPARTMENT STORE has been a great emporium of comfortable clothes serving Calistogans since 1904. It is located in two storefronts of the stone Fisher Building. Facing the building, the store on your right is for women, with New Options dresses, Blue Cactus, Caribe, and Jan Michaels designs. On the men's side Bruce Dill has Pendleton shirts, Levis, Dockers, Reyn Spooner, Paradise Found wild shirts, Back East, Johnny Cotton, and Tommy Bahama. ✢✧ *L. Funke & Son Department Store, 1417 Lincoln Avenue, Calistoga 94515; phone (707) 942–6235. Open 9:30 A.M.–6:00 P.M. Monday–Saturday, 11:00 A.M.–4:00 P.M. Sunday. Visa and MasterCard. Wheelchair-accessible.*

Right next to L. Funke is fun CAFÉ SARAFORNIA, a name made of the leftovers of Sam Brannan's combination of Saratoga and California to get Calistoga. Café Sarafornia is a very informal restaurant that opens onto the sidewalk and features champagne mimosas, oatbran pancakes, healthy omelets, special Five Alarm Chili, a good Thai chicken salad, a decent Caesar salad with anchovies extra, blue cheese pasta with grilled chicken, a Zinfandel burger, and Jalisco club sandwiches. The cheese blintzes are to die for. Baked muffins and breads are really special, as they come from owner Drake Dierkhising's Feed Store Again Bakery in Sonoma. (Drake is the brother of Alex, who owns Hydro Bar & Grill three doors down and All Seasons Café and Wine Shop across Lincoln Avenue.) Be prepared to wait in line on the sidewalk on weekends for breakfast. Locals love this place. ✢✧ *Café Sarafornia, 1413 Lincoln Avenue, Calistoga 94515; phone (707) 942–0555. Open breakfast, lunch, and dinner till closing. Beer and wine. Visa and MasterCard. Wheelchair-accessible.*

ONE SONG is a peaceful shop featuring fine gifts and natural wear such as a copper Greek fountain made to order for $1,500, Mishi natural clothing, P. Ching designs, earrings, and heavy candles that look like granite.

❧ *One Song*, *1407 Lincoln Avenue, Calistoga 94515; phone (707) 942–8959. Open 10:00 A.M.–6:00 P.M. daily winter; 9:30 A.M.–8:00 P.M. Monday–Thursday and Sunday, and till 9:00 P.M. Friday–Saturday summer. Visa, MasterCard, and American Express. Wheelchair-acessible.*

Alex Dierkhising's HYDRO BAR & GRILL at the corner of Lincoln and Washington is a locally popular pub and casual restaurant where you can enjoy hummus and veggies, steak sandwiches, burgers, and thick crust pizzas. Try the housemade spicy beer sausage with garlic aioli, the fabulously different lasagne with goat's milk cheese, tomatoes, spinach and roasted peppers. Hydro is handy because it serves a late night menu until 11:00 P.M. after everyone else has closed and its prices are reasonable from $4.95–$14.95. Those of you who need a beer break from all that wine can select from more than twenty microbrews. Hydro bills itself as "the place to party in Calistoga." So be warned. Breakfast too.

❧ *Hydro Bar & Grill*, *1403 Lincoln Avenue, Calistoga 94515; phone (707) 942–9777. Open 7:30 A.M.–closing. Full bar. Visa and MasterCard. Wheelchair-accessible.*

Take the time to walk west one block on Washington Street for a few minutes to the Wappo Bar Bistro and the Sharpsteen Museum. Don't miss Calistoga City Hall's honesty, with its decorative, band-aid approach.

The WAPPO BAR BISTRO is one of Calistoga's most interesting and widely publicized restaurants, with an exquisite patio-gathering place and a simple but elegant narrow dining room. Wappo is the anglicized version of Guapo, the name given by early Spanish speaking settlers to local American Indians.

Flavors come from Latin America, Africa, and the Mediterranean, so have on your adventure hat when you try Wappo. There are also plenty of standards with a twist, such as roasted pork sandwich with sweet and sour cabbage ($12) or grilled eggplant sandwich on focaccia with baked goat cheese ($10), but try the pan fried chicken livers on field greens salad with apple smoked bacon ($10.50) or the sensational Vatapa stew with scallops, shrimp, snapper, black beans and feta topped with peanut sauce and sauteed bananas ($12.50).

At dinner roasted vegetables with polenta and persillade ($12.50), Ugandan peanut chicken with roasted yams, banana and coconut ($15.50) is a taste trip, Hornada Ecuadoran braised pork with chile and beer with stuffed potato pancake and hominy ($15.75) is a marvelous experience, as is the osso bucco

CALISTOGA CITY HALL'S BAND-AID APPROACH

gremolata veal shanks with white wine and porcini mushroom sauce with risotto Milanese ($17.00). Caesar and local greens salads are also available for a little familiarity.

❧ *Wappo Bar Bistro, 1226B Washington Street, Calistoga 94515; phone (707) 942–4712, fax (707) 942–4741. Open 11:30 A.M.–2:30 P.M., 6:00 –9:30 P.M. Wednesday–Monday. Full bar. Visa, MasterCard, and American Express. Wheelchair-accessible.*

The City of Calistoga has done some very smart things. It moved one of Sam Brannan's cottages downtown and graciously allowed Bernice and Ben Sharpsteen, a major creator for Walt Disney, to build a museum of Calistoga and wine country history—the SHARPSTEEN MUSEUM—and threw in a senior center and police station to form an efficient and attractive small civic complex.

Ben Sharpsteen was an Academy Award winning animator, and producer and director for Walt Disney Studios, who retired with his wife to their ranch in Calistoga, which his grandmother had acquired in the 1800s. The ultimate fan of Sam Brannan, resort builder, promoter, pioneer, publisher, entrepreneur, soldier of fortune, and the person who brought the railroad to Calistoga and put it on the map, Sharpsteen dedicated his creative energies in "retirement" to designing and building the Sharpsteen Museum.

A side benefit to the public is that we get to view Sharpsteen's Academy Awards and loads of memorabilia from the early Disney studios, Sharpsteen's collections of California automobile license plates and hubcaps dating from wooden spoke carriages. In a well-planned compact space you will also see dioramas of Sam Brannan's original resort, which he called "The Saratoga of the Pacific," and which he built in 1859 when he bought a square mile of land containing the hot springs at the foot of Mount St. Helena, beginning the fad of "taking the waters in Calistoga." California + Saratoga = Calistoga. At one time his resort had a hotel and 13 cottages, a stable and racetrack, telegraph, bath house and pool, an observatory, a skating rink, riding trails, a distillery and winery, and a cooperage shop.

You can also learn from a Napa Valley Timeline, a beautifully restored stagecoach, a simulated barn interior with a collection of period farming tools, and then walk into the Brannan cottage to see what life was like, experience the simulated interior of a general store, kitchen, and blacksmith shop from the 1800s. The little shop at the entrance also stocks the best collection of Napa Valley history books and pamphlets available anywhere.

❧ *Sharpsteen Museum, 1311 Washington Street, Calistoga 94515; phone (707) 942–5911. Open 10:00 A.M.–4:00 P.M. daily summer, noon–4:00 P.M. daily winter. Admission fee: donation. No credit cards. Wheelchair-accessible.*

Walk back the short block to Lincoln Avenue and turn right (west) to continue your exploration of Calistoga's shops. Bella Tootsie sells Bass, Sam & Libby and kids shoes, sunglasses and rain boots in what was a glorious bank building. Nature Etc. purveys its educational nature toys and books as it does in Sonoma and St. Helena. The Candy Cellar sells not-made-here salt water taffy, Jelly Bellies and fudge from barrels, and Mr. Moon's offers a good kids' stop, or a stop for good kids with Beanie Babies, souvenirs, shirts, and body lotions.

For a little local color, you might want to follow the in-ground train tracks and saunter back to SUSIE'S BAR, truly a working men's and women's bar with "no beer on draught" and Napa Fairgrounds (in Calistoga) Sprint Car Races posters and fans. Pool tables and pinball machines complete the picture. The old tracks used to bring flour bins from the street back to the ovens when Susie's was a bakery fifty years and more ago.

❧ *Susie's Bar, 1365 Lincoln Avenue, Calistoga 94515; phone (707) 942–6710. Open 9:00–2:00 A.M. Full bar. No credit cards. Wheelchair-accessible.*

Nicola's Delicatessen serves hot or cold deli sandwiches, low cost breakfast and hot dogs and chili if you order at the counter. Mostly local kids hang out here. The T-Shirt Shop is one of the best of those, and then, we come to a must-stop, Napa Valley Ovens, the pride and joy of Fred Halpert of Brava Terrace (see page 142). NAPA VALLEY OVENS supplies most of the better restaurants and Bed & breakfasts, and offers fabulous creative breads, focaccia, quiche, hot cross buns, ice cream, sundaes, and smoothies.

✦✬ *Napa Valley Ovens, 1352 Lincoln Avenue, Calistoga 94515; phone (707) 942–0777. Open 7:00 A.M.–3:00 P.M. Wednesday–Monday. No credit cards. Wheelchair-accessible.*

In a town where many visitors come to pamper themselves and indulge in their bodies, WEXFORD & WOODS excels in offering pamper vehicles such as skin care products, including a whole section of products for men, meditation candles, lavender, natural herbal soaps, Hawaiian floral bath bars, and colorful paper flowers.

✦✬ *Wexford & Woods, 1347 Lincoln Avenue, Calistoga 94515; phone (707) 942–9729. Open 10:00 A.M.–6:00 P.M. Sunday–Thursday, 10:00 A.M.–9:00 P.M. Friday–Saturday. Visa and MasterCard. Wheelchair-accessible.*

Up some narrow stairs between Wexford & Woods and the Calistoga Bookstore a wooden butler beckons you to Upstairs Enoteca, Margaux Singleton's Wine Shop, and Lone Dog Fine Art & Antiques.

We especially enjoy the CALISTOGA BOOKSTORE, where you find great vacation reading and travel material, as well as school and art supplies, crayons, pads, and mood music.

✦✬ *Calistoga Bookstore, 1343 Lincoln Avenue, Calistoga 94515; phone (707) 942–4123. Open 10:00 A.M.–6:00 P.M. Sunday–Thursday, 10:00 A.M.–9:00 P.M. Friday–Saturday. Visa, MasterCard, and American Express. Wheelchair-accessible.*

Heading west, next comes the Lincoln Avenue Spa, Tammy's New Leaf ladies' clothes, and an extraordinary local art gallery, THE ARTFUL EYE. We loved the blown glass, hand painted platters, Steven Dixon jewelry, salt and pepper chess sets, books, wearable art clothing, wild-looking home accessories, and hand-carved lamps. Don't miss it.

✦✬ *The Artful Eye, 1333A Lincoln Avenue, Calistoga 94515; phone (707) 942–4743. Open 10:00 A.M.–6:00 P.M. daily. Visa, MasterCard, and American Express. Wheelchair-accessible.*

As you walk across the little bridge opposite the Calistoga Inn, there's an interesting clothing store facing the creek with colorful clothes and flags luring you down the wooden deck to THE BIRD'S EYE, featuring women's wear "to escape the ordinary." Women will find mostly hand made natural fiber clothing including lean to generous sizes and one-of-a-kind Calistoga-made jewelry, casual vacation clothes to glitzy sequined evening wear, Japanese wedding kimonos, and autographed Parisian scarves.

❧ *The Bird's Eye, 1307 Lincoln Avenue, Calistoga 94515; phone (707) 942–6191. Open 9:00 A.M.–6:00 P.M. Monday–Thursday, 9:00 A.M.–8:00 P.M. Friday–Sunday. Visa, MasterCard, and Discover. Wheelchair-accessible.*

Just across Cedar Street is PACIFICO RESTAURANTE MEXICANO, a refreshingly popular local Mexican restaurant that's best known for its signature fish dishes, particularly the sea bass with melon salsa ($14.95), grilled fresh fish tacos served on grilled corn ($12.50), grilled snapper or prawns sauteed several ways, and shrimp and fish ceviche ($8.25). You will find Oaxacan cheeses, grilled chicken tacos, red snapper tacos ($7.95), and even tamales stuffed with mushrooms, roasted poblanos, tomatoes and tomato chile salsa ($6.75). And for the less adventurouss, Salvador Gomez cooks good hamburgers served with a Caesar salad ($4.50).

Weekend brunch is exceedingly popular and features everything from Mexican buttermilk pancakes with maple syrup ($3.50) and huevos rancheros ($6.95) to shredded beef and scrambled eggs ($7.95), chorizo con huevos ($7.50), and huevos Oaxaqueños, an open face omelette with chayote, pasilla chiles and Chihuahua cheese with rancheras potatoes and tortillas or wheat toast ($6.95). Not too plain old eggs with potatoes and toast and American omelettes are also available.

The rooms are wide open and decorated with primary colors, with lots of Mexican masks; a fountain cools on hot days. The margaritas and Fiesta Hour (4:40–6:00 P.M. Monday–Friday) are famously good in this up-to-date spot owned by John Seeger of Boskos Italian restaurant down Lincoln.

❧ *Pacifico Restaurante Mexicano, 1237 Lincoln Avneue, Calistoga 94515; phone (707) 942–4400. Open 11:00 A.M.–10:00 P.M. Monday–Friday, 10:00 A.M.–10:00 P.M. Saturday–Sunday. Full bar. Visa and MasterCard. Wheelchair-accessible.*

CHAPTER 4

THE SILVERADO TRAIL

*A*s you turn down the Silverado Trail from Calistoga's *Lincoln Avenue at the Trailhead Deli and Juice Bar, don't miss the old, overflowing water truck on a mound "announcing" the Calistoga Mineral Water Company. Luella Ackerman founded the company in 1916 and sold it to Enrichetta and Giuseppe Musante in 1920.*

Giuseppe had a soda fountain and candy store called The Railway Exchange, where he sold ice cream, phosphates, and other soda-fountain goodies. One day in 1920 he was drilling for a well at his Railway Exchange and tapped into a geyser that blew him off his scaffold and burned him so badly that he had to be hospitalized. Giuseppe had discovered the Calistoga geyser, and he soon began to sell the mineral water from the geyser in his fountain. In 1924 he set up a bottling line and began selling Calistoga Sparkling Mineral Water.

The company passed through many owners, and in 1971 a Pepsi Cola truck driver named Elwood Sprenger bought the company when it was in one of its sad shape phases. Soon thereafter Perrier started advertising the glories of mineral waters in the United States; Perrier bought the company from Sprenger in 1980. In 1991 the Nestlé Corporation bought the Perrier Group, and Calistoga Mineral Water is now the top-selling water in the western United States.

The old truck is as close as you can get to the plant, and there are no tastings or tours—just an interesting story.

The Silverado Trail vintners and resorts refer to themselves as being along "The Road Less Traveled" on "the quiet side" of the Napa Valley. And they are right! The Silverado Trail feels more like the Sonoma Valley than busy Napa Valley. The Trail feels less commercial, or at least less hustle-bustle, more rural, and more peaceful. Cyclists will enjoy the generous marked bike lanes on both sides of the road as well as the fewer cars and seemingly more polite drivers than on Highway 29. We love it.

Most of the attractions on the Silverado Trail are highly reputed wineries and resorts, so prepare to enjoy. All of the crossroads go all the way across Napa Valley to Highway 29.

Half a mile south of the Calistoga Mineral Water Company, you come to Dunaweal Lane to your right, taking you to Clos Pegase, Sterling, and Stonegate wineries.

Just 0.2 mile past Dunaweal Lane (1.8 miles from Silverado Trail and Lincoln Avenue in Calistoga), don't miss CUVAISON WINERY on your left (east) side. Park and enter the home-like white-stucco building with a tile roof and Dutch door. The large parking lot and lush lawns—and gardens with plenty of picnic tables—encourage visitors to stay a while.

Founded in 1969 by two Silicon Valley engineers, Thomas Parkhill and Thomas Cottrell, Cuvaison is now owned by one of Switzerland's wealthiest men, Thomas Schmidheiny of Holderbank (supposedly the world's largest cement company). Money and good taste show throughout. Schmidheiny wisely bought acreage in Carneros, and most of the winery's grapes come from his vineyards in that prime growing region straddling the Sonoma–Napa County line.

Fine points: Cuvaison's cozy and elegant tasting room features a wine bar and shop with excellent selections of silver jewelry and corkscrews, books, and shirts. Membership in Club Cuvaison brings extraordinary discounts. There is a winery tasting fee of

CUVAISON ON THE SILVERADO TRAIL

$4.00. Featured wines: Chardonnay, Pinot Noir, Merlot, Cabernet Sauvignon. Owner: Thomas Schmidheiny. Winemaker: John Thacher. Cases: 63,000. Acres: 400.

❧ Cuvaison Winery, 4550 Silverado Trail, Calistoga 94515; phone (707) 942–6266, fax (707) 942–5732, Web site www.cuvaison.com. Open 10:00 A.M.–5:00 P.M. daily. Visa, MasterCard, and American Express. Wheelchair-accessible.

As you leave Cuvaison, turn left onto the road very carefully and go south on the Silverado Trail, to DUTCH HENRY WINERY, a true family operation of Kendall Phelps and Scott Chafen. Dutch Henry is an almost two-story building, nestled against the hillside on the east side of the road.

A former administrator of San Francisco's late French Hospital (now Kaiser), Kendall Phelps says they had to make up a name for the winery because he's not related to either of the prominent Kendall or Phelps wine families. Pity.

The Phelps' golden retriever and black Lab greet you and beg for you to steal the slobbery tennis ball from them and give it a toss. Rumor has it that there's a $5.00 fee to play with the dogs. While there's a small tasting room at the northern end of the building, the real action is in the large winery room, where you may enjoy barrel tastings with one of the owners.

Fine points: Tours consist of standing in the middle of the tank room and spinning yourself around, hopefully with Kendall's accompanying words and wry humor. He gives barrel tastings during the week, especially in slow season. If you like the wine, buy it here because it's your only chance. No tasting fee. Featured wines. Chardonnay, Gamay Beaujolais, Sauvignon Blanc, Pinot Noir, Merlot, Rosé, Petite Syrah. Owners: Kendall Phelps, Les Chafen and Scott Chafen. Winemaker: Kendall Phelps. Cases: 4,000. Acres: 16 and buy locally.

❧ Dutch Henry Winery, 4310 Silverado Trail, Calistoga 94515; phone (707) 942–5771, fax (707) 942–5512. Dog friendly. Open 10:00 A.M.–4:30 P.M. daily except Tuesday. Visa, MasterCard, and American Express. Wheelchair-accessible.

As you leave Dutch Henry, turn left onto the road, again with great caution, since traffic from your left is just coming over a little hill and won't see you until the last minute. Gun it.

Larkmead Lane comes in to your right 0.5 mile south of Dutch Henry. It will take you west to Hanns Kornell Champagne Cellars (see page 147). For now continue another 0.7 mile to one of the two smallest wineries in the Napa Valley, WERMUTH WINERY.

When we visited Wermuth, owner/winemaker Ralph Wermuth came out to our car and apologized because there were so many cars (four) parked at his winery's entrance. His wife, Smitty, who designed their label and poster, had "a few of the ladies over to lunch today." Believe the sign that says IF I'M NOT HERE, HONK HORN, I'M AROUND.—RALPH.

A Canadian doctor with a few intriguing eccentricities and interests, Ralph uses an eighteenth-century wood basket press. He "can't stand automatic things" and likens his winemaking methods versus more modern ones to rowing across a pond instead of using a motorboat.

Wermuth's tiny tasting room has a slanting wood ceiling and windows facing west, yellow walls, a green cement floor, and a worn wooden counter—all resembling a sauna in the summertime. It's well worth a stop for this slightly eccentric and different winemaking experience. Ralph will gladly show you around with a little notice.

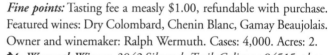

Fine points: Tasting fee a measly $1.00, refundable with purchase. Featured wines: Dry Colombard, Chenin Blanc, Gamay Beaujolais. Owner and winemaker: Ralph Wermuth. Cases: 4,000. Acres: 2.

➳ *Wermuth Winery, 3942 Silverado Trail, Calistoga 94515; phone (707) 942-5924. Open "loosely" 11:00 A.M.–5:00 P.M. daily. Visa and MasterCard. Wheelchair-accessible.*

Next you might like to visit ROMBAUER VINEYARDS, 1.6 miles south of Wermuth and 1.1 miles south of the intersection of Bale Lane, on the right (west) side of Silverado Trail. Turn right at Rombauer's sign. Be sure to stay to the right as you wind up the steep and beautiful driveway to Rombauer's pink cement-block building in a small forest—a 0.3-mile drive well worth the trip just to see the view, even if you aren't interested in Rombauer's limited production wines. Notice the "R" metal gate leading down a flowered path to the winery's caves.

Koerner Rombauer is a former Braniff International pilot who, with his wife Joan, bought this property in 1972. The grand-nephew of Irma Rombauer of *The Joy of Cooking* fame, Koerner spreads his "Joy of Wine" message through his wines, brochures, and T-shirts. The Rombauers' children, Koerner (K. R.) Rombauer III and Sheana, are both active in the winery. (Koerner Rombauer is now co-owner, with Richard Frank and the Kornell family, of Hanns Kornell Champagne Cellars. He also has an interest in Napa Cellars.)

Fine points: Rombauer's retail sales room is cozy, and Jim Kozier and Harvey Posert are among the most informative hosts in Napa Valley. The tasting fee is $5.00. Featured wines: Chardonnay, Cabernet Sauvignon, Merlot, Zinfandel, Cabernet Franc, Le

Meilleur du Chai ("The Best of the Cellar") Bordeaux blend. Owners: Koerner and Joan Rombauer. Winemaker: Gregory Graham. Cases and acres: Undefined.

❧ *Rombauer Vineyards, 3522 Silverado Trail, St. Helena 94574; phone (707) 963–5170, fax (707) 963–5752, Web site www.rombauervineyards.com. Open 10:00 A.M.–5:00 P.M. daily. Visa and MasterCard. The tasting room is wheelchair-accessible.*

As you leave Rombauer turn right (south) onto the Silverado Trail. On your left will be Chateau Boswell, a curious Elizabethan structure that is never open to the public.

Just 0.3 mile south of Rombauer's driveway and slightly past Chateau Boswell, turn right (west) into CASA NUESTRA WINERY. (This tasting room is open sporadically, due to the illness of owners Gene and Cody Kirkham's friend who hosts in the little yellow and white house.) In this sublime setting the winery blends in with the oak trees' new leaves and flowers, as if you are sitting in someone's picturesque yard.

Gene Kirkham is an amusing and committed civil-rights lawyer who mostly left the hustle and bustle in the mid-1970s for this once "remote" part of the Napa Valley. He works to keep the county from paving his gravel road. Go for the wines and to pick up the humorous and informative newsletter. After you read it once, you will want to be on their mailing list.

Fine points: There is a tasting fee of $2.00. Featured wines: Dry Chenin Blanc, Johannisberg Riesling, Cabernet Sauvignon, Cabernet Franc, Tinto, and Quixote blends. Owners: Gene and Cody Kirkham. Winemakers: Gene and Cody Kirkham. Cases: 1,000+. Acres: 20.

❧ *Casa Nuestra Winery, 3451 Silverado Trail, St. Helena 94574; phone (707) 963–5783. Open 11:00 A.M.–5:00 P.M. Friday–Sunday. Visa and MasterCard. Not wheelchair-accessible.*

A mile south of Casa Nuestra, DUCKHORN VINEYARDS is tucked away on the west side of the Silverado Trail, just before Lodi Lane. Only open for the sale of wine, Duckhorn's superb Merlot alone is worth many fans' whole trip to the Napa Valley, as are the Cabernets and the fun, bargain Decoy label line.

Fine points: Featured wines: Merlot, Cabernet Sauvignon. Owners: Margaret and Dan Duckhorn. Winemaker: Tom Rinaldi. Cases: 50,000. Acres: 200+.

❧ *Duckhorn Vineyards, 3027 Silverado Trail, St. Helena 94574; phone (707) 963–7108. Open for retail sales only 11:00 A.M.–4:00 P.M.*

Monday–Saturday. Tours available Saturday by appointment. Visa and MasterCard. Wheelchair-accessible.

As you leave Duckhorn, come back to the Silverado Trail and turn right (south). Cross the intersection with a stoplight at Deer Park Road, which to the east leads to Angwin. If you would like to try extremely fresh local fruit and vegetables, stop at the two little fair-weather produce stands on the western corners of the crossroads.

Along with Auberge du Soleil, just south of here, MEADOWOOD RESORT is one of the two most elegant places to stay in the Napa Valley, and even the whole of Northern California. To get there turn left (east) onto Howell Mountain Road and then left onto Meadowood Lane. The resort's excellent signage is extremely helpful to first time visitors. Follow the well-kept road past tennis courts, swimming pools, the golf course, and the perfectly manicured croquet courts. New England–style cottages and lodges dot the 250-acre wooded property, located at the foot of Howell Mountain. The resort's whole ambience feels like understated, elegant New England.

THE RESTAURANT AT MEADOWOOD and the Grill facing the golf course are legendary for the ultimate in sophisticated service, dining, and prices. The open beamed cathedral ceilings and bucolic views will enhance your dining experience. Most diners are guests at the resort, but the public is also welcome for Sunday brunch or dinner. Prix fixe dinner choices always include an excellent vegetarian dinner. Regulars usually indulge in the daily soufflé. Breakfast by the pool is especially exhilarating. The Grill is open for breakfast and lunch.

Fine points: All rooms have air conditioning, ceiling fans, private decks facing greenery, and every amenity imaginable, with the most expensive four-bedroom suites running about $2,000 per night. The spa and health facilities alone could keep you occupied for days.

🍇 *Meadowood Resort* and *The Restaurant at Meadowood, 900 Meadowood Lane, St. Helena 94574; phone (707) 963–3646 or (800) 458–8080. Visa, MasterCard, American Express, and Diners. Wheelchair-accessible, but call ahead for details.*

Don't miss JOSEPH PHELPS VINEYARDS, which is on the east side of the Silverado Trail. If you have visited Meadowood, turn left (south) carefully onto Silverado Trail and then turn left (east) onto Taplin Road and drive for 0.3 mile. If you didn't visit Meadowood, just go east on Taplin for 0.3 mile. Turn left through the wooden gate and take the paved road uphill for 0.5 mile. You have

MEADOWOOD RESORT

to make an advance appointment to tour and taste, but it's worth the effort to see the redwood barn and sophisticated wine production systems.

As you walk into the winery's courtyard, turn left to the barn and retail room. Take a whiff of the blooms from the wisteria covering the overhead trellis, which is made from century-old recycled bridge timbers. Just inside the door look to the left at the gorgeous Great Hall dining room. In good weather tastings are held out on the deck overlooking the Napa Valley; in bad weather, you get to taste in the dining room.

 Fine points: Knowledgeable and friendly hosts make the whole experience attractive. The entire place exudes Joseph Phelps' and his staff's love of what they are doing. Featured wines: Chardonnay, Sauvignon Blanc, Cabernet Sauvignon, Merlot; "Insignia" Bordeaux blends, "Vin du Mistral" Rhone Valley–style Syrah, Viognier, Grenach Rosé, Le Mistral, Muscat Marsanne. Owner: Joseph Phelps. Winemaker: Craig Williams. Cases: 100,000. Acres: 600.

🍇 *Joseph Phelps Vineyards, 200 Taplin Road, St. Helena 94574; phone (707) 963–2745 or (800) 707–5789, fax (707) 963–4831, e-mail jpvwines@aol.com, Web site www. jpvwines.com. Open for sales 9:00 A.M.–5:00 P.M., Monday–Saturday, 10:00 A.M.–4:00 P.M. Sunday. Tasting and tours by appointment. Visa, MasterCard, and American Express. Wheelchair-accessible.*

CHICKEN EN CROUTE
AND 1994 LOS CARNEROS CHARDONNAY
from Trey Blankenship, Joseph Phelps Vineyards

INGREDIENTS:

4 bone-in chicken breasts

4 oyster mushrooms

2 Roma tomatoes, sliced

4 sheets of Pepperidge Farm Frozen Puff Pastry

salt and pepper to taste

4 Red Bliss potatoes, diced

2 carrots, diced

2 sprigs fresh oregano, chopped

2 sprigs fresh tarragon, chopped

3 scallions, chopped

24 oz white wine

16 oz heavy cream

PREPARATION:

Allow the puff pastry to thaw. Place the four sheets on a baking sheet and then on each sheet place 1 of the mushrooms and a half of one tomato.

Season the chicken to taste. In a sauté pan cook the chicken breasts until almost completely done. Place one breast on each puff pastry. Fold in the corners of the puff pastry and seal so that no moisture will escape during baking. Bake the puff pastry as per instructions on the box.

While the chicken is in the oven, deglaze the chicken pan with white wine. Add the carrots and, on high heat, allow the wine and carrots to come to a boil. Add the fresh herbs and scallions. After 30 seconds, add the cream and potatoes. Cook on high for 2 minutes, stirring constantly. Turn the heat down to a simmer, and continue to reduce the sauce until the puff pastry is done. Distribute the sauce and vegetables over the chicken. Trey recommends serving in a large soup bowl. Serves 4.

MARIO PERELLI-MINETTI WINERY

Leaving Joseph Phelps, go back down Taplin Road to the Silverado Trail, turn left very carefully, and head south past Zinfandel Lane.

For a Wild West Italian experience, try **MARIO PERELLI-MINETTI WINERY**, whose sign on the Silverado Trail proclaims that it is AMERICAN OWNED, lest someone suspect otherwise because of the combination of Italian names. Turn right off the Silverado Trail at the sign and pass the family home, sometimes with kids riding their bikes through puddles, to the two-story stone building with a window sign announcing PARKING FOR ITALIANS ONLY. Patio tables and chairs invite you to the deck, and geraniums in window boxes set the cheerful tone.

The Perelli and Minetti families have been making wine since 1250 in Italy, and, as Jeff says, they have been making wine for 87 years in this country "without a computer, so who needs one?" Mario still delivers wine at age ninety. Notice the accordion and piano (go ahead!), and the Perelli-Minetti family tree of four generations in the United States (and proud of it) on the door.

Fine points: When the tasting room is full of tasters, this place almost sounds like an Old West bar. Manager Jeff Hansen is a comedian by nature and keeps everyone informed and laughing. He claims they make the "driest Chardonnay in the Napa Valley." The tasting fee of $2.50 is waived with purchase. Featured wines: All estate Chardonnay, Cabernet Sauvignon, William Harrison Cabernet Sauvignon, Red

Heritage, Cabernet Franc. Owner: Mario Perelli-Minetti. Winemaker: Bruce Bradley. Cases: 3,000. Acres: 9.

✒ *Mario Perelli-Minetti Winery, 1443 Silverado Trail, St. Helena 94574; phone (707) 963–8310, fax (707) 963–8762. Open 10:00 A.M.–5:00 P.M. daily. Visa and MasterCard. Wheelchair-accessible.*

When you leave the winery, turn right (south) onto Silverado Trail and continue for most of a mile to Rutherford Hill Road. Turn left (east) to visit Auberge du Soleil and Rutherford Hill Winery & Picnic Grounds.

Voted by *Gourmet* magazine readers in 1998 to be the ninth top hotel in the world, AUBERGE DU SOLEIL attracts the wealthy and famous from around the world. This is a modestly elegant resort where you can hide away in your cabin or mingle in the bar overlooking Napa Valley.

The atmosphere is Southern France/Mediterranean, and no wonder. Owner Claude Rouas, once of L'Etoile in San Francisco's Huntington Hotel and later of the successful Piatti Ristorante chain, hails from French Algeria. One brother, Maurice, co-owns Fleur de Lys in San Francisco; his other brother, Albert, created the late, great Le Beaujolais and now works at the Yountville (original) Piatti.

Check out the Auberge Boutique and the Gayle Houston Salon (by appointment). Tennis, swimming, massage, and full spa treatments are yours for the asking—and, of course, paying.

No detail is overlooked, and it's as if the staff spend all their time trying to anticipate new human or culinary needs. While meals here are expensive, Executive Chef Andrew Sutton offers both healthy and not so healthy foods. Meals are available morning, noon, and nighttime, too. Asterisks on the menu indicate vegetarian dishes. Two asterisks signal spa cuisine.

At breakfast Valencia orange juice is a mere $5.00, while the continental breakfast is $10.00. The All American, with eggs, meats, potatoes, and toast, is $16. The spa-cuisine half grapefruit and Quinoa crepe delivers only 274 calories and one gram of fat, for $15. Assorted meats and cheeses, "European style," is $15, while the Hillside Benedict is $17. Chocolate waffles, pancakes, lemon brioche French toast, huevos rancheros, lox and bagels, and Starbuck's coffee are also on the menu.

Lunch gets interesting, offering Seven Sparkling Sins—with osetra caviar, foie gras, Thai lobster, truffled quail egg, salmon, sturgeon, and oysters ($22–$37)—tempura ahi–salmon sashimi with sautéed shiitakes ($14.50), soups, Petaluma quail and baby-spinach salad ($12), steamed ginger cabbage–wrapped halibut ($26.50), or hazelnut-crusted rack of lamb ($36.50).

At dinner you can try the lobster sausage ($16.50), Hunan glazed boneless spareribs with red-cabbage kimchee ($13.50)—sooo good—and rosemary bacon–wrapped swordfish ($28.50). Or try the truffle, Swiss chard, and portobello–stuffed manicotti ($26.50) or horseradish grilled ribeye ($34). All desserts are spectacular and under $10.

❧ *Auberge du Soleil, 180 Rutherford Hill Road, Rutherford 94573; phone (707) 963–1211. Open for breakfast 7:00–11:00 A.M. daily; for lunch 11:30 A.M.–2:30 P.M. daily; for dinner 6:00–9:30 P.M. Monday–Friday, 5:30–9:30 P.M. Saturday–Sunday. Visa, MasterCard, American Express, and Diners. The restaurant is wheelchair-accessible, as well as some of the rooms in the resort.*

Just up the hill from Auberge du Soleil, enjoy RUTHERFORD HILL WINERY, set in what looks like a sophisticated, well-designed barn with rough wood walls. The windows frame perfect white clouds, and a century-old olive grove covers the hillside below to create the most romantic picnic grounds in Northern California. We once heard a young woman coming out the door of Rutherford Hill's tasting room remark, "I'm in heaven now" (to which her male companion responded, "You are?").

No wonder she felt so good. The tasting room is full of excellent wines (be sure to try the Merlot), Calistoga waters, iced tea, fudge and garlic sauces, chocolates, wine and food books, cigars, elegant leather cigar cases and cigar books, and marble ashtrays. Try to visit the largest man-made (Chinese labor) wine-aging caves in California, which go nearly a mile into the rock—the best part of Rutherford Hill's frequent tours.

Fine points: Founded by William P. Jaeger, Jr. Charles Carpy and Thomas Witter, Rutherford Hill was purchased in 1996 by the Terlato family of Chicago. The $4.00 tasting fee includes logo glass for regular wines; $6.00 for reserves. Featured wines: Chardonnay, Gewürztraminer, Pinot Noir, Sangiovese, Merlot, Cabernet Sauvignon, Zinfandel, Zinfandel Port. Owners: The Terlato Family. Winemakers: Kevin Robinson and Kent Barthman. Cases: 120,000. Acres: Undefined.

❧ *Rutherford Hill Winery, 200 Rutherford Hill Road, Rutherford 94573; phone (707) 963–7194 or (800) 726–5226, fax (707) 963–4231, e-mail rhw@nbn.com, Web site www.rutherfordhill.com. Open 10:00 A.M.–4:30 P.M. daily. Visa, MasterCard, American Express, and Discover. Wheelchair-accessible.*

In case you have been enjoying yourself just a little too much in the tasting room, drive carefully back down Rutherford Hill Road. Pay special caution to guests leaving Auberge du Soleil; they sometimes forget to look up the hill for oncoming cars.

Back down at the Silverado Trail, turn left (south) carefully and proceed to ROUND HILL VINEYARDS, which has one of the most interesting family stories in the Napa Valley. Turn into Roundhill's driveway and take the left side of the fork toward the retail-sales section. Check out the terracotta pot statues in the trees to the right of the parking lot.

A successful and popular buyer at Joseph Magnin's clothing stores in San Francisco, Virginia McInnis married Ernie Van Asperen and honeymooned at the Roundhill Resort in Jamaica. (Guess where the winery's name came from?)

A protégé of master marketeer and creative genius Cyril Magnin, Virginia now applies her substantial skills to developing Round Hill Vineyards and Van Asperen wines. With the help of industry veteran Mike Hardy, Virginia is following her vision to cease production and sale of Round Hill's generic wines, so there are some real bargains available here. Virginia is developing the Van Asperen Signature wines, with the first release in 1997 of its 400-case Cabernet Sauvignon, in addition to selling Round Hill and Rutherford Ranch wines.

Fine points: No wine tastings here. Featured wines: Van Asperen Chardonnay, Cabernet Sauvignon, Merlot, Zinfandel, Signature Reserve; Rutherford Ranch Chardonnay, Sauvignon Blanc, Cabernet Sauvignon; Round Hill Chardonnay, Sauvignon Blanc,

TERRACOTTA POT SCULPTURES WELCOME VISITORS TO
ROUNDHILL VINEYARDS

Cabernet Sauvignon, Merlot, White Zinfandel. Owners: Ernest and Virginia Van Asperen. Winemaker: Mark Swain. Cases: 400,000. Acres: 210.

🍇 *Round Hill Vineyards, 1680 Silverado Trail, St. Helena 94574; phone (707) 963–9503. Open 10:00 A.M.–4:30 P.M., sales only. Visa, MasterCard, American Express, and Discover. Wheelchair-accessible.*

If you are ready for a 10-mile round-trip detour adventure to the Rustridge Winery, Bed & Breakfast & Thoroughbred Home, with the Nichelini Winery thrown in, turn east up Conn Creek Road, which becomes Sage Canyon Road (Highway 128) opposite Villa Mt. Eden Winery.

If you want to continue on our tour without the long side trip, we offer a much shorter one here to Frog's Leap Winery and Caymus Vineyards on Conn Creek Road, which runs west along the side of Villa Mt. Eden Winery. Should you choose this alternative to the 10-mile trip, just skip the paragraphs below on Nichelini and Rustridge wineries.

If you want to go the long, exquisite, and winding way, after you pass Lake Hennessy on your left, take Chiles Valley Road (Pope Valley Road) northeastward and then turn back on Lower Chiles Road (Highway 128) to RUSTRIDGE RANCH & WINERY, BED & BREAKFAST, & THOROUGHBRED HOME. (The easier but less scenic way is to go "straight" up Sage Canyon to Highway 128 and turn left to Nichelini Winery and Rustridge.)

You truly feel as if you have arrived at someone's home when you drive into Rustridge's wandering, bumpy road, and you have! As you pass the home and B&B, tennis court and swimming pool—going slowly of necessity—hostess Alicia Perez will jump into her car and tail you as you follow the signs through the horse paddocks to the winery. This is a very personal winery with wine prizes and wines displayed on tables.

Winemaker Susan Meyer and her husband, thoroughbred racehorse jockey Jim Fresquez, combine their interests and talents most successfully on Susan's family ranch to raise racehorses and make good wine. Old horse equipment decorates the rails around the winery in this heavenly meadow high in the Chiles Valley. Picnics are encouraged on the lawns and at tables under a huge, shady oak tree. Try not to miss this experience!

 Fine points: The ranch has been breeding and training horses since the 1950s, with an occasional winner at Santa Anita. The winery has had several winners, too, especially its Cabernet Sauvignon. The tasting fee is $2.50. Featured wines: Chardonnay, Cabernet Sauvignon, Cabernet Zinfandel blend, Zinfandel, Late Harvest Riesling. Owners: Susan Meyer and Jim Fresquez. Winemaker: Susan Meyer. Cases: 2,000. Acres: 442 (50 in grapes).

꙳ **Rustridge Ranch & Winery, Bed & Breakfast,** *2910 Lower Chiles Valley Road, St. Helena 94574; phone (707) 965–2871 for winery, (707) 965–9353 for B&B, or (800) 788–0263, e-mail rustridg@napanet.net or rustridge@aol.com. Open 10:00 A.M.–4:00 P.M. daily. Visa, MasterCard, American Express, and Discover. Wheelchair-accessible.*

As you leave Rustridge, which you may not want to, turn left on Lower Chiles Valley Road to reach **NICHELINI WINERY**, one of the oldest in the Napa Valley. Founded in 1890, Nichelini is Bonded Winery No. 843, and the old Nichelini family home hangs over the edge of the hillside with the winery. Park in the gravel pullouts along the road (don't knock on the door of the white house—it's a private home). Walk down the steep driveway between the original dark, weathered wood winery and the house to the cellar level, where you will find a bar made of barrel wood and picnic tables on the grass near the creek. There's also a bocce-ball court for family and guests. Hello Italy!

 Fine points: Nichelini is famous for its Old Vine Zinfandel from eighty-year-old vines and is now owned by the grandchildren of Anton Nichelini, who say that Nichelini "is the oldest winery owned by the same family in the Napa Valley." No tasting fee. Featured wines: Old Vine Zinfandel, Cabernet Sauvignon, Merlot, Petite Syrah. Owners: Vic Wainwright, Greg Boeger, Joe Nichelini, and Toni Nicholini-Irwin. Winemaker: Greg Boeger. Cases: 3,000. Acres: 100.

꙳ **Nichelini Winery,** *2590 Sage Canyon Road, St. Helena 94574; phone (707) 963–0717. Open 10:00 A.M.–6:00 P.M. Sundays, holidays, and by appointment. Visa and MasterCard. Not wheelchair-accessible.*

After enjoying the Nichelini Winery, go back down to the Silverado Trail to resume your tour. Carefully cross the Silverado Trail to **VILLA MT. EDEN WINERY** and **CONN CREEK**, a newly remodeled, pink-stucco, state-of-the-art edifice and winery just south of the Conn Creek Road/Rutherford Cross Road.

(Or you can cross Silverado Trail to Conn Creek Road which becomes Rutherford Cross Road and visit Frog's Leap and Caymus, which are open by appointment.)

Villa Mt. Eden's origins date to the 1880s, when John Bateman planted the original eighty acres. Some of Bateman's original property was expanded by its next owner, George S. Meyer of Oakland, who began to make wine. California Wineries owned the No. 11 Bonded Winery in the early 1940s, and Jim and Ann McWilliams bought it in 1969 from Baron Constantine Ramsay. In 1995 Stimson Lane moved Villa Mt. Eden here, to sister winery Conn Creek's facility, and completed the ultimate renovation in 1998. Stimson Lane also

NICHELINI WINERY

planted 400 acres of vines in Monterey County and Napa Valley.

The elegant tasting room and winery, with the property lined by olive trees, looks across the Silverado Trail toward Auberge du Soleil, up the hill. You will find a pleasant tasting bar to the right, as you enter, and an attractive gift shop to the back. Colorful grapevine pottery and dishes rest on heavy wood furniture along with books and wining and dining accessories.

Fine points: Be sure to sample the Orange Muscat, only 4 percent alcohol and a great topping on ice cream or cheescake or dribbled into champagne. We enjoy just sipping it. No tasting fee. Featured wines: Villa Mt. Eden Pinot Blanc, Chardonnay, Pinot Noir, Zinfandel, Merlot, Cabernet Sauvignon, Orange Muscat; Conn Creek Winery Cabernet Sauvignon and Anthology Bordeaux–style blend. Owners: Stimson Lane (U.S. Tobacco). Winemakers: Mike McGrath for Villa Mt. Eden, David Moore for Conn Creek. Cases: 150,000 Villa Mt. Eden, 3,000 Conn Creek. Acres: 400 and buy from others.

🐌 *Villa Mt. Eden and Conn Creek, 8711 Silverado Trail, St. Helena 94574; phone (707) 944–2414, fax (707) 963–7840. Open 10:00 A.M.–4:00 P.M. daily. Visa, MasterCard, and American Express. Wheelchair-accessible.*

For a quick and delightful distraction, follow Conn Creek Road (also called Highway 128 and Rutherford Cross Road) down beside Villa Mt. Eden to the Napa Valley Grapevine Wreath Company, Frog's Leap, and Caymus wineries.

You come to brown-shingled NAPA VALLEY GRAPEVINE WREATH COMPANY on the first turn of Conn Creek Road off the Silverado Trail. The Wood family turns the wood of their Cabernet Sauvignon vines into other people's treasures, including baskets, hearts, crosses, wine holders, magic wands, and, by golly, wreaths. This is a wonderful recycling project, making the most of every part of the vine.

🐸 *Napa Valley Grapevine Wreath Company, 8901 Conn Creek Road (Highway 128), Rutherford 94573; phone (707) 963–8893, fax (707) 963–3325. Open 10:30 A.M.–5:30 P.M. Visa, MasterCard, and Discover. Wheelchair-accessible.*

Just around the bend west of the wreath company is FROG'S LEAP WINERY, in a big old barn built by C. T. Adamson in the late 1800s. Frog's Leap purposely doesn't have a sign on the road to make it a wee bit difficult for strangers to visit. Those in the know are welcomed. Just turn off Conn Creek Road when you see the biggest barn around.

Adamson made and sold bulk wine here, and for ninety-six years the building served as a farming center to store and dry cherries and prunes. In 1994 Frog's Leap moved here from the "frog farm" where they started by leaps and bounds.

The leaping frog on top of the winery's roof doubles as a weathervane. Park in the parking lot and walk to the back of the property on the left side of the barn (facing it) to the little Vineyard House retail room. If no one is there, venture through the raised vegetable and herb beds, and go past the lawn and barbecue to the office on the far side. The winery is only allowed to serve by appointment—so go right in and make one on the spot.

Fine points: Featured wines: Sauvignon Blanc, Chardonnay, Zinfandel, Merlot, Cabernet Sauvignon. Owners: Julie and John Williams. Winemaker: John Williams. Cases: 47,000. Acres: 40.

🐸 *Frog's Leap Winery, 8815 Conn Creek Road (Highway 128), Rutherford 94573; phone (707) 963–4704, e-mail Ribbitt@frogsleap.com. Open 10:00 A.M.–4:00 P.M. Monday–Friday, wine tasting by appointment. Visa, MasterCard, and American Express. Wheelchair-accessible.*

Farther down Conn Creek Road is CAYMUS VINEYARDS, the world-renowned producers of Special Selection Cabernet Sauvignons, which *Wine Spectator* rates in its "Top 10" as often as it does Chateau Margaux's. To get there drive south on Conn Creek from where the Rutherford Cross Road (Highway 128) intersects with it. Caymus is on the left (east) side of the street.

FROG'S LEAP WINERY'S LEAPING FROG
CHECKS WHICH WAY THE WIND BLOWS

To enter you must approach the gate, buzz, and inquire whether appointments are available. Or you can call ahead. Caymus schedules its appointments
carefully so that all guests can be treated privately. Wines are served in the
cream-colored dining room with brick floors to the right of the entrance.

The Charles Wagner family began farming here in 1906, and Chuck Wagner
was born and raised on the property, the son of Charlie and Lorna Wagner. The
Wagners named their winery in honor of the Caymus Indians. They show their
respect for the land by allowing their wines to develop primarily on their own.
Besides good wine you can purchase great logo hats ($13), shirts, corkscrews,
shirts, and the *Wine Spectator's Buying Guide and California Wine Book.*

Fine points: Featured wines: Special Selection Cabernet Sauvignon,
Conundrum dry white blend, Pinot Noir Blanc, Oeuil de Pedrille.
Owner and winemaker: Chuck Wagner. Cases: 54,000. Acres: 65.
❧ *Caymus Vineyards, 8700 Conn Creek Road, Rutherford 94573;
phone (707) 967–3010. Open 10:00 A.M.–4:30 P.M. daily, wine tasting by
appointment. Visa and MasterCard. Wheelchair-accessible.*

If you're famished, rush west on the Rutherford Cross Road to Rutherford
Grill at Highway 29. Otherwise, we recommend that you retrace your tracks

back to Silverado Trail by turning right when you leave Caymus and continuing back northeastward. When you get to the Silverado Trail, turn right (south) to continue.

Don't miss **MUMM NAPA VALLEY**, about a mile south of Villa Mt. Eden on the right (west) side of the Silverado Trail. Red flags hint that you have arrived at the winery, which was modeled after a turn-of-the-century barn with screened porches. Cyclists enjoy the bike rack. When you enter the winery, a gift shop is on the right. The tasting porch lies beyond, facing south and west and overlooking sumptuous vineyards and the Mayacamas Mountains. Sit at a table, and the champagne will be brought to you. Heaven!

The French champagne maker Mumm gave original Mumm Napa Valley winemaker Guy Deveaux, a native of Epernay in the heart of France's Champagne district, "carte blanche" to develop this estate sparkling wine works, and Mumm's vineyard along Highway 12 in Carneros between Sonoma and Napa is named for him. Joseph E. Seagram & Sons owns the French Mumm company as well as Mumm Napa Valley and Sterling Vineyards.

Mumm provides a whole cultural and educational experience, with tours through its demonstration vineyards and video monitors, as well as the fabulous Ansel Adams "The Story of a Winery" permanent photo exhibit in the Art Gallery. Adams's photo series resulted from his friendship with Otto E. Meyer, president of the wine division of Joseph E. Seagram & Sons.

The gift shop is a delight, with everything from books and maps to film and aspirin. The staff encourage individuality and fun. We found them to be the most friendly and helpful around.

 Fine points: Mumm Napa Valley's sparkling wines have been served at The White House to both France's Jacques Chirac and Britain's Tony Blair. Try to taste Mumm's four special still wines, Chardonnay, Pinot Noir, Rosé, and a dessert wine, which are only available here. The tasting fee of $3.50 will be applied to your purchase, or you can pay $7.50 for a sampler of three half-glasses. Featured wines: Blanc de Blancs, DVX, Brut Prestige, Blanc de Noirs, Chardonnay, Sparkling Pinot Noir, Pinot Noir, Rosé, dessert wine. Owners: Joseph E. Seagram & Sons. Winemakers: Greg Fowler, Senior Winemaker; Rob McNeil hands-on Winemaker. Cases: 200,000+. Acres: 1,200.

❧ *Mumm Napa Valley, 8445 Silverado Trail, Rutherford 94573; phone (707) 942–3434, fax (707) 942–3469. Open 10:30 A.M.–6:00 P.M. daily. Visa, MasterCard, American Express, and JCB. Wheelchair-accessible.*

When you leave Mumm turn right (south) onto the Silverado Trail. Watch carefully for **ZD WINES** just 0.3 mile south. ZD's tile roof is what you see from the road. Turn right (west) at the sign and park in the lot. Walk or roll along the path beside the winery by the lawns and tree roses in the patio to the large wood doors and the tasting room. White walls highlight the many soft-colored woods in the room and its Mexican-tile floor.

ZD was founded in the Carneros District in 1968 by aerospace engineers Norman de Leuze and Gino Zepponi, with $3,000 each. They obtained the first Sonoma County winery permit issued in twenty years and purchased grapes from Rene di Rosa to make wine "in Sonoma from grapes grown in the Carneros region of Napa." Ten years later they moved the winery here. Since Zepponi's tragic death in an automobile accident, the de Leuze family has developed ZD alone, with mother Rosa Lee and son Brett handling marketing. Robert serves as winemaker, and Julie is administrative director—and a fabulous cook.

We encourage you to visit this happy and modest atmosphere. Check out the tasteful and high-quality shirts and hats, ZD-logo cork pullers, and aprons.

Fine points: ZD provides small baskets of sliced bread to cleanse your palate between wines. The $5.00 tasting fee is refundable with purchase. ZD wines have been served at state dinners in The White House by three presidents. Featured wines: Chardonnay, Merlot, Cabernet Sauvignon, Pinot Noir. Owners: The de Leuze Family. Winemaker: Robert de Leuze. Cases: 30,000. Acres: 35.

ZD Wines, 8383 Silverado Trail, Napa 94558; phone (707) 963–5188, fax (707) 963–2640, e-mail info@zdwines.com, Web site www.zdwines.com. Open 10:00 A.M.–4:30 P.M. daily. Visa, MasterCard, and American Express. Wheelchair-accessible.

Almost 1 ½ miles south of ZD and on the left (east) side of Silverado Trail, you might want to visit **OAKVILLE RANCH WINERY**. Bob Miner, founder of the Oracle Corporation, and his wife Mary bought the intial acreage for this winery in 1989 and began making wines. In 1996 they purchased the adjacent property, the brand-new but never used Stratford Winery. After the recent death of Bob, the winery has been run by Mary and their nephew David Miner. The winery's Cabernets have received ratings of 90 or higher consistently since 1989.

Set slightly up the slope from the road, Oakville Ranch has a towering, vanilla façade. The pleasant tasting room (on the second floor—an elevator is available) is beige with light hardwood floors covered with oriental rugs. There is an excellent selection of books on a large dining table, and a glassed-in humidor to keep cigars at the perfect temperature. Walk down the hall toward the rest rooms and look through the windows to the barrel room with pinkish-beige walls. Relax on the Smith & Hawkin patio furniture and take in the spectacular Napa Valley view.

Oakville Ranch is in the process of removing 15,000 cubic feet of soil to create its caves. The mounds of dirt appear around the property and seem to be growing larger daily in front of the winery. The owner promises landscaping to come!

Fine points: The tasting fee is $3.00 for Oakville Cellars, $5.00 for estate wines. Featured wines: Chardonnay, Sauvignon Blanc, Pinot Noir, Zinfandel, Cabernet Sauvignon. Owner: Mary Miner. President: David Miner. Winemaker: Joe Cafaro is consulting winemaker. Cases: 4,500 estate wines. Acres: 80 of 300 in use.

❧ *Oakville Ranch Winery, 7850 Silverado Trail, Oakville 94562; phone (707) 944–9500, fax (707) 945–1280. Open 11:00 A.M.–6:00 P.M. Thursday–Sunday. Visa, MasterCard, and American Express. Wheelchair-accessible.*

GIRARD'S COPPER FOUNTAIN
AT ITS NEW ENTRANCE

Half a mile south of Oakville Ranch and on the other (west) side of Silverado Trail, stop in at **GIRARD WINERY**, a unique Napa Valley winery whose grape tonnage is 40 percent lower than the Napa Valley average, due to dry, rocky soil, pushing the fruit to more intensity and resulting in remarkable Chardonnay and Cabernet Sauvignon. Turn right onto the Oakville Cross Road to Girard's new entrance gate and follow the markers. For their first six years as vineyardists, the Girard family sold their grapes to Robert Mondavi. They built the winery here in 1980 and sold it in 1996 to Leslie Rudd, owner of Dean & DeLuca. Leslie has made major investments and improvements in the facility, including the new entrances to both the winery and the tasting room (notice the copper lily fountain), all new tanks, and an exquisitely peaceful tasting room with slate floors and heavy beams.

Fine points: A $5.00 tasting fee for five wines. Featured wines: Chardonnay, Chenin Blanc, Cabernet Sauvignon. Owner: Leslie Rudd. Winemakers: Mark Smith and David Ramey. Cases: 15,000. Acres: 44.

❧ *Girard Winery, 7717 Silverado Trail, Oakville 94562; phone (707) 944–8577, fax (707) 944–2823. Open 11:00 A.M.–4:30 P.M. daily. Visa, MasterCard, and American Express. Wheelchair-accessible.*

We highly recommend a slight detour west on Oakville Cross Road to Plumpjack, Groth, and the prized Silver Oak wineries.

The first of the three that you come to from the Silverado Trail is PLUMPJACK WINERY, a venture of San Francisco's Plumpjack Café owners and thirty-something movers and shakers: Plumpjack managing director and San Francisco supervisor Gavin Newsom and Bill and Gordon Getty.

Three-tenths of a mile from the Silverado Trail, turn north at the sign, take a sharp left in front of the winery building, and then turn right into Plumpjack's parking lot. Walk on rose-colored gravel through herb gardens and olive trees to the tasting room on the left of the tank house. Admire the shiny copper "chandelier" in the middle of the room.

Located in what used to be Jim and Ann McWilliams' Villa Mt. Eden Winery (now Stimson Lane's Villa Mt. Eden), Plumpjack has great picnic tables, Henry IV Shakespearean decor, and a youthful irreverence unusual in these parts. A fun stop.

Fine points: The logo shirts and hats are highest quality, as are the emerging wines. There's a $5.00 tasting fee. Featured wines: Chardonnay, Riesling, Petite Syrah, Cabernet Sauvignon. Owners: Gavin Newsom, Bill and Gordon Getty. Winemaker: Nils Venge. Cases: 6,000. Acres: 70.

❧ *Plumpjack Winery, 620 Oakville Cross Road, Oakville 94562; phone (707) 945–1220, fax (707) 944–0744, e-mail plumpjck@napanet.com. Open 10:00 A.M.–4:00 P.M. daily. Visa, MasterCard, and American Express. Gravel makes wheelchair-access difficult.*

Practically adjoining Plumpjack is GROTH VINEYARDS & WINERY, the baby of Judy and Dennis Groth, former CPA with Ernst Young & Co., former Executive Vice President of Atari and president of Atari's International Division, and one of the wine industry's truly nice guys. You can't miss the enormous rose-stucco Mission-style structure with its blue tile fountain and sweeping steps, designed by Napa architect Bob Gianelli.

When you enter the lovely cavernous rooms, the first thing you see is Suzanne Groth's vineyard painting called "Block One," which is on Groth's postcards and several other surfaces. Walk through the large dining room with its dramatic fireplace, Nino Barrucca serving platters and bowls, and seating for crowds. (Unfortunately, the dining room is used only for house and trade

GROTH VINEYARDS & WINERY'S IMPRESSIVE EDIFICE

events.) Through the arched windows you can see the barrel aging room. Walk out onto the patio to enjoy the view of vineyards to the north.

Judy and Dennis met in the first grade in Sunnyvale and are still together. They introduced the concept of winemakers getting equity (10 percent) in the winery instead of just being employees. With great success they hired Villa Mt. Eden's winemaker, Nils Venge, to create the wines, since they knew nothing about the process.

 Fine points: In 1988 Robert Parker called Groth "one of California's hottest wineries" and gave Groth's 1985 Cabernet Sauvignon a rare "perfect" score, immediately spiking the demand for Groth's 400 cases. The $3.00 tasting fee is refundable with purchase. Featured wines: Chardonnay, Sauvignon Blanc, Cabernet Sauvignon, Merlot. Owners: Dennis and Judy Groth. Winemaker: Michael Weis. Cases: 40,000. Acres: 165.

❧ *Groth Vineyards & Winery, 750 Oakville Cross Road, Oakville 94562; phone (707) 944–0290, fax (707) 944–8932. Open 10:00 A.M.–4:00 P.M. daily. Visa, MasterCard, and American Express. Wheelchair-accessible by entrance to left of stairs and elevator to second floor.*

Leaving Groth, turn right (west) onto Oakville Cross Road. Go about half a mile to the superb SILVER OAK WINERY. Turn left (south) into Silver Oak's double driveway, lined with olive trees and silver oaks, to what was once the Oakville Dairy. Silver Oak makes only Cabernet Sauvignon—and makes only the best Cabernet Sauvignon in the Napa Valley and possibly anywhere. Try to sneak a taste of its Meyer Family Port.

Partner, president, and winemaster Justin Meyer was once a teacher–coach member of the Christian Brothers religious order. He was "drafted" to work at Christian Brothers Winery instead of teaching. Experiencing every job in the winery, adding B.S. and M.S. degrees in viticulture and enology in addition to his M.S. in economics, Justin left the order after fifteen years to create his own winery, with the intent of making the best Cabernet in the world. He has. Having taught "Wine Appreciation" at Napa Valley College, he also wrote *Plain Talk about Wine*, a fun and user-friendly book about viticulture, enology, and wine appreciation. It is available in Silver Oak's tasting room.

Partner Raymond Duncan is an investor, Denver oilman, buffalo rancher, and co-owner of an art gallery. Ray and Justin began their endeavor in 1972 to plant and manage 750 acres that Ray owned in the Napa and Alexander Valleys. In 1975 they bought Franciscan Winery from bankruptcy. There they crushed and bottled Silver Oak's grapes from 1975 to 1981. They sold Franciscan to the Eckes Company of Germany in 1979.

SILVER OAK WINERY

So here they are in this elegant, stone monastery-looking winery. As you enter the dark tasting room, it might take your eyes a few moments to adjust from the sunlight outside. Tasters may sit on stone benches or upholstered black wrought-iron furniture.

Silver Oak also has a winery in Sonoma County's Alexander Valley in what was once the old Lyeth Winery facility. At both wineries Justin makes a masterful effort of creating a family among staff members. The results are readily apparent.

 Fine points: Be sure to look into the glassed-in Library Room, where Silver Oak's finest bottlings are stored. Sliding glass doors lead to the barrel and tank rooms, where the Cabernets are aged at least thirty months in American oak barrels. The tasting fee of $5.00 includes an elegant souvenir glass. Featured wines: Cabernet Sauvignon, Port. Owners: Justin Meyer and Raymond Duncan. Winemaker: Justin Meyer. Cases: 50,000. Acres: 220.

❧ *Silver Oak Winery, 915 Oakville Cross Road, Oakville 94562; phone (707) 944–8808, Web site www.SilverOak.com. Open 9:00 A.M.–4:00 P.M. Monday–Saturday. Visa and MasterCard. Wheelchair-accessible.*

As you leave Silver Oak, we suggest that you turn right (east) onto Oakville Cross Road and go back to the Silverado Trail. Turn right (south) onto Silverado Trail and turn left (east) to visit ROBERT SINSKEY VINEYARDS, up the hill to the left (east). Nestled in soft hills, the winery has ivy-covered stone walls, rose gardens, interesting half-circle benches, a half-circle fish pond (no coins, please), and great views. Enjoy the vegetable and herb gardens in the summer.

Robert Sinskey is a graduate of the Parsons School of Design in New York. He designed the winery and does all the graphics. His father, Dr. Robert Sinskey, was a partner in Acacia Winery in Carneros when the Chalone group bought it.

As you enter the cavernous tasting room and kitchen, hosts greet you as if you have just arrived in their home. Because Robert Sinskey believes so strongly in the importance of food and wine, he has a gorgeous professional kitchen right in the tasting room—and a house chef. You will see both a historic wood stove and ultra-modern ovens, wood-burning ovens, a television/video screen, a full range of professional pots and pans, and a magnificent view of Silverado Vineyards across the road.

Robert brings in restaurant chefs from all over the country to conduct cooking classes, including Michael Foley of Printer's Row in Chicago, Martin Oswald of Syzygy in Aspen, Chris and Eric from Blue Ribbon in New York, and Maria Helm of Plumpjack Café in San Francisco. Demonstration cooking classes cost $75 per person and include lunch paired with Robert Sinskey wines.

ROBERT SINSKEY VINEYARDS

Every year Robert Sinskey stages his fun Pinot Revival Show ("guaranteed to cure what ails you") so you and all can "hear the gospel according to Pinot," feast on "life sustaining creations," listen to "down home music," and "take The Pinot cure." It all takes place close to May 1 for $250 per person including six bottles of Carneros Pinot Noir. Get on the mailing list!

 Fine points: You can purchase the best olive oils and books here. The tasting fee of $5.00 includes a glass. Featured wines: Chardonnay, Pinot Noir, Merlot, Cabernet Sauvignon, Cabernet Franc, Zinfandel, Claret, Pinot Blanc. Owner: Robert Sinskey. Winemaker: Jeff Birnig. Chef: Andrew Turner. Cases: 31,000. Acres: 205.

Robert Sinskey Vineyards, 6320 Silverado Trail, Yountville 94558; phone (707) 944–9090 or (800) 869–2030. Open 10:00 A.M.–4:30 P.M. daily. Visa, MasterCard, and American Express. Wheelchair-accessible.

As you leave the winery, turn left (south) onto the Silverado Trail, and then turn right (west) on Yountville Cross Road, where you will find S. Anderson and Goosecross Cellars. (On your way south you will see Wine Cliff Cellars up the hill to the east, but it is not open to the public.) If you choose not to make this detour, just continue southward to Shafer and Silverado Vineyards.

Down the slight hill on Yountville Cross Road, and left into S. ANDERSON, a small family winery of great taste and flower-bedecked ambience. The exquisite lawns, rose-covered arbors, and gazebo with gravel patio made us want to move right in.

Owner Carol Anderson graduated from UC Davis's School of Viticulture and Enology and created S. Anderson Champagnes and Chardonnays. She still directs the winemaking. Her late husband Stanley supervised planting of the noble vinifera Chardonnay and Pinot Noir vineyards in the Stag's Leap and Carneros districts, as well as creation of the caves and winery. Son John oversees business and marketing, while his wife, Tracy, a graduate of the California Culinary Academy, is the winery's chef and chief entertainment organizer.

S. Anderson's caves hold 400,000 bottles of Champagne, Chardonnay, and Cabernet aging in the barrel. These are great places for candlelit parties and chamber-music concerts. The stone tasting room feels like a cave. Notice photographs of Stanley Anderson at the end of the bar.

 Fine points: Get on their mailing list for the terrific "S. Anderson News." There's a $5.00 tasting fee. Featured wines: Chardonnay, Brut Champagne, Blanc de Noirs, Rosé Champagne. Owner: Carol Anderson. Winemaker: David DeSante. Cases: 12,000. Acres: 120. *S. Anderson, 1473 Yountville Cross Road, Yountville 94599; phone (707) 944–8642 or (800) 4–BUBBLY, fax (707) 944–8020, Web site www.4bubbly.com. Open 10:00 A.M.–5:00 P.M. daily. Visa, MasterCard, and American Express. Wheelchair-accessible.*

As you leave S. Anderson, turn left onto Yountville Cross Road, and then turn right on State Lane to visit GOOSECROSS CELLARS, a fun, informal, and homey winery behind the old Gorsuch home. Goosecross is a rough translation of *Gorsuch,* an Old English name meaning "where the goose crosses the stream." Canadian geese cross the Napa Valley here in their migration north and south.

Two wooden geese in front of the house suggest that you go to the right and park beside the winery's tanks in back of the house. Ring the bell if you don't see anyone, and walk between the tanks to the tasting-room door, where Tyrone, a black Lab, greets visitors. The tasting room, gift shop, and winery are all one, which makes this stop especially fun.

Patt and Rey Gorsuch founded the winery and passed it on to their son and winemaker, Geoff, whose business partner is David Topper. As director of hospitality, Colleen Tatarian oversees the retail center as well as the popular "Wine Basics" classes.

LEMON TEA BREAD
from Carol Anderson, S. Anderson

INGREDIENTS FOR THE BREAD:

¾ cup milk	1 ½ tsp baking powder
1 Tbs lemon balm, finely chopped	¼ tsp salt
	6 Tbs butter, at room temperature
1 Tbs lemon thyme, finely chopped	1 cup sugar
	2 eggs, beaten
2 cups flour	1 Tbs lemon zest, grated

PREPARATION:

Set out butter to come to room temperature. Butter a 9x5x3-inch pan. Preheat oven to 325 F. Heat the milk with the chopped herbs and let steep until cool.

Mix the flour, baking powder, and salt together in a bowl. In another bowl, cream the butter and gradually beat in the sugar. Continue beating until light and fluffy. Beat in the eggs, one at a time. Beat in the lemon zest. Add the flour mixture alternately with the herbed milk. Mix until the batter is just blended.

Put the batter into the prepared pan. Bake for about 50 minutes, or until a toothpick inserted in the center comes out dry. Remove from the pan onto a wire rack that is set over a sheet of waxed paper. Pour the lemon glaze over the still-hot bread. Decorate with a few sprigs of lemon thyme.

INGREDIENTS FOR LEMON GLAZE:

juice of 2 lemons
powdered sugar

PREPARATION:

Put the lemon juice in a bowl and add the sugar, stirring until a thick, but still pourable, paste forms. Pour the glaze over the hot bread.

Fine points: You can purchase minor snacks such as Wisecrackers, cheese sticks, mustards, and olive oils. The tasting fee is $1.00 per wine per person. Goosecross never submits its wines to review by magazines or contests. Featured wines: Chardonnay, Cabernet Sauvignon. Owners: Geoff Gorsuch and David Topper. Winemaker: Geoff Gorsuch. Cases: 8,000. Acres: 10.5.

❧ *Goosecross Cellars, 1119 State Lane, Yountville 94599; phone (707) 944–1986 or (800) 276–9210, e-mail ct@napanet.net, Web site www.goose-cross.com. Open 10:00 A.M.–5:00 P.M. daily. Visa, MasterCard, and American Express. Wheelchair-accessible.*

Back to the Silverado Trail to a series of interesting and excellent wineries: Shafer, Silverado Vineyards, Pine Ridge Winery, Steltzner Vineyards, Stag's Leap Wine Cellars, Chimney Rock Winery, Clos du Val, and Signorello Vineyards.

Turn right (south) from Yountville Cross Road onto the Silverado Trail. To get to SHAFER VINEYARDS, turn left (east) at the Shafer sign and turn left again in 0.2 mile, keeping to the right side so that you will be on the upper part of the divided road. Continue for 1 mile, passing sensuous rolling hills, a valley, and vines circling knolls all around. You arrive at what looks like a two-story ranch home with a large oak tree in front. The working part of the winery is on your left. Just looking at the earth-colored stucco, stone, and natural wood relaxes visitors.

John Shafer left the publishing business in Chicago in 1972 and moved his family to this rocky, hilly vineyard in the Napa Valley. He discovered that what looked like lousy soil and water conditions turned out to stress vines and produce prized intense flavors in his wines. John's son Doug studied at UC Davis, graduating in enology and viticulture, and became Shafer winemaker in 1983. He was soon joined by Elias Fernandez as assistant winemaker. Now Elias is winemaker. Doug became president in 1994, when John became chairman of the board.

Dogs Jake, Rocky, and Charity form the welcoming committee. Be sure to collect the vast selections of printed information and recipes that Shafer makes available for free to visitors.

Fine points: Shafer wines have been served at The White House to Queen Elizabeth II and Prince Philip of Britain and to President Hosni Mubarak of Egypt. Shafer's Cabernet Sauvignon outranked those of Chateau Margaux, Chateau Latour, and Chateau Palmer at a blind tasting in Germany in 1993. No tasting fee. Featured wines: Chardonnay, Merlot, Firebreak, Cabernet Sauvignon, Sangiovese, Port. Owner and CEO: John Shafer. President: Doug Shafer. Winemaker: Elias Fernandez. Cases: 25,000. Acres: 500.

❧ *Shafer Vineyards, 6154 Silverado Trail, Napa 94558; phone (707) 944–2877, fax (707) 944–9454. Open 9:00 A.M.–5:00 P.M Monday–Friday, 9:00 A.M.–4:00 P.M. weekends, by appointment. Visa and MasterCard. Wheelchair-accessible by driving up behind the winery to the back.*

CHICKEN IN PHYLLO SALAD
from Shafer Vineyards

INGREDIENTS:

1 lb (4) chicken breasts, boneless and skinless	½ lb mixed greens
8 Tbs Balsamic vinegar	1 cup seedless white grapes, quartered
3 oz feta cheese	½ cup extra virgin olive oil
3 oz pine nuts, toasted	1 Tbs shallots, finely chopped
1 tsp fresh thyme	¼ tsp salt
2 oz unsalted butter	⅛ tsp pepper
5 sheets phyllo dough	

PREPARATION:

Heat 1 Tbs of oil in a pan. Brown both sides of seasoned chicken breasts. Add 4 Tbs of balsamic vinegar to deglaze and finish chicken in 350° F oven for about 15 minutes. Remove and allow to cool.

Cube chicken and mix with feta, pine nuts, and thyme. Lay one sheet of phyllo down and brush gently with melted butter. Repeat until there are four layers of phyllo. Spread mixture over ¾ of the exposed phyllo surface lengthwise. Roll lengthwise toward exposed area.

Brush one side of remaining phyllo and wrap the roll with it. Bake in oven-proof pan at 375° F for 15–20 minutes or until golden brown.

Remove from oven and let stand 5–10 minutes. Add shallots to 4 Tbs of balsamic vinegar in a bowl. Season and whisk well. While whisking add olive oil slowly. Toss greens and grapes with dressing. Slice roll into 12 pieces.

Place greens in center of plates and arrange 3 slices of phyllo roll on each. Serve immediately. Serves 4. Serve with Chardonnay.

SILVERADO VINEYARDS' COURTYARD ENTRANCE

SILVERADO VINEYARDS is 2 miles south of the Yountville Cross Road and just south of the road to Shafer Vineyards. Turn right (west) up Silverado's driveway to its gorgeous Italian gardens and courtyard, fountain, flowers, benches and Old World ambience. There are glorious views from the private knoll above the Napa Valley.

Long ago Walt Disney, Lillian Disney, Diane Disney Miller, and Ron Miller set out to grow some of the best grapes in the Napa Valley and to "deliver the best wine the Napa Valley could produce at a fair price." Named for an abandoned silver mine, Silverado symbolizes the Disney family's commitment to Napa wine. They see themselves as "prospecting," as Robert Louis Stevenson suggested winegrowers do, seeking viticultural paydirt.

Toward that goal, the Disneys brought in John Stuart before construction to take charge of technical design and vineyard development. Highly regarded by colleagues and wine reviewers, Jack is a fifth-generation Californian with a literature degree from Stanford and graduate training in viticulture and enology from UC Davis.

Do not miss this informally elegant experience, especially with the help of tasting-room expert Don Dodson.

BRAISED BEEF SHORT RIBS WITH FOIE GRAS, POTATO GALLETTE, AND WATERCRESS SALAD

from Chef Sean Knight, Pinot Blanc Restaurant
and Silverado Vineyards

INGREDIENTS:

4 lb beef short ribs, cut (by your butcher) 1 inch thick
2 Russet potatoes, peeled
2 white onions, peeled and chopped
2 carrots, peeled and chopped
1 celery stalk, chopped
6 thyme sprigs
1 bay leaf
10 whole black peppercorns
1 head garlic, split
1 qt beef or veal stock
1 cup Port wine
1 cup clarified butter
¼ cup olive oil
2 tsp balsamic vinegar
salt and pepper to taste
4–3 oz duck foie gras medallions (optional)
1 lb watercress, washed

PREPARATION:

Season the ribs with salt and pepper. Add 1 Tbs clarified butter to a large roasting pan and heat over high heat until pan is smoking. Carefully add the ribs to the pan and brown thoroughly on both sides.

When the ribs are brown, remove from the pan and add the chopped carrot, celery, onion, thyme, bay leaf, peppercorns, and garlic. Sauté until brown and deglaze with the Port wine, scraping all of the brown bits from the pan. Reduce the wine until almost all is evaporated.

Add the veal stock and bring to boil. Add the ribs to the pan, turn the heat to low, and simmer until the ribs are almost falling off the bone, occasionally skimming off all surface residue—approximately 2 ½ hours.

(continued on next page)

Braised Beef Short Ribs . . . (Continued)

Remove the ribs from the pan and keep warm. Strain the braising liquid through a fine strainer and discard all vegetables. Return the liquid to a sauce pan and reduce to 1 ½ cups.

While the sauce is reducing, bring the foie gras to room temperature.

Using a cheese grater, grate potatoes and remaining onion. Season with salt and pepper and, using a clean kitchen towel, squeeze out all excess liquid from potato–onion mixture. Heat a large, nonstick sauté pan over high heat and add ½ cup of the clarified butter. When the butter starts to smoke, carefully add the potato–onion mixture to the pan and, using a spoon, shape the potato mix into a round cake, packing it down at the same time to about 1 in thick. Turn heat down to medium and cook until the edge of the potato cake is golden brown. With one motion, flip the cake over and add ¼ cup clarified butter to the pan. Cook until the edges are golden brown, transfer to a baking sheet, and finish in a 400° F oven—approximately 10 minutes. Remove from oven, cut cake into quarters, and keep warm.

Heat a small sauté pan over high heat. Season the foie gras with salt and pepper and add to pan. Sear until golden brown, turn over, and brown other side. The foie gras should be rare, so cook on each side for only about 10–15 seconds.

To serve, place the potato wedges in the center of the plates. In a small bowl, toss the watercress with the balsamic vinegar, olive oil, and salt and pepper. Place a small salad on top of the potato wedge. Place the foie gras on the salad, then the rib on top. Bring sauce to a boil, season with salt and pepper, and spoon over ribs. Serves 4.

Fine points: Tasting fee $2.00 on weekends. Featured wines: Sauvignon Blanc, Chardonnay, Sangiovese Rosato, Sangiovese, Merlot, Cabernet Sauvignon. Owners: Diane Disney Miller and Ron Miller. Winemaker: Jack Stuart. Cases: 100,000. Acres: 348.

Silverado Vineyards, 6121 Silverado Trail, Napa 94558; phone (707) 257–1770, fax (707) 257–1538, Web site www.silveradovineyards.com. Open 10:30 A.M.–5:00 P.M. May 15–September 15, 11:00 A.M.–4:30 P.M. daily in winter. Visa, MasterCard, and American Express. Wheelchair-accessible.

As you come back down Silverado's driveway, turn right (south) again onto the Silverado Trail to PINE RIDGE WINERY, 0.4 mile down the road. Turn right (west) at Pine Ridge's sign. As you approach the winery, you get a feel of the place from the adult tire swings hanging from pine trees, among which you are welcome to stroll, swing, or picnic. There are even barbecues for your use.

A former Olympic skier with a degree in organic chemistry and an MBA, co-founder Gary Andrus is a self-proclaimed "wine geek" who grew up Mormon in Utah and worked three harvests in Bordeaux studying enology at Montpellier. Gary's wife and Pine Ridge co-founder, Nancy Andrus, is executive vice president for marketing. Nancy runs the Napa Marathon and frequently rides her Harley Davidson through the wine country.

PINE RIDGE WINERY

Be sure to walk through Pine Ridge's demonstration vineyard adjoining the south side of the parking lot and at the foot of the ridge covered with pines, and call ahead to make an appointment to tour the caves.

A new financial relationship with Leucadia Cellars, an East Coast investment firm, has led to a total makeover of Pine Ridge's tasting room and processing, what Gary calls "reinventing ourselves." They have now even bought a vineyard in Dundee, Oregon, near Drouhin, where they built Archery Summit Winery. They actually made Archery Summit's first Pinot Noir vintages here before the winery was completed.

Fine points: Take home some of Pine Ridge's Extra Virgin Olive Oil, made from its estate-grown olives. Pine Ridge uses olive trees as active participants in organic farming, since they attract blue-green sharpshooters (like grasshoppers) and keep them busy so they don't attack the vines. You might also enjoy the elegant Nicole Miller wine-label shirts. Tasting fee $5.00. Featured wines: Chenin Blanc, Eye of the Tiger, Chardonnay, Merlot, Cabernet Sauvignon, Cabernet Franc, Black Diamond Port. Owners: Gary and Nancy Andrus. Winemaker: Stacy Clark. Cases: 75,000. Acres: 310.

❧ *Pine Ridge Winery, 5901 Silverado Trail, Napa 94558; phone (707) 252–9777, fax (707) 253–1493. Open 11:00 A.M.–5:00 P.M. daily. Visa, MasterCard, American Express, and Discover. Wheelchair-accessible.*

Just 0.2 mile south on the east side of Silverado Trail is STELTZNER VINEYARDS. The winery is set in a new California/Mediterranean stucco structure, in a flat valley within view of the road. Turn left at the sign. The tasting room is the long, narrow entrance to Steltzner's caves which are dug into the hillside. The winery office building is topped with a three-story observation tower, offering a bird's eye view of the surrounding Stag's Leap region.

Rick Steltzner is a third-generation Californian who grew up in Livermore working part time for Wente Brothers Winery. He earned an MFA degree at Sacramento State College. Soon his life as an artist on St. Helena's Lodi Lane forced a change of career in order to stay in the Napa Valley.

STELTZNER VINEYARDS TOWER AND CAVE ENTRANCE

Rick bought some land in the Stag's Leap District in 1964 (smart move) and began to grow grapes, drawing on his childhood memories of his mentor, Ernest Wente. Since he turned out to be good at caring for vineyards, Rick established and managed vineyards for other growers and wineries. He then started his own wine-making operation in a converted prune-dehydrating shed. He now enjoys high ratings from many reviewers.

 Fine points: Tasting fee $2.50. Featured wines: Sauvignon Blanc, Chardonnay, Claret, Merlot, Cabernet Sauvignon, Sangiovese, Merlot Grappa. Owners: Richard and Christine Steltzner. Winemaker: Charles W. Hendricks. Cases: 15,000. Acres: 100.

❧ *Steltzner Vineyards, 5998 Silverado Trail, Napa 94558; phone (707) 252–7272, fax (707) 252–2079. Open 10:00 A.M.–5:00 P.M. Monday–Saturday, noon–4:30 P.M. Sunday. Visa and MasterCard. Wheelchair-accessible.*

As you leave Steltzner, turn left (south) very carefully and head south on the Silverado Trail for half a mile to STAG'S LEAP WINE CELLARS, whose sign comes up quickly down a little hill on the left (east). Stag's Leap's world-class Cabernet Sauvignon won the Paris Bicentennial Tasting in 1976, causing French judges at the blind tasting to proclaim "At last a good French wine!"

Stag's Leap is actually an old Indian name given to a rock formation on the hillside and later applied to the local wine appellation. Be sure to notice co-owner Barbara Winiarski's artistic sandstone floors in the reception hall, as well as her gardens and comfortable design concepts. Employees and visitors enjoy picnic lunches at tables, and children are offered juices.

Founder Warren Winiarski was born in Chicago of Polish parents. His last name means "from the vine" or "winemaker's son." Warren should have known that, since his father made dandelion wine and fruit cordials in their home basement, he was fated to make elegant wines someday instead of following his liberal arts degree or the political history and theory he studied in Italy. While a liberal arts lecturer at the University of Chicago, he and his wife, Barbara, began to think of farming as an alternative to big-city life.

The Winiarskis moved to California in 1964. Warren first worked as an apprentice for Lee Stewart at Souverain Winery, then as assistant winemaker for Robert Mondavi in 1966, while looking for land similar to Nathan Fay's, whose wines he admired greatly. He found forty-four acres next to Fay Vineyard. Partly planted by Barbara and their children, it is now Stag's Leap Vineyards.

 Fine points: The Smithsonian Institution recently completed a year-long project of recording life at Stag's Leap. The $5.00 tasting fee includes a glass. Featured wines: Chardonnay, Sauvignon Blanc, Cabernet Sauvignon, Merlot, White Riesling. Owners:

Warren and Barbara Winiarsky. Winemaker: Michael Silacci. Cases: 150,000. Acres: 105.

✤✣ *Stag's Leap Wine Cellars, 5766 Silverado Trail, Napa 94558; phone (707) 944–2020. Open 10:00 A.M.–4:30 P.M. daily. Visa, MasterCard, and American Express. Wheelchair access to left of steps from parking lot.*

Next in our progression southward on the Silverado Trail is CHIMNEY ROCK WINERY, located in a large, white, monastic-looking building, a replica of a South African winery with the Dutch Huguenot architectural influence of Capetown. Drive 0.8 mile south of Stag's Leap Wine Cellars and turn left when you see the signs.

Poplar trees line the buildings. You can sip in the beautiful courtyard, but no picnicking is allowed.

Co-owner Sheldon (Hack) Wilson developed the Pepsi market throughout Africa as the founding bottler on the African continent. He also served as president of Pepsi United Bottlers for Los Angeles, Mexico, and Puerto Rico. Hack explored vineyard property in Bordeaux but directed his attention to the Napa Valley with the encouragement of his friend the late Alexis Lichine.

Hack purchased the Chimney Rock Golf Course and the adjacent mountain in 1980, bulldozed nine holes (seventy-five acres), and planted his vineyard estate. (The remaining nine-hole golf course is open to the public just south of the winery.)

 Fine points: Behind the counter in the tasting room, you can get up close and personal with special-label Chimney Rock bottles made for the final cast party of *Cheers*; parties for television shows *Wings* and *Empty Nest*; the movie *Victor-Victoria*; the Long Beach Grand Prix; and NBC's *Today* show. Tasting fee $3.00 per glass. Featured wines: Chardonnay, Fume Blanc, Cabernet Sauvignon, Cuvee, Elevage. Owners: Stella and Sheldon Wilson. Winemaker: Douglas Fletcher. Cases: 30,000. Acres: 50.

✤✣ *Chimney Rock Winery, 5350 Silverado Trail, Napa 94558; phone (707) 257–2641 or (800) 257–2641, fax (707) 257–2036. Open 10:00 A.M.–5:00 P.M. daily. Visa, MasterCard, and American Express. Wheelchair-accessible.*

Right next door, to the south of Chimney Rock, is CLOS DU VAL, which means "a small vineyard estate in the valley"—appropriate for a family whose roots are in France. As you approach the winery, notice the American and French flags, loads of California poppies, magnolia trees, a little lake, roses along the paths, and an herb garden of lavender, rosemary, and thyme.

Owner John Goelet descends from a distinguished French wine family. His mother, Anne Marie Guestier, was a descendant of Francois Guestier, who

CLOS DU VAL

worked for the Marquis de Segur, owner of Chateaux Lafite and Latour. His son, Pierre Francois Guestier, owned Chateau Beychevelle and was a partner in the Barton & Guestier wine firm.

Goelet was introduced to Bernard Portet, a native of the Medoc region of Bordeaux and then a recent graduate in agronomy, viticulture, and enology from the renowned University of Montpellier in France. Portet came from a family involved in winemaking in Cognac and Bordeaux for generations. The two men searched the world and decided that this was the perfect site for their winery.

The interesting Clos du Val wine labels introduce you to the Three Graces—Aglaia (Splendor), Euphrosyne (Mirth), and Thalia (Good Cheer)—daughters of Zeus and Eurynome, and thought to be the loveliest figures of Greek mythology. When the Greek gods planned a banquet, the Three Graces were the first to be invited. They subsequently enchanted the gods, and no banquet was complete without them. Clos du Val hopes you will feel the same way about their wines.

Don't miss the Ronald Searle whimsical wine illustrations commissioned by John Goelet in 1977, which you can purchase for a bargain $9.00 in the fun and elegant tasting room. Check out the specially etched wine bottles.

Fine points: Clos du Val also sponsors the Napa Chamber Music Series in S. Anderson's champagne caves. Tasting fee $5.00. Featured wines: Semillon, Chardonnay, Zinfandel, Sangiovese, Merlot, Cabernet Sauvignon. Owner: John Goelet. Winemaker and President: Bernard Portet. Cases: 60,000. Acres: 270.

❧ *Clos du Val, 5330 Silverado Trail, Napa 94558; phone (707) 259–2200, fax (707) 252–6125, Web site www.closduval.com. Open 10:00 A.M.–5:00 P.M. daily. Visa, MasterCard, American Express, and Discover. Wheelchair-accessible.*

A mile and a half south of Clos du Val, also on the east side of Silverado Trail, you will find newish, tiny, and elegant SIGNORELLO VINEYARDS. Its driveway is lined with plum trees and Italian junipers as you climb the driveway through vineyards. The modest, tasteful Italian decor includes painted arches and a glass desk in the cozy vestibule.

The tasting bar is right in the tank and aging room. Tasting is hosted by Linda Swearingen, who knows all the wine and restaurant gossip in Napa Valley—a very valuable person. You will enjoy the scale of everything here.

Fine points: You can't miss the Dan Marino football jersey personally signed to owner Ray Signorello. Signorello's wines receive high ratings from the *Wine Spectator*. Tasting fee $5.00. Featured wines: Chardonnay, Semillon, Petite Syrah, Merlot, Cabernet Sauvignon, Pinot Noir. Owners: Ray Signorello Sr. and Jr. Winemakers: Steve Devitt and Ray Signorello, Jr. Cases: 8,000. Acres: 100.

❧ *Signorello Vineyards, 4500 Silverado Trail, Napa 94558; phone (707) 255–5990. Open 11:00 A.M.–5:00 P.M. Friday–Sunday, by appointment. Visa and MasterCard. Wheelchair-accessible.*

The most southern winery on the Silverado is homey VAN DER HEYDEN, the pride and joy of Andre and Sande Van der Heyden and their family. Van der Heyden claims to be the only winery in the world that produces a Late Harvest Cabernet Sauvignon. It, like all their wines, is sold only here in the tasting room.

To get here turn right (west) at the multicolored flags to the Van der Heyden home. There are lots of RVs near the vineyard. The small, homemade, slightly funky tasting room is in the rear. Cut wooden Dutch people hold signs directing you to the tasting room. If the American flag is out, the winery is open.

House cats sit on needlepoint chairs and Oriental rugs, and the ceiling is taped together here and there, but who's looking? A football signed by the whole San Francisco '49ers football team sits in a glass case, alongside Dutch porcelain figurines.

A former furniture-business owner, Van der Heyden first made wine in his basement and gave winemaking classes in a Piedmont, California, lawyer's basement. He sells lots of his wine in Holland, a result of the Dutch ambassador to the United States taking some of these wines home. He also does wine-tasting cruises and tastings in conjunction with Holland America Line.

Fine points: This place is a don't-miss, once-in-a-lifetime experience. Andre sells chocolate truffles for $1.50 to accompany sips of his rare Late Harvest Cabernet Sauvignon. Tasting fee $2.50. Featured wines: Chardonnay, Cabernet Sauvignon, Late Harvest Cabernet Sauvignon. Owner, winemaker, "and janitor and everything in between": Andre Van der Heyden. Cases: 2,000. Acres: 15.

Van der Heyden, 4057 Silverado Trail, Napa 94558; phone (707) 259–9473. Open 10:00 A.M.–6:00 P.M. daily. Visa, MasterCard, American Express, Discover, and JCB. Wheelchair-accessible.

Barely south and across the Silverado Trail from Van der Heyden, you might want to stop into the SODA CANYON STORE for excellent sandwiches and salads, Seattle's Best Coffee espresso drinks, last-minute supplies, and lots of local color.
Soda Canyon Store, 4006 Silverado Trail, Napa 94558; phone (707) 252–0285. Open 6:00 A.M.–7:00 P.M. Monday–Friday, 6:30 A.M.–7:00 P.M. Saturday, 7:00 A.M.–7:00 P.M. Sunday. Visa and MasterCard. Wheelchair-accessible.

Hardman Avenue, which leads to Silverado Golf Course and Resort and William Hill Winery, is off to the left (east) from Silverado Trail, 1 mile south of the Soda Canyon Store. Hardman follows the ups and downs of the local landscape and runs right into the SILVERADO COUNTRY CLUB, a vast resort focused on golf at two courses. If you are a golf devotee, this is it in Northern California.

Individuals own the cottages here and rent them to guests through the club. The restaurant is elegant, and locals like the Sunday brunch.
Silverado Country Club, 1600 Atlas Peak Road, Napa 94558; phone (707) 257–0200. Visa, MasterCard, American Express, Discover, Diners, and Carte Blanche. Wheelchair-accessible.

Turn left onto Atlas Peak Road when you reach Silverado Country Club and follow WILLIAM HILL WINERY's signs up the hill. Here you can inhale the most spectacular view in the southern Napa Valley.

William Hill began his winery in 1976, developing prize vineyards on the Silverado Bench, and produced excellent Chardonnay and Cabernet Sauvignon.

NAPA VALLEY VIEW FROM WILLIAM HILL WINERY

He built this new winery in 1990. It was so impressive that the Wine Alliance of William Hill, Atlas Peak, Clos du Bois, and Callaway in Southern California were bought by Hiram Walker and Allied Domecq in 1991.

Try to visit Friday through Sunday, when the staff offer food and wine pairings, which might include tapenades and fresh local strawberries. Enjoy relaxing, tasting the wines, and soaking in the view from wrought-iron tables and chairs on the patio.

 Fine points: William Hill's wine labels all feature biologically accurate representations of the Chardonnay, Cabernet Sauvignon, and Merlot vine leaf appropriate to the wine in the bottle, with interesting explanations of the leaf's qualities. No tasting fee. Featured wines: Chardonnay, Merlot, Cabernet Sauvignon. Owner: Wine Alliance (Hiram Walker). Winemaker: Jill Davis. Cases: 90,000. Acres: 130.

↬ *William Hill Winery, 1761 Atlas Peak Road, Napa 94558; phone (707) 224–4477, fax (707) 224–4484, Web site www.williamhillwinery.com. Open 10:00 A.M.–4:30 P.M. daily. Visa, MasterCard, and American Express. Wheelchair-accessible.*

Now take yourselves back to the Silverado Trail, head south (left) to Trancas Boulevard, turn right (west), and you're on your way back to Highway 29.
Salud!

CHAPTER 5

WHERE TO STAY IN THE NAPA VALLEY

ere we list each establishment's price range, valid from late spring into fall; prices are typically lower the rest of the year. The prices also vary between weekdays and weekends and are subject to change without notice. Many places require a two-day minimum.

NAPA

Hotels, Motels, and Inns

The hostelries in the city of Napa are all of good quality and are listed here in order, based on the distance from Highway 29.

EMBASSY SUITES—NAPA VALLEY, 1075 California Boulevard, Napa 94558; phone (707) 253–9540, fax (707) 253–9202; 205 suites in three Mediterranean style stories; $144–$234. Restaurant in atrium, giant fireplace in lobby, indoor and outdoor pools, several meeting rooms open on a court, some smoking rooms. No pets, but you can enjoy watching swans float by in the pond.

BEST WESTERN ELM HOUSE INN, 800 California Boulevard, Napa 94558; phone (707) 255–1831, fax (707) 255–8609; 16 large units in three stories; $109–$189. Some fireplaces, whirlpool, spa, continental breakfast. No pets.

NAPA VALLEY TRAVELODGE, 853 Coombs Street, Napa 94558; phone (707) 226–1871, fax (707) 226–1707; 44 units; $75–$95. Small pool. No pets.

THE CHABLIS INN, 3360 Solano Avenue, Napa 94558; phone (707) 257–1944, fax (707) 226–6862; 34 units, some efficiencies; $70–$130. Pool, spa, whirlpool, continental breakfast, free movies. No pets.

NAPA VALLEY MARRIOTT, 3425 Solano Avenue, Napa 94558; phone (707) 253–7433, fax (707) 258–1320; 191 units; $104–$199. Recently renovated for several million dollars. Harvest Café Restaurant, heated pool, two lighted tennis courts, spa, conference facilities, free movies. No pets.

NAPA VALLEY BUDGET INN, 3380 Solano Avenue, Napa 94558; phone (707) 257–6111; 58 rooms; $56–$124. Pool. Pets OK.

THE CHATEAU, 4195 Solano Avenue, Napa 94558; phone (707) 253–9300, fax (707) 253–0906; 115 units; $85–$100. Pool, spa, meeting facilities, free movies. No pets.

JOHN MUIR INN, 1998 Trower Avenue, Napa 94558; phone (707) 257–7220; fax (707) 258–0943; 59 units in three stories, some efficiencies; $75–$160. Pool, continental breakfast, free movies, conference room, under 14 free. No pets.

BEST WESTERN INN, 100 Soscol Avenue, Napa 94558; phone (707) 257–1930, fax (707) 255–0709; 68 units, including deluxe; $85–$165. Pool, whirlpool. No pets.

Bed and Breakfasts

These entries are listed from downtown Napa to farther out in the countryside. They are an architectural historian's delight. Almost all are nonsmoking and require a two-night minimum stay on weekends.

THE BEAZLEY HOUSE, 1910 First Street, Napa 94558; phone (707) 257–1649; 11 darkly romantic rooms; $125–$215. This 1902 Colonial Revival was Napa's first B&B (in 1981). Fireplaces, spas, low-fat gourmet breakfasts, complimentary tea and other goodies, wonderful gardens, parking area. No pets.

THE 1801 INN, 1801 1st Street, Napa 94558; phone (707) 224–3739; 5 rooms; $125–$215. A 1903 Queen Anne Victorian, air conditioning, breakfast, snacks. Parking on premises.

THE OLD WORLD INN, 1301 Jefferson Street, Napa 94558; phone (707) 257–0112; 8 rooms; $115–$150. A Victorian house. One room with whirlpool, some canopied beds. Outdoor spa, air conditioning, complimentary tea time, wine and cheese social in evening, chocolate dessert buffet. No pets.

CEDAR GABLES INN, 486 Coombs Street, Napa 94558; phone (707) 224–7969, fax (707) 224–4838; 6 rooms; $129–$189. Sixteenth-century–style shingled English Manor house built in 1892. Four rooms with whirlpools, some fireplaces. Breakfast in dining room or sun porch. No pets.

HENNESSEY HOUSE B&B INN, 1727 Main Street, phone (707) 226–3774, fax (707) 226–2975; 10 rooms; $129–$189. An 1889 Queen Anne Victorian and carriage house, originally owned by Dr. Edwin Hennessey, an early city mayor; National Register of Historic Places. Several spas, some fireplaces and patios, sauna. Breakfast in dining room with stamped tin ceiling. No pets.

THE BLUE VELVET MANSION, 443 Brown Street, Napa 94558; phone (707) 253–2583, fax (707) 257–8205; 14 rooms, 1 2-room suite; $145–$285. Well-preserved 1886 Queen Anne Victorian in center of city. Antiques, breakfast in dining room, massage, champagne available in room. Stunning gardens, gazebo. No pets.

CHURCHILL MANOR, 485 Brown Street, Napa 94558; phone (707) 253–7733, fax (707) 253–8836; 10 rooms; $85–$165. This 1889 Second Empire mansion (with classic columns) on a downtown acre is surrounded by lawns and gardens; National Register of Historic Places. Twelve-foot carved ceilings, verandas, air conditioning, croquet. Wine and cheese each evening, complimentary tandem bikes. No pets.

McCLELLAND-PRIEST B & B, 569 Randolph Street, Napa 94559; phone (707) 224–6875 or (800) 290–6881; Web site www.historicinnstravel.com; 5 rooms; $159–$259. An 1879 house, elegantly decorated. Large suites, Jacuzzis, fireplaces. Full breakfast, evening wine receptions.

LA BELLE EPOQUE, 1386 Calistoga Avenue, Napa 94558; phone (707) 257–2161; 6 rooms; $119–$179. An 1893 Queen Anne Victorian; 2 rooms with fireplaces. Air conditioning, parking on site, antiques, stained-glass windows. Evening free wine tasting in the rustic wine cellar; breakfast in the sunroom or dining room. No pets.

ARBOR GUEST HOUSE, 1436 G Street, Napa 94558; phone (707) 252–8144; 5 rooms; $95–$165. A 1906 Colonial style home, with choice of fireplace or spa in carriage house or garden patio units. Antiques, flowering arbors. No pets.

THE NAPA INN, 1137 Warren Street, Napa 94558; phone (707) 257–1444; 6 rooms; $140–$210. An 1899 Victorian on residential street, stained-glass windows. Spacious parlors, player piano, some special rooms (including the huge upstairs Grand Suite) with antiques (including clock collection), some with fireplace. Complimentary sherry, breakfast in dining room. Not recommended for children. No pets.

CHARDONNAY LODGE, 2640 Jefferson Street, Napa 94558; phone (707) 224–0789; 20 rooms; $38–$95. Recently renovated.

STAHLECKER HOUSE, 1042 Easum Drive, Napa 94558; phone (707) 257–1588; 4 rooms; $125–$185. Country inn beside running creek; 1 room has spa, 3 with fireplace. Canopy beds, sun deck, volleyball, croquet, Ping-Pong.

CANDLELIGHT INN, 1045 Easum Drive, Napa 94558; phone (707) 257–3717; 9 rooms; $85–$195. A 1929 English Tudor with modern amenities, in park on the bank of Napa Creek. Fireplaces, whirlpools, 1 private sauna, patios, pool. No pets.

OAK KNOLL INN, 2200 East Oak Knoll Avenue, Napa 94558; phone (707) 255–2200; 3 large rooms; $250–$315. French-style country inn built in 1984. Open-beamed ceilings, brass beds, lavish views of surrounding vineyards. Pool, hot tub, croquet. Given 4 kisses by "Best Places to Kiss in Northern California."

INN ON RANDOLPH, 411 Randolph Street, Napa 94558; phone (707) 257–2886; 5 rooms; $119–$249. Lovingly restored 1860 landmark Gothic Revival Victorian. Some fireplaces, canopy beds, double or deep-soak whirlpools. Private decks, gazebo in garden. Southern-style breakfast.

LA RESIDENCE COUNTRY INN, 4066 Highway 29, Napa 94558; phone (707) 253–0337; 20 rooms (including 4 suites); $175–$275. An 1870 Gothic Revival mansion and "French Barn" on 2 wooded acres. Full breakfast in sunny dining room, pool, Jacuzzi, fireplaces. No smoking; not for children.

BROOKSIDE VINEYARDS B&B, 3194 Redwood Road, Napa 94558; (707) 944–1661, fax (707) 252–6690; 3 rooms; $105–$135. A 1955 California Mission style set in vineyard, patio, gazebo. One room has fireplace. No pets.

COUNTRY GARDEN INN, 1815 Silverado Trail, Napa 94558; phone (707) 255–1197, fax (707) 255–3112; 8 rooms; $135–$210. An 1860 carriage house beside river. Some rooms have fireplace or whirlpool. Full breakfast, plus champagne, afternoon wine, and hors d'oeuvres.

Resorts

SILVERADO COUNTRY CLUB RESORT, 1600 Atlas Peak Road, Napa 94558; phone (707) 257–0200, fax (707) 257–5400; 260 units; $150–$280, with condos up to $750. Two dining rooms, restaurant, lounge, room service, lush 1220-acre grounds. Three pools and internationally famous golf courses (you might see Johnny Miller at practice). AAA 4 diamonds; no pets.

YOUNTVILLE

Hotels, Motels, and Inns

VINTAGE INN, 6541 Washington Street, Yountville 94599; phone (707) 944–1112, fax (707) 944–1617; 80 rooms; $175–$325. Built in 1970s, several buildings designed by Kipp Stewart. All units have fireplace, balcony or patio, whirlpool tub, handcrafted furniture. Two tennis courts, pool, whirlpool, complimentary breakfast and newspaper. AAA 4 diamonds. Pets OK with deposit.

NAPA VALLEY LODGE, 2230 Madison Street, Yountville 94599; phone (707) 944–2468, fax (707) 944–9362; 55 rooms; $152–$325. Spanish-style buildings, elegant lobby with large fireplace, conference facilities. Many fireplaces, 3 2-bedroom units, some balconies, pool, sauna, whirlpool. Complimentary champagne, breakfast buffet. AAA 4 diamonds; part of northern California Woodside Hotel chain. No pets.

NAPA VALLEY RAILWAY INN, 6503 Washington Street, Yountville 94599; phone (707) 944–2000; $65–$125. An unusual inn constructed of nine old railroad cars transformed into elegant suites fit for a nineteenth-century rail baron, each with bath, brass bed, love seats, and antiques. No pets.

VILLAGIO INN & SPA, on Washington Street, Yountville 94599; phone (707) 945–4545; 112 rooms; $185–$270. Brand new sister to nearby Vintage Inn. Fireplaces, balconies, patios, spa, sauna, massage, hydrotherapy, lap pool. Wine bar, champagne breakfast, meeting rooms. No pets.

Bed and Breakfasts

OLEANDER HOUSE, 7433 St. Helena Highway (Highway 29), Yountville 94599; phone (707) 944–8315; 5 rooms; $115–$160. Two-story French Country home built in 1982, rooms with views. No smoking. No pets.

MAISON FLEURIE, 6529 Yount Street, Yountville 94599; phone (707) 944–2056, fax (707) 944–9362 or 944–9342; 13 rooms; $110–$190. If you're looking for a colorful past, this is the place. Built of fieldstone and brick in 1873 as an inn, it became a bordello, then a speakeasy during Prohibition, and later the local 4-H meeting hall. Wine and hors d'oeuvres in the afternoon, free bikes, pool. Once known as the Magnolia, in 1994 it was purchased by Roger and Sally Post who restored the inn in French Country style. No smoking. No pets.

PETIT LOGIS INN AND B&B, 6527 Yount Street, Yountville 94599; phone (707) 944–2332; 5 rooms; $95–$175.

BORDEAUX HOUSE, 6600 Washington Street, Yountville 94599; phone (707) 944–0889; 7 rooms; $115–$145. Air conditioning, some fireplaces and balconies. No smoking. No pets.

BURGUNDY HOUSE, 6711 Washington Street, Yountville 94599; phone (707) 944–0889; 5 rooms; $110–$135. An 1893 French-style stone inn originally built as a brandy distillery. No smoking. No pets.

THE WEBBER PLACE, 6610 Webber Street, Yountville 94599; phone (707) 944–8384, fax (707) 944–8383; 4 rooms; $89–$119. This reconstructed farmhouse dates back to 1850 (earlier than when the town was laid out, in 1855). No smoking. No pets.

TRUBODY RANCH, Yountville 94599; phone (707) 255–5907; 3 rooms; $115–$195. A restored 1872 Victorian farmhouse on a 140-acre vineyard; original antiques. Air conditioned, continental breakfast. No pets.

HILLVIEW COUNTRY INN, Yountville 94599; phone (707) 224–5004; 3 rooms; $125–$175. A century-old farmhouse in the middle of vineyards, with farm furniture. Country breakfast, air conditioned, evening refreshments. No pets.

RUTHERFORD

Hotels, Motels, and Inns

RANCHO CAYMUS, 1140 Rutherford Cross Road, Rutherford 94573; phone (707) 963–1777, fax (707) 963–5387; 26 rooms; $135–$295. Beautifully designed Spanish-style, with tiled roof, open-beam ceilings, courtyard, gardens, hand-crafted furniture from Mexico and Ecuador, many balconies and fireplaces. Continental breakfast. No pets.

Resorts

AUBERGE DU SOLEIL, 180 Rutherford Hill Road, Rutherford 94573; phone (707) 963–1211; 50 rooms (19 are suites); $275–$2,000 (!). Southern France country style with wooden shutters. Private entries, terraces, refrigerators, wet bars, elegance throughout. This resort is set on 33 hillside acres among olive trees, and grew from the world-famous Auberge Du Soleil restaurant. If price is no object, then this is the tops in Napa Valley luxury. Three tennis courts, pool, spa, exercise room, whirlpool. Not recommended for children. No pets.

ST. HELENA

Hotels, Motels, and Inns

HARVEST INN, One Main Street, St. Helena 94574; phone (707) 963–9463, fax (707) 963–4402; 54 rooms; $195–$366. Tudor-style stone building situated in vineyard. Two pools, Jacuzzis, many fireplaces, wet bars, balconies, some rooms with whirlpool tubs. Elegant, oak-lined main lobby, "Harvest Centre," has wine bar and dance floor. AAA 4 diamonds. Small pets OK if call ahead.

EL BONITA MOTEL, 195 Main Street (Highway 29), St. Helena 94574; phone (707) 963–3216, fax (707) 963–8838; 42 rooms, some efficiencies; $77–$140. Free movies, pool, sauna, whirlpool. Award-winning garden with sweeping lawn. Small pets OK.

VINEYARD COUNTRY INN, 201 Main Street (Highway 29), St. Helena 94574; phone (707) 963–1000, fax (707) 963–1794; 21 rooms, all suites; $205. All rooms in this beautifully appointed French Country inn have wood-burning fireplaces, wet bar and fridge; most have balconies. Pool, spa. Breakfast included in dining room. No pets.

THE INN AT SOUTHBRIDGE, 1020 Main Street (Highway 29), St. Helena 94574; phone (707) 967–9400; 21 large rooms; $195–$335. Designed by architect William Turnbull, Jr., with a winery theme, and completed in 1995. Each unit has vaulted ceiling, fireplace, and balcony. Spa, lap pool; room service from Tomatina Restaurant. No pets.

HOTEL ST. HELENA, 1309 Main Street (Highway 29), St. Helena 94574; phone (707) 963–4388, fax (707) 963–5402; 18 rooms; $145–$275. This 1881 historic hotel had deteriorated into a fleabag before it was recently rebuilt and lovingly restored with its original nineteenth-century feeling. Rooms are above a commercial arcade. Antique furnishings, air conditioned. Four rooms share baths. Continental breakfast, complimentary wine. No pets.

WINE COUNTRY INN, 1152 Lodi Lane, St. Helena 94574; phone (707) 963–7077; 25 rooms; $146–$268. Most rooms in this New England–style inn have antiques, balconies or decks. No king-size beds. Fireplaces operate in off-season. Pool, spa, buffet breakfast. No pets.

Resorts and Spas

St. Helena has two resorts, which are also spas providing mineral and mud baths and a variety of healthy "treatments" to bring pleasure and tone up your system.

MEADOWOOD NAPA VALLEY, 900 Meadowood Lane, St. Helena 94574; phone (707) 963–3646, fax (707) 963–3532; 99 rooms; $320–$540, some 2-room suites. Adirondack-style lodges and cottages on 250 acres. Each room has vaulted ceiling, skylight, deck, wet bar, refrigerator. Two pools, sauna, whirlpool, 7 tennis courts, 2 championship croquet courts with teaching professional, 9-hole golf course, playground. Starmont Restaurant, Fairway Grill. Spa treatments available to public as well as resort guests. AAA 4 diamonds. No pets.

WHITE SULPHUR SPRINGS, 3100 Sulphur Springs Road, St. Helena 94574; phone (707) 963–8588; 14 rooms and 9 cottages; $85–$125. The oldest resort in Napa County, established in 1852. Set in a canyon, surrounded by redwood and fir trees on 330 acres with a natural spring of warm sulphur waters perpetually feeding a large soaking pool. Some shared bathrooms; kitchenettes in cottages. Continental breakfast. Hiking trails, picnic areas. Spa treatments.

Bed and Breakfasts

THE INK HOUSE, 1575 St. Helena Highway South (Highway 29), St. Helena 94574; phone (707) 963–3890; 7 rooms; $95–$175. An 1884 Italianate Victorian, in Register of Historic Places. Full breakfast, complimentary wine and brandy. Parlors, grand piano, pump organ, observatory on roof for full view of valley vineyards. Pool table, video library. No smoking. No pets.

ROSE GARDEN INN, 1277 St. Helena Highway South (Highway 29), St. Helena 94574; phone (707) 963–4417; 4 rooms; $110–$155. Turn-of-the-century farmhouse set among vineyards and a walnut grove. Fireplaces in living and dining rooms. No smoking. No pets.

SHADY OAKS COUNTRY INN, 399 Zinfandel Lane, St. Helena 94574; phone (707) 963–1190, fax (707) 963–9367; 4 rooms, 2 in 1920s Craftsman house and 2 in 1880s-era stone winery; $145–$195. Antiques, patio with pillars entwined by century-old wisteria. Champagne breakfast, home-baked bread, complimentary wine in evening. No smoking. No pets.

ZINFANDEL INN, 800 Zinfandel Lane, St. Helena 94574; phone (707) 963–3512; Web site: zinfandelinn.com; 3 rooms; $125–$295. English Tudor–style house. One room has whirlpool, another a stone fireplace. Gazebo, aviary.

LA FLEUR B & B, 1475 Inglewood Avenue, St. Helena 94574; phone (707) 963–0233; 3 rooms; $165.75. An 1882 Queen Anne Victorian in the midst of a working vineyard and winery. Buffet breakfast in solarium or on deck. No pets.

VIGNE DEL UOMO FELICE, 1871 Cabernet Lane, St. Helena 94574; phone (707) 963–2376; 3 rooms; $100. Stone French Country cottage. Continental breakfast, maid service, fresh fruit in season, croquet. No smoking. No pets.

SUNNY ACRES B & B, 397 Main Street (Highway 29), St. Helena 94574; phone (707) 963–2826; 2 rooms; $125–$150. Restored 1879 Victorian originally built for Dr. George Belden Crane, one of the valley's first grape growers, in midst of 20 acres of vineyard. Air conditioned, full breakfast in dining room. No smoking. No pets.

AMBROSE BIERCE HOUSE, 1515 Main Street (Highway 29), St. Helena 94574; phone (707) 963–3003; 2 rooms, 1 suite; $99–$159. An 1872 Victorian where once lived acerbic journalist Ambrose Bierce. Antiques, brass beds, air conditioned. Continental breakfast, complimentary sherry. No pets.

CHESTELSON HOUSE, 1417 Kearney Street, St. Helena 94574; phone (707) 963–2238; 3 rooms; $102–$148. A 1902 Victorian, air conditioned. One suite has 2-person whirlpool. Owner Jackie Sweet's breakfasts have won raves. Evening treats. No smoking. No pets.

CINNAMON BEAR B & B, 1407 Kearney Street, St. Helena 94574; phone (707) 963–4653; 3 rooms; $115–$165. A 1904 Craftsman house. Full breakfast. Veranda around house, air conditioned. No pets.

BYLUND HOUSE, 2000 Howell Mountain Road, St. Helena 94574; phone (707) 963–9073; 2 rooms; $95–$175. Modern Italian villa with sweeping valley views, balconies. One room in tower with separate entrance. High poster beds, air conditioned. Continental breakfast. No smoking. No pets.

VILLA STREET HELENA, 2727 Sulphur Springs Avenue, St. Helena 94574; 3 rooms; $145–$245. Tuscan hilltop villa with panoramic view of Napa Valley.

Antiques, private entrances, library, courtyard, 20 wooded acres. Continental breakfast in solarium, complimentary wine. No pets.

HILLTOP B & B, 9550 St. Helena Road, St. Helena 94574; phone (707) 944–0880; 4 rooms; $105–$175. Modern ranch house in the Mayacamas Mountains 6 miles west of town. Hot tub, deck with views. Full breakfast. No smoking. No pets.

OLIVER HOUSE COUNTRY INN, 2970 Silverado Trail North, St. Helena 94574; phone (707) 963–5566; 4 rooms, 2 with fireplaces; $75–$250. Swiss Bavarian chalet. Private entrances, air conditioned, large parlor, antiques. Full breakfast. No smoking. No pets.

GLASS MOUNTAIN INN, 3100 Silverado Trail North, St. Helena 94574; phone (707) 963–3512; 3 rooms; $165–$295. Shingled house with steeple roof, 1 room with whirlpool. Full breakfast, complimentary champagne and truffles. Old wine cave on premises. No pets.

SPANISH VILLA, 474 Glass Mountain Road, St. Helena 94574; phone (707) 963–7483; 3 rooms; $125–$175. Spanish-style country inn. Continental breakfast in galleria. No smoking. No pets.

BARTELS RANCH, 1200 Conn Valley Road, St. Helena 94574; phone (707) 963–4001; 4 rooms; $95–$275. Rock-and-redwood ranch house set on 60 acres. One suite has Jacuzzi. Fireplace, sauna, game room, library. Full breakfast. No pets.

ELSIE'S CONN VALLEY INN, 726 Rossi Road, St. Helena 94574; phone (707) 963–4614; 3 rooms; $125–$275. Rose garden, views. Complimentary wine, cheese, and fruit in room. Refrigerator, barbecue. No pets.

ERIKA'S HILLSIDE, 285 Fawn Park Road, St. Helena 94574; phone (707) 963–2887; 3 suites; $95–295. Swiss chalet on 3-acre hillside garden, terraced rock walls, shaded by oak trees. Hot tub, fireplace, views. German specialties served in garden room. No pets.

WINE COUNTRY VICTORIAN, St. Helena; phone (707) 963–0852; 2 rooms in classic Victorian and 1 in cottage on woodland estate; $110–$150. Decorator furnishings. No pets. Call for reservations and directions.

CALISTOGA

Spas, Resorts, Baths

Nowadays the spas and baths are the centerpieces of the resorts in Calistoga. In most cases you do not have to stay at the resort to enjoy spa privileges. Here we list only those places with lodging.

DR. WILKINSON'S HOT SPRINGS RESORT, 1507 Lincoln Avenue, Calistoga 94515; phone (707) 942–4102; 42 rooms, many with kitchenettes; $89–$129 weekdays, $99–$139 weekends, $129–$139 for the Victorian suite. Pools (for guests only), spa treatments. No pets.

INDIAN SPRINGS RESORT AND SPA , 1712 Lincoln Avenue, Calistoga 94515; phone (707) 942–4913; 16 cottages; $150–$180. Calistoga's oldest continuing resort. Pool, 16 acres with palm trees. Spa treatments. Site of centuries-old Indian sweat house. No pets.

CALISTOGA VILLAGE INN AND SPA, 1880 Lincoln Avenue, Calistoga 94515; phone (707) 942–0991, fax (707) 942–5306; 41 rooms and cottage; $75–$175. Mineral water spa and pool with views of hills, whirlpool, sauna, children's wading pool. Spa treatments. Restaurant, conference center. Free movies. No pets.

EUROSPA, 1202 Pine Street, Calistoga 94515; phone (707) 942–6829; 16 rooms; package prices only (room for 2, spa treatment, and meal) $189 Sunday–Thursday; $279 Friday–Saturday. Pool, Jacuzzi. Spa treatments. No pets.

GOLDEN HAVEN HOT SPRINGS AND RESORT, 1713 Lake Street, Calistoga 94515; phone (707) 942–6793, Web site www.Goldenhaven.com; 30 rooms, many with kitchenettes; $65–$135. Set in oaks with gardens. Whirlpools, saunas, heated pool, Jacuzzi. Spa treatments. No pets.

SILVER ROSE INN AND SPA, 351 Rosedale Road, Calistoga 94515; phone (707) 942–9581; 20 rooms; $145–$240 Monday–Thursday, $165–$260 Friday–Sunday. Packages available. Rooms split between 2 lodges, on knoll and in vineyard. Individually decorated rooms with "themes," some balconies. Pool in shape of wine bottle. Whirlpool, exercise room, tennis courts, putting green, complimentary bottle of wine from private wine cellar. Spa treatments. Not for children. Facilities for lodging guests only. No pets.

Hotels, Motels, and Inns

CALISTOGA INN, 1250 Lincoln Avenue, Calistoga 94515; phone (707) 942–4101; 17 rooms; $49–$60. An 1882 pioneer hotel in heart of town, above restaurant and brewpub. Shared bathrooms and showers. Complimentary wine and beer. No pets.

ROMAN SPA, 1300 Washington Street, Calistoga 94515; phone (707) 942–4441; 60 rooms, 26 with kitchens, 1 with 2 bedrooms; $69–$178. Beautiful gardens, next door to International Spa. No pets.

CALISTOGA SPA HOT SPRINGS, 1006 Washington Avenue, Calistoga 94515; phone (707) 942–6269; 57 units, all with kitchenettes; $87–$132. Air conditioned, 4 outdoor mineral pools, weight room, aerobics room. No pets.

MOUNT VIEW HOTEL, 1457 Lincoln Avenue, Calistoga 94515; phone (707) 942–6877; 34 rooms; $80–$205. Restored 1919 Mission Revival Hotel with some cottages. Once Calistoga's prestigious European Hotel, it is listed in the National Register of Historic Places. It now has 9 elegant suites with period furniture, redecorated Art Deco lobby. Pool, whirlpool, continental breakfast in room. Connected to Catahoula Restaurant and Mount View Spa. No pets.

HIDEAWAY COTTAGES, 1412 Fairway, Calistoga 94515; phone (707) 942–4108; 17 cottages, some with kitchenettes; $89–$94, 1 at $165. Air conditioned, 2 outdoor pools, no breakfast, grass courtyard. Next to Dr. Wilkinson's Hot Springs Resort. No pets.

COTTAGE GROVE INN, 1711 Lincoln Avenue, Calistoga 94515; phone (707) 942–8400, fax (707) 942–2653; 16 cottages; $150–$195. Each cottage with fireplaces, 2-person Jacuzzi, ironing board, air conditioned. Continental breakfast, evening wine in lounge. Historically on promenade of Sam Brannan's resort of mid-1880s. No pets.

BEST WESTERN STEVENSON MANOR INN, 1830 Lincoln Avenue, Calistoga 94515; phone (707) 942–1112; 34 rooms; $80–$189. All rooms with refrigerators, some with fireplaces and whirlpools. Pool, sauna, whirlpool, courtyard, gazebo. Complimentary breakfast and newspaper. No pets.

COMFORT INN NAPA VALLEY NORTH, 1865 Lincoln Avenue, Calistoga 94515; phone (707) 942–9400, fax (707) 942–5262; 54 rooms, many with views; $70–$135. Sauna, small pool, whirlpool. Free breakfast. Preregistration urged to get scenic rooms. No pets.

CARLIN COUNTRY COTTAGES, 1623 Lake Street, Calistoga 94515; phone (707) 942–9102, fax (707) 942–2295; 15 rooms, 8 with kitchens; $89–$175. No pets.

Bed and Breakfasts

LARKMEAD COUNTRY INN, 1103 Larkmead Lane, Calistoga 94515; phone (707) 942–5360; 4 rooms; $138. Early 1900s Palladian-style house. One room with king-size brass bed. Grand views. Smoking OK. No pets.

THE ELMS, 1300 Cedar Street, Calistoga 94515; phone (707) 942–9476, fax (707) 942–9479; 7 rooms; $125–$175. An 1873 French Second Empire–style house, listed in National Register of Historic Places. Varied amenities in rooms such as decks, patios, fireplaces, "whirltubs." Full breakfast, afternoon wine, evening port. No smoking. No pets.

LA CHAUMIERE, 1301 Cedar Street, Calistoga 94515; phone (707) 942–5139; 2 rooms, plus a log cabin; $135–$185. A 1932 Cotswold cottage with lush garden, patio. One unit has sitting room. Patio, full breakfast, wine and cheese in afternoon, port or sherry in evening. Expansion coming. No pets.

HOTEL D'AMICI, 1436 Lincoln, Calistoga 94515; phone (707) 942–1007; 4 suites; $150–$250. Formerly Brannan's Loft. In 1998 the Pestoni family— long-time owners of the hotel and Rutherford Grove Winery—completely remodeled this venerable inn and changed its name. Three rooms; 2 have fireplaces, 2 have balconies. "Extended" continental breakfast. No pets.

BRANNAN COTTAGE INN, 109 Wapoo Avenue, Calistoga 94515; (707) 942–4200; 6 rooms, including 2 suites; $95–$160. An 1860 Greek Revival inn, the only survivor from Sam Brannan's Hot Springs Resort. The oldest building in Calistoga, fully renovated in 1990s, listed in National Register of Historic Places. Private entrances, air conditioned, antiques. Shaded courtyard and garden, noted for varied breakfasts. No smoking. Pets negotiable.

SLEEPY HOLLOW B & B INN, 911 Foothill Boulevard, Calistoga 94515; phone (707) 942–4760, fax (707) 963–0181; 2 rooms; $100. Country-style inn. Continental breakfast. No smoking. No pets.

CHRISTOPHER'S INN, 1010 Foothill Boulevard, Calistoga 94515; phone (707) 942–5755; 13 rooms, including 3 suites; $135–$200. Country Georgian–style inn. Five rooms have fireplaces. Separate entrances, Laura Ashley comforters. Croquet under the trees. Continental breakfast served in room. No smoking. No pets.

CALISTOGA'S WINE WAY INN, 1019 Foothill Boulevard, Calistoga 94515; phone (707) 942–0680; 6 rooms; $80–$150. A 1915 Craftsman home. Gazebo, air conditioned. Full breakfast, wine in the evening. No pets.

THE PINK MANSION, 1415 Foothill Boulevard, Calistoga 94515; phone (707) 942–0558, fax (707) 942–0558; 6 rooms; $85–$155. An 1875 Victorian house. Three suites have fireplaces. Air conditioned, indoor pool and whirlpool. Full breakfast, complimentary wine and cheese. No smoking. Pets on approval.

CALISTOGA WAYSIDE INN, 1523 Foothill Boulevard, Calistoga 94515; phone (707) 942–0645; 3 rooms; $140 Monday–Thursday, $150 Friday–Sunday. A 1920 Spanish-style home with waterfall into pond, gardens for meditation. Full breakfast, offer of wine, sherry, herb tea, parlor with fireplace. No smoking. No pets.

CULVER'S A COUNTRY INN, 1805 Foothill Boulevard, Calistoga 94515; phone (707) 942–4535; 6 rooms; $140–$160. An 1875 Victorian—Registered Historical Landmark. Fireplace in living room, player piano. Pool. Full breakfast, sherry in evening. No smoking. No pets.

CALISTOGA COUNTRY LODGE, 2883 Foothill Boulevard, Calistoga 94515; phone (707) 942–5555, fax (707) 942–5864; 6 rooms; $105–$145. A 1910 Southwest-style lodge. Two rooms share bath; 2 rooms with fireplaces. Pool, spa. Full breakfast, evening wine and cheese. No smoking. No pets.

FOOTHILL HOUSE, 3037 Foothill Boulevard, Calistoga 94515; phone (707) 942–6933, fax (707) 942–5692, 4 suites; $135–$275. An 1897 renovated farmhouse and cottage. Private entrances. Two suites with whirlpool, all with fireplace or wood-burning stove, refrigerator, antiques, 4-poster beds. Full breakfast inside or on terrace, evening wine and cheese. No smoking. No pets.

SCARLETT'S COUNTRY INN, Calistoga; phone (707) 942–6669; 3 suites; $110–$175. Lawns, pines, vineyards, pool, fireplace, air conditioned. Full breakfast, afternoon refreshments. Children stay free. No pets. Call for reservations and directions.

TRAILSIDE B & B, 4201 Silverado Trail North, Calistoga 94515; phone (707) 942–4106; 3 suites; $120–$150. A 1930s farmhouse with fireplaces, vineyard, air conditioned, pool. Home-baked bread served with breakfast "fixings" to cook in each kitchen. No pets.

QUAIL MOUNTAIN B & B, 4455 North St. Helena Highway, Calistoga 94515; phone (707) 942–0316; 3 rooms; $130–$150. Set about 300 feet above highway, on 26 acres up wooded mountain. Floor-to-ceiling windows to enjoy view. Individual decks and baths, solarium, pool. Full breakfast, complimentary wine. No pets.

Ranches

MOUNTAIN HOME RANCH, 3400 Mountain Home Ranch Road, Calistoga 94515; phone (707) 942–6616; 7 cabins without hot water, 7 hotel rooms, 8 cabanas; $65.00 for 2, plus $7.00 for each additional person. Two pools, tennis court, sulphur spring, on 260 acres dotted with oaks and pines. Breakfast. Pets OK.

TRIPLE-S RANCH, 4600 Mountain Ranch Road, Calistoga 94515; phone (707) 942–6730; 7 cabins; $65. Hiking, bocce ball. Restaurant serves breakfast, thick dinner steaks, vegetarian, pasta. Full bar. Pets OK.

ANGWIN

Bed and Breakfast

FOREST MANOR, 415 Cold Springs Road, Angwin 94508; phone (707) 965–3538; 3 rooms; $169–$315. In English Tudor inn on 20 acres, vaulted ceilings, fireplaces, refrigerators. Whirlpool in honeymoon suite. Pool, verandah. Full breakfast. No pets.

CHAPTER 6

BEYOND WINE TASTING

*W*ining *and dining and general gastro-touring are primary activities in the Napa Valley, but there are many other wonderful things to do in this heaven on Earth. Here we tell you about where to find some of the favorites, including ballooning, biking, horse-back riding, gliding, and golfing. We also describe less active pursuits, such as getting spa treatments, meandering through farmers' markets, and taking river cruises. So here we go—up, up, and away.*

BALLOONING

Ballooning is best and most peaceful in the early morning, when winds are calm and the air is cool. Most balloon flights in the Napa Valley end with brunch in a restaurant, and some include champagne. Most flights cost $115–$185 for adults and $150 for children ages one to sixteen. Here's an alphabetical list of balloon-flying companies. All of them encourage you to bring cameras and personal video equipment.

ADVENTURES ALOFT OF THE NAPA VALLEY, P.O. Box 2500 at Vintage 1870, Yountville 94599; phone (707) 944–4408 or (800) 944–4408, e-mail ballooning@nvaloft.com, Web site www.nvaloft.com. Claims "the world's most experienced pilot team" and offers a seated champagne breakfast hosted by your pilot.

BONAVENTURA BALLOON COMPANY, 133 Wall Road, Napa 94558; phone (707) 944–2822. Has been used and recommended by *Forbes* magazine, Universal Studios/ABC-TV, and *Gourmet* magazine. Includes champagne.

CALISTOGA BALLOON ADVENTURES, P.O. Box 932, Calistoga 94515; phone (707) 942–2282 or (800) 400–0162. Hour-long flights from Calistoga meadow; you are allowed to pitch in for the balloon setup if you wish; the price includes brunch at Café Sarafornia in Calistoga. The whole experience lasts three to four hours.

NAPA VALLEY BALLOONS, P.O. Box 2860, Yountville 94599; phone (707) 944–0228 or (800) 253–2224. The hour-long flight with Napa's oldest ballooning company culminates with a catered sparkling-wine brunch.

BICYCLE RIDING AND BIKE RENTALS

Napa Valley is an ideal locale for biking as, except for a few slight climbs, it's pretty flat. The heavy traffic makes cycling on Highway 29 hazardous, but bike lanes run the full length of the Silverado Trail. The Trail also has fewer cars and a generally quieter ride and ambience than Highway 29.

Here's an alphabetical list of bike rental (and repair) shops. Most charge about $25.00 a day, or $7.00 an hour for rentals.

BICYCLE TRAX, 796 Soscol Avenue at the corner of Third Street, Napa 94559; phone (707) 258–8729. Voted "Best Bike Shop in the Napa Valley."

BIKE TOURS OF THE NAPA VALLEY, 4080 Byway East (at Trower), Napa 94559; phone (707) 255–3377 or (800) 707–2453. Bike rentals and tours, including half-day or one-day guided tours.

PALISADES MOUNTAIN SPORT, 1330 Gerard, Calistoga 94515; phone (707) 942–9687. Mountain and hybrid bike rentals and expert mechanics available including drop-in.

ST. HELENA CYCLERY, 1156 Main Street, St. Helena 94574; phone (707) 963–7736, fax (707) 963–5099. Rentals of hybrid bicycles for touring; the rental fee includes helmet, lock, water-bottle cage, rear rack, and a bag to carry picnic supplies.

YOUNTVILLE BIKE RENTALS, Vintage 1870 on Washington Street, Yountville 94599; phone (707) 944–9080. Includes helmet and a map of Napa Valley and its wineries.

BOCCE BALL

When was the last time you played bocce ball? Give it a try. Public bocce courts are located right in downtown Yountville, south of new hotels and The Diner on the west side of Washington Street. Take the Yountville exit off

Highway 29, turn right (east) to Washington Street, and turn right (south) again. The bocce ball courts will be on your right. Bocce balls are available at a small rental fee. Call Brent Randol (707) 483–3630 to schedule free games.

HANG GLIDING

CALISTOGA GLIDERS, 1546 Lincoln Avenue, Calistoga 94515; phone (707) 942–5000, fax (707) 942–4520. Your affable glider pilots recommend that you "surf the invisible waves of air breaking over the mountains as your glider swoops and soars on silent wings." Go ahead! Open every day, weather permitting, Calistoga Gliders will have you take off heading down the Napa Valley from its northern tip, bounded on both sides by low hills, with vineyards and wineries below. Maximum combined weight is 340 pounds. The cost ranges from $79 for one person for twenty minutes to $179 for two people for thirty minutes.

GOLFING

Not surprisingly, Napa Valley has lovely golf courses. Most of the courses are open to the public; two are not.

Courses Open to the Public

AETNA SPRINGS GOLF COURSE, 1600 Aetna Springs Road, Pope Valley 94567; phone (800) 675–2115. Nine holes, driving range, picnic and BBQ facilities, forty-five minutes north of Napa. From Highway 29, turn east on Deer Park Road opposite the Culinary Institute of America. From the Silverado Trail, turn east at the stoplight. Go up Deer Park Road for 12 miles into Pope Valley. Turn north on Pope Valley Road and continue for 3.6 miles. Turn left on Aetna Springs Road. Continue 1 mile to the golf course. Greens fees: $13 weekdays, $18 weekends.

CHARDONNAY CLUB, 2555 Jamieson Canyon Road (Highway 12 between American Canyon and Highway 80), Napa 94558; phone (707) 257–8950. Two eighteen-hole courses, lovely setting, restaurant. Greens fees: $60 weekdays, $80 weekends.

CHIMNEY ROCK GOLF COURSE, 5320 Silverado Trail, Napa 94558; phone (707) 255–3363. Nine holes surrounded by Chimney Rock's vineyards, Cathy's

Cafe. Greens fees: $18 weekdays, $22 weekends; twilight (cooler) play $13 weekdays, $17 weekends.

MOUNT ST. HELENA GOLF, Napa Valley Fairgrounds, Calistoga 94515; phone (707) 942–9966. Flat nine holes, BBQ area, RV park, seniors' programs, snack bar. Greens fees: $12 weekdays, $18 weekends; seniors $9 weekdays, $12 weekends.

NAPA MUNICIPAL GOLF COURSE at John F. Kennedy Park, 2295 Streblow Drive, Napa 94558; phone (707) 255–4333. Eighteen holes, cocktail lounge, restaurant, outside deck. Greens fees: $15 residents, $21 nonresidents weekdays; $20 residents, $25 nonresidents weekends.

Private Courses

MEADOWOOD RESORT, 900 Meadowood Lane, St. Helena 94574; phone (800) 458–8080. Open to members and resort guests only. Members of other clubs may play. Nine holes. Greens fees: $35.

SILVERADO COUNTRY CLUB, 1600 Atlas Peak Road, Napa 94558; phone (707) 257–0200. Open to members and resort guests only. Greens fees: resort guests $115, members of reciprocal clubs $135, including cart.

TENNIS

The climate in Napa Valley makes for some fantastic tennis. Try out these courts on your visit. They are open to the public and are available on a first-come, first-serve basis.

Public Courts

CALISTOGA PUBLIC TENNIS COURTS, Stevenson and Grant Streets; phone (707) 942–2838. Four courts, lighted at night.

NAPA PUBLIC COURTS, Napa Valley College (Highway 12 south of Napa); phone (707) 257–9529 and at Vintage High School, 1275 Trower Avenue, Napa High School, 2475 Jefferson Street, and Silverado Middle School, 1133 Coombsville Road, all in Napa.

ST. HELENA PUBLIC TENNIS COURTS, Robert Louis Stevenson School, 1316 Hill View Place; St. Helena High School, 1401 Grayson Avenue; Crane Park off Crane Avenue; phone (707) 963–5706.

Private Courts

MEADOWOOD RESORT, 900 Meadowood Lane, St. Helena 94574; phone (707) 963–3646. Courts open to members and guests only.

SILVERADO COUNTRY CLUB AND RESORT, 1600 Atlas Peak Road, Napa 94558; phone (707) 257–0200. Courts open to members and guests only.

TOURS

Every entrepreneur in the Napa Valley is some sort of tour guide, some more reputable than others. Here we identify a few—but perhaps our book will help you be your own best guide.

NAPA VALLEY WINE TRAIN, 1275 McKinstry at Soscol Avenue, Napa 94559; phone (707) 253–2111 or (800) 522–4142. The Wine Train is a more than three-hour, 36-mile ride up the spine of the Napa Valley along the tracks built by Samuel Brannan for the Napa Valley Railroad Company in 1864 and last owned by the Southern Pacific. It is also an elegant gourmand trip into the past, with plush railroad cars and the best Napa Valley wines and excellent food served in a 1917 Pullman Dining Car.

Many locals don't like the Wine Train, and some people demonstrate this dislike with signs along the route. They feel that the Train competes with local restaurants (which, of course, it does, like any other food purveyor). But Golden Grain (Rice-a-Roni) Macaroni Company and Ghirardelli Chocolate president Vincent de Domenico perseveres with his Wine Train. (Mrs. de Domenico told Kathleen, "He never had a model train as a child.") It runs at 11:30 A.M. and 6:30 P.M. weekdays, 8:55 A.M. and 12:30 and 6:00 P.M. weekends. The food is excellent and reasonably priced. Reservations are necessary—and mandatory for the winemakers' lunches on Fridays. Jackets suggested on dinner train. Prices range from $25 to $60; a children's menu is available.

GRAND ROMANCE NAPA RIVER CRUISES, Main and Third Street Dock, Napa 94558; phone (707) 554–2100 or (800) 750–7501. An enterprising group captured one of the old Petaluma riverboats and restored it to recapture the glamour and romance of the golden days of paddlewheeler travel. Two-and-a-half-hour cruises on the Napa River include lunch or dinner at $34.95 or $39.95 per person, leaving from Napa; or you might enjoy the Sunset Dinner Dance ($49.95), Sunday Champagne Brunch Cruise ($29.95), or the Music Cruise on Sunday afternoons ($15.95), all departing from the Vallejo Waterfront.

BRIDGEFORD FLYING SERVICE (Napa Valley Airport; 707–224–0887 or 707–644–1658) offers sensational tours by air in its Cessna Skyhawk or Cessna Centurion, for groups of any size. Fly over the Napa Valley, Lake Berryessa, Golden Gate Bridge and San Francisco Bay, and along the Pacific Coast and the Russian River in Sonoma County. Make up your own tour—they'll fly you.

ANTIQUE TOURS LIMOUSINE SERVICE, phone (707) 226–9227. Tour in elegantly restored, 1947 convertible Packard limousines for an unforgettable Gatsby-esque experience. The cars are equipped with stereo, electronic bar, champagne bucket, gourmet picnic lunch, and privacy window. These limos accommodate up to six passengers in the rear, and two more up front. Rates: $60 per hour weekdays, $80 per hour weekends, both with three hour minimums. Let your guides select the wineries to visit, or go to those of your choice.

ROYAL COACH LIMOUSINE SERVICE, INC., (800) 995–7692, has basically the same features as Antique Tours, but without lunch, and featuring more traditional cars. Executive Limousine, (707) 257–2949, offers sedans,.stretches, and super-stretches for transportation and wine tours, as do Napa Valley Crown Limousine, (707) 257–0879, (707) 226–9500, and (800) 286–8228; Classic Limousine, (707) 253–0999; Odyssey Limousine, (800) 544–1929; Premier Limousine, (707) 226–2106; and Napa Valley Limousine Services, (707) 258–0689, which also has "licensed bodyguards."

BEAU LIMOUSINE NAPA WINE TOURS; phone (800) 387–2328, Web site www.beaulimousine.com. Choose from a variety of packages, from a $49 five-hour wine tour to a $168 dinner on the Wine Train and a five-hour wine tour. Prices are based per person ($168 per person, with a minimum of six people) and include champagne. Stretch limousine or "limousine party bus."

DESTINATION: NAPA VALLEY HISTORICAL TOURS, phone or fax (707) 965–1808. Covers history and historical wineries, native cultures and pioneer settlers, St. Helena's 19th-century architecture, Calistoga spas and silver mines, enology, stone bridges, water towers, Victorian homes, landmarks, and ranchos; $39 for a half-day tour.

NAPA VALLEY HOLIDAYS, phone (707) 255–1050, uses "mini-coaches" to wineries, hiking trails, restaurants; $30 per person.

VILLA CA 'TOGA HOUSE TOUR, from Sharpsteen Museum, 1311 Washington Street, Calistoga 94515; phone (707) 963–4171. Artist Carlo Marchiori conducts a tour once each May. Shuttle buses from the Sharpsteen Museum; $20 donation to the museum. The museum also sells detailed books for self-guided auto or foot tours.

SPAS

Calistoga majors in spas, mud baths, massages, and mineral baths from the natural wells located in the area. Spas abound in Napa Valley; some provide lodging, while others are day spas. Here we tell you about a few of the best. They all take major credit cards and reservations.

CALISTOGA SPA HOT SPRINGS, 1006 Washington Street, Calistoga 94515; phone (707) 942–6269. Four outdoor mineral pools, mud and mineral baths, steam bath, blanket sweat, massage, exercise equipment, aerobics. Fifty-seven rooms, all with kitchenettes.

DR. WILKINSON'S HOT SPRINGS, 1507 Lincoln Avenue, Calistoga 94515; phone (707) 942–4102. A spa with 1950s character; mud baths, mineral whirlpool baths, steam rooms, massage, facial salon, indoor mineral pool, two outdoor swimming pools. Forty-two rooms, some with kitchenettes.

INDIAN SPRINGS, 1712 Lincoln Avenue, Calistoga 94515; phone (707) 942–4913, fax (707) 942–4919. Three thermal geysers, sixteen acres of volcanic ash, old Native and Wappo Indian sweat lodges; mud, steam, naturally heated Olympic-size swimming pool. Seventeen cottage suites.

LAVENDER HILL SPA, 1015 Foothill Boulevard, Calistoga 94515; phone (707) 942–4495 or (800) 528–4772. Intended for couples; Fango mud bath, massage, seaweed bath and herbal blanket wrap, aromatherapy, mineral-salt bath, mini-facial, foot reflexology. No lodging.

MOUNT VIEW SPA AT THE MOUNT VIEW HOTEL, 1457 Lincoln Avenue, Calistoga 94515; phone (707) 942–5789 or (800) 772–8838. Euro-spa featuring Fango mud bath for two, massage, facial, body wrap, outdoor pool and mineral Jacuzzi. Thirty-four elegant rooms.

NANCE'S HOT SPRINGS, 1614 Lincoln Avenue, Calistoga 94515; phone (707) 942–6211. Mud bath, mineral bath, massage, indoor mineral pool. Twenty-four rooms, all with kitchenettes.

FARMERS' MARKETS

Every week three farmers' markets attract locals and visitors alike to the freshest of fresh vegetables and flowers from the Napa Valley and other prime California agricultural sources.

NAPA CHEF'S MARKET, at the Napa Town Center, on and off First Street, Napa 94558; phone (707) 255–8073; Friday 4:00–9:00 P.M., May–September. Good family fun in this downtown mall atmosphere. Many different vendors set up on First Street, in the walkways within the open-air mall. Napa Valley chefs give cooking demonstrations at 6:00 P.M., and local bands play live music.

NAPA DOWNTOWN FARMERS' MARKET, in the parking lot on West Street between First and Pearl Streets, Napa 94558; phone (707) 252–7142; Tuesday 7:30 A.M.–noon, May–October. This market features some local produce in a neighborhood atmosphere. If you time it right, you can stay on for lunch at nearby restaurants.

To get to the ST. HELENA FARMERS' MARKET, in Crane Park, turn west off Highway 29 onto Grayson Avenue between the A&W root-beer restaurant and St. Helena High School, St. Helena, 94574; phone (707) 252–2105, Fridays 7:30–11:30 A.M. May–October. This market has the most gourmet atmosphere and delicacies; a must for food lovers visiting the Napa Valley.

CHAPTER 7

HISTORY OF THE NAPA VALLEY

Once upon a time there were no grapevines, no wineries, and no wine in Napa Valley. There was just a long, narrow valley—no more than 5 miles wide at any point—with a river meandering southward down to a gigantic bay sheltered from the ocean. At the head of the valley was a dark mountain, which, at 4,343 feet, was the highest for a hundred miles in any direction.

Within the shadow of that mountain, along the shores of the river, beneath the canopy of thousands of oak, fir, and redwood trees, and in the hills that bordered the valley, lived more than 5,000 Native Americans. Their ancestors had first migrated to the valley more than 7,000 years earlier.

By the time Europeans discovered the valley, it was home to several peoples, including a Coast Miwok tribe (which the Mexicans named Wappos, a corruption of the Spanish *guapos*, meaning "brave ones"). These people called themselves Mayacamas. They lived northwest of the Pomo and Wintun groups, who had come across the hills from the Sacramento Valley. Tribelets included the Callajomans, near St. Helena and Oakville; the Caymus, around Yountville; the Napa (spelled *Nappa* by the first white settlers), between the river and present-day Napa city; the Ulcas, east of the Napa River; and the Suscol, south toward the bay. A Miwok band, the Huichica, spilled over from Sonoma Valley in the southwest, in what is now called the Carneros District. To the southeast, at the present-day city of Vallejo and beyond, lived the brave and combative Suisun.

Hunters and gatherers, these peoples lived on game, fish, roots, berries, and a rough bread made from acorns ground with a mortar and pestle. There was no agriculture. Simple thatched huts provided shelter from late autumn to early spring; then they set up outdoor camps for hunting and fishing closer to the shores of rivers, streams, and the bay.

Like most Natives of northern California, these first denizens of the Napa Valley were far more hygienic than the white invaders, bathing every day. The men and boys regularly and purposely perspired in a sweathouse, waiting until the heat was nearly unbearable before rinsing off in a cold stream. These buildings doubled as a meeting place for the elders. It was an existence lived in harmony with nature.

FATHER ALTIMIRA "DISCOVERS" THE VALLEY

San Francisco Bay was "discovered" in 1769 by a company of Spanish soldiers led by Gaspar de Portola, who had accidentally bypassed Monterey Bay. Portola sent his chief explorer, Sergeant Jose Ortega, circling the bay to find a route to Drake's Bay to the north. Ortega stopped at Carquinez Strait, across the bay from the delta of the Napa River, and turned back. Thus Napa Valley remained little more than a rumor to the outside world for another fifty years.

The Spanish landed a squad of soldiers at Bodega Bay in 1810. They marched overland and then south through Sonoma Valley just west of the Mayacamas hills from Napa Valley. Sonoma Creek had overflowed, and the soldiers reported that Sonoma Valley was too marshy for settlement. In 1817 a small mission was built in San Rafael as a sanitarium for sick Indians.

When the Mexicans gained independence from Spain in 1822, their government was anxious to counter possible Russian movement from Fort Ross at Bodega Bay, and the Franciscan friars wanted to found a northern mission where food could be produced. A young Spanish priest, Father Jose Altimira, was sent from Mission San Francisco de Assisi (Mission Dolores) in Yerba Buena with a troop of mounted soldiers to locate a likely site. Altimira passed through San Rafael on June 16, 1823, and headed over the first range of hills to the Petaluma plain. He then led his party over the next range of hills eastward and for two days explored Sonoma Valley.

Altimira and his military escort turned east again and rode over the hills more or less along the route of current Highway 121—they were the first non-natives to see the Napa Valley. It was July 1, 1823. After crossing the Napa River, they climbed a hill east of the present-day site of Napa State Hospital, from which they could see the sweep of the southern valley. After another day of exploration, they returned to the Sonoma Valley. There Altimira set up an altar at what is now Cline Cellars on his way back to Mission Dolores. A few weeks later he returned to Sonoma Valley to start the construction of Mission San Francisco Solano. It was dedicated on April 4, 1824.

The Napa Valley was just too distant from the mission in San Rafael to be considered for a new mission location. However, this verdant valley and its "pagan natives" easily came within the expanding control of the Sonoma mission. According to legend, Father Altimira brought a sack of mustard seed to sprinkle along the way, in order to be able to find and return to his route at a later time. This is probably apocryphal, since Altimira and his military leader, Francisco Castro, took daily notes describing their route. However, each year Napa Valley displays a yellow carpet of mustard, much of which is planted by vineyardists and celebrated with an annual festival.

Altimira sailed back to Spain in 1826, unwilling to take Mexican citizenship. He left behind fields of grain; fruit trees; cattle, sheep, and hogs; and 3,000 grapevines. His principal vineyard was planted next to the Sonoma mission, but a few vines were planted in the Napa plain. These were the so-called Mission grapes, which made adequate but unexciting wine for the use of the Mission fathers.

Some 1,300 Natives were baptized between 1823 and 1834, and as many as 700 lived under serf-like conditions in or around the Sonoma mission, supposedly learning agriculture and manufacturing (like adobe bricks). The whip was used to enforce rules and punish runaways. Most of the Indians in the Napa Valley avoided living at the mission, although many were baptized there.

VALLEJO AND THE MEXICAN LAND GRANTS

In 1834 the Mexican government decreed that the missions be "secularized" and their lands and buildings taken over by the government. Sent north from Monterey was twenty-nine-year-old Lieutenant Mariano G. Vallejo, who assumed control of the mission lands covering the region from present-day Petaluma, through Sonoma Valley, and all of Napa Valley.

The first American to settle in the Napa Valley was George C. Yount, guided there in 1831 by twenty-four-year-old frontiersman Guy Freeman Fling, who had "gone native," living with Indians around Monterey and adopting their ways. As he stood on the cusp of Mount St. Helena (not yet so named), Yount reputedly announced to the wind that "in such a place I would like to live…." A North Carolinian with a wandering foot, he had left his wife Eliza and their three children in Missouri one day in 1826 to lead a pack train to New Mexico—and never returned. He hunted everything from elk to otters, for a time made shingles, and in 1833 became sort of a jack-of-all trades for both the San Rafael and Sonoma missions.

When Mariano Vallejo took command of Sonoma, he contracted with Yount to make shingles for the roofs of the mission building he was having restored, and for his own palatial adobe facing the Sonoma eight-acre plaza that he had made the centerpiece of the pueblo. Yount told Vallejo that his one desire was to have land of his own, and he knew just the place. He was baptized by the Catholic priest in San Rafael and began exploring Napa Valley in earnest. With Vallejo's endorsement, on March 23, 1836 Yount received a grant of 11,814 acres in the heart of the Valley, called Rancho Caymus after the Caymus tribe. With the labor of Natives from the Sonoma mission, he built a two-story block-house that served as both a home and a bastion from which Indian attacks could be repelled.

In May 1836 Vallejo gave two grants to Nicolas Higuerra: one where Napa City now stands, and another in the Carneros—a total of 2,638 acres. Higuerra built an adobe house and planted beans.

A native Californio, born in Monterey like General Vallejo, was Cayetano Juarez, who had come to Sonoma as a seventeen-year-old soldier in 1827. He received a two-square league (8,865 acre) grant called Tulucay, on the east shore of the Napa River, southeast of present-day Napa city. Juarez built an adobe house. Today it is the oldest building still standing; it currently houses the Old Adobe Restaurant.

The next beneficiary of the largesse of General Vallejo was brother Salvador Vallejo. Salvador was granted the traditional two square leagues, which comprised two tracts, called the Trancas and the Jolopa. They were north and northeast of what is now the center of Napa, generally called the Napa Rancho. He built a good-sized adobe home for himself off what is now called the Silverado Trail, and two more for ranch workers. Later he received an additional 6,652 acres.

The Berryessa family received two large grants in 1836 totaling over 17,000 acres. This land was called the Mallocomas (or Mayacamas), which covered the northern end of the Valley, including today's Calistoga. In 1843 they acquired an even bigger grant, more than 35,000 acres, much of which was then Berryessa Valley and is now under man-made Lake Berryessa. This grant was, oddly, named Las Putas Rancho (puta is Spanish for "whore"). The name survives as Putah Creek.

Edward Bale was an eccentric, twenty-nine-year-old English physician when he landed in Monterey from a ship out of Boston. For a couple of years, he prac-ticed medicine in Monterey. He wooed and wed the young niece of General Vallejo, Maria Soberanes, converted to Catholicism, and became a naturalized Mexican citizen. While in Monterey he obtained a permit to open a drug store but began selling liquor, which was against the law. For this he was arrested and fined. Despite Bale's indiscretion, Vallejo appointed him "Surgeon of the California Forces," since he was the only doctor around. Bale and his wife moved to Vallejo's headquarters in Sonoma.

But Bale soon ran afoul of brother-in-law Salvador, accusing him of making a pass at Bale's wife, who was also Salvador's niece. Salvador administered a whipping to Bale. A battered and humiliated Bale responded with two shots at Salvador, missed, and was thrown into what passed for a jail in Sonoma. Through the intervention of the British consul in Monterey, no punishment was meted out.

Despite all this discord, in 1841 General Vallejo arranged a two-square league grant for Bale in Napa Valley—perhaps to get him out of town—between the grants to Yount and the Berryessas, and including the future site of St. Helena. It was officially given the unusual name of Carne Humana—literally "human flesh" (and you thought Whore's Ranch was bad)—which was apparently a corruption of an Indian name for the area. The Spanish and English ears for native tongues were notoriously weak, and the newcomers seemed to care little for the names the Natives gave to land that was being stolen from them.

In the area where Highway 121 links Napa and Sonoma Counties today, another expatriate American, Jacob Leese, who happened to be married to Vallejo's sister Rosalie, received the Huichica grant in exchange for property in Yerba Buena (San Francisco), where he was a trader, and moved to Sonoma.

In 1843 Dr. Bale built a house on his rancho with Indian labor. His neighbor Yount had received some good news in 1841: After 15 years his wife had obtained a divorce for desertion. He also received an additional land grant, timberlands in the hills called La Jota ("The J"), including what is now the community of Angwin.

Two Americans settled and received grants beyond the eastern hills. William Pope, a former trapper and hunter in the southwest who had been living in the Los Angeles pueblo with his Mexican wife and children, was given Pope Valley. Pope had only six months to enjoy his land, for he suffered a near-amputation of his leg when an ax slipped, and he bled to death. The other to receive a land grant was Colonel John Chiles, an old Indian fighter and guide across the plains as early as 1841, who brought Yount's children from Missouri in 1843. The following year he received the Chiles Valley grant. He continued his guiding work, settled permanently with his family in 1852, and built a flour mill.

Napa Valley benefited from the stability of land titles, for all the grants were confirmed promptly by the state land commission formed in 1851, a remarkable result when compared to some land grant disputes that dragged on for as long as 30 years.

THE DEHUMANIZATION OF THE INDIANS

But what of the original residents: the Wappo, Pomo, Coast Miwok and all their sub-nations, the Mayacamas, Caymus, Suscol, Huichica, and Nappa?

Many of the Indians had become restless under mission life. They often ran away, only to be hunted down by the Mexican soldiers assigned to the Sonoma mission. Between 1837 and 1839 a smallpox epidemic killed hundreds of Natives, who lacked immunity to the European malady. Other diseases, such as cholera, and the consumption of hard liquor (unknown to the Indians before the Europeans came) reduced the population.

Fearful of Indian attacks, Mariano Vallejo initially put the problem in the hands of his heavy-handed brother Salvador, who used his small troop of soldiers to show force. In the one outright battle between Mexican soldiers and the Indians in the Soscol (a Spanish spelling of Suscol) area, the Natives lost more than 200, against the deaths of only two Mexicans.

However, General Vallejo soon entered into peace treaties or alliances with several of the chiefs of neighboring tribes. The most valuable of these arrangements was a long-term pact with Chief Solano (a name given when he was baptized at the mission) of the Suisun. The imposing Solano stood 6 feet 7 inches and was probably the biggest Native in Northern California. He was smart and loyal to Vallejo. The Suisun were willing to fight off any tribes that had any ideas of threatening the Mexican settlement. It was Solano who arrested Dr. Bale when he ran off after shooting at Salvador Vallejo.

Nevertheless, the Natives had become dehumanized in the eyes of Salvador and his squad, as well as some of the early settlers. In 1841, responding to reports of cattle being stolen by Natives in the upper Napa Valley, a group of soldiers and settlers under the direction of Salvador Vallejo surrounded a sweat house near Mount St. Helena. As the Indian men and boys stepped out, one by one they were shot and killed—more than a hundred in all. An entire village lost its menfolk.

That cowardly massacre was probably the low point in the history of pre-statehood California, but it was not an isolated case. Several years later one of the Kelsey brothers—Andrew—and his partner were killed by Indians in revenge for mistreatment of Indian workers and the kidnapping of an Indian girl. In response, U.S. troops surrounded Moth Island on Clear Lake and killed all the Indians there, including women and children. One hundred and fifty Natives were massacred in this tragic incident.

George Yount, on the other hand, was friendly with the Indians. He hired them to build his blockhouse and an adobe home two years later. In turn they taught him various skills. Only once were shots fired at Yount's blockhouse. Most settlers found that the Indians were good workers and trustworthy if treated fairly and given respect.

Eventually, some of the Native survivors were induced to move to a reservation in Mendocino County, established in 1856.

GEORGE YOUNT

In 1841 the Russians at Bodega Bay sent an exploring party eastward to Mount St. Helena, where they planted a copper tablet memorializing the visit on the mountain's western peak and raised a Russian flag. That symbolic effort was the last Russian move to enlarge their influence in California, and they soon sold Fort Ross to John Sutter.

The origin of the name St. Helena has several versions. In 1823 Father Altimira declared that it looked like "Saint Helena on her bier," referring to the sculptured tomb of the saint at the abbey in Rheims. Some suggest that it was named for Saint Helena, patron saint of Russian royalty. Others theorize that the name honored the wife of the governor-general of Siberia and Fort Ross or for a ship of that name that brought supplies to Fort Ross. Take your pick, but Altimira was there first.

THE BEAR FLAG REVOLT

Meanwhile, by 1840 wagon trains were beginning to wend their way west, mostly to Oregon. The Kelsey family train (including Ben Kelsey's wife, Nancy, the first white woman to cross the plains) came down from the Columbia River in 1844 to the Napa Valley. Those who trekked over the Sierra Nevadas stopped at Sutter's Fort and then dispersed from there. Other Americans arrived by ships that were anchoring in San Francisco Bay.

By 1846 about 10 percent of the population of Alta California were transplanted Americans. The Mexican governor of the province announced that new American immigrants were not welcome.

In Napa Valley there were maybe a dozen houses and a non-Native population of less than fifty. In the area of what is now Napa city, there were neither buildings nor white people.

U.S. president James K. Polk had an acquisitive eye on California and the Southwest. Captain John C. Fremont ("The Pathfinder") was roaming about southern Oregon beyond the reach of Mexican authorities, with a crew of "topographical engineers," including scout Kit Carson, with secret orders. In early June 1846 Fremont rode south to Sutter's Fort, where he encountered an irregular company of twenty-two American settlers desirous of throwing off Mexican rule. Fremont urged them to intercept a herd of horses being sent by General Vallejo to General Jose Castro in Santa Clara, and they did so.

Now with first-class mounts, the Americans decided they would capture Sonoma, the frontier capital of Mexican authority. Led by Ezekiel Merritt, a Fremont man, they set out for Sonoma and on June 13 stopped at the Bale rancho in Napa Valley, where they met a group of Napa Valley settlers, whose spokesman was John Grigsby. Eleven of the Napa Valley men, including Grigsby, three Kelsey brothers (Ben, Sam, and Andy), and teenager Nathan Coombs, agreed to become part of the force. Late at night the thirty-three riders headed westward over the hills.

They galloped into the Sonoma plaza shortly after dawn on June 14. General Vallejo was asleep. In the words of historian Bernard deVoto, "Sonoma was a tiny cluster of adobe houses and could have been captured by Tom Sawyer and Huck Finn."

Awakened by the whoops and hollers of a rowdy-looking band of armed riders, Vallejo invited in the leaders. He offered them brandy and wine and spoke of having a discussion on a "friendly" basis until interrupted by Merritt, who announced that they "meant business" and intended to set up an independent California government. Merritt also placed under arrest General Vallejo, his brother Salvador, brother-in-law Jacob Leese, and his secretary Victor Prudon.

Nevertheless, General Vallejo ordered wine for all the men under Merritt's command. Some of the men drank too much and began talking about looting, until William Ide, the co-leader of the Grigsby-Ide wagon train, made a stirring speech reminding the invaders that their goal was to form a republic free of Mexico. His oratory caused them to elect Ide the first and only president of the Republic of California.

President Ide prepared a proclamation printed in English and Spanish, while William Todd (nephew of Mary Todd Lincoln) made a flag out of a petticoat and a chemise, drew a red star in the corner, ran a strip of red flannel along the bottom, and drew a bear, which looked for all the world like a misshapen pig. With "poke juice" he printed in the words CALIFORNIA REPUBLC, but then had to blot out the last syllable to insert the missing "I." The concept of a bear flag was apparently the idea of Napa Valley's Peter Storm, who in later years would display his version with a bear standing on its hind legs. Vallejo and his aides were taken to Sutter's Fort and put in jail, where they languished for two months.

The California Republic lasted just twenty-five days. Before June was over Fremont showed up in Sonoma and incorporated the Bear Flaggers into what he called the California Battalion, making Grigsby commander of one of three companies. On July 9 Navy lieutenant Joseph W. Revere, grandson of Paul Revere, rode into the plaza with the news that Monterey had been captured by the U.S. Navy and that he had been ordered to raise the American flag at Sonoma. Down came the Bear Flag from its pole in the plaza, and up went the stars and stripes.

Although Fremont, Revere, and the American naval commanders acted as if there was a war on, they did not know for sure. On May 13, 1846 the United States had declared war on Mexico, supposedly over a border dispute along the Rio Grande. However, official news of the war did not reach Monterey until the second week in August.

When the Mexican War ended with the Treaty of Guadalupe Hidalgo in 1848, California became American land, but officially neither a territory nor a state. All Californios were granted full benefits of American citizenship; and the vast majority of former Mexican citizens, including the Vallejos and the Napa Valley Californios, swore loyalty to the United States.

NATHAN COOMBS LAYS OUT NAPA

George Yount, in 1837, and Dr. Bale, in 1846, built grist mills for grinding grain into flour, as well as lumber mills. The Bale grist mill still exists in Bale Grist Mill Historical Park on Highway 29 between St. Helena and Calistoga. Yount's blockhouse, adobe house, and mills are no more, but they are commemorated by a stone monument just north of Yountville on Yount Mill Road.

The principal commercial activities in the Valley before 1850 consisted of cattle raising (hides for leather always made for good business), grain (wheat, barley, beans, and corn), a few orchards, the beginning of a lumber industry, and some quarrying. A primitive embarcadero was built on the Napa River from which Nicolas Higuerra shipped lime on a small sail-powered freight boat as early as 1844.

Nathan Coombs was a young man from Massachusetts who came to the Sacramento Valley in 1843, worked on a ranch, married the boss's daughter, and in 1845 moved to the Napa Valley. Coombs and John Grigsby were hired by pioneer Higuerra in 1847 to build his adobe residence to replace the thatch-and-mud cabin he had built himself. In payment, Higuerra gave them a large plot of land on the Napa River. Coombs soon bought out Grigsby's interest.

Just twenty-one, Coombs laid out the proposed town of Napa on his newly acquired property, using James Hudspeth as surveyor. Then Coombs began to sell lots. The first building erected was Harrison Pierce's Empire Saloon (first things first!), on Third Street near the Napa River. The streets were not marked clearly, and the saloon was framed out in the middle of Main Street and had to be rolled to its proper location. In 1848 J. T. Thompson opened the first store at the foot of Main Street, followed by a store built for Vallejo and Frisbie (the general and his son in law), and a spate of others in 1849. The spelling of "Napa" with a single "p" was settled, and the use of "Nappa" was abandoned by 1851.

NATHAN COOMBS

The California Gold Rush brought almost all Napa business and expansion to a halt between late 1848 and early 1850. With the discovery of easy gold at Sutter's Mill near Coloma, Napa was virtually deserted by those who rushed to locate a claim and a fortune. Most would be disappointed, but Napa eventually benefited by the influx of immigrants pouring into northern California through San Francisco.

The Napa Valley's first school was established in 1847 by a survivor of the snow-trapped Donner Party, Sarah Graves Fosdick, the first American schoolteacher in California, who taught outdoors under the trees on the Bale property until a school was built for her in 1849. The first public elementary school opened in Napa in 1855.

In 1848 a ferry service across the Napa River was instituted. The first steamboat from San Francisco arrived at the Napa embarcadero at Soscol in 1850, and two years later it blossomed into regular commercial runs three times a week. From there stages and wagons transported passengers and goods northward. Soscol was a natural port, since the Napa River was still navigable there at low tide. Roads from Napa to Sonoma and Vallejo were improved in the early 1850s.

Napa County was one of the original twenty-seven California counties created in September 1850. It originally included present-day Lake County, which was split off in 1861. In 1872 a small slice of Lake County was returned to Napa in a county-line adjustment. The first official census in 1850 numbered Napa County's population at 405, with 159 in the town of Napa. In two years it would multiply five times.

With increased population came crime. The most spectacular case stemmed from a minor lawsuit in 1850 between pioneers George Yount and Isaac Howell, which Justice of the Peace S. H. Sellers had decided in Howell's favor. A few days later a relative of Yount's, Hugh McCaully, encountered Judge Sellers at a store and began giving him an earful about the decision. The judge, who was sitting on a barrel, in effect told McCaully to "get lost." In response, McCaully pulled a large knife and stabbed Sellers in the back. The judge died instantly, and McCaully was tried, convicted, and sentenced to hang.

The killer's friends went to the state capital, which was in nearby Benicia (named for General Vallejo's wife) for that year, and convinced the governor to issue a reprieve. Friends of the slain judge were in Benicia and heard about the reprieve, so they chartered a little steamer to race to Napa, while the officer coming with the governor's order headed overland. To delay the officer, they stopped long enough to disable the ferry so that it could not cross the Napa River, thus forcing the officer to ride upstream to the Trancas area before crossing. In the meantime the judge's friends invaded the temporary jail, located above a general store at Main and Second, threw a rope over a rafter, and lynched McCaully. No witnesses could be found.

Coombs built the American Hotel in 1850, the first hostelry in the Valley, which was followed by the Napa Hotel and inns connected with new saloons. Some of the enterprises were run in structures that were half wood and half tent, but were soon replaced by something more substantial. Restaurants, a blacksmith shop, a butcher shop, and houses—a couple built of brick—made their appearance in the early 1850s.

Unfortunately, the quality of so-called streets did not match the development of businesses and homes, for they were unimproved mudholes part of the year, and rough trails in summer. Vehicles were constantly getting stuck or tipping over. Inadequate bridges were built across neighboring creeks and the Napa River. Most of them collapsed or were swept away in heavy rains.

Coombs started a freight shipping line and from his ranch, The Willows, became the state's leading breeder of thoroughbred racehorses. He served two terms in the State Assembly. When he died at age fifty-one in 1877, his funeral was the largest in the city's history, with a cortege of 150 carriages and a procession of fifty Napa County pioneers.

THE BIRTH OF ST. HELENA

In 1849 Dr. Bale died, at just forty-one years of age, leading to the sell-off of portions of his property in the 1850s. One of the early buyers was Henry

Still. In 1853 Still built a home and a general store in the middle of the upper portion of the Napa Valley. Trouble was, the population was so sparse that he could look miles in each direction and seldom spot a customer. So Still devised a remarkable strategy: He would give away—free, gratis—a lot of land to anyone willing to start a business on the property. Shortly there were takers—a shoe shop, a blacksmith, a wagon-building and -repair business, a hotel, and then two saloons. Houses soon followed, and the Baptists and the Cumberland Presbyterians built churches. The town of St. Helena had been born.

The county rejoiced when the rough trail up the center of the Valley was designated a county road, and development work began in 1852. Five years later a stagecoach service operating throughout the county and over the hills to Clear Lake was founded by William F. Fisher, who had been a station agent for Coombs. However, the main county road was not fully improved with gravel and oil until 1860. A telegraph line was strung between Vallejo and Napa in 1858, seven years before the telegraph reached the west coast from the east in 1865.

THE FIRST TRICKLE OF WINE

Still no wine? Well, barely. George Yount brought a few cuttings from the Sonoma mission vineyard when he first received his land grant in 1836, and he planted and nurtured these vines into a small vineyard, primarily for table grapes. He made a little bit of wine for serving to guests, with the grapes in leather bags stomped by foot.

John M. Patchett was fifty-three years old when he arrived at Napa in 1850, after gradually making his way west. He purchased a hundred-acre tract in 1852. It became known as "Patchett's Addition" to Napa between First Street and Laurel west of Jefferson. On it he planted a vineyard of Mission grapes and an orchard. In 1857 he crushed enough Mission grapes to produce six barrels and 600 bottles of wine, charging $2.00 a gallon. He built the Valley's first winery in 1859, a 50-by-33-foot stone structure in the city of Napa

Napa Valley's first nurseryman was Simpson Thompson, a Pennsylvanian who arrived in 1852 and, with his brother, William, purchased a hundred acres of the Soscol Rancho south of the town. With a system of ditches and dikes, he established orchards and a great variety of fruit-bearing trees and plants, including forty-five varieties of grapevines by 1856. Just north of Napa at Oak Knoll, another orchardist, Joseph Warren Osborne, was also experimenting, in his case with 3,000 vines of European varietals, including Zinfandel, by the late 1850s.

Hungarian Augoston Haraszthy had fled his home country after an abortive attempt by army officers to liberalize the autocratic rule of the Hapsburgs. In

Wisconsin, Illinois, and San Diego and San Mateo, California, he had unsuccessfully searched for the ideal location for growing wine grapes equal to those of Europe. He wangled a job as the director of the U.S. mint in San Francisco, but was sacked when accused of keeping the gold-dust sweepings. One of his assistants at the mint was a German immigrant, Charles Krug, who also dreamed of making wines like those back home.

Haraszthy visited the old Mission vineyard and Vallejo's little home vineyard at Sonoma in 1856. He believed that he had found the soil and climate he had been seeking. He purchased land and planted a vineyard, which he named Buena Vista, and crushed some purchased grapes in 1858. Ironically, he had to look to Napa Valley for cuttings of European varietals (vinefera) to plant his vineyard in Sonoma. He purchased cuttings of a relatively unknown varietal, Zinfandel—from either or both Simpson Thompson and Joseph Osborne—and planted them at Buena Vista.

In 1863 Osborne was shot and killed in his orchard by a disgruntled laborer in a dispute over a bounced paycheck. The murderer was convicted in a jury trial and became the first person legally hanged in Napa County.

Haraszthy inveigled the governor of California to appoint him official emissary to vineyardists in Europe so that he could explore the potential of bringing varietals to supplant the second-rate-tasting Mission grapes. He returned in 1861 with 100,000 seedlings for Sonoma and for distribution throughout California. Haraszthy's pioneering efforts launched California's commercial wine business big time and gave Sonoma Valley a running head start.

However, Napa Valley was already getting on the wine-grape bandwagon, without Haraszthy's help. Patchett, Thompson, and Osborne may have been first, but others were soon also busy. The number of vines climbed from 22,000 in 1856 to 90,000 in 1858, when there were thirteen grape growers in the Valley, including the Valley's first woman vintner, Lolita Bruck, in the St. Helena area.

Charles Krug had emigrated from Germany to Philadelphia when he was twenty-two, went back to participate in the democratic uprisings in 1848, and then returned to the United States when those efforts were crushed, winding up in California in 1852. He planted a small vineyard in San Mateo County, south of San Francisco, as had Haraszthy, and then became an assistant to the Hungarian at the U.S. Mint. Krug followed Haraszthy to Sonoma and planted 16,000 vines on land he had purchased next to Haraszthy's Buena Vista.

Using an apple press at Patchett's place, Krug crushed some grapes for wine in 1858. The next year he made a little wine for Dr. Bale's widow, and in 1860 he became winemaker for George Yount's small vineyard. Then, in rapid succession, Krug put his Sonoma vineyard up for sale in August 1860, became

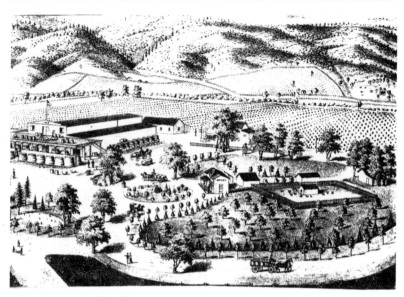

CHARLES KRUG WINERY – 1870S

engaged to Caroline Bale—heiress to a substantial portion of the unsold lands of the late doctor—and married her the day after Christmas.

The newly wed Krug found himself master of a tract of 800 acres, and he planted 15,000 vines there in 1861. Within a few years he extended the planting to 60,000 vines, two-thirds in European varietals. Starting with a crude 14-by-20-foot wine cellar, each year Krug expanded, until he eventually built a new, concrete two-story winery.

Parallel to Krug's vineyard development was the operation of Dr. George Belden Crane, a physician '49er from New York, who had been director of the City and County Hospital in San Jose before moving to Napa Valley in 1858. Crane planted vines in St. Helena—the first in that township—and produced 300 gallons of varietal wines in 1864, a year before Krug's first vintage. Crane hired Swiss-born Henri Alphonse Pellet away from Patchett to manage his vineyard, where he planted sixty varieties.

Highly respected for his viticulture knowledge, Pellet eventually created Pellet & Carver Winery, with financing from partner D. B. Carver. Pellet also built the first steam-powered mill in the Valley. He later was elected city trustee of St. Helena and to two terms as a county supervisor.

Various pioneers had begun planting small vineyards along with orchards and grain, including John York, David Hudson, and George Tucker. Cattle raising suffered a blow in the late 1860s from legislation that permitted fencing of open spaces. The number of cattle in Napa County dropped from more than 10,000 to 5,000 by the end of the decade. However, well into the 1870s dairies were still the leading agricultural occupation in the Napa Valley.

George Yount died in 1865, leaving a will that provided that several thousand of his acres be divided into fifty-acre parcels and sold at public auction. The sun had set on the day of the giant land-grant ranchos. Two years after his death, the community that had grown up around his home, which he had named Sebastopol, officially changed its name to Yountville.

SAM BRANNAN'S CALISTOGA, SARAFORNIA

In 1848 John York had discovered natural hot springs on the Bale property. This was later named White Sulphur Springs, and a hotel catering to the wealthy of San Francisco was erected in 1855. When it burned down in 1859, it was rebuilt, and the grounds were developed by one Swen Alstrom, who built cottages and other amenities, including a private telegraph line to the financial district of San Francisco. He was neither the first nor the last to recognize the potential for various Napa Valley hot springs and mineral waters.

Sam Brannan was something of a rogue. He arrived in 1846 at the village of Yerba Buena, in charge of a shipload of Mormons and money to purchase land for Mormon colonies in California. He used some of those funds to acquire property for his own account. He opened a general store in the future San Francisco but needed more population to make it the success he envisioned.

While visiting Sutter's Fort, Brannan heard the details of James Marshall's gold discovery at Sutter's Mill. John Sutter was desperate to keep it quiet, fearing that an influx of settlers would overrun his inland empire. Brannan, with his eye on the gold ring, did not care what Sutter wanted to hide, for the Mormon colonist wanted California—just acquired by the United States—to be flooded with immigrants, who would be his customers. So he took a small bag of gold dust back to San Francisco and dramatically rode through the center of the little village shouting, "Gold. Gold at the American River." The secret was out, the gold rush began, and Brannan emerged a rich man.

Learning of the hot waters that bubbled to the surface in the northern part of the Napa Valley (actually then called The Springs Township), in 1859 Brannan paid top dollar for a large parcel of property. He immediately began development of a resort for the recreation of the people of the San Francisco Bay Area—particularly the wealthy. He spent money on bathhouses, into which was pumped sulfurous hot water from the ground, twenty-five cabins, and a lavish community plan. After several drinks one night, he described his scheme to create a west coast resort in the mode of the upscale Saratoga in New York: "It'll be the Calistoga of Sarafornia," he slurred. And the name stuck.

Brannan's Calistoga resort opened with a huge splash in 1862, when a chartered ship full of guests from San Francisco was met by coaches and carriages that carried them from the dock in Vallejo to a huge feast. There was champagne for the rich and influential—and free kegs of beer and barbecue for the multitudes. They found a racetrack, swimming pool, skating rink, exotic landscaping tended by Japanese gardeners, and an observatory from which to view the entire utopia. There was a private water reservoir, a distillery for making brandy, a winery, and 100,000 newly planted vines.

Almost immediately businesses to support this operation were attracted to Calistoga. But the road north of St. Helena was still too bumpy for the tender backsides of the ladies whom Brannan hoped to attract. What he and the Valley needed was a railroad. The legal means were in place.

CALIFORNIA'S FIRST TRAIN

Ex-judge Chancellor Hartson from Napa was elected to the State Assembly for the 1864 session. Shortly before taking office Hartson organized the Napa Valley Railroad Company. Assemblyman Hartson's number-one priority was to shepherd a bill chartering the company with the right to receive subsidies of between $5,000 and $10,000 per mile, to be guaranteed by a bond issue submitted to the voters of Napa County. What the proposed railroad needed was a promoter, and Brannan was that man.

The bond issue was adopted easily, $60,000 was subscribed to meet additional costs (including $30,000 advanced for railroad cars by the corporation's directors), and farmers along the proposed route gladly donated the right-of-way.

The inaugural train ran from Soscol to Napa in June 1865—the first railroad in California. With the help of another Hartson bill, the Napa Valley Railroad was extended to Calistoga by August 1868. Winery owners were ecstatic, since they and other agriculturists could ship cheaply and travel from doorstep to San Francisco via rail and ferry in just six hours. In 1869 the Napa Valley line was connected to a railway running from Vallejo to Sacramento, and shortly thereafter with the transcontinental railroad.

But life was going downhill for the enthusiastic Brannan. In April 1868, when he personally tried to foreclose on a neighboring mill, the owner shot Brannan, hitting him eight times from neck to hip. Brannan almost died. Still, as the first train arrived in Calistoga in August, Brannan had recovered sufficiently to throw a party at his resort for 3,000 celebrants. It was to be his last hurrah.

To finance the elegance of his Calistoga Hot Springs resort and extravagant living, Brannan had borrowed heavily, with the resort put up as security. The Sacramento Savings Bank finally foreclosed in the early 1870s. In 1879 the bank began selling off twenty-five- to 200-acre parcels. His wife divorced him, he drank more heavily, and died impoverished in Southern California.

Calistoga (population 1,259 in 1880) and the railroad were his heritage to the Napa Valley.

The Napa Valley Railroad also went into foreclosure and was purchased by the California Pacific, and through a series of mergers eventually became part of the Southern Pacific.

PIONEER DAYS IN THE '60S AND '70S

Crimes in Napa Valley during the 1860s and 1870s were often exotic. There was the case of the adventurer Gilbert Jenkins, for instance, who killed the father of a seventeen-year-old woman of both beauty and wealth whom he hoped to seduce with her dad out of the way. Not only was he caught, but he owned up to eight murders across the country before he was hanged.

Winery owner John Patchett was slipped knock-out drops in his drink so that he would be unconscious; then two masked men terrified his housekeeper, ransacked his home, and burglarized the houses of the public administrator and a former judge. Hunters spotted two suspicious men by a cave in the hills. A notorious ex-con named "Black Jack" Bowen and his partner were soon surprised by a posse and packed off to San Quentin Prison.

When the manager of a bar with a bordello upstairs fired at some unruly customers outside and killed one, he was soon taken from jail by a small mob. They hanged him from a tree, apparently to prevent a trial in which testimony of witnesses would have revealed the names of the customers of the bawdy house. A conspiracy of silence protected the lynchers.

With a population in which men outnumbered women ten to one, in the 1860s Napa County held the distinction of having the most prostitutes per capita of any county in California.

To illuminate Napa city, a gas company was founded in 1867, with sixty-five customers. Lamps on principal streets were lit by a lamplighter who rode around town at dusk. The first public library opened in 1870. An imposing stone library (The Goodman Library) erected in 1902 is now the home of the Napa County Historical Society.

Adding to the tourist attraction of the Valley was the discovery in 1870 of the petrified forest—ancient trees turned to stone—by "Petrified Charlie" Evans, northwest of Calistoga.

NAPA WINES GROW AND GO NATIONAL

On the heels of Krug and Crane came Jacob Schram, an unlikely vintner in an unlikely place, who purchased his first land in Napa Valley in 1862. A barber by trade, Schram landed in New York from Germany in the mid-1850s and headed to San Francisco. Upon visiting Napa Valley Schram became convinced that he could succeed at making wine. The only land he could afford was a chaparral- and tree-studded slope of the Mayacamas north of St. Helena. He cleared a patch of land himself, cut hair at White Sulphur Springs resort on weekends to put food on the table, and in 1863 planted his first vineyard. By 1867 he had 14,000 vines.

Schram's first vintage encouraged another German, San Francisco wine merchant Gottlieb Groezinger, to buy vineyard land, plant vines, and produce wines. Groezinger was particularly interested in improving the quality of California wine to provide real competition for European wines being sold on the east coast market. A San Francisco outfit, Kohler & Frohling, had begun shipping some California wines and brandy around the Horn to New York as early as 1857, but the price received (75 cents a gallon on average) was well below that of French and German products, and the reputation for quality was shaky at best.

Schram and Groezinger were the harbingers of a new wave of winemakers in the Napa Valley, including brothers John and Theodore Sigrist in Brown's Valley, west of Napa, who built a winery with a capacity of 100,000 gallons. John Lewelling was a noted nurseryman, whose brothers had brought west the seedlings that launched Oregon's agriculture. He had planted orchards in what he called Fruitvale (now a neighborhood in Oakland) and gave up his post as a county supervisor in Alameda County to move to Napa Valley, where he planted orchards and 35,000 vinifera grape vines in St. Helena.

By 1866 there were 700,000 grape vines in Napa County. However, wheat, particularly in Berryessa Valley, was still the leading farm product, ground into flour by local mills.

Alexander J. Cox, a printer who came west as a soldier with the regiment that took over Sonoma during the Mexican War, had started a newspaper there called *The Sonoma Bulletin*, which he shut down in 1855. He carted his old press to Napa and, on July 4, 1856, began publishing the four-page *Napa*

County Reporter, which was erratically issued until 1858, when Cox moved on to Healdsburg. New ownership, led by the hard-drinking but popular writer R. T. Montgomery, took over and acquired a new press. For several years it was an influential newspaper. It went out of business in 1888.

The Napa Register came out as a weekly in August 1863 and went through a series of ownership changes. Popular from the outset, in December 1872, under new publisher G. W. Henning, the Register became a daily. It is still Napa's principal newspaper. Other journalistic attempts failed after short runs, including The Pacific Echo, a rabidly anti–President Lincoln paper—which died the day of Lincoln's death.

The St. Helena Star was founded in 1874 as a weekly newspaper. It has been in continuous publication ever since—one of the oldest weeklies in the state. Another survivor of the numerous pioneering publication efforts in the county is The Weekly Calistogan, which first came off the press in 1877.

Cinnabar, the ore that contains quicksilver, was discovered in Pope Valley in 1861, and later near Oakville. Various attempts were made to mine and process the ore, but the work stumbled along for a decade under various companies until the major mining efforts were consolidated under the Napa Mining Company in 1873. For more than sixty years thereafter, quicksilver was profitably mined in substantial amounts. Commencing in 1871 there was some coal mining in the hills, but it never reached major proportions.

Silver mining in Napa County was a flash in the pan. In 1872 a vein of silver was discovered north of Calistoga, on the southeast slope of Mount St. Helena, near the toll road to Lake County. Alexander Badlam, a nephew of Sam Brannan, staked a claim, laid out a small town called Silverado City, dug a mine, and built a mill to process the ore. This activity triggered a silver rush, which drew 1,500 people, a host of mining claims in the hills, the Silverado Hotel, a stage station, several businesses, and the inevitable saloons. The silver was played out by the autumn of 1875 (the total was a puny $92,000 worth), and the population disappeared. The county mining recorder Sam Chapman bought the deserted Silverado Hotel.

Chinese laborers had first arrived in the Valley after they had been drawn to the gold diggings in the mountains as early as 1849. By the time they had helped substantially to build the transcontinental railroad, completed in 1869, at least 400 had settled in the Valley. Grouped in "Chinatowns" on the outskirts of Napa, St. Helena, and Calistoga, they provided the brawn for building stone fences (which still exist), planting vineyards, digging mines, and harvesting crops. Some worked as cooks, gardeners, and household servants, while a few operated their own laundries. When the Chinese Exclusion Act was enacted in 1882, barring further immigration, Terrell Grigsby, owner of Occidental

Winery in Browns Valley, personally fought off a mob intent on chasing out his Chinese workers. The wine industry needed their loyal, inexpensive labor. Eventually, most Chinese migrated to the cities.

THE BUILDING BOOM

The Uncle Sam Wine Cellar was founded in 1870, in a large building at the corner of Main and Fourth Streets in Napa, with a storage capacity of 500,000 gallons for the bulk wine it made from the grapes of several growers. The structure still stands, albeit substantially altered. A young widowed mother, Josephine Marlin Tychson, built a winery in 1881 called Lodi Vineyards, which is now Freemark Abbey. California's first full-time female winemaker, Mrs. Tychson produced wine for fifteen years.

Napa was chosen by a state commission as the site of the State Hospital for the Insane (now called Napa State Hospital). A five-story Gothic institution with seven towers was subsequently erected on spacious grounds southeast of Napa city, where Father Altimira had first camped. Despite its rococo façade it was extremely modern in amenities for the time (fire hydrants on every floor, lots of toilets, central steam heating, and gas lighting). In 1875 it opened to handle more than 600 patients.

A courthouse of classic design was dedicated in February 1879, built for a cost of $51,000 in downtown Napa. Amazingly, it still functions as Napa County's courthouse, almost without change from the day it opened, except that a nonfunctional tower was added and then later removed. An elevator has been installed, but most people climb the sweeping staircase to the richly paneled courtrooms. No other California courthouse has served as long.

In Napa city the luxurious Palace Hotel, with seventy rooms, all with baths and fireplaces, opened in 1875 at the corner of Third and Soscol. When the old Napa Hotel, dating from 1851, burned down in 1884, it was immediately replaced by a brick structure just south of the Opera House. There was also the wooden Revere House, which was the largest building in Napa to collapse during the 1906 San Francisco earthquake.

Napa Valley was fortunate that Mark Strong, a photographer with an artistic eye and feel for history, came to town in 1886. From then on, almost to the day of his death in 1946, Strong recorded on film the changes in the city and Valley.

With the transcontinental railroad's completion in 1869, it became easy to ship goods to the east, and practical to travel to New York and other business centers. Dr. Crane visited his native New York to promote Napa Valley wines,

PALACE HOTEL IN THE 1870S

met with skepticism, and was discouraged. Charles Krug followed, and his enthusiasm carried the day. Krug's greatest contribution was to convince the eastern wine distributors that the best wines in the Western Hemisphere came from the Napa Valley.

Krug, Jacob Beringer (Krug's former winemaker who launched his own winery, Beringer Brothers, in 1875), and M. G. Ritchie established the Napa Valley Wine Company to combine forces to distribute wines. Krug not only made contacts in New York but found distributors in St. Louis, Kansas City, and Georgia. John Lewelling and H. W. Crabb, who had followed Lewelling from Alameda County to found his Hermosa Vineyards in Oakville, emulated the Krug/Beringer/Ritchie example by contracting with eastern distributors. Lewelling and Crabb pioneered the shipment of grapes packed in freight cars filled with ice.

The results are in the statistics. By 1873 Napa Valley wines were being shipped to the east coast by the carload. The gallonage of wines vinted reached almost 500,000 that year, a far cry from the piddling 8,745 in 1860. Still, Napa County continued to trail Sonoma County production. In 1877 Napa produced 640,000 gallons and Sonoma, 2,500,000. But that was soon to change. Total shipments of California wine to the midwest and east coast climbed to 1,243,000 gallons in 1878. In 1880 Crabb produced 300,000 gallons and Krug, 280,000. While Krug was the chief publicist for Napa's wines, Crabb became the Valley's most innovative experimenter. He later gave twenty acres to the University of California for enological testing.

STEVENSON AND OTHER CHARACTERS

An itinerant Scottish travel writer, Robert Louis Stevenson, showed up in Calistoga in the summer of 1880, on a honeymoon with his wife Fanny, a widow he had just married in Monterey. The Stevensons lived for most of the time at the old hotel in the ghost town of Silverado. He spent much of the summer nursing his wife, who suffered from a non-lethal form of cholera, and writing letters requesting payments from his publisher. The writer and winemaker Schram became friends who talked for hours. Three years later Stevenson burst on the literary world with his novel *Treasure Island*, in which the physical description of the island's interior was based on Mount St. Helena. In November and December 1883, Stevenson had two articles published in the magazine *Century Illustrated* about the Stevensons' stay, which were later issued in a small volume entitled *Silverado Squatters*.

The tubercular Stevenson died in 1894, before anyone in the Valley paid any attention to this book. His death was reported in just half a dozen lines in the *St. Helena Star*, with no mention at all in the *Register* or *Calistogan*.

Several prominent characters moved to the Valley during this period, including S. Clinton Hastings, chief justice of the California Supreme Court and founder of the state's first law school, Hastings College of the Law in San Francisco (now part of the University of California system); and Lilburn W. Boggs, former governor of Missouri, who had come west expecting to be appointed first governor of California. The highest west coast office that Boggs achieved was alcalde (mayor/judge) of Sonoma. Former speaker of the Assembly, and losing candidate for governor and U.S. Senate, Morris M. Estee built a winery on Atlas Peak in 1885 (it is still used for wine storage).

Former Union general and U.S. senator John F. Miller purchased a large parcel east of Napa, upon which he built a fourteen-room mansion, which he named La Vergne, for the Civil War battle in which he had lost an eye. Today it is the Silverado Country Club.

San Francisco socialite Lillie Hitchcock Coit spent a lot of time driving her coach at breakneck speed and throwing parties at the mansion her father had built for her at his spread on Larkmead in St. Helena. Loving to ride to fires, she became an honorary firefighter with her own uniform. She willed funds to build Coit Tower atop Telegraph Hill in San Francisco.

Concerned with the condition of disabled veterans of the Civil War, the San Francisco chapter of the Grand Army of the Republic (GAR), with the assistance of a Mexican War veterans group, bought 910 acres just west of Yountville for $17,500 in 1881. With donated funds, the Veterans' Home Association opened its first building in 1884, to house forty-two veterans. Soon the legislature approved expense payments of $150 a year for each resident. The Veterans' Home expanded rapidly but was always short of funds. Finally, in 1897 the state took over the Home's operation, when it was the residence for 800 veterans.

OF BERINGER, NIEBAUM, AND BANDITS

Over the hills to the west, disaster struck the vineyards of Sonoma Valley, where *phylloxera*, a louse that attacked vine roots, caused most vineyards to wither and die between 1876 and 1879. For the first time Napa County surpassed Sonoma County in wine production. Napa vineyardists breathed a collective sigh of relief that they had been spared. Their elation would prove to be premature.

New and larger wineries were constructed in the late 1870s and early 1880s. Jacob Beringer, with financing from brother Frederick in New York, built a three-story winery with a deep, cool cave in St. Helena. Nearby, John C. Weinberger erected a winery in 1876, which he soon enlarged to hold 180,000 gallons—it is now the location of the Markham Winery. In 1874 Napa grocer Giuseppe Migliavacca became the first Napa resident of Italian heritage to develop a major winery, and he was followed by Vittorio Sattui in 1885 and Anton Nichelini shortly thereafter. As early as 1882 some Valley growers began using smudge pots to ward off extreme frosts—now often replaced by more environmentally acceptable wind machines. In 1888 Greystone Winery in St. Helena became the first run by electricity from a gasoline-powered generator.

Gustave Niebaum, a Finnish sea captain, had made a fortune in the northern Pacific fur trade, and was a partner with San Francisco investors in the Alaska Commercial Company. When he became interested in winemaking, he had the time, money, and inclination to be a perfectionist. West of the hamlet of Rutherford, on what had been Yount's Caymus Rancho, Niebaum found a poorly maintained attempt at a winery, which he bought. Its name: Inglenook (Scottish for "a seat by the fire.")

During the early 1880s Niebaum expanded and cleared his acreage, went to Europe and brought back cuttings, read every book he could get in any language about winemaking, ordered the best equipment, and created cellars to maintain constant temperatures. And, to house it all, he had constructed an imposing stone mansion that overlooked the plain. Seven years after Inglenook's first wine release, Niebaum's winery was given the award for "excellence and purity" at the Paris Exposition in 1889. Other Napa Valley wineries brought home twenty medals—including a gold for Migliavacca—more than any American wine region. Napa Valley had secured its place on the international wine map.

Stagecoaches and delivery wagons that climbed the hills from Napa Valley to Lake County were occasionally robbed in the 1880s. In the '90s the high-waymen became a plague, time and again forcing drivers to "throw down the box" and passengers to empty their pocketbooks. In May 1895 one of a pair of robbers beat up a Chinese passenger, immediately casting suspicion on one Buck English, known to be a foul-mouthed Sinophobe. Sheriff George McKenzie put together a four-man posse, which included twenty-three-year-old District Attorney Ted Bell. They trailed English to the village of Monticello in Berryessa Valley. A Wild West–style chase followed, in which English was punctured by fifty-two shotgun pellets before being captured more dead than alive.

A couple of years later, David Dunlap, the leader of the local Democratic party, was elected sheriff. With prior experience as a sheriff in Nevada, Dunlap looked like a Central Casting version of the western lawman: tall, erect, with a drooping mustache and steel-blue eyes. A new gang of stage robbers went into business, and the frustrated sheriff kept losing their tracks in the hills. One newspaper began referring to Dunlap as "no catch-em Dave." Finally, he and his deputies chased down and arrested the county's last highwayman. (The newspaper was unimpressed, calling the sheriff "no catch-em Dave, except once.")

Frank Coombs, son of Nathan Coombs, was the county's most successful political figure. He was elected district attorney in 1880 at age twenty-seven as a Republican. His next successes were his election to the state assembly on seven occasions between 1887 and 1927. Coombs was twice chosen speaker of the assembly; was appointed U.S. minister to Japan in 1892; served a term in Congress; and for several years was U.S. attorney for Northern California.

His son, another Nathan Coombs, was elected state senator as a Republican in the 1950s. The sister of Senator Coombs married the son of Sheriff David Dunlap. Their union produced four sons; a farmer and three lawyers. One of them, Frank Dunlap, was Napa city attorney for many years. Another, Democrat John F. Dunlap; was elected to four terms as state assemblyman and served four years as state senator in the 1970s. He and his wife, Janet, still reside on a portion of founder Nathan Coombs' ranch.

KRUG'S DEATH AND THE BATTLE AGAINST *PHYLLOXERA*

A slump in wine prices drove Charles Krug into bankruptcy in 1885—he had gotten easy credit based on his reputation—and forced the sale of his winery to a San Francisco banker. His wife, Caroline, went from eccentricity—like her father Dr. Bale—into outright insanity before she died in December 1885. The man who loved to talk to reporters lost the power of speech. The "Father of Napa Valley Wines" died on November 1, 1892.

The insidious *phylloxera* had made its migration gradually from Sonoma Valley into vineyards in the Carneros region, shared by Sonoma and Napa Valleys by 1890. In 1893 a report commissioned by the state Board of Viticultural Commissioners revealed that 244 out of 577 Napa County vineyards showed signs of the voracious louse, listing locations and owners. The battle line had advanced northward from the Carneros region past St. Helena.

Napa's winegrowers benefited from Sonoma's experience with the bug, since Sonoma growers had found some root stock resistant to *phylloxera*. There was also the expertise available from the University of California's new enological study department. The state board pointed out that Judge John Stanly's vineyards in Carneros had not been harmed by the louse since they were planted in *Riparia* roots, proving they were resistant, as Sonoma Valley vintner Julius Dresel had claimed as early as 1878. The judge became a vocal advocate of *Riparia*.

University of California professor Arthur Hayne argued that the root stock *Rupestris* was superior to *Riparia* in California soil. Although most growers were slow to accept Hayne's view, George Schonewald met with remarkable success with grafting to *Rupestris*. A new face on the scene, French immigrant Georges de Latour, in 1900—the depth of the *phylloxera* calamity—ordered millions of *Rupestris* root stock from France, which he sold throughout Northern California.

While Napa wines continued to win medals through the 1890s at various state and national expositions, by the turn of the century, there remained fewer than 5,000 acres in vines. Grape and wine production had become disastrously low. Although some growers switched to fruit growing—French prunes were a new favorite—others began pulling vines in favor of replanting first with *Riparia* and then *Rupestris* root stock.

There were other industries in the Valley besides winemaking, however. There were fruit orchards, olive groves, dairying, the resort business, the bottling of mineral waters, and the processing of leather, which dated back to the 1860s. In fact, "Napa Leather" became a dictionary definition for soft leather.

Newcomer de Latour, barely speaking English and previously perpetually near-broke, became the leader of Napa Valley's winery resurgence. With the profits from his chancy purchase of root stock—primarily on credit—he finally had some funds to purchase property and build a winery, which he opened in Rutherford in 1907, named Beaulieu Vineyards, meaning "beautiful place."

De Latour planted extensively, obtained the endorsement of the San Francisco Catholic Archdiocese for use of his wine by churches, bottled bulk wine under his label while waiting for vines to mature, and soon was vinting large amounts of Bordeaux-type wines. By 1910 Beaulieu was Napa Valley's most famous winery—a far cry from the days when de Latour, a chemist trained in France, scraped out a living by making cream of tartar from wine-barrel leavings.

Victory over the *phylloxera* bug encouraged new investors who built large wineries. The Salmina family built Larkmead, and Antonio Forni leased and rejuvenated Josephine Tychson's winery and vineyards, which had been stripped by the root louse.

The 1903 invention of a machine that would mass-produce glass bottles made bottles cheap and plentiful. This allowed each winery to identify its product with labels on the bottles and increased the Napa Valley wine exposure and popularity in the marketplace. Annual wine production in Napa County was reaching 4 million gallons.

It appeared that there were clear skies ahead for the Napa Valley wine industry. But there was one cloud on the horizon. It was called Prohibition.

PROHIBITION SHUTS DOWN THE WINERIES

What started as a movement to close down saloons, by the second decade of the century had become a crusade, with accelerating political momentum, to put an end to all alcohol manufacture and sale. In 1914 and 1916 Prohibition ballot propositions were rejected by California voters, but the margin was increasingly close. Many winemakers, as producers of the drink of moderation, hoped that, if alcohol were prohibited, wine would be exempt as "food."

Congress passed the Eighteenth Amendment on December 18, 1917, and submitted it to the state legislatures. The California Assembly and Senate approved it on January 11, 1919, and five days later the last necessary state legislature ratified Prohibition, to take effect in 1920. There were exceptions: Wine for sacramental and medicinal purposes could be made and sold (on the technicality that it was not used for "beverage purposes"), and limited production of wine—200 gallons a year—for personal use was permitted.

The sacramental-wine exemption became a saving grace for de Latour and his Beaulieu, since he had one of ten permits to provide wine for church altars (Sebastiani and Wente were two others in Northern California).

More than 120 wineries in Napa County officially shut down. Grape growers could still ship grape juice or grapes—sometimes with the warning not to add yeast, which might cause "illegal fermentation." Many tore out their vines and substituted prunes, cherries, or walnuts. Dairy farms grew and converted to pasteurization.

Of course, like many Americans, there were winemakers who sneered at Prohibition as a joke, and they continued to make wine far in excess of personal needs. Although local law enforcement and federal officials were primarily concerned about halting the bootlegging of hard liquor, wine occasionally became the target. One day the revenuers raided large storage tanks on Dunaweal Lane (near what is now Hanns Kornell) and delighted in smashing them with axes. The resulting wine flood turned the road into what old-timers still call "the river of red."

The Sawyer Tanning Company, which had been in business since 1872, expanded with new products such as patent-leather shoes and softball covers. In 1915 Napans Peter Jensen and Edwin Pridham invented the loudspeaker, which they named Magnavox. As the company grew it moved to Indiana.

Napa County was essentially on hold: Between 1910 and 1930 the population increased slightly, from 19,800 to 22,879. In the 1920s the number of residents of the city of Napa actually dropped, from 6,757 in 1920 to 6,437 in 1930.

The Napa Valley Railroad eliminated passenger service in 1929, and the electric line from Vallejo to Calistoga shut down in 1939, giving way to the bus and automobile. (Vincent DeDomenico, famed for Rice-a-Roni, would buy the old railway from S. P. in 1987 and put the Wine Train for tourists into operation in 1991—running from Napa to Calistoga with gourmet meals, beverages, and sightseeing.)

REPEAL AND RECOVERY

Like the rest of the nation, the Napa Valley was stagnant after the onset of the Great Depression in 1929. The resort business was hurt by the lack of personal income available for entertainment, and agriculture suffered from low prices. One hope would be the repeal of Prohibition, which finally occurred on December 7, 1933.

Beaulieu Vineyards was first out of the gate, since it had been making sacramental wine during the twelve years of Prohibition and because shrewd de Latour built up a large pre-repeal inventory of wine, which he could ship immediately. Close on his heels was forty-three-year-old Louis M. Martini, a tall, blonde native of Italy, who since 1922 had run a company at Kingsburg in the San Joaquin Valley that made grape concentrate for sale to amateur winemakers. Martini built a winery in St. Helena, planted vineyards of Cabernet Sauvignon and Zinfandel in both Napa and Sonoma Counties, and began producing full-bodied wines at modest prices. They were an instant success. He was a founder of the California Wine Institute and the prime mover in creating a gathering of winery owners, which became the Napa Valley Vintners Association.

The leadership of Inglenook devolved on the grand-nephew of founder Captain Niebaum, young John Daniel. The handsome 1933 Stanford engineering graduate felt obligated to restore the old winery's preeminence and honor the legacy of Captain Niebaum. He studied viticulture with Sonoma wine sage Carl Bundschu. When John's aunt died in 1937, he took full command of the winery (owned jointly with his sister, who was not interested in its operation). Daniel hired an expert winemaster, George Deuer, diversified wine vintages, joined the Wine Institute Board in 1941, and put "Napa Valley" on Inglenook labels, which were vintage-dated.

Charles de Latour got another step on the competition in 1938, when he induced Andre Tchelistcheff to leave Paris and work for Beaulieu as a winemaster. Tchelistcheff was a dapper Russian refugee from the Communist regime who had studied agronomy in France and was an expert on grapes. Despite doubts about coming to America, Andre, his wife, and child came to Napa, in part because he had been impressed by the quality of an Inglenook Gewürztraminer he had tasted.

He cleaned up Beaulieu Winery, had tanks scrubbed, set up a laboratory, and insisted on new equipment, including a corking device. His taste buds for wines were remarkable, and Beaulieu's quality rose. For the next forty years he would be the United States' ruling authority on wines and winemaking. His prestige was so great—and his comments so direct—that his advice was sought by generations of winemakers. His influence on disciples like Joe Heitz, Mike Grgich, and Warren Winiarski raised the standard that winemasters expected. Tchelistcheff ushered in the era of the professional winemakers, who were often graduates of the University of California at Davis.

The vacant Krug winery was just a piece of real estate to its San Francisco owners. They leased it to Louis Stralla, a hotel man with Las Vegas connections, who made and sold bulk wine. Beringer was back in business with absentee ownership. On land owned by the Catholic order for three-quarters of a century, the Christian Brothers were making wine and brandy. They would gain fame under the legendary winemaker Brother Timothy. But it was still the Depression, and the wine industry was only a shadow of what it would become.

Cesare Mondavi was an Italian immigrant who had settled in Lodi, California, where he shipped grapes to home winemakers around the country during Prohibition. Shortly after repeal he bought a small, vacant stone winery in St. Helena. Cesare sent his older son, Robert, fresh out of Stanford, to build up a bulk wine business there. Robert soon was crushing enough grapes to yield a million gallons a year. At the urging of his sons, Robert and Peter, Cesare bought the dilapidated Krug winery and property for $87,000 (mostly borrowed) in 1943, on the condition that Robert, as general manager, and Peter, as winemaker, would run the winery.

THE 1940s AND BEYOND

In 1940 the Basalt Rock Company was awarded a contract to make boats and oil barges for the navy. After World War II Basalt began large-scale production of oil and gas pipe, then sold its plant to Kaiser Steel, which in turn sold to Oregon Steel Mills in 1987. A military airport south of Napa city was built during the war and became Napa County Airport in 1946.

Famous people living in the valley included Jessamyn West, wife of Superintendent of Schools Harry McPherson, who wrote *Friendly Persuasion* in 1940. Her book became a best-seller and a popular movie. West (the outspoken Democratic cousin of Republican Richard Nixon) also authored another best-seller, *The Witch Diggers*. M. F. K. (Mary Frances Kennedy) Fisher, was already famous for her classics on food appreciation and travel like *How To Cook a Wolf,* when she moved to St. Helena in the early 1960s. During the time she lived there, she wrote regularly for *The New Yorker* magazine. Canadian writer Arthur Hailey lived in a large house overlooking St. Helena while writing several of his very popular novels like *Airport, Hotel,* and *The Bankers* in the 1970s and 1980s, before leaving for a home in the Bahamas.

Scarcely noticed in 1947 was the purchase of the old Sutter Home Winery by Mario Trinchero and his family from New York. Mario and his brother were so strapped for cash that they could not pay the $12,000 for the century-old Victorian next to the vineyards on Highway 29 in St. Helena.

In the meantime, John Daniel came to love Inglenook, but his beautiful wife, Betty, came to hate it. Isolated from the city society she enjoyed, she suffered depression, began drinking too much, and became involved in notorious affairs—a ski instructor, an Air Force officer, an abusive Umatilla Indian— which eventually led to their divorce. In 1964 John finally sold Inglenook—it had never made much of a profit—to United Vintners, whose management promised to maintain Inglenook's integrity. With the winery out of his system, John and Betty reconciled and remarried. But United Vintners turned the main building into a storage house and began producing jug wine under the venerable Inglenook name. Soon thereafter John Daniel died of a heart attack, induced by an overdose of barbiturates. The cause was considered suicide, but some said that it was really a broken heart.

BIG BUSINESS AND BIG WINNERS

The sale of Inglenook was an omen. Big corporations were attracted to the existing wineries and had the bucks to make tempting offers. Soon Heublein, Coca-Cola, Seagrams, Nestlé, R. J. Reynolds, and Grand Metropolitan of London (which had bought Reynolds, which had bought Heublein) became owners. There would be others. Some cared about excellent wines; others were primarily interested in profits.

Tensions existed between brothers Robert and Peter Mondavi at Charles Krug Winery even before their father, Cesare, died. It was almost inevitable that Robert, as "Mr. Outside," and Peter, as "Mr. Inside," would not agree. Robert was outgoing and willing to spend money for promotion, while Peter was cautious and introverted. Robert was demanding and impatient, and his relationship to his wife Marge, who had been his high school sweetheart, became strained.

The brothers argued over the future participation of their sons in the business. In 1965, when Robert set up a corporation to establish a small winery for his sons, which he called Robert Mondavi, Peter and mother Rosa—who owned the majority of the stock in Krug—pulled the plug. Robert was put on involuntary "leave," which really meant that he was out.

Robert Mondavi lined up financing, bought property in Oakville on Highway 29, and built a winery. The family split had a much greater impact on Napa Valley than the addition of another winery. It meant that Robert Mondavi was turned loose to promote himself, his winery, his wines, and Napa Valley.

The elegant mansion and grounds created by General Miller in the last century was purchased in 1967 by Amfak Corporation. Amfak spent $100 million to turn the estate into the private Silverado Country Club, with two golf courses designed by Robert Trent Jones, 400 condos, a spacious clubhouse, tennis courts, and a renovated mansion.

May 24, 1976, was a landmark date for Napa Valley wines. At a prestigious blind tasting in Paris that day, the Cabernet Sauvignon of Stag's Leap Cellars (Warren Winiarski, owner and winemaker) was rated the "Best Red," and the Chardonnay of Chateau Montelena (James Barrett, owner and winemaker) was named best of the white Burgundies. Their competition was the elite wineries' best from Bordeaux and Burgundy, including Chateau Mouton-Rothschild. These tasting triumphs proved that Napa Valley wines belonged among the best international wines and signaled that Napa Valley wineries should shift toward varietals rather than "jug" wines. Within the next twenty years, sales from Napa varietals leapt from $150 million to $2.5 billion.

THE POLITICS OF PRESERVATION

Political controversies over the future of Napa County broke out in the late 1960s and continued for the next thirty years. The first scrimmage came in 1968, when the Board of Supervisors had to decide whether to authorize "agricultural preserves" pursuant to the recently adopted state Williamson Act. Under that act, an owner of agricultural land could contract with the county to keep the property in agriculture (and not a subdivision) perpetually until ten years after the owner filed a notice of intent to cancel the contract. In return, the county would give the owner a property-tax reduction.

The Board of supervisors had to pass an ordinance agreeing to county participation. "Ag preserves" are common today, but were novel in the 1960s. Those Napans concerned with overdevelopment were in favor of permitting such preserves in Napa County, as were some vintners, including Louis Peter Martini, of the new generation of Martinis, and Jack Davies, who had just purchased the old Schramsberg winery, which he and his wife, Jamie, were restoring. However, other winery owners had joined with those who felt that no one had a right to tell others what they could do with their land, including ex-owner John Daniel. At the crucial meeting of the board, one winery owner was so abusive to the supervisor from St. Helena, fence-sitter Julius Caiocco, that Julius voted to make it unanimous to approve agricultural preserves, saying "Nobody's gonna shake a finger at me."

In 1972, supported by a coalition of environmentalists and neighborhood organizations, Virginia (Ginny) Simms, John Tuteur, and Henry Wigger were elected to the Board of Supervisors. They had pledged to enact zoning that would limit home sites on rural hillsides to forty acres per home. That limitation was adopted in 1973. For the next two decades, bitter supervisorial elections—unlimited development versus limited growth—were held every two years, with the Board split one way or the other each term. The hillside limitation bounced down to twenty acres and then back up to forty. In 1989 a pro-development board majority abruptly dismissed the entire Planning Commission and fired the county's long-time planning director.

Another area of conflict needed to be resolved. Volker Eisele, with a Ph.D. from UC Berkeley, and his landscape architect wife, Liesel, had bought an old vineyard and rusty winery. He soon organized the Napa Valley Grape Growers Association, to represent the position of independent growers not employed by major wineries. The local growers were concerned with the use of the Napa Valley address on bottles of wine made from so-called foreign grapes shipped in from outside the county. This was particularly true of wineries that had a second label with wine of lower quality. The growers' proposal: In order to use a Napa address or Napa appellation, or to become a new or expanded winery in Napa County, 75 percent of the wine had to be vinted from grapes grown in the county.

The 240 members of the growers' association were unanimous in favor, but the wineries were divided. It took almost three years of discussions, a moratorium on new winery permits, and two supervisorial elections before a compromise—first proposed by the growers—was adopted by the Board of Supervisors in the county's "definition" of wineries for permits. The ordinance allowed already existing wineries to continue any practices they were employing (including use of "foreign" grapes), but new wineries had to use 75 percent Napa grapes and could not have public tours and tastings. It did allow food to be served for promotional services. Any expansion of an existing winery had to meet the 75 percent requirement. In part, this explains the reason why many wineries today—even elegant facilities like Joseph Phelps—require visitors to call ahead for an appointment for tasting, to avoid the "open to the public" tasting-room prohibition.

As the 1990s opened there was an important shift of sentiment: More and more vineyardists and winemakers became convinced that subdivisions and vineyards did not mix. Since Napa Valley wineries were a crucial business as well as a great tourist draw, maintaining the beauty of the hills and restricting the areas available for malls, outlet centers, and subdivisions made economic as well as aesthetic sense.

THE NEW WAVE

Napa Valley saw many changes in the 1980s and 1990s. Robert Mondavi won a large judgment against his brother Peter and the Krug winery. A lawsuit that began over the use of the Mondavi name on a company Peter set up climaxed in a ruling that Robert was owed millions for being forced out of Charles Krug. In 1980 he married Margrit Biever, who worked closely with him in developing his Robert Mondavi Winery. With his financial and personal conflicts in the past, Robert Mondavi had more time to spend as spokesman of Napa Valley wines to the world. He was not the only one, but certainly was the most ubiquitous.

Robert Trinchero, the son of Mario, who had bought little Sutter Home, experimented with making a white wine from Zinfandel grapes, after trying dozens of different varieties. He came out with 350 cases of his "invented" White Zinfandel in 1974. He caught the popular trend toward whites and surpassed the 4-million-cases mark early in the 1990s, to become Napa Valley's largest producer. The headquarters is in the lovely Victorian house that his father and uncle could not afford to buy for $12,000.

Motion picture director Francis Ford Coppola (*The Godfather, Peggy Sue Got Married, Apocalypse Now*) purchased—some say "rescued"—Inglenook from Heublein, changed the name to Niebaum-Coppola Estate, and created a museum of cinematic history. Art and wine were linked with architectural innovation, exhibits and museums, including avant-garde Clos Pegase and the winery/art museum called The Hess Collection.

More and more people from other disciplines and professions—doctors, lawyers, Silicon Valley pioneers, businesspeople, a rocket scientist—planted grapes and opened wineries, all dedicated to a search for quality. There were several new owners and winemakers who had grown up with European wine traditions. The number of wineries rose at a dizzying pace, as did the ratings by such magazines as *Wine Spectator* and *Wine Enthusiast*.

Resort business was also making a comeback. In the 1980s Auberge du Soleil and Meadowood, both rated among the best resorts in the world, became instant tourist magnets. Old mansions were being converted to bed and breakfasts every year. Upscale restaurants were drawing crowds. The Culinary Institute of America, the nationally known school for high-caliber chefs, purchased the old Greystone Cellars, restored the facility exquisitely, and opened its western campus in 1995.

Finally, in 1998 the voters passed a bond issue to pay for rerouting the Napa River to prevent the periodic flooding that has swept the city of Napa regularly since the days of Nathan Coombs.

The population of Napa Valley now exceeds 150,000—compared to the 5,000 native Americans living there when Father Altimira surveyed the Valley from a hill in the Soscol, or when George Yount built his blockhouse. The glory is that the natural beauty remains.

CHAPTER 8

THE NAPA VALLEY LIST OF LISTS

n this chapter we give you lots of handy information that we like to have ourselves when traveling, and we hope that it comes in handy for you, too. In each case, we list the best available.

WINERIES

Following is the list of all Napa Valley wineries open to the public. The list groups the wineries by communities, with Los Carneros included in Napa. The mailing addresses here might appear confusing, since some wineries are physically closer to one town, while their addresses are technically in another. Be sure to check or use detailed directions and maps. An * means you must make an appointment prior to visiting because the winery is not open for drop-in tasting.

Napa

Acacia Winery, 2750 Las Amigas Road, Napa 94559; phone (707) 226–9991. Open 10:00 A.M.–4:30 P.M. Monday–Saturday, noon–4:30 P.M. Sunday.

Bayview Cellars, 980 Pearl, Napa 94558; phone (707) 255–8544. Open 10:00 A.M.–5:00 P.M. Monday–Saturday, 11:00 A.M.–4:00 P.M. Sunday.

*Bouchaine Vineyards, 1075 Buchli Station Road, Napa 94558; phone (707) 252–9065. Open 10:00 A.M.–4:00 P.M. Monday–Friday; call for appointment.

Carneros Creek Winery, 1285 Dealy Lane, Napa 94559; phone (707) 253–9463. Open 10:00 A.M.–5:00 P.M. daily.

Chateau Potelle, 2875 Mount Veeder Road, Napa 94558; phone (707) 255–9440. Open noon–5:00 P.M. Friday–Monday.

Chimney Rock Winery, 5350 Silverado Trail, Napa 94558; phone (707) 257–2641. Open 10:00 A.M.–5:00 P.M. daily.

Clos Du Val, 5330 Silverado Trail, Napa 94558; phone (707) 259–2200. Open 10:00 A.M.–5:00 P.M. daily.

*Crichton Hall, 1150 Darms Lane, Napa 94558; phone (707) 224–4200. Open 10:00 A.M.–5:00 P.M. Monday–Friday; call for appointment.

Codorniu Napa, 1345 Henry Road, Napa 94559; phone (707) 224–1668. Open 10:00 A.M.–5:00 P.M. daily.

Domaine Carneros, 1240 Duhig Road, Napa 94559; phone (707) 257–0101. Open 10:30 A.M.–6:00 P.M. daily.

Domaine Filipe, 5400 Old Sonoma Road, Napa 94559; phone (707) 255–5585. Open 10:00 A.M.–5:00 P.M. daily.

*Domaine Montreaux, 4242 Big Ranch Road, Napa 94558; phone (707) 253–2802. Call for appointment.

Hakusan Sake Gardens, One Executive Way, Napa 94558; phone (707) 258–6160. Open 10:00 A.M.–5:00 P.M. every day except Wednesday.

The Hess Collection, 4411 Redwood Road, Napa 94558; phone (707) 255–1144. Open 10:00 A.M.–4:00 P.M. daily, including art exhibit.

Mont St. John Cellars, 5400 Old Sonoma Road, Napa 94559; phone (707) 255–8864. Open 10:00 A.M.–5:00 P.M. daily.

Monticello Cellars, 4242 Big Ranch Road, Napa 94558; phone (707) 253–2802. Open 10:00 A.M.–4:30 P.M. daily.

Newlan Vineyards & Winery, 5225 Solano Avenue, Napa 94558; phone (707) 257–2399. Open 10:00 A.M.–4:30 P.M. daily.

Pine Ridge Winery, 5901 Silverado Trail, Napa 94558; mail P.O. Box 2508, Yountville, 94599; phone (707) 252–9777. Open 11:00 A.M.–5:00 P.M. daily.

RMS Distillery (Carneros Alambic Distillery) 1250 Cuttings Wharf Road, Napa 94559; phone (707) 253–9055. Open 10:00 A.M.–5:00 P.M. daily.

*Saintsbury, 1500 Los Carneros Avenue, Napa 94559; phone (707) 252–0592. Call for appointment.

Signorello Vineyards, 4500 Silverado Trail, Napa 94558; phone (707) 255–5990. Open 11:00 A.M.–5:00 P.M. daily.

Stag's Leap Wine Cellars, 5766 Silverado Trail, Napa 94558; phone (707) 944–2020. Open 10:00 A.M.–4:30 P.M. daily.

Steltzner Vineyards, 5998 Silverado Trail, Napa 94558; phone (707) 252–7272. Phone 10:00 A.M.–5:00 P.M. Monday–Saturday, noon–4:30 P.M. Sunday.

Trefethen Estate Vineyards, 1160 Oak Knoll Avenue, Napa 94558; phone (707) 255–7700. Open 10:00 A.M.–4:30 P.M. daily.

Truchard Vineyards, 3234 Old Sonoma Road, Napa 94559; phone (707) 253–7153. Call for appointment.

Van Der Heyden, 4057 Silverado Trail, Napa 94558; phone (707) 259–9473. Open 10:00 A.M.–6:00 P.M. daily.

William Hill Winery, 1761 Atlas Peak Road, Napa 94558; phone (707) 224–4477. Open 10:30 A.M.–4:30 P.M. daily.

ZD Wines, 8383 Silverado Trail, Napa 94558; phone (707) 963–5188. Open 10:00 A.M.–4:30 P.M. daily.

Yountville

Cosentino Winery, 7415 St. Helena Highway, Yountville 94559; phone (707) 944–1220. Open 10:00 A.M.–5:30 P.M. daily.

Domaine Chandon, 1 California Drive, Yountville 94599; phone (707) 944–2280. Open 10:00 A.M.–9:00 P.M. daily except winter, November–April.

Goosecross Cellars, 1119 State Lane, Yountville 94599; phone (707) 944–1986. Open 10:00 A.M.–5:00 P.M. daily.

Havens Wine Cellars, 2055 Hoffman Lane, Yountville 94599; phone (707) 945–0921. Call for appointment.

Mayacamas Vineyards, 1155 Lokoya Road, Yountville 94599; phone (707) 224–4030. Open 8:00 A.M.–4:30 P.M. Monday–Friday. Call for appointment.

Monticello Cellars, 4242 Big Ranch Road, Yountville 94599; phone (707) 253–2802. Open 10:00 A.M.–4:30 P.M. daily.

Moss Creek Winery, 6015 Steele Canyon Road, Yountville 94559; or P.O. Box 4066, Napa 94558; phone (707) 252–1295. Call for appointment.

Plam Vineyards, 6200 Washington Street, Yountville 94558; phone (707) 944–1102. Open 9:00 A.M.–5:00 P.M. daily, 9:00 A.M.–3:00 P.M. Sunday. Call for appointment.

Robert Sinskey Vineyards, 6320 Silverado Trail, Yountville 94558; phone (707) 944–9090. Open 10:00 A.M.–4:30 P.M. daily.

S. Anderson, 1473 Yountville Cross Road, Yountville 94599; phone (707) 944–8642. Open 10:00 A.M.–5:00 P.M. daily.

Shafer Vineyards, 6154 Silverado Trail, Yountville 94599; phone (707) 944–2877. Open 9:00 A.M.–5:00 P.M. Monday–Friday, 9:00 A.M.–4:00 P.M. Saturday–Sunday. Call for appointment.

Silverado Vineyards, 6121 Silverado Trail, Yountville 94558; phone (707) 257–1770. Open 10:30 A.M.–5:00 P.M. daily, May 15–September 15; 11:00 A.M.–4:30 P.M. rest of the year.

Oakville

Cardinale, 7585 St. Helena Highway, Oakville 94562; phone (707) 945–1391. Open 10:30 A.M.–4:00 P.M. daily.

Chateau Potelle, 2875 Mt. Veeder Road, Oakville 94562; phone (707) 255–9440. Open noon–5:00 P.M. Friday–Monday.

Girard Winery, 7717 Silverado Trail, Oakville 94562; mail P.O. Box 105, Oakville 94562; phone (707) 944–8577. Tasting room at 677 St. Helena Highway, St. Helena 94574; phone (707) 963–5711. Open 11:00 A.M.–4:30 P.M. daily.

Groth Vineyards & Winery, 750 Oakville Crossroad, Oakville 94562; mail P.O. Box 390, Oakville 94562; phone (707) 944–0290. Open 10:00 A.M.–4:00 P.M. daily.

La Famiglia di Robert Mondavi Winery, 1595 Oakville Grade, Oakville 94562; phone (707) 944–2811. Open 10:00 A.M.–4:30 P.M. daily.

Napa Cellars, 7481 St. Helena Highway, Oakville 94562; phone (707) 944–2565 or (800) 535–6400. Open 10:00 A.M.–6:00 P.M. Friday–Sunday.

Napa Wine Company, 7840 St. Helena Highway, Oakville 94562; phone (707) 944–1710. Open 10:00 A.M.–3:30 P.M. Wednesday–Sunday.

Oakville Ranch Winery, 7850 Silverado Trail, Oakville 94562; phone (707) 944–9500. Open 11:00 A.M.–6:00 P.M. Thursday–Sunday.

*Opus One Winery, 7900 St. Helena Highway, Oakville 94562; mail P.O. Box 6, Oakville 94562; phone (707) 944–9442. Call for appointment.

Pepi Winery, 7585 St. Helena Highway, Oakville 94562; phone (707) 945–1391. Open 10:30 A.M.–4:00 P.M. daily.

Plumpjack Winery, 620 Oakville Cross Road, Oakville 94562; phone (707) 945–1220. Open 10:00 A.M.–4:00 P.M. daily.

Robert Mondavi Winery, 7801 St. Helena Highway, Oakville 94562; phone (707) 226–1335 or (800) MONDAVI. Open 9:00 A.M.–5:00 P.M. daily, May–October; 9:30 A.M.–4:30 P.M. daily, November–April.

Silver Oak Winery, 915 Oakville Cross Road, Oakville 94562; phone (707) 944–8808. Open 9:00 A.M.–4:00 P.M. Monday– Saturday.

Turnbull Wine Cellars, 8210 St. Helena Highway, Oakville 94562; phone (707) 963–5839 or (800) 887–6285. Open 10:00 A.M.–4:30 P.M. daily.

*Vine Cliff Winery, 7400 Silverado Trail, Oakville 94562; phone (707) 944–1364. Open 10:00 A.M.–4:30 P.M. Monday–Friday. Call for appointment.

Rutherford

Beaulieu Vineyards, 1960 St. Helena Highway South, Rutherford 94573; mail P.O. Box 219, Rutherford 94573; phone (707) 967–5200. Open 10:00 A.M.–5:00 P.M. daily.

Cakebread Cellars, 8300 St. Helena Highway, Rutherford 94573; mail P.O. Box 216, Rutherford 94573; phone (707) 963–5221. Open 10:00 A.M.–4:30 P.M. daily.

Caymus Vineyards, 8700 Conn Creek Road, Rutherford 94573; phone (707) 967–3010. Open 10:00 A.M.–4:30 P.M. daily. Tastings available by appointment.

*Frog's Leap Winery, 8815 Conn Creek Road, Rutherford 94573; mail P.O. Box 189, Rutherford 94573; phone (707) 963–4704. Open for sales 10:00 A.M.–4:00 P.M. Monday–Saturday. Tastings available by appointment.

Grgich Hills Cellar, 1829 St. Helena Highway, Rutherford 94573; mail P.O. Box 450, Rutherford 94573; phone (707) 963–2784. Open 9:30 A.M.–4:30 P.M. daily.

Mumm Napa Valley, 8445 Silverado Trail, Rutherford 94573; mail P.O. Box 500, Rutherford 94573; phone (707) 942–3434. Open 10:30 A.M.–6:00 P.M. daily.

Niebaum–Coppola, 1991 St. Helena Highway, Rutherford 94573; phone (888) COPPOLA. Open 10:00 A.M.–5:00 P.M. daily.

Peju Province, 8466 St. Helena Highway, Rutherford 94573; phone (707) 963–3600. Open 10:00 A.M.–6:00 P.M. daily.

Quail Ridge Cellars & Vineyards, 1155 Mee Lane, Rutherford 94573; mail P.O. Box 460, Rutherford 94573; phone (707) 963–9783. Open 11:00 A.M.–6:00 daily, summer; 10:00 A.M.–5:00 P.M. daily, winter.

Rutherford Grove Winery, 1673 St. Helena Highway, Rutherford 94573; phone (707) 963–0544. Open 10:00 A.M.–4:30 P.M. daily.

Rutherford Hill Winery, 200 Rutherford Hill Road, Rutherford 94573; phone (707) 963–7194. Open 10:00 A.M.–4:30 P.M. daily.

St. Supery Vineyards & Winery Discovery Center, 8440 St. Helena Highway, Rutherford 94573; phone (707) 963–4507. Open 9:30 A.M.–6:00 P.M. daily.

Sequoia Grove Winery, 8338 St. Helena Highway, Rutherford 94573; phone (707) 944–2945. Open 10:00 A.M.–5:00 P.M. daily.

Staglin Family Vineyard, 1570 Bella Oaks Lane, Rutherford 94573; mail P.O. Box 680, Rutherford 94573; phone (707) 963–1749. Open 10:30 A.M.–5:00 P.M. daily.

Sullivan Vineyards, 1090 Galleron Road, Rutherford 94573; phone (707) 963–9646. Open 10:00 A.M.–5:00 P.M. daily.

*Swanson Vineyards, 1271 Manley Lane, Rutherford 94573; mail P.O. Box 459, Rutherford 94573; phone (707) 944–0905. Call for appointment.

Villa Mt. Eden, 8711 Silverado Trail, Rutherford 94573; phone (707) 963–9100. Open 10:00 A.M.–4:00 P.M. daily.

St. Helena

*Anderson's Conn Valley Vineyards, 680 Rossi Road, St. Helena 94574; phone (707) 963–8600. Call for appointment.

Beaucanon Napa Valley, 1695 St. Helena Highway South, St. Helena 94574; phone (707) 967–3520. Open 10:00 A.M.–5:00 P.M. daily.

Beringer Vineyards, 2000 Main Street, St. Helena 94574; phone (707) 963–4812. Open 9:30 A.M.–5:00 P.M. daily.

*Calafia Cellars, 629 Fulton Lane, St. Helena 94574; phone (707) 963–0114. Call for appointment.

Casa Nuestra, 3451 Silverado Trail, St. Helena 94574; phone (707) 963–5783. Open 11:00 A.M.–5:00 P.M. Friday–Sunday.

*Chappellet Winery, 1581 Sage Canyon Road; phone (707) 963–7136. Call for appointment.

Charles Krug Winery, 2800 North Main Street, St. Helena 94574; mail P.O. Box 191, St. Helena, 94574; phone (707) 967–2200. Open 10:30 A.M.–5:30 P.M. daily.

Chateau Boswell, 3468 Silverado Trail, St. Helena 94574; phone (707) 963–5472. Open 10:00 A.M.–5:00 P.M. Friday–Sunday, May–November.

*Chateau Woltner, 3500 Silverado Trail, St. Helena 94574; phone (707) 963–1744. Call for appointment.

*David Arthur Vineyards, 1521 Sage Canyon Road, St. Helena 94574; phone (707) 963–5190. Call for appointment.

*Domaine Charbay Winery & Distillery, 4001 Spring Mountain Road, St. Helena 94574; phone (707) 963–9327. Open 10:00 A.M.–4:00 P.M. daily. Call for appointment.

*Duckhorn Vineyards, 3027 Silverado Trail (office at 1000 Lodi Lane), St. Helena 94574; phone (707) 963–7108. Open 11:00 A.M.–4:00 P.M. Monday–Saturday; tours on Saturday by appointment; sales, no tasting.

Edgewood Estate Winery, 401 St. Helena Highway South, St. Helena 94574; phone (707) 963–7293. Open 11:00 A.M.–5:30 P.M. daily.

Ehlers Grove and *Cartlidge & Brown*, 3222 Ehlers Lane, St. Helena 94574; phone (707) 963–3200. Open 11:00 A.M.–5:00 P.M. daily.

Flora Springs Wine Company, 1978 West Zinfandel Lane, St. Helena 94574; tasting room at 677 St. Helena Highway, St. Helena 94574; phone (707) 967–8032. Open 10:00 A.M.–6:00 P.M. daily.

Folie á Deux Winery, 3070 North St. Helena Highway, St. Helena 94574; phone (707) 963–1160. Open 10:00 A.M.–5:00 P.M. daily.

Franciscan Vineyards, 1178 Galleron Road, St. Helena 94574; mail P.O. Box 407, Rutherford 94573; phone (707) 963–7111. Open 10:00 A.M.–5:00 P.M. daily.

Freemark Abbey Winery, 3022 St. Helena Highway North, St. Helena 94574; mail P.O. Box 410, St. Helena 94574; phone (707) 963–9694. Open 10:00 A.M.–4:30 P.M. daily; restaurant.

Heitz Wine Cellars, 436 St. Helena Highway, St. Helena 94574; phone (707) 963–3542. Open 11:00 A.M.–4:30 P.M. daily.

**Joseph Phelps Vineyards*, 200 Taplin Road, St. Helena 94574; phone (707) 963–2745. Open 9:00 A.M.–5:00 P.M. Monday–Saturday, 10:00 A.M.–4:00 P.M. Sunday; tasting by appointment on morning and afternoon tours; calls welcomed for same-day appointments.

Louis M. Martini, 254 St. Helena Highway South, St. Helena 94574; mail P.O. Box 112, St. Helena 94574; phone (707) 963–2736 or (800) 321–WINE. Open 10:00 A.M.–4:30 P.M. daily.

Markham Vineyards, 2812 St. Helena Highway North, St. Helena 94574; mail P.O. Box 636, St. Helena, 94574; phone (707) 963–5292. Open 10:00 A.M.–5:00 P.M. daily.

Mario Perelli–Minetti, 1443 Silverado Trail, St. Helena 94574; phone (707) 963–8310. Open 10:00 A.M.–5:00 P.M. daily.

Merryvale Vineyards, 1000 Main Street, St. Helena 94574; phone (707) 963–2225 or 963–7777. Open 10:00 A.M.–5:30 P.M. daily; seminars 10:30 A.M. Saturday and Sunday.

Milat Vineyards, 1091 St. Helena Highway South, St. Helena 94574; phone (707) 963–0758. Open 10:00 A.M.–6:00 P.M. daily.

*Newton Vineyard, 2555 Madrona Avenue, St. Helena 94574; phone (707) 963–9000. Open 11:00 A.M. Friday. Call for appointment.

Nichelini Winery, 2950 Sage Canyon Road, St. Helena 94574; phone (707) 963–0717. Open 10:00 A.M.–6:00 P.M. Saturday, Sunday, and holidays; other times, call for appointment.

Prager Winery & Port Works, 1281 Lewelling Lane, St. Helena 94574; phone (707) 963–7678. Open 10:30 A.M.–4:30 P.M. daily.

Raymond Vineyard & Cellar, 849 Zinfandel Lane, St. Helena 94574; phone (707) 963–3141 or (800) 525–2659. Open 10:00 A.M.–4:00 P.M. daily.

*Robert Keenan Winery, 3660 Spring Mountain Road, St. Helena 94574; mail P.O. Box 142, St. Helena 94574; phone (707) 963–9177 or 963–9178. Call for appointment.

Rombauer Vineyards, 3522 Silverado Trail, St. Helena 94574; phone (707) 963–5170. Open 10:00 A.M.–5:00 P.M. daily.

*Round Hill Vineyards, 1680 Silverado Trail, St. Helena 94574; phone (707) 963–9503. Open 10:00 A.M.–4:30 P.M. daily; sales; no tasting.

Rustridge Ranch and Winery, 2910 Lower Chiles Road, St. Helena 94574; phone (707) 965–2871. Open 10:00 A.M.–4:00 P.M. daily.

St. Clement Vineyards, 2867 St. Helena Highway North, St. Helena 94574; mail P.O. Box 261, St. Helena, 94574; phone (800) 331–8266 or 967–3033. Open 10:00 A.M.–4:00 P.M. daily.

*Schweiger Vineyards, 4015 Spring Mountain Road, St. Helena 94574; phone (707) 963–4882; call for appointment.

*Smith–Madrone Vineyards, 4022 Spring Mountain Road, St. Helena 94574; phone (707) 963–2283. Open 10:00 A.M.–4:00 P.M. Monday–Saturday; call for appointment.

*Spottswoode Vineyard and Winery, 1902 Madrona Avenue, St. Helena 94574; phone (707) 963–0134. Call for appointment.

*Stony Hill Vineyard, 3331 St. Helena Highway North, St. Helena 94574; mail P.O. Box 308, St. Helena, 94574; phone (707) 963–2636. Call for appointment.

Sutter Home Winery, 100 St. Helena Highway South, St. Helena 94574; mail P.O. Box 248, St. Helena, 94574; phone (707) 963–3104. Open 9:30 A.M.–5:00 P.M. daily.

*Tudal Winery, 1015 Big Tree Road, St. Helena 94574; phone (707) 963–3947. Open 10:00 A.M.–4:00 P.M. daily. Call for appointment.

*Van Asperen Vineyards, 1680 Silverado Trail, St. Helena 94574; phone (707) 963–5251. Call for appointment.

V. Sattui Winery, 111 White Lane, St. Helena 94574; phone (707) 963–7774. Open 9:00 A.M.–6:00 P.M. daily, March–October; 9:00 A.M.–5:00 P.M. daily, November–February; includes deli.

Villa Mount Eden and *Conn Creek*, 8711 Silverado Trail, St. Helena 94574; phone (707) 944–2414. Open 10:00 A.M.–4:00 P.M. daily.

Whitehall Lane Winery, 1563 St. Helena Highway, St. Helena 94574; phone (707) 963–9454. Open 11:00 A.M.–6:00 P.M. daily.

Calistoga

Chateau Montelena, 1429 Tubbs Lane, Calistoga 94515; phone (707) 942–5105. Open 10:00 A.M.–4:00 P.M. daily.

Clos Pegase, 1060 Dunaweal Lane, Calistoga 94515; phone (707) 942–4981. Open 10:30 A.M.–5:00 P.M. daily.

Cuvaison Winery, 4550 Silverado Trail, Calistoga 94515; mail P.O. Box 384, Calistoga 94515; phone (707) 942–6266. Open 10:00 A.M.–5:00 P.M. daily.

Dutch Henry Winery, 4310 Silverado Trail, Calistoga 94515; phone (707) 942–5771. Open 10:00 A.M.–4:30 P.M. daily except Tuesday.

*Graeser Winery, 255 Petrified Forest Road, Calistoga 94515; phone (707) 942–4437. Open 11:00 A.M.–5:00 P.M. daily. Call for tasting appointment.

Hanns Kornell Champagne Cellars, 1091 Larkmead Lane, Calistoga 94515; mail 3522 Silverado Trail, St. Helena 94574; phone (707) 942–0859. Open 10:00 A.M.–4:30 P.M. daily.

*Hansfahden Wineries, 5300 Mountain Home Ranch Road, Calistoga 94515; phone (707) 942–6760. Call for appointment.

*Helena View Johnson, 3500 Highway 128, Calistoga 94515; phone (707) 942–4956. Open 10:00 A.M.–5:00 P.M. Saturday and Sunday. Call for appointment.

*Robert Pecota Winery, 3299 Bennett Lane, Calistoga 94515; mail P.O. Box 303, Calistoga 94515; phone (707) 942–6625. Call for appointment.

*Schramsberg Vineyards, 1400 Schramsberg Road, Calistoga 94515; phone (707) 942–4558. Open 10:00 A.M.–4:00 P.M. daily. Call for appointment.

Sterling Vineyards, 1111 Dunaweal Lane, Calistoga 94515; mail P.O. Box 365, Calistoga 94515; phone (707) 942–3344. Open 10:30 A.M.–4:30 P.M. daily.

Stonegate Winery, 1183 Dunaweal Lane, Calistoga 94515; phone (707) 942–6500. Open 10:00 A.M.–4:30 P.M. daily.

*Storybook Mountain Vineyards, 3835 Highway 128, Calistoga 94515; phone (707) 942–5310. Open by appointment Monday–Saturday.

Traulsen Vineyards, 2250 Lake County Highway, Calistoga 94515; phone (707) 942–0283. Open 10:00 A.M.–5:00 P.M. Monday–Thursday.

Vigil Vineyards, 3340 Highway 128, Calistoga 94515; phone (707) 942–2900 or (800) 94–VIGIL. Open 10:30 A.M.–4:30 P.M. daily.

Vincent Arroyo Winery, 2361 Greenwood Avenue, Calistoga 94515; phone (707) 942–6995. Open 10:00 A.M.–4:30 P.M. daily.

Wermuth Winery, 3942 Silverado Trail, Calistoga 94515; phone (707) 942–5924. Open 11:00 A.M.–5:00 P.M. daily.

Deer Park

Deer Park Winery, 1000 Deer Park Road, Deer Park 94576; phone (707) 963–5411. Open 10:00 A.M.–4:00 P.M. daily. Call for appointment.

*Viader Vineyards, 1120 Deer Park Road, Deer Park 94576; mail P.O. Box 280, Deer Park, 94576; phone (707) 963–3816. Call for appointment.

Angwin

*Dunn Vineyards, 805 White Cottage Road North, Angwin 94508; phone (707) 965–3642. Call for appointment.

*Summit Lake Vineyards & Winery, 2000 Summit Lake Drive, Angwin 94508; phone (707) 965–2488. Call for appointment.

SOME FINE WINERIES
GENERALLY NOT OPEN TO THE PUBLIC

Many Napa Valley wineries do not have tasting or sales facilities, but produce some of the best wines in the world. You can purchase their wines at fine wine shops, try them in restaurants, or get on winery mailing lists for newsletters and other special mailings.

Altamura Winery, 1700 Wooden Valley Road, Napa 94558; mail P.O. Box 3209, Napa 94558; phone (707) 253–2000.

Andretti Winery, 4162 Big Ranch Road, Napa 94558; phone (707) 259–6777.

Araujo Estate Wines/Eisele Vineyard, 2155 Pickett Road, St. Helena 94574; phone (707) 942–6061.

Atlas Peak Vineyards, 3700 Soda Canyon Road, Napa 94558; phone (707) 252–7971. Wine may be ordered at William Hill.

Azalea Springs Vineyards, 4301 Azalea Springs Way, Calistoga 94515; mail 2790 Broadway, San Francisco, CA 94115; phone (707) 942–4811 or (415) 346–3300.

Bacio Divino Cellars, 2610 Pinot Way, St. Helena 94574; phone (707) 942–8101.

Barnett Vineyards, 4070 Spring Mountain Road, St. Helena 94574; phone (707) 963–7075.

Benessere Vineyards, 1010 Big Tree Road, St. Helena 94574; phone (707) 963–5853.

Buehler Vineyards, 820 Greenfield Road, St. Helena 94574; phone (707) 963–2155.

Burgess Cellars, 1108 Deer Park Road, St. Helena 94574; mail P.O. Box 282, St. Helena 94574; phone (707) 963–4766.

Cain Vineyard & Winery, 3800 Langtry Road, St. Helena 94574; phone (707) 963–1616.

Colgin Cellars, 7830 St. Helena Highway (Highway 29), St. Helena 94574; mail 9601 Wilshire Boulevard, Suite 1200, Beverly Hills, CA 90210; phone (707) 963–0999 or (310) 786–1889.

Corison Wines, P.O. Box 427, St. Helena 94574; phone (707) 963–0826.

Dalla Valle Vineyards, 7776 Silverado Trail, Oakville 94562; mail P.O. Box 329, Oakville 94562; phone (707) 944–2676.

Diamond Creek Vineyards, 1500 Diamond Mountain Road, Calistoga 94515; phone (707) 942–6926.

Diamond Mountain Vineyard, 2121 Diamond Mountain Road, Calistoga 94515; phone (707) 942–0707.

Dominus Estate, 2570 Napanook Road, Yountville 94599; mail P.O. Box 3327, Yountville 94599; phone (707) 944–8954.

Far Niente, 1 Acacia Drive, Oakville 94562; mail P.O Box 327, Oakville 94562; phone (707) 944–2861.

Farella–Park Vineyards, 2222 North Third Avenue, Napa 94558; mail 235 Montgomery Street, San Francisco, CA 94104; phone (415) 954–4411.

Frazier, 40 Lupine Hill Road, Napa 94558; phone (707) 255–3444.

Grace Family Vineyards, 1210 Rockland Road, St. Helena 94574; phone (707) 963–0808.

Grandview Cellars, 1328 Main Street, St. Helena 94574; phone (707) 967–9480.

Harlan Estate, 1551 Oakville Grade, Oakville 94562; mail P.O. Box 352, Oakville 94562; phone (707) 944–1441.

Harrison Vineyards, 1527 Sage Canyon Road, St. Helena 94574; phone (707) 963–8271.

Honig Cellars, 850 Rutherford Road, Rutherford 94573; phone (707) 963-5618.

Jaeger Family Wine Co., 4324 Big Ranch Road, Napa 94558; phone (707) 255–4456.

Jarvis Vineyards, 2970 Monticello Road, Yountville 94599; phone (707) 255–5280.

Lang & Reed Wine Company, 1961 Vineyard Avenue, St. Helena 94574; mail P.O. Box 662, St. Helena 94574; phone (707) 963–3758.

Larkmead Vineyards, 1145 Larkmead Lane, St. Helena 94574; mail P.O. Box 309, St. Helena 94574; phone (707) 942–6605.

Livingston Wines, 1895 Cabernet Lane, St. Helena 94574; phone (707) 963–2120.

Lokoya Wines, 7585 St. Helena Highway (Highway 29), Oakville 94562; mail P.O. Box 328, Oakville 94562; phone (707) 944–2807.

Long Meadow Ranch Winery, 1775 Whitehall Lane, St. Helena 94574; phone (707) 963–4555.

Louis Corthay Winery, 996 Galleron Road, Rutherford 94573; phone (707) 963–2384.

Luna Vineyards, 2921 Silverado Trail, Yountville 94599; phone (707) 255–5862.

Mount Veeder Winery, 1999 Mount Veeder Road, Yountville 94599; phone (707) 963–7111. Wines available at Franciscan Estate.

Newton Vineyard, 2555 Madrona Avenue, St. Helena 94574; phone (707) 963–9000. Oakford Vineyards, 1575 Oakville Grade, Oakville 94562; mail P.O. Box 150, Oakville 94562; phone (707) 945–0445.

Oliver Caldwell Cellars, 3480 St. Helena Highway (Highway 29), St. Helena 94574; phone (707) 963–2037.

Pahlmeyer Winery, 101 South Coombs Street, Napa 94558; mail P.O. Box 2410, Napa 94558; phone (707) 255–2321.

Paoletti, 4501 Silverado Trail, Calistoga 94515; phone (707) 942–0689 or (310) 476–7379.

Paradigm, 683 Dwyer Road, Oakville 94562; mail P.O. Box 323, Oakville 94562; phone (707) 944–1683.

Quintessa (Franciscan), 1178 Galleron Road at Highway 29, Rutherford, 94573; mail P.O. Box 407, Rutherford 94573; phone (707) 963–7111. Can order at Franciscan Estate.

Reverie on Diamond Mountain, 1520 Diamond Mountain Road, Calistoga 94515; phone (707) 942–6800.

Screaming Eagle, P.O. Box 134, Oakville 94562; phone (707) 944–0749.

Seavey Vineyards, 1310 Conn Valley Road, St. Helena 94574; phone (707) 963–8339 or 788–0800.

Silverado Hill Cellars, 3105 Silverado Trail, Napa 94558; mail P.O. Box 2640, Napa 94558; phone (707) 253–9306 or 253–9307.

Spring Mountain Vineyard, 2805 Spring Mountain Road, St. Helena 94574; phone (707) 967–4188 or 967–4190.

Stag's Leap Winery, 6150 Silverado Trail, Napa 94558; phone (707) 944–1303 or 944–4493. Not to be confused with the older Stag's Leap Cellars.

Star Hill Winery, 1075 Shadybrook Lane, Napa 94558; phone (707) 255–1957.

Tulocay Winery, 1426 Coombsville Road, Napa 94558; phone (707) 255–4064.

Turley Wine Cellars, 3358 St. Helena Highway, St. Helena 94574; phone (707) 963–0940.

Villa Encinal Winery, 620 Oakville Crossroad, Oakville 94562; phone (707) 944–1465.

Vineyard 29, 2929 Highway 29 North, St. Helena 94574; phone (707) 963–9292.

Volker Eisele Family Estate, 3080 Lower Chiles Valley Road, St. Helena 94574; phone (707) 965–2260.

Von Strasser Winery, 1510 Diamond Mountain Road, Calistoga 94515; phone (707) 942–0930.

W Winery, 1001 Silverado Trail, St. Helena 94574; mail 3268 Villa Lane, Napa 94558; phone (707) 259–2800.

EVENTS AND FESTIVALS

The dates and times of regular events and festivals change from year to year. We encourage you to call the phone numbers listed for information.

February–March

Napa Valley Mustard Festival celebrates mustard in the vineyards at various locations, including the Culinary Institute of America, the Niebaum–Coppola Vineyards, and the Napa Fairgrounds in downtown Napa. The World Wide Mustard Competition is a big deal, with results announced with great fanfare at the opening party. It's all kicked off by the *Blessing of the Balloons* at Domaine Chandon Winery, 1 California Drive, Yountville 94599; phone (707) 259–9020, 944–8793, or 938–1133.

Taste of Yountville, along Washington Street in Yountville; phone (707) 944–0904. This event celebrates Yountville's claim that it has more world-class restaurants per square foot than any other town in the United States. And we are the beneficiaries, because they all cook and serve their delicacies at tables along the street. Lots of music and fun if it isn't raining.

April

Calistoga Maifest, Calistoga Fairgrounds; phone (707) 942–6524. This event takes place the first weekend in April (of course) and benefits the Rotary High School Scholarship Fund. Entertainment includes the Al Gruber band and mariachis. German and American food is available as well as German and local beers. Open noon–9:00 P.M.

April in Carneros, at all Carneros District wineries along the Sonoma–Napa border, promotes and celebrates the Carneros appellation with new wine releases, food, cigars, music, and general gustatory bliss; phone (800) 825–9475.

June

Beringer Celebrity Golf Classic, Chardonnay Golf Club, 2555 Jamieson Canyon Road east of Highway 12, Napa 94558; phone (707) 255–0950. This event benefits Justin–Siena Catholic High School in Napa, with big-name athletes mixing with lesser-known golfers. The fee is $375 to play with a celebrity of some sort.

Napa Valley Wine Auction, Meadowood Resort, 900 Meadowood Lane, St. Helena 94574; phone (707) 942–9783. This is the ultimate wine auction in the United States. The auction raises funds for local hospitals. The long weekend event includes barrel tastings, dinners with winemakers and owners, a Napa Valley collaborative chefs' dinner at Meadowood, and the auction itself. Most guests think the nearly $1,500 ticket price is well worth it.

Silverado Concours D'Elegance, Silverado Country Club, 1600 Atlas Peak Road, Napa 94558; phone (707) 428–3355; $10 in advance, $12 at the gate. This benefits the Children's Hospital of Oakland. Nearly 300 classic cars and their owners assemble to strut, wine and dine. A fun event for all who enjoy a little elegance, old and new.

Vintage 1870 Father's Day Invitational Auto Show, at Vintage 1870 in Yountville; phone (707) 944–2451. The name pretty much says it all.

July

Meadowood Croquet Classic, Meadowood Resort, 900 Meadowood Lane, St. Helena 94574; phone (707) 963–3646. Meadowood is the only winery with croquet courts and a full-time croquet pro. The U.S. Croquet Association holds this annual event of events, dressed all in white, of course. Inquire about new events and admission.

Napa Valley Shakespeare Festival, Rutherford Grove Winery, 1673 St. Helena Highway, St. Helena 94574; phone (707) 963–0544. The festival recently moved to this lovely site, with Shakespeare being performed on the lawn under huge shade trees.

August

Napa Town and Country Fair, Napa Exposition Grounds, 575 Third Street, Napa 94558; phone (707) 253–4900. This is a truly local fair, more homey than a county fair for the southern end of the Napa Valley, featuring everything you would expect from 4-H projects living and cooked, carnivals, kids' games, wine tasting, cotton candy, and even a rodeo and—gads—a demolition derby.

September

Napa Symphony on the River, Third Street at the bridge, Napa; phone (707) 258–8762. Come here to celebrate life and music, with music from 7:00–9:00 P.M., food and fireworks in Veterans Park—it's a general down-home great time, held the Sunday of Labor Day weekend.

October

Calistoga Beer & Sausage Fest, Napa County Fairgrounds, 1435 North Oak Street, Calistoga 94515; phone (707) 942–0795. On the second weekend in October, twenty-four microbreweries from around Northern California show and pour, along with sausage- and mustard-making companies, local restaurants, and chili cook-off; $20 for everything, in toto. A wild-and-wooly time.

Harvest Festival, Hometown Style, Adams Street, St. Helena; phone (707) 963–5706. This is a resurrected and underpublicized local celebration of the grape harvest, held the last Saturday in October, with arts and crafts, run, carnival, and a pet parade (our favorite).

Old Mill Days, Bale Grist Mill State Historic Park, 3369 St. Helena Highway, St. Helena 94574; phone (707) 942–4575. Coopers, storytellers, millers, fiddlers, weavers, kids, and grownups all pretend it's 130 years ago. Why not. Great mill tours, grinding of flours of several kinds. A good healthy day.

November

Festival of Lights, Vintage 1870, Yountville; phone (707) 944–1171. This is held the Friday after Thanksgiving all over town, with Christmas carols, roasted chestnuts, Santa, street musicians and actors, and of course wine and food. Lots of fun for visitors and locals alike. The next day, Saturday, Santa moves on to Napa's Christmas Parade, beginning by the Cinedome multiplex theater at Pearl and Soscol. The parade and Santa, and a few throngs of locals, end up at the Napa Town Center to make the shopping season official and have a wee bit of sustenance.

Napa Valley Wine Festival, Napa Valley Country Club, 3385 Hagen Road, Napa 94558; phone (707) 253–3511. This event, held the first weekend in November, benefits the Napa Valley Unified School District. There are golf and tennis, fifty Napa Valley wineries, huge pasta dinner, and student music. A fun, charitable event. Tickets cost $30 in advance, $35 at the door.

ANTIQUES

Antique Fair, 6512 Washington Street, Yountville; phone (707) 844–8440

Elrod Antiques, 3000 St. Helena Highway; phone (707) 963–1901

Neighborhood Antique Collective, 1400 First Street, Napa; phone (707) 259–1900

European Country Antiques, 1148 Main Street, St. Helena; phone (707) 963–4666

Hacienda Hardware, 1989 St. Helena Highway, Rutherford; phone (707) 963–8850 .

Jack Cole Antiques and Curios, 805 Washington Street, Calistoga; phone (707) 942–6712

Mandrake's Antiques, 6525 Washington Street in Vintage 1870, Yountville; phone (707) 944–9479

Red Hen Antiques, 5091 St. Helena Highway, Napa; phone (707) 257–0822

St. Helena Antiques, 1231 Main Street, St. Helena; phone (707) 963–5878

Tin Barn Collective, 1510 Lincoln Avenue, Calistoga; phone (707) 942–0618

BOOKSTORES

Book Cellar, 1254 Main Street, St. Helena; phone (707) 963–3901

Bookends Book Store, 1014 Coombs Street, Napa; phone (707) 224–1077

Calistoga Book Store, 1343 Lincoln Avenue, Calistoga; phone (707) 942–4123

Main Street Books, 1315 Main Street, St. Helena; phone (707) 963–1338

Napa Children's Book Company, 1239 First Street, Napa; phone (707) 224–3893

Volume One Used Books, 1405 Second Street, Napa; phone (707) 252–1466

CAMPGROUNDS

Bothe-Napa Valley State Park, Highway 29 south of Calistoga and adjoining Bale Mill State Park; phone (707) 942–4575 or (800) 444–PARK for state park reservations. Forty-nine tent and RV sites, nine tent only sites; picnic tables, fire pits and barbecues; rest rooms; showers; wheelchair-accessible; $1.00 fee for pets; $3.00 fee for swimming pool.

Calistoga Ranch Club Resort & Campground, 580 Lommel Road south of Calistoga; phone (707) 942–6565. Sixty tent only spaces, 84 RV sites, and some cabins. Enjoy 167 acres of trails, forest, fishing, swimming pool, and games. Facilities include barbecues, rest rooms, and showers.

Napa County Fairgrounds, 1435 North Oak Street, Calistoga; phone (707) 942–5111. Tents and RVs. Walk to downtown Calistoga. Pets OK on leash.

Napa Fairgrounds, 575 Third Street, Napa; phone (707) 253–4905. Spaces for motor homes and 500 campers with cars. Facilities include rest rooms and showers; grocery store and laundromat nearby.

LAUNDROMATS

Launder World, 703 Lincoln Avenue, Napa; phone (707) 252–9130
Napa Coin Laundry, 1132 Imola Avenue, Napa; phone (707) 254–8817

NIGHTCLUBS (SORT OF)

These are microbreweries, restaurants, and bars that occasionally have music.

Ana's Cantina, 1205 Main Street, St. Helena; phone (707) 963–4921. A local hangout featuring Mexican and El Salvadoran food and real drinks; rock, reggae, and country.

Calistoga Inn & Restaurant and *Napa Valley Brewing Company*, 1250 Lincoln Avenue, Calistoga; phone (707) 942–4101. Music in the bar Tuesday, Friday, and Saturday nights; on the patio occasionally in summer.

Club Bacchus, 1853 Trancas, Napa; phone (707) 258–1145. Disc jockey '50's funk Thursday–Saturday.

Downtown Joe's, 902 Main Street, Napa; phone (707) 258–2337. Microbrewery/restaurant with a lively rock, pop, and blues scene Thursday–Saturday. A $3.00 cover on weekends.

Hydro Bar & Grill, 1403 Lincoln Avenue, Calistoga; phone (707) 942–9777. Stays open late for great food, romantic bar-style jazz; Dixieland jam on Thursday.

Lord Derby Arms, Highway 29 (Lincoln Avenue) and Silverado Trail, Calistoga; phone (707) 942–9155. A distinctly British pub and hangout where local Irish singer John Kelley performs weekends.

Planet Rock, 3392 Solano Avenue, Napa; phone (707) 252–8200. Disc jockey, dancing with music style changing nightly. A $5.00 cover some nights. Call ahead for current details.

PHARMACIES

Longs Drugs, 1558 Trancas Avenue, Napa; phone (707) 253–7906

Silverado Pharmacy, 1348 Lincoln Avenue, Calistoga; phone (707) 942–5115

Smith's St. Helena Pharmacy, 1390 Railroad Avenue, St. Helena; phone (707) 963–2794

Vasconi's Drugs, 1381 Main Street, St. Helena; phone (707) 963–1444

PICNIC SUPPLIES

Cantinetta Tra Vigne, 1050 Charter Oak Avenue, St. Helena; phone (707) 963–8888

Genova Delicatessen & Ravioli Factory, 1550 Trancas, Napa; phone (707) 253–8686, fax (707) 253–2487

Giugni Grocery Company, 1227 Main Street, St. Helena; phone (707) 963–3421

Oakville Grocery, 7856 St. Helena Highway, Oakville; phone (707) 944–8802

Pometta's, 7787 Highway 29, Oakville; phone (707) 944–2365

Sattui Winery, South St. Helena Highway, St. Helena; phone (707) 963–7774

Soda Canyon Store, 4006 Silverado Trail, Napa; phone (707) 252–0285

INDEX

ABOUT THE
AUTHORS

*K*athleen and Gerald Hill are native Californians who divide their time between Sonoma in the northern California wine country and Vancouver Island, British Columbia. As a team the Hills wrote *Sonoma Valley: The Secret Wine Country, Victoria and Vancouver Island: The Almost Perfect Eden, Northwest Wine Country: Wine's New Frontier, The Real Life Dictionary of the Law, The Real Life Dictionary of American Politics,* and an international exposé, *The Aquino Assassination.* Kathleen is the author of *Festivals USA* and *Festivals USA—Western States,* and she has written articles for *The Chicago Tribune, San Francisco Magazine, Cook's Magazine, San Francisco Examiner Magazine, James Beard Newsletter* and other periodicals, while Gerald was editor and co-author of *Housing in California.* Gerald also practices law to support their writing habit.

Kathleen earned an A.B. at University of California at Berkeley, a Certificat from the Sorbonne in Paris, and an M.A. at Sonoma State University. Gerald holds an A.B. from Stanford University and a Juris Doctor from Hastings College of the Law, University of California.